Windows®
Server 2003

Best Practices
for Enterprise Deployments

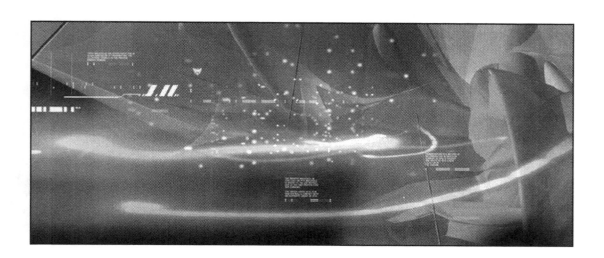

About the Authors

Danielle Ruest is a workflow architect and process consultant focused on people and organizational issues for large IT deployment projects. During her 22-year career, she has led change-management processes, developed and delivered training, and managed communications programs during process-implementation projects. Danielle is the co-author of numerous articles and presentations as well as *Preparing for .NET Enterprise Technologies*, a book on mastering change in the enterprise.

Nelson Ruest is an enterprise architect specializing in infrastructure design. He is a Microsoft Certified Systems Engineer and Microsoft Certified Trainer. The goal of his 22-year career has been to assist organizations in mastering the technologies they depend upon. He is also a frequent guest speaker at Comdex and other conferences in North America. Nelson is the co-author of numerous articles as well as *Preparing for .NET Enterprise Technologies*.

Both work for Resolutions Enterprises (http://www.Reso-Net.com/), a Canadian consulting firm that provides services in the architectural and project management fields.

About the Technical Editor

Stephane Asselin has been involved with information technology for the past 11 years, with a majority of his time focused on hardware and networking configurations. He has done infrastructure assessment and host hardening on Microsoft technologies for five years. He is a Certified Information Systems Security Professional (CISSP) and a Microsoft Certified Systems Engineer (MCSE). More recently, he has been involved in supportability reviews for government agencies to help them prepare for their Windows Server 2003 migration. He is currently a senior technical account manager for Microsoft Corporation.

Windows® Server 2003

Best Practices for Enterprise Deployments

Danielle Ruest
Nelson Ruest

McGraw-Hill/Osborne

New York / Chicago / San Francisco
Lisbon / London / Madrid / Mexico City / Milan
New Delhi / San Juan / Seoul / Singapore / Sydney / Toronto

The McGraw·Hill Companies

McGraw-Hill/Osborne
2100 Powell Street, Floor 10
Emeryville, California 94608
U.S.A.

To arrange bulk purchase discounts for sales promotions, premiums, or fund-raisers, please contact
McGraw-Hill/Osborne at the above address. For information on translations or book distributors outside the
U.S.A., please see the International Contact Information page immediately following the index of this book.

Windows® Server 2003: Best Practices for Enterprise Deployments

1234567890 CUS CUS 019876543

ISBN 0-07-222343-X

Publisher	Brandon A. Nordin
Vice President & Associate Publisher	Scott Rogers
Acquisitions Editor	Franny Kelly
Project Editor	Patty Mon
Acquisitions Coordinators	Emma Acker
	Martin Przybyla
Technical Editor	Stephane Asselin
Copy Editor	Lunaea Weatherstone
Indexer	Karin Arrigoni
Computer Designers	Carie Abrew, Lucie Ericksen
Illustrators	Melinda Moore Lytle, Michael Mueller,
	Danielle Ruest, Lyssa Wald
Series Design	Roberta Steele
Cover Series Design	Jeff Weeks

This book was composed with Corel VENTURA™ Publisher.

If there is one thing we have learned in our 22 years of experience, it is that even if technology is constantly changing, one thing remains the same: we must always take the time to master a technology before implementing it. But, even before that, we must fully comprehend our needs. The best way to achieve this is to work as a team. Including personnel from all areas of the enterprise can only make a better product in the end.

Thus we dedicate this book to you, the reader, in hopes that it will help you achieve this goal.

Contents at a Glance

Contents

Preface

Windows Server 2003 is a graphical environment. As such, many of its operations are wizard-based. We recommend you use the wizard interface even though there may be command-line equivalents. The reason for this is because a wizard enforces best practices and standard operating procedures automatically. The wizard always uses the same steps and always provides the ability to review your actions before they are implemented.

This does not mean that you need to dally on screens that only provide information. Read them at least once and when you're familiar with their content, move on to the screens where you need to perform actions.

We cannot emphasize standard operating procedures enough. An enterprise network simply cannot be built on ad hoc procedures. This is one of the reasons for this book. It provides best practices and standard procedures for building an enterprise network with Windows Server 2003. We hope you find it useful.

Comments can be sent to **WindowsServer@Reso-Net.com**.

Acknowledgments

We would like to thank all of the people who helped make this book a reality, especially Stephane Asselin of Microsoft Premier Support, our technical reviewer. Thanks for all of your constructive ideas. We would also like to thank Charles Gratton of Hewlett-Packard Canada for giving so much of his personal time and dedication to let us test Windows Server 2003 on various hardware configurations.

Thanks also to Microsoft's development and marketing team for Windows Server 2003 for all of their help in finding the right solution when issues arose. Specifically, we'd like to thank Jan Shanahan, Jill Zoeller, Jenna Miller, Jackson Shaw, Kamal Janardhan, and B.J. Whalen.

Thanks to VMware Corporation for providing us with the software required to create our entire technical laboratory. Thanks also to all of the other manufacturers that provided us with pre-release software tools so that we could cover enterprise needs as much as possible. You'll find yourselves within the book.

Finally, thanks to McGraw-Hill/Osborne for all their patience and dedication in helping us make this a better book. Franny, it was fun to be part of your team.

Introduction

Building an enterprise network is no small task. Worse, it seems you have to start over every time the server operating system changes. This book provides a structured approach that lets you create a brand new enterprise network that is built on the best features of Microsoft's new operating system (OS), Windows Server 2003. This network is built in a parallel environment that does not affect your current production network. Then, when you're ready to make the migration, it outlines how to take security principals, documents, data, and applications and move them from your legacy network to the new, parallel environment. This way, you can immediately begin to profit from the best of this powerful OS.

To achieve this goal, the book is divided into ten chapters, each building on the concepts of the previous chapters to finally cover all of the elements required to build your new network. The core concept of this book is its focus on enterprise features—only those features that are relevant to an enterprise environment. Microsoft used a similar approach when they decided to remove such features as Universal Plug and Play and scanner drivers from the OS because they are not server features and are not relevant in an enterprise. Similarly, this book discards the features that are not intended for the enterprise from Windows Server 2003's more than 400 new features and improvements.

Each chapter includes both discussion points and step-by-step implementations. Each chapter is chock full of best practices, checklists, and processes. In addition, each chapter ends with a Chapter Roadmap—a graphical illustration of the elements covered in the chapter, relevant figures, and tools found on the companion Web site (http://www.Reso-Net.com/WindowsServer/). The chapters are divided into the following topics:

- **Chapter 1: Planning for Windows Server 2003** gives an overview of the processes you need to prepare your migration to the new OS. It discusses the various elements you must have on hand before you proceed.

- **Chapter 2: Preparing for Massive Installations of Windows Server 2003** identifies the four supported installation methods for Windows Server 2003 and helps you choose the most appropriate massive installation method for your organization.

- **Chapter 3: Designing the Active Directory** reviews all of the requirements of an Active Directory and outlines the steps required to build it. It uses different scenarios to help you understand the most complex concepts of this powerful enterprise network feature.

- **Chapter 4: Designing the Enterprise Network IP Infrastructure** focuses on TCP/IP, the core communication protocol of the enterprise network. Then it begins the parallel network installation.

- **Chapter 5: Building the PC Organizational Unit Infrastructure** looks at the elements you need to put in place to manage PCs with Active Directory. It begins the discussion on Group Policy, a discussion that will not end until Chapter 8.

- **Chapter 6: Preparing the User Organizational Unit Infrastructure** examines how to manage user objects through Active Directory. It includes an extensive discussion of the use of groups within an enterprise network.

- **Chapter 7: Designing the Network Services Infrastructure** covers the services the network is to deliver to users. It outlines how these services should be built and identifies how they should be implemented.

- **Chapter 8: Managing Enterprise Security** focuses on one element and one element only: security. It introduces a new system, the Castle Defense System, which can be used to simplify security policy design and implementation.

- **Chapter 9: Creating a Resilient Infrastructure** is concentrated on making sure your services are always available. As such, it covers both redundancy and disaster recovery.

- **Chapter 10: Putting the Enterprise Network into Production** tells you how to migrate users from your legacy network to the new, parallel environment you created. In addition, it begins a discussion of the new and revamped IT roles you will require now that you are running a network through Active Directory.

Migrating to a new server OS is not a task that should be taken lightly. This is why you should make sure your project team includes all of the right players. These should focus on at least two groups: the first will work at the elaboration of the network architecture and the second will focus on the preparation of installation procedures and perform the installation itself. The technical project team should include architects, system administrators, installers, user representatives, support personnel, developers, and project managers. You should make sure you involve your current administrative and operational staff in this project. This will help you recover the best of the existing network and help them learn more about the new operating system they will soon be using.

In addition, you need to make sure that you involve the right stakeholders in your project. Not having the right stakeholders can be as disastrous as not making the right technical decisions.

Finally, managing a project of this magnitude can be complex and can give you the impression it is never-ending unless you structure it properly. Thus, each chapter has been designed to help you structure the technical activities needed to perform the migration. This does not mean that every chapter needs to be addressed in a sequential order. Though this is possible and even appropriate in some cases, in very large organizations it would improperly stretch the project timeline. Some chapters require the participation of your entire technical project team, but others do not because they are focused on specific areas of technical expertise. Figure 1 illustrates a sample timeline distribution for the activities found in each chapter. It lets you divide the technical project team into appropriate

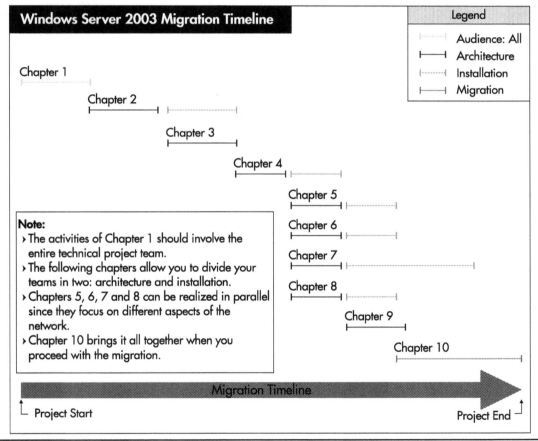

Figure 1   The Windows Server 2003 Migration Timeline

subgroups to shorten the overall project timeline while still achieving your goal: doing the best implementation you can so that all can profit from an improved networking environment.

The Companion Web Site

This book is powered by a companion Web site: **http://www.Reso-Net.com/WindowsServer/**. It lists dozens of job aids, forms, checklists, blueprints, spreadsheets, and other tools that are designed to help you in your network migration. All are readily available to everyone. These tools are listed on a per chapter basis to help you locate them more easily. Make sure you connect and download these items; they will definitely simplify your migration project.

CHAPTER 1

Planning for Windows Server 2003

IN THIS CHAPTER

Preparing the enterprise network is a complex process, even more so now that Windows is in its second post-NT edition. With Windows NT, decisions were relatively simple because the choices were limited. But with Windows Server 2003 (WS03), this is no longer the case.

It's not surprising since the network has evolved today from being a loosely coupled series of servers and computers to being an integrated infrastructure providing and supporting the organization's mission. This evolutionary process is not unlike that of the telephone. At first, telephone systems were loosely coupled. Today, worldwide telecommunications systems are much more complex and complete.

Similarly, networks are now mission-critical. The enterprise network, in fact, has become a secure, stable, redundant infrastructure that is completely oriented toward the delivery of information technology services to the enterprise. These services can range from simple file and print systems to complex authentication systems, storage area networks, or application services. In addition, these services can be made available to two communities of users—internal users over whom you have complete control of the PC, and external users over whom you have little or no control.

That's why moving or migrating to Windows Server 2003 is much more of a network infrastructure design project than one dealing simply with upgrading to a new technology. Each time you change a technology that is as critical as the operating system (OS) of your network, it is important, if not essential, to review corporate needs and requirements, review the features and capabilities of the new OS, design a comprehensive architecture and implementation plan, then move on to the actual implementation. In addition, aligning a project of this magnitude with the business strategies of the organization will make the transition more easily accepted and more profitable for the enterprise. Too many organizations cannot fully profit from the benefits of an enterprise network because they have never taken the time to perform each of these steps. As a result, they don't benefit from the maximum potential or performance of their network.

In fact, planning and preparing for the implementation of Windows Server 2003 should be 80 percent planning, preparing, and testing, and 20 percent implementing. This applies whether your enterprise has one or one million users. It's just a matter of degree of importance. If your enterprise is an enterprise of one, you'll still want to take the time to prepare properly, but you probably won't take the time to invest in automating procedures. You'll still want standard operating procedures, but you probably won't involve a series of technicians and architects to validate them. You'll still want to design based on architectural models, but you won't take the time to design them yourself.

Building an enterprise network with Windows Server 2003 consists of designing the network architecture and its implementation procedure while identifying opportunities for and using standard operating procedures. The enterprise network infrastructure is thus divided into service delivery areas that must be supported by a structure for network administration and management. For each aspect of this infrastructure, it is essential to have a complete understanding of the features that Windows Server 2003 offers in this area. It is also important to identify which of these features offer the best cost/benefit scenario for the enterprise.

For example, very few enterprises using Windows today can live without Active Directory. For organizations of all sizes, it is always better to take the time to centralize all authentication and authorization services than to keep them distributed through the use of workgroups because if a change is required, you only have to make it in one central place. Thus, the organization that requires an enterprise-level network infrastructure will not invest in workgroups, they will invest directly into Active Directory, bypassing workgroups altogether. This enterprise-level approach is the one that will be used throughout the elaboration of the Enterprise Architecture for Windows Server 2003.

Windows Server 2003

As the 22nd edition of Windows, this version is designed specifically for servers. It is a successor to Windows 2000 Server and uses the same core code as its predecessor. In this case, Microsoft did not perform a complete rewrite of the Windows 2000 code (as was done with the Windows NT code when Windows 2000 was designed). This means that WS03 is a natural evolution from Windows 2000. Several of the new features of WS03 are simply improvements over their Windows 2000 counterparts.

If you are experienced with Windows 2000, you will find it easier to move to WS03. If you are coming from another operating system or even from Windows NT, you'll have to begin by mastering the basic concepts of this new Windows platform. There are four versions of Windows Server 2003:

- **Windows Server 2003, Standard Edition (WSS)** Supports four-way symmetric multiprocessing and up to 4 gigabytes (GB) of memory. Aimed at file and printer sharing, Internet connectivity, small-scale application deployment, and collaboration.

- **Windows Server 2003, Enterprise Edition (WSE)** Supports either 32- or 64-bit processing—it offers native support for the Intel Itanium processor, up to eight processors and 32 GB of memory in 32-bit mode and 64 GB of memory in 64-bit mode. Also supports eight-node clustering. Aimed at infrastructure support, as well as application and Web services support.

- **Windows Server 2003, Datacenter Edition (WSD)** Supports either 32- or 64-bit processing, up to 64-way symmetric multiprocessing on custom hardware. Supports 64 GB of memory in 32-bit mode and 512 GB of memory in 64-bit mode. Can also support eight-node clusters. WSD is available only with the purchase of a WSD-compatible system from an original equipment manufacturer. Aimed at business-critical and mission-critical applications demanding the highest level of scalability and availability. The list of approved manufacturers is available at http://www.microsoft.com/windows2000/datacenter/howtobuy/purchasing/oems.asp.

- **Windows Server 2003, Web Edition (WSW)**   A new edition of the Windows server operating system, WSW is focused on providing a trimmed-down and secure Web server supporting ASP.NET and the .NET Framework for Web services. Supports two-way multiprocessing and up to 2 GB of memory in 32-bit processing mode only.

While Windows 2000 offered more than 200 new features over Windows NT, WS03 offers more than 400 improvements on Windows 2000. Improvements have been made in a wide range of categories, including security, management, file storage, printing, server sizing, administration, even Active Directory. One of the major advantages of WS03 will be server consolidation. It is designed to help organizations do more with less. For example, Microsoft has tested WS03 clusters supporting more than 3,000 printer queues and both the Enterprise Edition and Datacenter Server have proven that the Windows platform can perform along with the best on the market in terms of processing power (see http://www.tpc.org for more information).

> **QUICK TIP**
>
> *If you are new to .NET, an article demystifying Microsoft's .NET initiative can be found at http://www.Reso-Net.com/WindowsServer/.*

The .NET Framework is a core part of WS03. Deployment of the enterprise XML Web services on Windows Server 2003 includes configuration and administration of the underlying .NET Framework as well as installation, configuration, and administration of supporting UDDI services.

Building the Foundation of the Network

The server operating system is the core of the Enterprise Network. When looking to replace this operating system, it is important to ensure that every aspect of the services that the network will provide has been covered. The best way to do this is to use the "lifecycle" approach. Two lifecycles are important here:

- **Server lifecycle**   The cycle an individual server undergoes when it is introduced into the network.
- **Service lifecycle**   The cycle services must undergo from the moment they are first introduced into the network until their retirement.

The server lifecycle, especially, will let you design the basic structure of all servers. This will form the basis for the server construction model. The service lifecycle will help you identify the different services required within your network. Once these are identified and prepared, you can then focus on network stability. Since many operations within the network are performed by a variety of personnel, network stability is greatly enhanced by the use of standard operating procedures (SOPs). It ensures that best practices are always used to perform operations.

The Server Lifecycle

As mentioned previously, building a network is 80 percent planning and preparation and 20 percent implementation. The process of building servers is the same. Servers are designed to meet specific requirements within your network. More will be discussed on this topic later, but for now, it is sufficient to say that, like all network components, servers have a lifecycle within the enterprise network. It begins with the Purchasing Process, then moves on to the IT Management Process to end with its Retirement from service.

The Purchasing Process covers purchase planning, requisition, and procurement. In this process, the enterprise should focus on several factors such as volume purchasing of servers, requests for proposal, minimum requirements for server hardware, hardware provider add-ons, and growth strategy. These processes can be supported by functionality and reliability testing of hardware and applications in the network environment. For this process to be a success, the purchasing department and IT must cooperate and work closely together.

One of the driving factors of this process is the volume buying approach. Servers, like PCs, should always be bought in lots. They should never be bought piecemeal. The main objective of this process in an enterprise network is to reduce diversity as much as possible. When servers are bought in lots, you can expect the manufacturer to ship machines that are configured as identically as possible. In this way, you can simplify and standardize the server building and maintenance process. More and more organizations are even moving to partnerships with server manufacturers to further decrease diversity within their server hardware families.

Once the Purchasing Process is complete, the server lifecycle moves on to the IT Management Process. Here IT personnel become responsible and take ownership of the server until its retirement. The process begins with the reception of the server and its entry into the corporate inventory database. This should include information such as purchase date, receipt date, purchase lot, warranty, and service contracts, among other items. Next begins the server construction. Here servers go through the staging process. At this point, only generic software elements are loaded onto the server. These would include the operating system, anti-virus software, management software, resource kit tools—everything that is either completely generic or includes an enterprise license and thus does not entail additional costs.

Next, the server is configured. This phase covers the application of the server software—software that will support the server's specific role within the enterprise.

The final preparation phase is server testing. This should include stress testing as well as configuration acceptance testing. Once this testing phase is complete, the server is ready for production.

Putting the server into production often means recovering information such as Security Settings from another server and migrating it to the new machine. Once this is performed, the server officially enters its production cycle. IT management for the server becomes focused on routine administrative tasks, software updates and service pack application, and performance and capacity monitoring. All are performed on a scheduled basis. This phase will also include server repairs if required. Though most every task will focus on remote operations, some repairs may require shutdown and physical access to the server. It is indeed very hard to upgrade server memory remotely. This is an area that has changed with Windows Server 2003; now all shutdowns can be documented and justified through a verbose shutdown dialog box called the Shutdown Event Tracker.

Finally, after its lifecycle is complete, the server reaches obsolescence and must be retired from the network. It is then replaced by new servers that have begun a new lifecycle within the enterprise network.

The Service Lifecycle

IT service lifecycle models abound in the industry. Microsoft first published an IT service lifecycle management model in a white paper entitled "Planning, Deploying and Managing Highly Available Solutions," released in May 1999 (search for the document name at http://search.microsoft.com/).

This model identified four phases of service lifecycle management:

- **Planning** Identifying and preparing solutions for deployment
- **Deployment** Acquiring, packaging, configuring, installing, and testing deployment strategies
- **Production** Problem, change, optimization, and administration management within the production network
- **Retirement** Replacement/upgrade planning and removal of obsolete technologies and processes

While the original Microsoft model provided a sound starting point for IT service lifecycle management, the test of time proved that it required some minor modifications to fully illustrate the lifecycle of a service within an enterprise network. This new model is illustrated in Figure 1-1.

This service lifecycle model is still based on the same four phases with refinements within both the planning and the Preparation and Deployment Phases. Each of these two phases was increased in size to better reflect their importance to the process since planning and preparation take on more and more importance in network architectures today.

▶ **NOTE**

Microsoft has made their model evolve as well. It is now fully incorporated into the Microsoft Operations Framework. More information on this framework is available at http://www.microsoft.com/business/services/mcsmof.asp.

In addition, several processes and procedures where added to each of these two phases. Rationalization—a process focused on decreasing the number of servers and applications in the enterprise—was added to the initial planning process in order to reduce diversity. Rationalization affects not only server hardware through server consolidation practices, but also the applications and

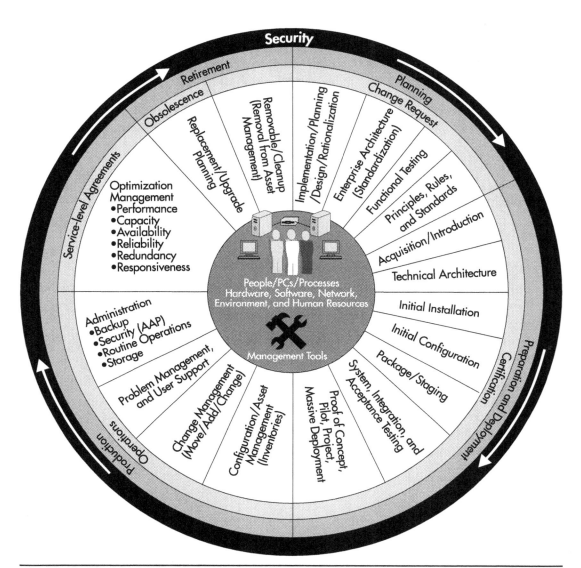

Figure 1-1   The service lifecycle is divided into four phases: Planning, Preparation and Deployment, Production, and Retirement.

utilities that run on these servers. The latter focuses on reduction through the selection of one and only one application to provide a given function within the network. One of the great opportunities for rationalization is when organizations move from Windows NT to Windows Server 2003. In NT, many third-party software products were required to have an efficient and effective network. In WS03, while third-party products are still required, a vast number of these utilities are no longer needed since the operating system includes so many new features.

Functional testing is now focused on proof-of-concept testing—that is, testing the concepts that emerge from the previous activity, which is Enterprise Architecture. It also involves application compatibility testing—testing current applications to see if they will operate with the new service. The outcome of this stage should be a complete impact report on existing products that will be required within the new network. This report should include upgrade procedures or replacement recommendations if the product is not compatible with the new OS.

The design of the Enterprise Architecture mainly involves analysis of the needs and requirements of the organization, the features of the new service, and the elaboration of the principles, rules, and standards that will be applied to its use within the enterprise. This stage also focuses on Standardization, another process which concentrates on the reduction of diversity, but this time, specifically within the service that is to be delivered.

Preparation and Deployment have also been enhanced with the addition of the Technical Architecture Process, which follows or can occur at the same time as the Acquisition Process. The Technical Architecture provides the technical parameters which will be applied to the service during its installation and during the rest of its lifecycle within the network. It is based on the orientations outlined in the Enterprise Architecture and simply details the specifics of the implementation.

The lifecycle then moves on to installation and initial configuration, and packaging/staging. Packaging is used if the service relies on a software product or an addition to the current network. Staging is used if the service relies on a new operating system. In the Windows Server 2003 implementation process, you will use both packaging and staging since you will begin with initial installation or staging of your servers, then follow with the application of the function or role the server will play in your network. Packaging is often used to automate the software or service installation process.

Testing is the next stage, which involves several different levels. System testing validates that the service operates in a standalone environment. Integration testing validates the service's coexistence with other services on the same machine or in the same network. Acceptance testing gives the final user approval rights to the service as it is packaged and prepared.

Finally, the service is ready for deployment. This can be done in several stages. Another proof-of-concept (POC) can be done to perform a final validation of the service in use. The target audience for this POC usually consists of the project team and some of its closest associates. This is followed by a pilot project that tests all aspects of the deployment methodology. Massive deployment follows a successful pilot project.

Not all services must undergo the proof-of-concept stage. This stage is only applied if the target population for the service is extremely large (1,000 or more users). If target populations are smaller, you may want to proceed with only a pilot project before deployment. There are, however, very few cases when you should proceed directly to deployment without either a POC or a pilot project. An example would be if you need to deploy a security patch in an emergency. Even then, you would need to do a minimum amount of testing before proceeding to deployment.

Once the service is deployed, it enters the Production Phase of its lifecycle. Here you must manage and maintain a complete inventory of the service, manage changes to the service, manage problems and support users of the service, and generally administer the service. You must also manage the service-level agreements for this service. This involves performance and capacity analysis, redundancy planning (backup, clustering, failsafe, and recovery procedures), availability, reliability, and responsiveness analysis of the service.

The final phase of the IT service lifecycle is Retirement. When the service reaches a certain degree of obsolescence, it must be retired from the network because its operation costs often outweigh the benefits it brings to the network.

Of special note is the security element, which surrounds the entire service lifecycle. Security has a special position in this lifecycle because it encompasses much more than just software and hardware. Security is a process in and of itself, as you will discover in Chapter 8.

Both the server and service lifecycles will be used throughout this book. The server lifecycle will help with the construction and delivery of the servers you build with WS03. The service lifecycle will apply more specifically to the roles or configurations you give to your servers as you prepare them for deployment. To simplify this process, you will need another model, the Server Construction and Management Model.

A New Model for Server Construction and Management

The use of an architectural model can greatly simplify the architectural design process for the construction and management of servers (and PCs) in your enterprise network. Such a model should outline the services required in the network and should group these services into appropriate categories or layers. In addition, to properly reflect the service and security nature of these groupings, and to outline that they are designed to provide access to resources within the network, the name of the model should describe its purpose. This model proposed here is called the Point of Access to Secure Services (PASS) model.

▶ **NOTE**

This model was first outlined in Preparing for .NET Enterprise Technologies, *by Ruest and Ruest (Addison-Wesley, 2001) and was originally called the "Service Point of Access or SPA Object Model." It has been renamed the PASS model here to better reflect its intended purpose.*

The model is based on an existing and well-known service model: the International Standards Organization's OSI Networking Reference model. The OSI model has been modified to better suit the needs of distributed environments. It is a good source model because it is well-known in the industry. It describes networking between clients and servers through a series of layers, with each layer having its own set of functional services. Interactions between layers are based on using common services, and interactions are limited to the layers immediately adjacent to any given layer.

In the PASS model, each layer offers a set of services to the others. Each layer interacts with the other and each layer has a specific function. This layered model can be applied to the core elements of a distributed environment, either PCs or servers. The content of the PASS model is divided into ten layers, similar to those of the OSI model:

- Physical
- Core operating system

- Networking
- Storage
- Security
- Communications
- Common productivity tools
- Presentation
- Role-based commercial software and/or corporate applications
- Ad hoc commercial software and/or corporate applications

The PASS model represents a design that is very similar to the OSI model, with the addition of three extra layers. This model begins to demonstrate how you can construct and present IT technologies in understandable ways. Even though all of the layers are related to each other in specific ways, some have a stronger relationship than others. By examining the content of each layer, you can see that some layers need to be implemented on every server while others aim at specific servers (see the ten layers of the PASS Model at http://www.Reso-Net.com/WindowsServer/). This "common" versus "specific" components approach must influence the ten-layer model. To provide a clear construction model, the ten layers must be regrouped into sections that are meant for every server and sections that are meant for specific groups of servers.

For this, the model must be restructured into four basic sections. This diagram can serve as a map for server design and deployment. This is the PASS model. Its four sections are:

- **Physical**   Standard physical components.
- **System Kernel**   All components that are common to all servers.
- **Role-based applications and software**   Components which are installed on a server on a role basis—that is, the role the server plays in the network. Roles can be based on commercial software, for example, Microsoft .NET Enterprise Server products, or they can be based on corporate applications. The difference between the two is often related to security levels. Commercial software is often available to all users and corporate applications are often restricted to specific users.
- **Ad hoc applications and software**   In some instances, there are highly specialized IT requirements for a server that are not necessarily related to its role within the enterprise. These are included in the ad hoc layer.

The final layer of the PASS System Kernel, the presentation layer, provides the interface requirements for the server at both the user and the administrative level. At the core of this model is the concept of standardization, specifically within the Physical and System Kernel layers. Standardization does not mean reduction; it simply means doing everything in a single unified manner. This alone can vastly reduce costs in the IT enterprise. The PASS model clearly displays the mechanisms that can be used to construct servers so long as standards are available to support all of the processes that it identifies.

This model is illustrated in Figure 1-2. As you can see, its construction is closely tied to the server lifecycle presented earlier.

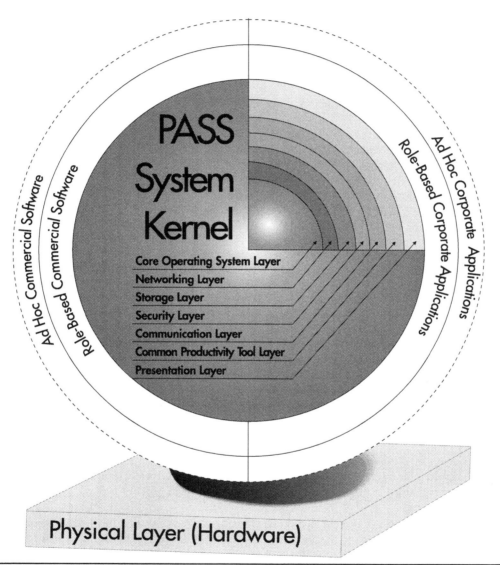

Figure 1-2   The PASS model

The Benefits of the PASS Model

Using a single model for the outline of technical services provided by both PCs and servers has several major advantages. First, by using layers and specifically including a presentation layer, it forms the framework for user and technology interactions within a Windows distributed environment. Second, it outlines that there should be no difference in the approaches used to manage and maintain PASS objects (PCs or servers). Third, it outlines how to construct both servers and PCs. Fourth, it outlines a framework that will allow the systems to evolve with time through structured management approaches. In addition, each of the four major layers of this model provides distinct benefits.

Standardizing the physical layer ensures that the organization has modern tools to perform its IT tasks. It also ensures the control of obsolescence within the organization. In addition, reducing the diversity of hardware within the organization reduces costs since fewer device drivers need to be maintained for each type of peripheral. With Windows Server 2003, you'll even want to aim for the inclusion of peripherals that can all be certified—that is, those which include device drivers that are digitally signed by the manufacturer guaranteeing their stability. When stability is the top priority, reducing the number of potential problem sources is critical. The physical layer should always be based on industry standards such as those outlined by the Desktop Management Task Force (DMTF). More information on the DMTF and the standards they promote can be found at http://www.dmtf.org/. Microsoft also provides detailed hardware specifications for Windows products at http://www.microsoft.com/hwdq/hcl/.

The System Kernel is the layer that will save the corporation the most because it provides the framework for the integration of common PASS services into a single unit. This means the organization must begin by devising the technical content of each of the kernel's sublayers, the rules and guidelines governing them, and their personalization or interaction with other sublayers. This information can then be used to interactively create model systems that will serve as sources for the automated installation of all servers in the enterprise network. Using new disk imaging or remote installation technologies, the complete Kernel can be captured into a single installation phase. This image can then be deployed to every server within the network and provide a single unified standard. More on this approach will be discussed in Chapter 2.

But automation is not the only requirement. Planning is essential since the new system will be made available to all users. Here the corporation will need to identify the content of each sublayer using structured guidelines (see "Using the PASS Model" section later in this chapter). Only corporate-wide software components will be included in the System Kernel. At this stage, it will also be vital to properly preconfigure the presentation layer for the model system that serves as the source device before reproduction. If IT is a service, then this is the most important layer of the entire model. It is the one aspect of the system that users will interact with on a daily basis. Presentation does not stop at the desktop. Every element users can see on a system should be standardized. The corporation saves through the definite reduction in retraining. If all hard disks, all desktops, all menus, and all display features are all standardized on all servers, corporate users, even administrators and technicians will always be able to quickly perform work on any given server within the network. For newcomers, the corporation can train them how to use the corporate systems, not how to use basic Windows.

The role-based software and application layer has two parts: commercial software and/or corporate applications. The commercial software portion contains everything that does not have a mission-critical role. It benefits from the rationalization process and thus provides single applications for any given IT task. This layer can save time and money since software and applications are grouped as functional families of products and tools that provide specialized services. Thus deployment of these applications can be performed through the assignment of the family of applications to groups of servers within the corporation.

The corporate application section of this layer focuses on mission-critical business roles. Once again, it is the guidelines of the presentation section that tie this application section to the entire system. Here application deployment costs are considerably reduced because once again, families of applications can be deployed to groups of servers within the network. The major difference between this section and the role-based commercial software section is restricted access. Users of corporate applications must be authorized since they can have access to confidential information through these applications.

All staging and administration approaches for Windows Server 2003 should make use of the PASS model.

A Structured Approach: Using Standard Operating Procedures

To reduce costs and improve network stability, the corporation must implement standard operating procedures (SOPs). SOPs not only ensure stability within a network, but can also greatly reduce costs. Having documented SOPs, even for interactive or manual procedures, can vastly reduce the margin of error when performing the procedure. A well-designed SOP will also supply a contact point for reference if something goes wrong during its operation.

But technical staff often does not have the time or budget required for documenting and standardizing procedures and operations. Because of this, people find it easier to simply remember everything and know who to refer to if a problem arises. While this approach works and has given proven results, its major drawback lies with the availability of key personnel—when this personnel is not (or no longer) available, the knowledge disappears from the enterprise. On the other hand, it is often difficult for organizations to budget for SOP documentation. It is a time-consuming process whose benefits are not always immediately apparent to managers.

SOPs in the form of checklists and detailed procedural steps will be used here as much as possible. Thus, you can save considerable time and effort by simply incorporating these checklists and procedures into the standard operating procedures you prepare for your particular situation.

A standard operating procedure is a documented set of instructions to be followed to complete a given procedure. It focuses on maximizing efficiency during operational and production requirements. Once implemented, SOPs can help provide guaranteed service levels and become the basis for the elaboration of service-level agreements.

When well defined, SOPs allow an organization to measure the time it takes to perform a given task. SOPs are also used to simplify troubleshooting since every process is the same everywhere. Finally, SOPs provide redundancy and reduced costs in administration since all network technicians and administrators use the same processes wherever they are located and no retraining is required. Thus, the SOPs you write will also become the core of any technical training program you provide to the staff in your enterprise.

SOP Best Practices

Here are some concepts to keep in mind when writing or adapting SOPs:

- All SOPs must meet the definition of an SOP: a documented set of instructions to be followed to complete a given procedure.
- Incorporate safety and environment variables into the how-to steps.
- Keep SOPs as short as possible. This will ensure that they are followed. The actual SOP should include no more than 6 to 12 steps to be effective. If an SOP goes beyond 10 steps, consider these solutions:
    - Break the long SOP into several logical sub-job SOPs.
    - Prepare the longer comprehensive training SOP first to get a picture of what training is required. Then decide how to break it into shorter sub-job SOPs.
    - Make the long-form SOP a training document or manual to supplement the shorter sub-job SOPs.
    - If you write shortcut SOPs, explain the reason behind certain steps to provide understanding of the importance of following all the steps in the proper order.
- Write SOPs for people who work in different interpersonal circumstances:
    - For people who work alone
    - For two or more people who work as a team
    - For people who will supervise other people doing a job
    - For people who are not familiar with rules generally understood by your employees
- Consider the age, education, knowledge, skill, experience and training, and work culture of the individuals who will be performing the SOP steps.
- Forecast future effects and steps at certain points in the SOP to tell readers things they should know in advance (upcoming steps that require caution, precision, timing, and personal attention).
- Once the SOP is completed, have several workers test it and give you feedback.
- Review the effectiveness of SOPs after a few weeks and make necessary changes if field practice suggests that descriptions should be improved.
    - Review and update SOPs when processes and equipment are changed.
    - When new equipment is installed, take the opportunity to write a new SOP, incorporating the good from the old, and adding what is necessary to satisfy the new equipment.
- Rely on the expertise of your staff to create and test the SOPs. You can, of course, supplement this expertise with external help.
- Ensure that all SOPs have a designated owner and operator.

- Illustrate the steps in an SOP as much as possible. It is always easier to follow a diagram than written instructions.

> **QUICK TIP**

A sample standard operating procedure and an SOP model are available at http://www.Reso-Net .com/WindowsServer/. You will also find sample WS03-specific SOPs. They are designed to help you in your SOP preparation process.

Enterprise Network Architectures

This completes the basic architectural structure for the design of the enterprise network. This included the examination of several models—the server lifecycle, the service lifecycle, the PASS model—and the outline of the standard operating procedure strategy to be used. Every architectural process begins with the necessity for change. The advent of Windows Server 2003 is the impetus for change within your enterprise network infrastructure. But the technology alone is not the sole object of the change. When designing Enterprise Architectures, organizations must take several additional processes into account. A thorough examination of the existing network, its current problems, the business objectives of the organization, and industry best practices must be combined with a complete understanding of the feature set of the new technology to form the decisions that will make up the architecture you devise. This process is illustrated in Figure 1-3. Thus the next step is to examine the Windows Server 2003 family in depth to identify opportunities for change.

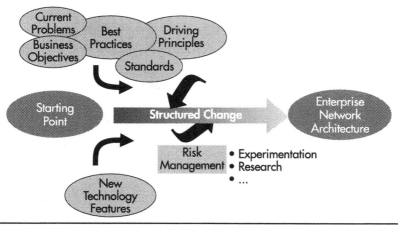

Figure 1-3 Designing an Enterprise Network Architecture involves input from several sources.

Building on Windows 2000: The WS03 Model

Since Windows NT, Microsoft has divided its server family of operating systems into several different products. Such is the case for the Windows Server 2003 family. As mentioned previously, the WS03 family includes four different editions. In addition to offering the standard features that have made Windows famous—complete and powerful network operating system, platform for the execution of applications from 16- to 64-bit, powerful authentication services, and more—the WS03 family offers major improvements over both Windows 2000 and Windows NT. The Windows Server 2003 family is at the same level as the Windows XP client family.

Despite its 32-bit programming model and its core construction protecting the operating system kernel from access by applications, Windows NT never did gain the reputation for stability it should have. For the past two generations of Windows server operating systems, Microsoft has endeavored to ensure that stability is at the core of the operating system. This goal was achieved to a certain degree with Windows 2000 and has been vastly improved with Windows Server 2003.

WS03 also includes a new structure for service offerings: the WS03 add-in. These feature packs are released after the core system and most are free to users of WS03. They include tools supporting communication, collaboration, application integration, and more. For example, the Real-Time Communications server can be added to WS03 to create a new communications infrastructure. SharePoint Team Services can help create team collaboration. Active Directory in Application Mode can be used for application integration. More services will come out in time.

The core WS03 system also supports secure mobile data communications and improved streaming media delivery. It is more stable and reliable than even Windows 2000. With proper server construction, you can ensure that the only downtime is scheduled downtime. WS03 also includes full integration with other components of Microsoft's .NET technology family:

- Integration between Microsoft .NET Passport with Active Directory, allowing organizations to integrate Passport services to their e-commerce strategy
- Native support for SOAP-based message parsing in Microsoft Message Queuing (MSMQ)
- Integration of the COM+ programming model within the .NET Framework

These are only a few of the new features available in WS03, but to understand them properly, you need to be able to compare them to both Windows NT and Windows 2000. If you haven't implemented Windows 2000 yet, you'll want to jump directly to WS03 and immediately profit from its enhancements over Windows 2000. If you are running Windows 2000 today, you may decide that some of the key features of WS03 justify the move. Whichever the case, it will be important to review the complete list of new features for WS03 before you begin your implementation.

As you will see, there are a lot of improvements throughout all of the feature categories of this operating system. But since there are four different versions of WS03, it is also important to understand which version supports which feature.

▶ *NOTE*

Microsoft provides a feature sorter at http://www.microsoft.com/windowsserver2003/evaluation/ features/featuresorter.aspx. But if you prefer a Microsoft Word version of the feature list, you can find one at http://www.Reso-Net.com/WindowsServer/. This table lists the new features and improvements of WS03 compared to Windows NT4 and Windows 2000. Microsoft also provides a feature per edition table at http://www.microsoft.com/windowsserver2003/evaluation/features/compareeditions.mspx.

As you will learn, not all features are supported by all versions of WS03. In fact, clear distinctions emerge when you compare the Web, Standard, and Enterprise Editions of WS03. The Datacenter Edition falls within its own category since it relies on custom hardware, something that not everyone will require.

Choosing a Windows edition to install was simpler in Windows NT. Most often, you installed Windows NT Server itself. Other editions were used only when specific needs or requirements demanded them. With WS03, you will definitely want to apply the proper edition when installing a server since this affects security, the number of default services installed, and operating system cost.

Throughout your discovery of this new OS, you will also find that the major areas for improvement in the WS03 family are security, reliability, performance, manageability, and integrated Web services. These will be discussed in greater length throughout the development process of the Enterprise Network Architecture.

The information found on the Microsoft Web site gives a lot of details, but serves more as a starting point than anything else. If you are working on the architecture phase of your WS03 implementation project, you will want to have more information available to you in a readily available format. One of the best ways to do this is to install help from another operating system on your PC. This option is available only on Windows XP and the WS03 family because it makes use of Windows XP's new Help and Support engine.

The WS03 help can be installed from any WS03 Installation CD by using the Options button of the Help and Support and selecting the appropriate choice from the menu it presents (see Figure 1-4).

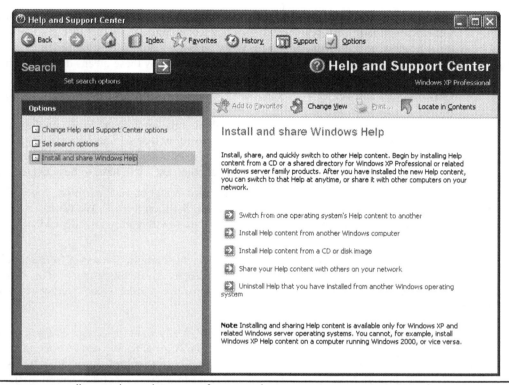

Figure 1-4 Installing Help and Support from another operating system on Windows XP.

You can install Help content from all versions of the WS03 family so that you can search for information on each directly from your PC. A complete installation procedure can be found at http://www.Reso-Net.com/WindowsServer/.

Product Activation

Product activation is a core component of the WS03 family of products. If you purchase a retail version of any version of WS03 or a new server including the operating system, you will have to activate the product. While there are a lot of discussions on the pros and cons of product activation, one thing is sure: Microsoft needs to implement anti-piracy technologies to protect its copyrights. Activation will not be an issue for anyone acquiring WS03 through volume licensing programs such as Open License or Select License because copies of WS03 acquired by these means do not require activation. But everyone else will have to deal with activation at some point in time.

Activation only becomes an issue in a few situations:

- If you partition your server's hard disk drive and install multiple instances of WS03 on the same server, you will need to activate each one. In fact, Microsoft will detect them as one single installation since the hardware components do not change between installations, but since each installation must operate independently of one another, each will have to be activated.

- If you partition your disk and install different instances of WS03 on each partition, you will have to activate each of them. For example, if you install WSE on drive C, WSW on drive D, and WSS on drive E, each will have to be activated and each will require an independent license.

- If you have a total server crash and no backups, and thus must rebuild the server from scratch, the activation will use the same license, but you will have to activate the product again. Worse, in this situation, you will most likely have to call the activation number since Internet activation may not work.

What if you just want to test the operating system and don't really want to activate it? Each retail copy of WS03 includes a 30-day grace period before activation. A lot of testing can be done in 30 days. If you really need a longer period than 30 days, you should use a multiple installation license such as those provided through MSDN subscriptions (http://msdn.microsoft.com/subscriptions/) or the Direct Action Pack (http://members.microsoft.com/partner/salesmarketing/PartnerMarket/ActionPack/).

The Windows Server Enterprise Architecture

Moving to Windows Server 2003 is a major technological undertaking. The scope of the project will vary depending on the size of your network, the number of servers it holds, and the number of users it serves. But in all cases, it is a significant project with significant costs. This is one of the main reasons it should not be taken lightly. Of course, everyone involved in an operating system upgrade project will do their utmost to deliver a great product (the new network), but not everyone will automatically be ready to invest themselves fully into the new operating system.

This is why the first and foremost activity you should perform when preparing the Windows Server 2003 implementation process is to define your project vision. A vision will help you define your own goals for the implementation. It will help define the scope of the change you want to implement and the direction you need to take. Microsoft, through the Microsoft Solutions Framework, uses the SMART approach for vision definition. SMART is an acronym for Specific, Measurable, Attainable, Result-oriented, and Timed. The vision statement you define should include all of these elements—it should specify what you want to do in measurable and attainable steps, be result-oriented, and specify the time it will take to make the change. It should also include information about service delivery, usually to users. For example, a vision statement for a Windows Server 2003 implementation might be:

"Design and deploy a structured and standardized enterprise network based on Windows Server 2003's inherent capabilities to improve our capacity to meet business and user needs, and complete the project within the next year."

This vision includes all of the elements described above. In addition, it is short, easy to understand, and easy to remember.

The vision statement helps ensure that the implementation project aims for the right objectives. One of the great failings of technological projects is that they don't always take full advantage of the technology's capabilities. For example, with the coming of Microsoft Internet Explorer 4, everyone had the Active Desktop at their disposal. But most organizations never made use of this technology at all, even when the Active Desktop provided the best possible solution. In situations of low network bandwidth, using the Active Desktop instead of a roaming profile made a lot of sense, despite industry resistance to the technology.

In this light, it is clear that for the enterprise Windows XP Professional is the client of choice for WS03. Of course, WS03 works with down-level clients, but if you want to take full advantage of the capabilities of WS03 in your enterprise network, you should make sure that you deploy or use Windows XP Professional on your client PCs.

In short, the vision is there to ensure that you don't forget that you're implementing a *new* technology—a technology that has surpassed the one you're replacing and that often provides lots of new ways to do things. The worst that can happen is that you don't keep this in mind and continue to use old methods when newer, more efficient ones are available, simply because you don't know or don't want to know that they exist. Don't let this happen to your project! Don't adapt the new technology to your old methods; adapt your old methods to the new technology.

▶ **NOTE**

This is not the only project-related aspect of a new network implementation, but since project management is not the focus of this book, you may want to refer to Preparing for .NET Enterprise Technologies, *by Ruest and Ruest (Addison-Wesley, 2001) for more information.*

Designing the Enterprise Network Architecture

Every network infrastructure project must begin with the design of the architecture for that project. This is where you make the architectural decisions that will affect how you will make use of the technology you are moving to. Before you work with Windows Server 2003, you'll have to design the architecture of your network. There are a lot of elements to consider and decisions you need to make before you perform your first production installation of WS03.

The Enterprise Network Architecture (ENA) design must begin by looking at the enterprise itself to identify the business needs that drive the type of services your network has to deliver. In fact, you must follow the basic steps of this design process before you are ready to deploy WS03. Every aspect of the network will have to be designed and every need must be taken into consideration. The blueprint in Figure 1-5 outlines the process to use for the design of an Enterprise Network Architecture. It is concentrated on three basic steps:

- Identify business requirements
- Identify technical requirements
- Design the solution

It is also important to remember is that the ENA is a product and should be treated as such. This means it must be iterative. As with any development project, it is a good idea to use versioning techniques when building the ENA. This way, you can aim for smaller steps as you build and prepare your environment. For example, begin with the implementation of Active Directory and the more basic WS03 features in version one, then introduce real-time communications in version two, and so on. Don't try to do everything at once!

As you can see, the design of the solution (step 3) must cover ten elements. These elements form the structure of this book. Using the server and service lifecycles (Figure 1-1), this book will focus on two of the four lifecycle phases: Planning and Preparation and Deployment. By the end of this book, your network should be ready for production.

The ENA blueprint is based on the structure of Exam 70-219 in the Microsoft Certification exam guide. This exam, "Designing a Microsoft Windows 2000 Directory Services Infrastructure," is concentrated on designing the Active Directory for organizations of all sizes. To do so, the designers must know and fully understand the nature of the business and the technical environment that Active Directory will be installed into. The same applies to the enterprise network. This blueprint has been used in a number of different enterprise network implementation projects with excellent results. The first two phases of this blueprint, the analysis components, apply just as well to network design as to AD design, as you'll see in Chapter 3.

The blueprint shows that the design of the solution begins with the planning activity. This activity leads to the initial architecture. Since the architecture is crucial to the project (there's nothing to implement if you don't have an architecture), it becomes valuable for the organization to use and write a standard operating procedure for this process.

The Architectural Design Process

The Architectural Design Process supports the introduction of a new service into the enterprise network. It is performed by architects, planners, and system administrators. Two types of architectures are required when implementing a new technology: the Enterprise Architecture (which is focused on orientations, rules, and standards for the service) and the Technical Architecture (which is focused on the technical details of the service implementation). Both use similar procedures with small variations.

Begin with the review of the existing situation and a review or creation of comprehensive inventories. If inventories are up to date, this process is greatly facilitated since it can concentrate on its objective instead of getting sidetracked into actually performing inventory collection. The situation review should also list existing problems and issues that can be addressed by the new service being introduced. Make sure the review also focuses on the positive elements of the existing situation. This ensures that what is being done well continues to be so.

Analysis

1 Business Requirements

2 Technical Requirements

Solution Design

3 Enterprise Network Architecture

1- Business Model
- ‣ Organization Model
- ‣ Organization Goals
- ‣ Products & Services
- ‣ Geographic Scope
- ‣ Organization Processes

2- Organization Structure
- ‣ Management Model
- ‣ Organization Structure
- ‣ Vendors/Partner/ Customer Relationships
- ‣ Acquisition Plans (Business)

3- Organization Strategies
- ‣ Business Priorities
- ‣ Projected Growth and Strategy
- ‣ Legal Implications
- ‣ Tolerance for Risk
- ‣ TCO Objectives

4- IT Management
- ‣ Centralized/ Decentralized Management
- ‣ Funding Model
- ‣ Outsourcing/ In-house?
- ‣ Decision-making Process
- ‣ Change Management Process

1- Existing/Planned IT Environment
- ‣ Organization size
- ‣ Number of Users
- ‣ Resources Location
- ‣ Network Geographic Distribution and Links
- ‣ Available Bandwidth
- ‣ H/S Performance Requirements
- ‣ Data Patterns
- ‣ Network Roles and Responsibilities
- ‣ Security Issues

2- Impact of Enterprise Network
- ‣ Existing Systems and Applications
- ‣ Planned Upgrades/Rollouts
- ‣ IP Infrastructure
- ‣ Technology Support Structure
- ‣ Current Planned Network & System Management
- ‣ Authentication Services

3- Client/PC Desktop Management
- ‣ End User Requirements
- ‣ Technology Support for End Users
- ‣ Required Client Environment
- ‣ Internal/External Client Base

1- Planning
- ‣ Review Requirements
- ‣ Review new Products Features
- ‣ Create Initial Architecture
- ‣ Prepare for the Installation

2- Installation
- ‣ Preparation
- ‣ Initial Installation
- ‣ Automating Installations
- ‣ Server Staging

3- AD Infrastructure
- ‣ AD Design
- ‣ AD Installation
- ‣ AD Management

4- IP Infrastructure
- ‣ Network Settings
- ‣ Connection Management
- ‣ IP Addressing
- ‣ Name Resolution

5- PC Management Strategy
- ‣ Managing Objects with Group Policy
- ‣ Software Installation
- ‣ Environment Management

6- User Support Infrastructure
- ‣ User Management (Accounts, Groups, Authentication)
- ‣ User Environment Management

7- Shared Resources & Internetworking
- ‣ Sharing Folders
- ‣ Sharing Printers
- ‣ Sharing Applications
- ‣ Auditing Resources
- ‣ Internet Information Server
- ‣ IP Routing
- ‣ Remote Access

8- Security Infrastructure
- ‣ Security Policy Design
- ‣ Security Resources
- ‣ IIS Security
- ‣ Public Key Infrastructure (PKI)

9- Resilience Management
- ‣ Disaster Recovery
- ‣ Troubleshooting Strategy
- ‣ Redundancy Planning

10- Network Administration
- ‣ Administration Design
- ‣ Remote Administration
- ‣ Routine Tasks
- ‣ Performance Management
- ‣ Directory Management

Figure 1-5   The blueprint for Enterprise Network Architecture Design

The architectural design process is supported by a series of tools, such as the Help and Support information mentioned earlier, but its most important tool is the technological laboratory. This is where you will reproduce existing environments and test all migration procedures. It will also be important for you to review product documentation and perhaps even attend training classes.

▶ **QUICK TIP**

A sample SOP for this process is available at http://www.Reso-Net.com/WindowsServer/.

Don't forget the objective of the architecture during this process: it is to solve problems, improve service levels, and stay within budget. Make sure you involve other groups, especially the groups targeted by the solution, in your solution design process.

Performing a Situation Review and Needs Analysis

As you can see, the starting point of any change is the current situation, and the best place to start a review of the current situation is with inventories. You need to create extensive lists of the items the inventory must cover. Like the blueprint in Figure 1-5, it should begin with the identification of business-related information, and then move on to the details of the technical environment for which you will need to design the solution.

For the Windows Server 2003 Enterprise Network Architecture, your analysis will need to focus on two additional areas:

- If you intend to perform a migration from an existing environment, you will need to perform an extensive server inventory to identify which servers can be rationalized, which can be retired and replaced, and which services will require entirely new servers. You will also need a detailed inventory of the services and functions each existing server performs. This will mean detailing the actual users on each server, information stored on the server, security parameters for that information, and so on.

- If you are implementing a new network, you will need to clearly identify the business requirements in order to properly scale the servers you will deploy.

Don't hold back on this activity, as it is the driving force for the solution you design.

▶ **QUICK TIP**

You can find a detailed inventory list at http://www.Reso-Net.com/WindowsServer/.

The Changing Role of Servers

One of the major objectives of each new version of Windows Microsoft releases is to support new hardware and advances in hardware technology. In terms of servers, these advances are considerable. Today, basic hardware performance for a server is no longer a limitation or an issue. Most servers today are multiprocessing servers—servers that can be scaled through the addition of more CPUs. Servers today also support "hot add" features such as random access memory and hard disks without having to stop the server. In addition, storage technologies have evolved into storage area networks (SAN) or network access storage (NAS) which are very easy to scale transparently.

Microsoft has helped considerably with the release of Windows 2000 and especially Windows Server 2003. Windows 2000 removed 75 reboot scenarios compared to Windows NT. WS03 is even more stable. Network modifications no longer require reboots, and the addition of a very powerful plug-and-play engine means adding most hardware also does not require a reboot.

As organizations move to WS03, they will be able to take advantage of the latest advancements in server hardware such as Intel's Itanium microchip (http://www.intel.com/itanium/). Both WSE and WSD offer native support for new Itanium-based servers operating with 64-bit processing. All of the versions of WS03 support the new "headless" server concept—servers without direct physical links to either monitors or input devices. There is also the concept of the "blade" server, which uses a large number of medium-performance processors in a multiprocessing system that provides redundancy, scalability, and peak-load processing. Once again, WS03 is designed to take advantage of these new capabilities since all versions of Windows Server 2003 have multiprocessing capabilities to some degree. In fact, Microsoft and Intel continuously work hand in hand to develop the guidelines for server creation with each new generation of Windows. Before you make your server decisions, you should definitely read the latest news on this collaborative effort. Microsoft publishes this information on their Web site at http://www.microsoft.com/hwdev/.

Consolidating Servers with Windows Server 2003

A server today provides a function. It is not a product. Many organizations have taken to single instance servers when working with Windows NT. The approach was reasonable. Though NT itself was a solid product, many of the operations organizations performed with it made it unstable. Often, the best way to deal with this instability was to dedicate the server to one specific role. Unfortunately this approach serves to increase the number of servers in the organization. Many existing Windows NT servers are never used to their full capacity. In many cases, the server rarely exceeds 15 percent utilization! The coming of Windows 2000 and especially Windows Server 2003 allows organizations to review traditional server approaches and aim for increased server consolidation.

Consolidation involves fatter servers and thinner clients because servers today are more manageable and more scalable. Consolidation also offers great advantages. You have fewer servers to manage. You can improve service levels because it is easier to maintain the operation of a few centralized servers than it is for several distributed servers. There is less downtime since servers tend to be centralized and provide easier physical access. Applications can be deployed more rapidly because most of the code resides on the server itself. And it is easier to standardize because fewer physical elements are involved.

There are four justifications for consolidation:

- **Centralization**   Relocating existing servers to fewer sites.
- **Physical consolidation**   Many smaller servers are replaced with fewer, more powerful servers.

- **Data integration**   Several distributed databases are consolidated into a single data repository.
- **Application integration**   Multiple applications are migrated to fewer, more powerful servers. Applications must have a certain degree of affinity before this integration can occur.

In addition, consolidation can take the form of implementing several "virtual machines" on a single server. Despite its many advances, Windows Server 2003 still doesn't support the simultaneous operation of multiple instances of the same application on a single server. But using technologies such as VMware Corporation's VMware Workstation or Server software, you can take better advantage of a single server's hardware by installing multiple instances of Windows Server 2003 or even older operating systems inside virtual machines. These machines act and operate exactly in the same manner as a physical machine and can be visible to the entire network. This means that they can provide additional services to users from a single physical server. For example, if you need to run SQL Server 2000 on your Windows Server 2003, but you still have legacy applications that have not been upgraded from SQL Server version 7, you can install SQL 2000 on the physical installation of WSS or WSE, create a virtual machine on the same server, and install an instance of SQL 7 inside that machine. You can then have the two instances of SQL Server running and delivering services to users from the same physical machine. The same applies to applications that run on NT, but not on WS03. If you don't have time to convert them, run them in NT virtual machines.

If you are among those who have servers performing at no more than 15 percent of their capacity, VMware is definitely a great tool to give you more service from the same hardware. VMware products can be found at http://www.vmware.com/.

Finally, Microsoft Windows Server 2003 Enterprise and Datacenter Editions offer improved clustering functionality over Windows NT and Windows 2000. Clustering services are now loaded by default during installation and are dynamic. This means that when you activate or modify clustering services with WSE or WSD, you no longer need to restart the cluster. In addition, WS03 cluster services are Active Directory aware—that is, they are published within the Active Directory and made available to all users in the same way that nonclustered services are. In Windows 2000, this posed a problem since printers installed on a cluster could not be published in the directory.

Thus clustering and server consolidation should be one of the objectives you keep in mind when designing your WS03 Enterprise Network Architecture. To do so, you need to group servers by function to see which logical groupings are available for consolidation purposes. This is where the PASS model illustrated previously in Figure 1-2 becomes most useful.

Using the PASS Model

As mentioned before, the PASS model makes it easier to conceive and manage servers. To do so, you need to concentrate on two elements:

- The Server Kernel or all of the elements that will be common to all servers
- Role-based server configurations—all of the applications or functions that can be consolidated onto similar servers

Designing the Server Kernel

The Server Kernel is designed to deliver all of the services that are common to all servers. The decision to include a component is based on corporate need as well as licensing mode for the component. If your organization owns a corporate license for a server component, it should be included in the kernel. If your corporation requires a specific function on all servers, the technology supporting it should be included in the kernel. Kernel contents also include the default server configuration. Finalizing the configuration elements of the server and capturing them in an "image" of the Server Kernel can greatly simplify the deployment process for new servers. This configuration should also include the preparation of the presentation section of the server. Making sure that all new user environments created on the server have immediate access to server management tools and server utilities simplifies the server management process as well.

Table 1-1 outlines the suggested content for the Server Kernel.

Sublayer	Suggested Contents
Operating system (provides basic system services)	Windows Server 2003, Enterprise Edition (most versatile edition) Service Packs and/or hot fixes, if applicable Specific drivers (video, power management, printing, etc.) DLLs (Visual Studio DLLs, .NET Framework CLR, others) Open/TrueType fonts
Networking (to apply network standards)	Unique protocol Server identification (host name, NetBIOS name, machine name) Domain membership Startup, shutdown, logon, logoff scripts Routing and remote access tools
Storage (to standardize the way information is presented)	Identical physical drives Identical logical disks (including the local tree for software and the local tree for data) Network tree (based on the Distributed File System or DFS)
Security (to standardize access control)	System owner User profiles and default Group Policies Local (NTFS) and network access rights and permissions Central access control management Group Policy management Antivirus software Intrusion detection and auditing tools
Communications (to standardize the way users interact with each other)	Email client Browsers (home page, internal corporate favorites, proxy/firewall controls) Communication tools to users (message from management, from IT, etc.) Data collection tools

Table 1-1   Potential Content for the Server Kernel

Sublayer	Suggested Contents
Common productivity tools (to standardize common tools)	Office automation (current version of Office managed through groups and profiles) Generic graphics and image capture tools Appropriate Service Packs Support tools Resource Kit tools
Presentation (to standardize the way users interact with the system)	Active Desktop components Menus and Quick Launch area and shortcuts Default User profile and presentation Resource Kit tools

Table 1-1   Potential Content for the Server Kernel *(continued)*

Configuring Server Roles

Next, you need to identify server roles or functions. This is done by grouping service types by service affinity. Certain types of services or functions do not belong together, while others naturally tend to fit in the same category. For servers, you will have roles that are defined by the type of software they run, and thus the type of service they deliver. Seven main categories emerge:

- **Identity Management Servers**   These servers are the core identity managers for the network. They contain and maintain the entire corporate identity database for all users and user access. For WS03, these would be servers running Active Directory services. This function should not be shared with any other unless it is a core networking function such as name resolution, though in some cases it may be found on a multi-purpose server.

- **Application Servers**   These servers provide application services to the user community. Windows Server 2003 examples would be SQL Server, Commerce Server, and so on. These will of course also include your corporate applications.

- **File and Print Servers**   These servers focus on the provision of storage and structured document services to the network. As you will see, these functions are greatly expanded in Windows Server 2003 and form the basis of information sharing within this technology.

- **Dedicated Web Servers**   These servers focus on the provision of Web services to user communities. In fact, Windows Server 2003 Web Edition is specifically designed to meet these needs.

- **Collaboration Servers**   These servers provide the infrastructure for collaboration within the enterprise. Their services can include SharePoint Team Services, Streaming Media Services, and Real Time Communications.

- **Network Infrastructure Servers**   These servers provide core networking functions such as IP addressing or name resolution, including support for legacy systems. They also provide routing and remote access services.

- **Terminal servers**   These servers provide a central application execution environment to users. Users need only have a minimal infrastructure to access these servers because their entire execution environment resides on the server itself.

In addition, server placement comes into play. Placement refers to the architectural proximity or position of the server in an end-to-end distributed system. Three positions are possible:

- Inside the intranet
- In the security perimeter, often referred to as the demilitarized zone (DMZ) though the perimeter often includes more than just the DMZ
- Outside the enterprise

Finally, you could add a last server category, the Failsafe Server. This type of server is in fact an exact copy of each of the above categories, but is made of dormant servers that wake up whenever there is a failure within the network. The nature of your business and the level of service you need to provide to users and customers will determine if this last category is required in your enterprise network.

Each of these elements will have to be taken into consideration during the elaboration of the solution you design with Windows Server 2003.

Migration Considerations

It is important to identify the migration path you will use to move from your existing network to the WS03 enterprise network. There are several techniques that can be used to migrate from one network operating system to another. Of course, if you're implementing a new network based on WS03, migration considerations are not your primary concern.

Migrating from an existing operating system would be very easy to do if you could do it while everyone is on vacation or during an annual shutdown of operations. Unfortunately, you will most likely be performing migrations during normal business operations. In addition, you'll have to make the migration process transparent to users and to the business process. Quite a challenge!

Migrations, as opposed to new installations, must take a few factors into consideration. First, you have to ensure that you provide, at the very least, exactly the same service levels users are currently experiencing in your network. Of course, your major goal will be to improve the user network experience, but you should ensure that whatever happens, you will not reduce service levels. This is one of the reasons why you must include user representatives in your network design project. They will help keep you focused. After all, the network is there as a service to them.

Second, you have to ensure that you provide comprehensive training programs at all levels of your organization. If you're moving from Windows NT to WS03, you'll find that the major training task is technical, not user oriented. While users do experience new features such as interface improvements, it is mostly in manageability and reliability that WS03 improvements abound. Technical staff will have to undergo extensive training. They will have to be prepared well before you implement the new network. In addition, you'll probably want to ensure that the user training program you deliver occurs at the time you migrate. The best migration results occur when user training is synchronized with the migration program. If you're running Windows 2000, training will be reduced since the main difference for users is the interface.

Third, you'll want to ensure that all of your applications run properly in WS03. If you're running Windows NT, you'll need to test applications thoroughly to ensure that they operate properly under the new operating system. One of the major reasons for this is the new security model in Windows 2000 and WS03. Users are much more restricted in WS03 than they ever were in NT, thus applications that run under NT do not necessarily run under WS03. More on this topic will be covered in Chapter 7. But there are other advantages in using WS03. WS03 offers an application compatibility mode that is the same as the one offered by Windows XP. This is something that wasn't available in Windows 2000. Applications should run better in WS03 than in Windows 2000, but nevertheless, you will discover that several of your applications will need to be upgraded or otherwise modified to run properly. Rationalization is a great help here because it means less upgrades. Both rationalization and extensive application compatibility testing should be part of your project.

Fourth, you'll want to determine if you upgrade your systems or if you perform clean installations. The decision will depend on a lot of factors, but the most valuable approach is the new installation. New installations simply offer better stability and reliability since they give you the opportunity to clean up your existing systems.

Finally, you'll need to consider how to migrate your directory and authentication services. WS03 includes an improved Active Directory Migration Tool (ADMT). Version 2 of this tool allows for migration of user accounts and passwords from Windows NT and Windows 2000. It is a good tool for domain consolidation and migration. More on this topic will be discussed in Chapter 10.

These aren't the only considerations you'll have to take into account when migrating, but they are a good starting point. More on this topic will be discussed throughout this book.

Upgrade versus Clean Installation

As mentioned earlier, there are some impacts to consider when deciding to upgrade or perform a new installation. Most depend on the status of your current network. Table 1-2 outlines the potential upgrade paths for all versions of WS03.

▶ **NOTE**

There is no upgrade path to Windows Server 2003, Web Edition.

Though the upgrade is much easier to perform than a clean installation, when you upgrade from Windows NT to WS03, you will lose some functionality. Windows Server 2003 no longer uses the WINNT folder. It has finally moved to a Windows folder. In addition, like Windows 2000, WS03 uses the Documents and Settings folder to store user profiles. If you upgrade from NT, profiles will be maintained in the WINNT/Profiles folder. This has a bearing on the proper application of Group Policy settings. More on this topic will be discussed in appropriate chapters, but the recommendation is strong: If you are migrating from Windows NT to WS03, prepare to perform clean installations.

The impact isn't the same if you upgrade from Windows 2000. WS03 and Windows 2000 share the same code base, so an upgrade is in fact quite possible, but *not* if you performed an upgrade to Windows 2000 from Windows NT. In the latter case, you will be facing the same problems you would

From the Following Versions of Windows...	...to a Windows Server 2003 Version
Windows NT Server version 4.0 with Service Pack 5 or later	Standard Edition
Note: Any Windows NT version earlier than 4.0 must first be upgraded to Windows NT version 4.0 with Service Pack 5	Enterprise Edition
Windows NT Server version 4.0, Terminal Server Edition, with Service Pack 5 or later	Standard Edition
Note: If you need full Terminal Server functionality, you must upgrade to Windows 2003, Enterprise Edition	Enterprise Edition
Windows 2000 Server	Standard Edition
	Enterprise Edition
Windows NT Server version 4.0, Enterprise Edition, Service Pack 5 or later	Enterprise Edition
Windows 2000 Advanced Server	
Windows 2000 Datacenter Server	Datacenter Edition
Windows 9x, Me, 2000 Professional, XP Home or Professional	No upgrade path
	These are workstation operating systems
	Upgrades must be performed as clean installs

Table 1-2   Upgrade Paths to WS03

if you upgraded directly from NT to WS03. Of course, in this case, you probably already know all the things you can't do with your Windows 2000 network.

Upgrading from a Windows 2000 network that was implemented as a clean install is quite acceptable, even recommended. In fact, this is the easiest upgrade path since WS03 supports an in-place upgrade and the process can be made quite transparent to users.

There is no upgrade path from any of the workstation or desktop versions of Windows to WS03. WS03 is a server and network operating system. Windows 9x, Me, 2000 Professional, and both editions of XP are not designed to perform the same type of work that WS03 is.

Using the Technological Lab as a Testing Ground

The final preparation activity for your WS03 enterprise network project is the preparation and implementation of a technological laboratory. Since application compatibility testing and proofs of concepts are an integral part of the design and preparation process, the technological laboratory is crucial.

The laboratory should contain enough technologies to be able to properly reproduce the organization's existing IT infrastructure. It should include technologies that are as recent as possible. Most often, organizations use recovered equipment that is not the latest and greatest. This only limits the potential benefits of this lab because its purpose is to work with new technologies. New technologies always require more powerful hardware. If you plan to purchase new equipment for your implementation project, it is a good idea to prepurchase a few systems and use them for laboratory testing.

The lab must also include quick setup and recovery strategies. For example, if technicians are working on a case study that requires the staging of an Active Directory and Windows Server 2003 infrastructure, you won't want them to have to rebuild it from scratch every time they return to the laboratory. One of the best ways to provide this capability is to use interchangeable disk drives. This allows each technical group to prepare and store their own working environment, which saves considerable time.

Another method is to use disk-imaging technologies. This requires a powerful storage server because each environment must be stored independently for the duration of the tests.

If access to hardware is an issue, you might consider using virtual machines with VMware. All that is required to design a complex network system based on virtual machines is a few very powerful servers. For example, with a single dual processor Pentium server and one gigabyte of RAM, it is possible to design an entire Active Directory distributed forest. It's not tremendously fast, but for testing purposes, it works extremely well.

In addition, the laboratory will require a special station or stations that are disconnected from the laboratory network and connected to the internal network and the Internet. These stations serve for documentation, research, and software downloads. Ideally, these stations are positioned throughout the lab for ready access by technicians.

The most important aspect of the lab will be its activity coordination and resource sharing. Most organizations cannot invest as much as they would like in a laboratory, therefore, most must use timesharing strategies to ensure that technical staff have ready access to the resources they need for testing purposes. Good coordination and structured testing methods can only ensure better testing results.

> **QUICK TIP**
>
> *A sample laboratory datasheet that can be used for the testing portion of the preparation phase for your project can be found at http://www.Reso-Net.com/WindowsServer/.*

Figure 1-6 illustrates a sample testing laboratory. This lab reproduces a typical internal network with a minimum of equipment. Internal TCP/IP addresses can be used since it does not connect to the external world. More servers can be added to test the migration strategy you will devise, but these can be older and more obsolete systems since you will not be doing performance testing with them.

Using a Testing Strategy

Since creating an enterprise network is 80 percent planning and preparation and 20 percent implementation, the laboratory is one of the key elements of your future network. To ensure that your preparation phase goes well, you should use very strict testing strategies. Most testing strategies include several stages, each focused on a specific type of test. When building and preparing the enterprise network, you should use the following test types:

- **Discovery**   The first test is always an interactive discovery of a new technology. This phase lets you identify the elements of the Technical Architecture for the product.

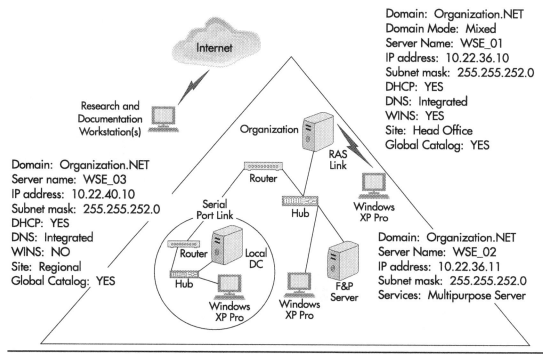

Figure 1-6   A testing lab should be as complete as possible.

- **System test**   Once the first stages of discovery have been performed, you move to automation of an installation process. This test focuses on evaluation of the automated procedure by itself.

- **Security issue identification**   Are there any security issues with the product as installed during system tests? If so, they must be taken into consideration.

- **Functional test**   Does the product operate as expected? If not, you must go back to the beginning.

- **Integration test**   How does the product behave when merged with other products it may have to coexist with? Are there modifications required to the installation?

- **Acceptance test**   Does the final client or user approve of the product as designed and installed? If not, you must modify the installation and configuration.

- **Deployment test**   Is remote distribution of this product required? If so, a deployment test must be performed to ensure that it behaves as expected during remote installation.

- **Uninstall test**   If uninstallation will eventually be required, it should be tested both interactively and remotely.

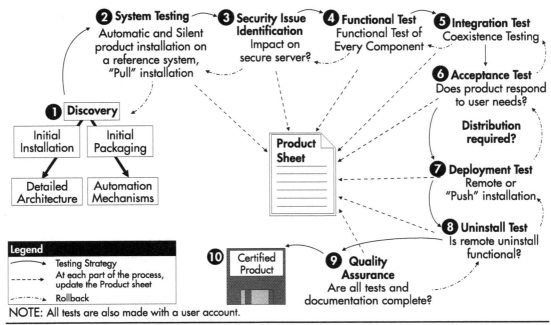

Figure 1-7   The Product Testing Strategy

- **Quality assurance**   Once all tests have been performed, a final quality assurance test should be performed. Is all documentation correct and complete? Have all testing procedures been followed correctly? These are some of the questions that must be answered during this phase before final release of the product to the enterprise.

Each testing phase is important. If, for any reason, your product fails at any testing stage, it must be rolled back to the previous stage and corrections must be applied. This process is illustrated in Figure 1-7. Following strict guidelines and rigorous testing procedures will only make your final product all the better. This is one of the definitions of enterprise-ready networking.

Moving On

Your preparations are now complete. You've starting working on the architectural design of your WS03 enterprise network. You have identified that a lifecycle approach is the best method to use to prepare for the migration to WS03. Now you're ready to move on to the first stage of the implementation, the analysis of the installation methods used for Windows Server 2003. This is what is covered in the next chapter.

Best Practice Summary

This chapter recommends the following best practices:

- Use the Server Lifecycle to prepare and plan for servers in your Enterprise Network Architecture.
- Use the Service Lifecycle to prepare and plan for services within your enterprise network.
- Use the PASS model to identify both common and specific components for server construction and management.
- Use standard operating procedures to document or automate all procedures within your network. This way, you can be sure of the outcome of the operation.
- Learn about the product you are about to deploy. Identify differences to existing products and see how they apply to your environment.
- Design an Enterprise Network Architecture *before* you install your new systems.
- Use the Architectural Design Process SOP to design your Enterprise Network Architecture.
- Write a project vision for yourself so you and your audience can know where you're going and what you're doing.
- Don't forget to look at new ways of doing things when moving to a new technology.
- Use a clean installation if you are moving from Windows NT to Windows Server 2003 or if you upgraded from Windows NT to Windows 2000.
- Prepare and use a technological laboratory throughout the project to perform proofs of concepts and test the solutions you design.
- If you need to perform a new inventory for this project, don't forget to keep it up to date from now on.

Chapter Roadmap

Use Figure 1-8 to review the contents of this chapter.

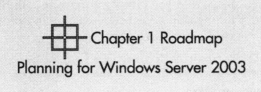
Chapter 1 Roadmap
Planning for Windows Server 2003

 The Windows Server 2003 Family
Building the Foundation of the Network
Lifecycle Approach:
  › The Server Lifecycle
  › The Service Lifecycle **(Figure 1-1)**
A New Model for Server Construction and
Management Model
  › The Benefits of the PASS Model **(Figure 1-2)**
Structured Approach - Using SOPs
  › SOP Best Practices
Enterprise Network Architectures **(Figure 1-3)**
Building on Windows 2000: The Windows Server 2003 Model
  › Finding more information - Install Help and Support **(Figure 1-4)**
  › Product Activation

Tools on the Companion Web Site
  ▫ Microsoft Word version of the
    WS03 improvements and new
    features
  ▫ Help and Support procedure
  ▫ A sample standard operating
    procedure (SOP)
  ▫ SOPs Blueprint
  ▫ The ten layers of the PASS model

 The Windows Server Enterprise Architecture
Designing the Enterprise Network Architecture **(Figure 1-5)**
  › The Architectural Design Process
  › Performing a Situation Review and Needs Analysis
  › The Changing Role of Servers
  › Consolidating Servers with Windows Server 2003
  › Using the PASS Model
    › Designing the Server Kernel
    › Configuring Server Roles
  › Migration Considerations
  › Upgrade versus Clean Installation
  › Using the Technological Lab as a Testing Ground **(Figure 1-6)**
    › Testing Strategy **(Figure 1-7)**

**Tools on the Companion Web Site**
  ▫ Enterprise Network Design Blueprint
  ▫ SOP: Architectural Design Process
  ▫ Inventory table of contents for
    Situation Review
  ▫ A sample Laboratory Data Sheet

 Moving on

 Best Practice Summary

Figure 1-8   Chapter Roadmap

CHAPTER 2

Preparing for Massive Installations of Windows Server 2003

IN THIS CHAPTER

W indows Server 2003 offers several significant improvements in installation methods compared to Windows 2000, and especially compared to Windows NT. Four installation methods are now available with WS03:

- Manual or interactive installation
- Unattended installation through an answer file
- Disk imaging with the System Preparation Tool
- Remote installation through the Remote Installation Service

Two of these, disk imaging and remote server installation, are new to Windows Server 2003. In addition, WS03 brings new features to the unattended installation method.

Each method is appropriate for specific situations; some can even be combined together for improved effectiveness and efficiency. But before you select the installation method, you need to consider the method you will use if you are migrating from an existing network. Once again, you need to make architectural decisions before you move on to the installation itself.

When you move to the WS03 enterprise network, you'll need to work with three major categories of systems:

- **Identity Management Servers**   These include domain controllers or the systems that contain and maintain the corporate identity database for users and other network objects.
- **Member Servers**   All other servers in the network fall into this category. These include the other six categories of servers mentioned in Chapter 1, such as Application Servers, File and Print Servers, Web Servers, and so on.
- **Personal Computers**   These include all of your workstations, including mobile devices.

In the case of Windows Server 2003, you'll be mostly concerned with the first two categories, but despite the fact that WS03 is a server operating system, implementing it in your network will also involve some operations on your PCs. Everything depends on the migration strategy you choose to use. In fact, you need to make some critical decisions *before* you begin installing servers.

Choosing the Migration Approach

First, you need to decide *how* you want to migrate: will you perform new installations or upgrades? Chapter 1 discussed this issue at length. If you are moving from Windows NT to Windows Server 2003, or if you are moving from a Windows 2000 network that was upgraded from Windows NT, you should take advantage of this opportunity to perform new installations everywhere. If you have already performed new installations when you migrated from Windows NT to Windows 2000, you can simply perform in-place upgrades of your Windows 2000 systems.

The answer to this first question will greatly influence the choices you make during your migration. If you need to perform new installations, you can't simply upgrade existing servers, because it will be difficult to design a migration approach that will not disrupt normal operations. There are methods that could simplify the migration process. For example, you could stage a new server using a separate network, give it the name of an existing server in your network, and replace the old with the new. But this approach has some issues. Even though the new server has the same name, it will not be seen as the same machine within your network because WS03 does not use the machine name to communicate and identify a server. Rather, it uses the security identifier (SID), a random identity number that is generated at installation. This identifier will never be duplicated on a given network and will never be the same between two machines that were installed using one of the four supported installation methods.

If you want to take advantage of WS03 to implement a new network, using new principles and a new architecture, you should consider the Parallel Network Approach. This is the safest approach because it involves the least risk. It focuses on the implementation of a new, parallel network that does not touch or affect the existing environment. Ongoing operations are not affected because the existing network is not removed or modified. The Parallel Network Approach is based on the acquisition of new machines that are used to create a migration pool. This migration pool becomes the core of the new network. Then, as you put new systems in place to replace existing services, you can recover machines from the existing or legacy network and rebuild them before adding them to the new network. This process is illustrated in Figure 2-1.

The parallel network has several advantages. First, it provides an ongoing rollback environment. If, for some reason, the new network does not work properly, you can quickly return to the legacy environment because it is still up and running. Next, you can migrate groups of users and machines according to your own timetable. Since the existing network is still running, you can target specific groups without having to affect others. Finally, since the existing network is still running, you can take the time to completely master new technologies and services before putting them in place.

It does have some disadvantages, though. It costs more than doing an in-place upgrade. But if you want a better return on investment (ROI) at the end of your project, you will want to take the time to redesign your network to take full advantage of new WS03 features. It is also more time consuming

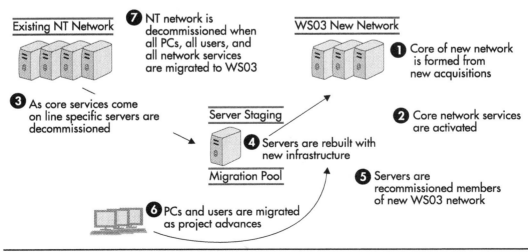

Figure 2-1   The Parallel Network Migration Approach

since the process of putting a second network in place is complex. On the other hand, it will give you the opportunity to take the time to design appropriately. The parallel network is a harder sell in a migration project, but its advantages far outweigh its disadvantages in most situations. In the case of a migration from Windows NT to WS03, its advantages are clear. Table 2-1 compares the upgrade to the parallel network. The Parallel Network Implementation Process is outlined in Chapter 4.

Choosing What to Migrate First

Of course, if your existing network is based on Windows 2000 and you have taken the time to perform a proper migration to this operating system, your migration path to WS03 will be much simpler. What you'll want to determine is which systems you will migrate first: Identity Servers, Member Servers, or PCs? For one category of systems, PCs, the answer is easy. If you're already using Windows XP Professional, you won't have to touch PCs until you've migrated the servers the PCs are linked to. But the question still remains between Identity and Member Servers: which to do first? Since Windows Server 2003 supports multiple operating modes and is compatible with Windows NT version 4 as well as Windows 2000, you could choose to migrate each category of server in any order. Figure 2-2 illustrates the migration "slide-rule." This concept shows that Identity Servers, Member Servers, and PCs can be migrated in any order. It also displays the relative migration timelines for each type of system, graphically demonstrating the duration of each migration process compared to each other. The slide-rule is used to demonstrate that each migration process can be moved from one place to another on the project timescale allowing you to begin with the process that suits your organization best.

Identity Servers First

In Windows Server 2003, migrating Identity Servers means working with Active Directory, the same as in Windows 2000. If you're already running Windows 2000, this step should be relatively easy to perform since you can upgrade a Windows 2000 domain controller and run a "mixed" environment of Windows 2000 and Windows Server domain controllers. Then when all your servers are migrated to

Parallel Network	Upgrade
Advantages	
Provides ongoing rollback environment	Lower costs
Migrate groups and users on an "as you need" basis, even support and administrative groups	Simpler to design since all services exist already
	A single network to manage
Migrate at your own speed	Dual support methods disappear faster
Take advantage of new system features immediately	
Implement features in "native" mode	
Can deal with existing issues	
Faster ROI	
Disadvantages	
Higher costs at first	No "simple" rollback method
Design is more complex because it's a completely new network	Must migrate users all at once when upgrading PDC
	Gain only the new features that work in "mixed" mode
Two networks to manage	Carry on existing issues into new network
Dual support methods last longer	Slower ROI

Table 2-1   Parallel Network versus Upgrade

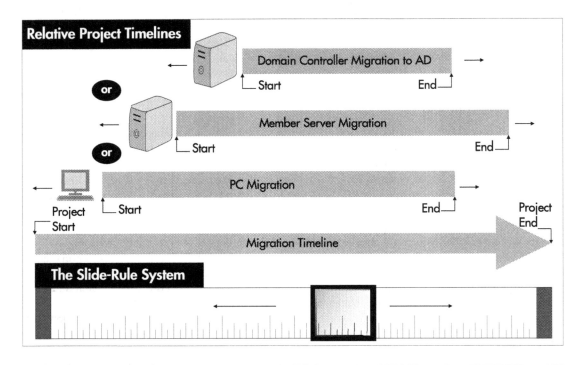

Figure 2-2   The migration slide-rule

WS03, you can activate the "native" directory mode for this version of Windows. While Windows 2000 could operate either in a mixed NT and 2000 mode or a native 2000 mode, WS03 now has two new Active Directory modes. More will be covered on this topic in Chapter 3, but it is sufficient to say for now that WS03 has four Active Directory modes:

- Mixed mode with NT, 2000, and WS03
- Mixed mode with 2000 and WS03, which is the Windows 2000 native mode
- Native WS03 domain mode
- Native WS03 forest mode

Switching to native mode is not something that is done lightly. You can only do so when you've verified that legacy domain controllers are either upgraded or decommissioned and that all other conditions are met.

If you're currently running a Windows NT network, migrating Identity Servers first will mean implementing Active Directory. You'll have to make sure you're ready before taking this step. Active Directory is to the Windows NT SAM what a handheld computer is to a full-fledged notebook. You can do a lot of stuff with the handheld, but there is so much more you can do with a real computer. And if your experience is with a handheld, you'll need a bit of training before you discover everything you can do with the notebook.

The same applies to Active Directory. If you're moving from NT to WS03, you'll need to take significant training and fully understand your needs before you can implement AD. But in either case, there are significant advantages for doing the Identity Servers first:

- Every Windows version from 98 on can participate in an Active Directory, though older versions require the installation of a client pack.

▶ *CAUTION*

Windows 95 and Windows NT 4 Service Pack 3 or earlier cannot participate in a WS03 domain because they do not support its security protocols.

- Member Servers running Windows NT and Windows 2000 also work in a WS03 Active Directory structure.

- The number of machines required to operate the identity environment is often significantly less than for other purposes.

- Every machine from Windows NT 4 on must *join* a Windows network. This joining process must be performed whenever Member Servers or PCs are installed. This process is also unique to each identity environment. Thus if you migrate the identity environment first, you will only need to join machines to the new directory environment once.

- Active Directory is the basis of a WS03 network. It makes sense to put it in place before putting anything else in place. That way, you can ensure that there is little or no "garbage" in your Directory Database.

The full migration approach to Active Directory is covered in Chapters 3 and 4.

Member Servers First

If you're working with a Windows NT network, chances are that you have a lot more domain controllers than you need in your network. Windows NT had serious limitations in terms of member services. You often had to install a server as a domain controller just to make it easier to manage or because applications required direct access to the domain security database. Member Servers are significantly different in Windows Server 2003. Now you can make full use of the member role and significantly reduce the number of Identity Servers in your network. In fact, one of the questions you'll have to ask yourself when replacing network services is "Should this be a Member Server only?"

Chapter 1 identified six categories of member servers: Application Servers, File and Print Servers, Dedicated Web Servers, Collaboration Servers, Network Infrastructure Servers, and Terminal Servers. Each of these must take its own migration path to Windows Server 2003. Because of this, you would only migrate Member Servers first if you had a minimal network infrastructure in place and if you have already begun the migration process for server-based corporate applications. If, for example, you have very few existing Member Servers that have minimal load, it might be appropriate to migrate them first and simply get both performance and stability improvements from Windows Server 2003. If your corporate applications are based on commercial software products that already have "designed for Windows Server 2003" logo compatibility, you might decide to do these first as well (see http://www.microsoft.com/winlogo/ for more information). Or if you initiated a corporate application redevelopment effort to adapt them to Windows Server 2003 and they are now ready, you might consider migrating Application Servers first. But these are the only conditions where you will want to migrate Member Servers first. In addition, you'll need to ensure that each server you migrate supports WS03. You might even want to take advantage of this opportunity to upgrade server RAM, add additional processors, or increase disk space.

Even though it does not have the scale of an Active Directory implementation project, the migration of Member Servers will also require time for reflection and consideration. For example, File and Print Servers are easier to migrate than Application Servers, but they still require significant preparation. Since both file and print services are controlled through access rights, you'll need to take a full inventory of all access rights if you are replacing an existing server with a new one. You might even decide that you want to take the time to redefine access rights to your file and print services—perform a cleanup—to ensure that your security levels are appropriate, especially on confidential information.

If you're using third-party quota management tools in Windows NT, you'll also need to upgrade them to work with Windows Server 2003 since NT and WS03 do not use the same file system drivers. More on this will be covered in Chapter 7, but this might be a good place to consider using third-party migration products such as NetIQ's Server Consolidator or Aelita's Server Consolidation Wizard. Both tools let you stage a new File and Print Server, mirror information and data between an existing server and the new server, and then migrate users and PCs to the new server remotely so that you can decommission the old system. Microsoft offers information on third-party products for Windows systems at http://www.microsoft.com/windows2000/partners/serversolutions.asp.

Next, you'll want to consider migration approaches for application services. These fall into two major categories: commercial and corporate application services. For commercial software, you'll need to identify if product updates are required and available. For corporate applications, you'll need to identify which portions need to be modified in order to properly operate on the WS03 platform. To improve stability, Microsoft modified the application execution infrastructure of Windows. Windows NT had several stability issues; one of the most important was that Windows NT's application execution environment allowed applications to write to critical portions of the system's disk. In NT, applications were allowed to write to the WINNT and the WINNT\System32 and, of course, the Program Files folders. What's worse, users were given some access to the WINNT folder since their profiles were stored under it.

Microsoft changed this entire infrastructure with Windows 2000. Windows Server 2003 continues to build on this new infrastructure. Applications do not write to any of these folders. Every file that needs to be modified while a user is making use of an application is now stored in the User Profile. This profile is now located in the Documents and Settings folder. In this way, anyone who damages their profile does not affect anyone else using the system. The Windows (WS03 installs to the Windows folder and not the WINNT folder) and Program Files folders are locked and in read-only mode to applications. This new architecture is illustrated in Figure 2-3. The same changes have been included in the registry. Only User sections are modified during application operation.

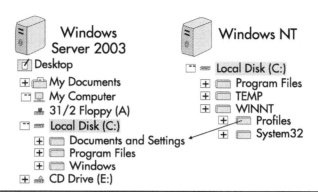

Figure 2-3   The new Windows Server 2003 application execution folder structure

Commercial applications that are modified to use this new architecture are often also modified to support every aspect of the Microsoft Designed for Windows Server 2003 Logo program. This means that they will provide an integrated installation mechanism based on the Windows Installer service and that they will be self-healing. User applications that have not been modified to work with this structure will simply not operate properly on Windows Server 2003 unless everyone is given an account with elevated privileges, something no enterprise network would allow.

If you must run legacy applications on Windows Server 2003, you will need to unlock the system's core folders and the registry. While this may be acceptable for applications that are intended for users, it is totally unacceptable for applications that are designed to support your network environment. Products like third-party quota managers, backup, antivirus, and monitoring software should all be Logo certified.

If you have a lot of applications that need to run in legacy mode, you might want to perform a general unlocking operation. This means resetting the WS03 security to be compatible with Windows NT. WS03 includes a Security Template, COMPATWS.SDB, that can be applied in an automated manner to all systems. If you only have a few legacy applications or if you prefer to maintain tighter security (this is highly recommended), you can work to identify which files and folders need to be unlocked for the application to work and create a small security settings script that can be applied after installation, unlocking only the actual files that need it.

The best approach is to have user applications that are compatible with the WS03 security strategy, so you don't need to compromise security in any way. Whatever you do, you will need to sit down and test each of your applications to ensure that they work properly in the WS03 environment. You'll also have to ensure that each and every one is tested using an account with only user privileges (see Figure 1-7). This will avoid any nasty surprises during deployment.

Since you need to test every application, you might consider repackaging their installation to be compatible with the Windows Installer service. This operation automatically gives self-healing capability to every application, not to mention that any application using the Windows Installer service can also be deployed through Active Directory. More on this will be covered in Chapter 5. Both commercial and corporate applications will need to be treated as subprojects during your migration. Once again, you can use the parallel network to install new Application Servers and then migrate your member services to these new servers. You will need to carefully plan each service migration. Microsoft

Exchange, for example, provides a centralized email service that is not simple to migrate and that is difficult to address through a simple software upgrade. The same applies to line of business applications. The impact of migrating from one version of a widely used application to another is always significant and must be managed.

Given these considerations, it is most likely that you will not migrate Member Servers first. But when you do, you will want to use a Member Server migration timeline such as the one illustrated in Figure 2-4. You can begin the migration of either type of server whenever you want to, but you will need a subproject for each server type. You may decide to begin with corporate applications since as you can see, you will require time to convert existing applications before the migration can take place and to do so, you need to put development servers in place.

Detailed Inventories

Whichever you migrate first, Identity Servers or Member Servers, the first thing you'll need is a detailed inventory of everything that is on every server. Chapter 1 detailed the general inventories you need to build an enterprise network. One of these inventories relates to the servers themselves. Each one includes access control lists, files and folders, installed applications, installed services, and which

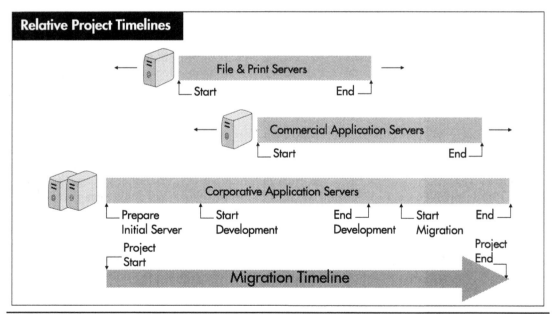

Figure 2-4   The Member Server migration timeline

of these will be required in the new configuration. This inventory should be performed in two phases. The first should be at the beginning of the project. This first inventory is less detailed. It is used to give you a general picture of the services and service points that are required in the new network.

The second is much more precise and should occur as close as possible to the moment you will migrate the server. Servers are complex environments that are constantly changing, especially if users are assigned to them. A good place to start is with server documentation. If you are already using standard documentation procedures for each of your servers, you'll probably want to update them to take into account modifications brought by Windows Server 2003. If you're not using standard server documentation approaches, now's a good time to start.

> ### QUICK TIP
>
> *A complete Windows Server Data Sheet is available at http://www.Reso-Net.com/ WindowsServer/. You can use it to document both legacy and parallel network server construction.*

You'll also need to review other inventories during your project, especially the network service inventory. This last inventory will be essential for the building of a parallel network. Now you begin to see the value of maintaining ongoing inventories, because performing all of these inventories from scratch at the beginning of a migration project really slows you down. It's amazing how many companies are in exactly this situation every time they begin such a project.

Security Considerations

The Server Data Sheet (available at http://www.Reso-Net.com/WindowsServer/) will also be useful in the support of your efforts to build a secure network. One of the first principles of security implementation is "Know your servers!" Too many people have servers that are not secure simply because they don't know what is installed on them. Also, make sure you only install exactly what you need on the server. If a service isn't required by the server's function, then keep it off the server. A service that isn't installed is a lot more secure than a service that is simply turned off.

> ### CAUTION
>
> *Be especially cautious here. Removing unwanted services can easily turn into dead machines. Make sure you have carefully studied each service's function and dependencies before you remove it.*

Once again, use the Server Data Sheet to detail every service and its function. Windows Server 2003 offers a useful feature (originally from Windows 2000) in the ability to display a service's dependencies. You can identify when a service is required simply to support another. To view dependency information, display the properties of any service using the Computer Management Microsoft Management Console (MMC).

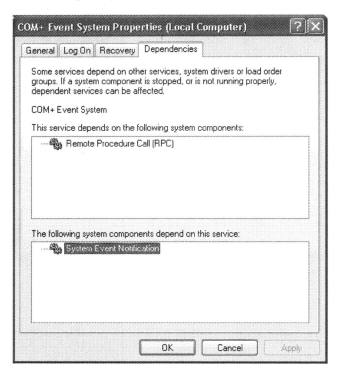

In addition, you can export the services list to complete your documentation. This list is exported in comma- or tab-delimited format and can be viewed and manipulated with tools such as Microsoft Excel. It is an excellent idea to complete your documentation in the Server Data Sheet with the exported service list.

Licensing Considerations

Like Windows NT and Windows 2000, Windows Server 2003 supports two licensing modes:

- **Per Server**   This mode configures the number of licenses based on the maximum number of users or computers that will connect to the server at a given time. This can be less costly if properly managed since only the people using the system on an ongoing basis need a license.
- **Per Device or Per User**   This mode configures the number of licenses based on the number of PCs and users in your organization. Since each PC and/or user has a license, they can use any server system.

Per server licensing can be less expensive than per device or user. But it is a lot more overhead to manage and it provides less satisfying results for users. Per server can be compared to workgroups in that it is a distributed licensing mode. Each server has its own licenses that are independent of other servers. So for Server A you can have 10 licenses and for Server B you can have 50. The problem with this is that as soon as an 11th person wants to use Server A or a 51st person wants to use Server B, they get an error message and can either wait for a license to be freed up or ask a systems administrator to add more licenses. The systems administrator must constantly verify that each server has the appropriate number of licenses.

Per device or user licensing is the recommended licensing mode for the enterprise network because it is worry-free. Since each PC or user has a license, there is no need to fiddle with servers to tune their licensing requirements. A single, central licensing server generates the number of licenses required for the entire network.

Installing and Configuring Servers

As mentioned earlier, Windows Server 2003 supports four installation methods. It goes without saying that despite all the improvements Microsoft has made to these installation methods, the very first method you will use is the interactive installation. That's because the very first thing you need to do is discover what happens when you install WS03. You also need to discover what is installed by default, what you want to add or remove from the installation, and which elements you want to configure.

Preparing for Massive Installations

Anyone who has installed any version of Windows since Windows NT is familiar with the various elements that must be identified before beginning the installation process. First, Windows Server 2003 requires a minimum hardware level. The minimum hardware requirements for each version of WS03 are identified in Table 2-2.

Requirements	Web Edition	Standard Edition	x86 Enterprise Edition	Itanium Enterprise Edition	x86 Datacenter Edition	Itanium Datacenter Edition
Minimum CPU speed	133 MHz	133 MHz	133 MHz	733 MHz	400 MHz	733 MHz
Recommended CPU speed	550 MHz	550 MHz	733 MHz	733 MHz	733 MHz	733 MHz
Minimum RAM	128 MB	128 MB	128 MB	128 MB	512 MB	512 MB
Recommended minimum RAM	256 MB	256 MB	256 MB	256 MB	1 GB	1 GB
Maximum RAM	2 GB	4 GB	32 GB	64 GB	64 GB	512 GB
Minimum number of processors	1	1	1	1	8	8
Multiprocessor support	Up to 2	Up to 4	Up to 8	Up to 8	Up to 64	Up to 64
Disk space for setup	1.5 GB	1.5 GB	1.5 GB	2.0 GB	1.5 GB	2.0 GB

Table 2-2   Microsoft's Minimum and Recommended Hardware Requirements for WS03

Requirements	Web Edition	Standard Edition	x86 Enterprise Edition	Itanium Enterprise Edition	x86 Datacenter Edition	Itanium Datacenter Edition
Disk space for network-based setup	1.7 GB	1.7 GB	1.7 GB	2.2 GB	1.7 GB	2.2 GB
Approximate disk space after setup	1.3 GB	1.3 GB	1.3 GB	1.7 GB	1.3 GB	1.7 GB
Minimum video mode	VGA	VGA	VGA	VGA	VGA	VGA
Recommended minimum video mode	SVGA	SVGA	SVGA	SVGA	SVGA	SVGA

Table 2-2   Microsoft's Minimum and Recommended Hardware Requirements for WS03 (continued)

▶ **NOTE**

The disk space required after setup depends, of course, on the amount of RAM on the system and thus, of the size of the paging file.

It goes without saying that you won't install servers that only meet minimum requirements. In fact, if you're planning on putting together an enterprise network, they won't be at Microsoft's recommended levels either. If you're wise, you'll either simply double Microsoft's recommendations and use that as a starting point or perform a formal Server Sizing Exercise. This exercise will help you determine the hardware and software configuration for each of your servers. It will tell you what size server you need, where it is needed, and what it should deliver in terms of services. When configuring servers, don't forget to take the following items into consideration:

- **Identify server bases**   Identify where your client groupings are. You will need to position your servers where you have a concentration of clients or users.

- **Number of users per server**   Identify a maximum number of users per server. To provide a given level of service, you need to ensure that there are never more than the specified number of users, depending on this server's services. On average, organizations set up one server per 250 users, but this depends on the server's function because with WS03, servers can support thousands of users.

- **Maximum acceptable server load**   Determine the speed of response you want from a server when providing a given service. This load must take into consideration the maximum number of users as well.

- **Server variance**   The location of the server is also important to consider because it often serves to determine the nature of the server. Most servers located at headquarters or in large regional offices will tend to be single-purpose servers—they will either perform one role or another. Servers in smaller regional offices, on the other hand, are often multipurpose servers.

If a regional office has fewer users than the minimum number of users per server that you determined earlier, more than one server would be too costly and will rarely be budgeted. So if you have only one server and you have a series of different services that must be delivered, you need to configure a multipurpose server. Multipurpose server configurations will differ from single-purpose servers because they are isolated. As such, they often need to be independently recoverable.

- **Minimum server capacity**   Determine the minimum hardware capacity you want for your servers. Remember that you don't want to change them for some time. The purpose of your network is to deliver services to your user base. Like most people, you'll want to provide a quality service. Take this into consideration when you determine the minimum server capacity. Capacity planning should identify items such as number and size of the processors, amount of RAM, and disk size. Each item is influenced by the decisions you've made before: How many users will the server cover? Where will the server be located? Will it be single or multipurpose?

- **Multiprocessing**   In most cases, you will use multiprocessing servers, servers that have more than a single processor. You'll have to take care here, since there is a clear demarcation between multiprocessor systems. The Standard Edition supports only four processors. All systems with five to eight processors require the Enterprise Edition. This will have an impact on your server budget.

- **RAM sizing**   The rule is simple: the more RAM you have, the better your server will perform. Thus, RAM is not an item you should skimp on. It all depends on the function of any given server, but it is a good rule of thumb to double Microsoft's minimal recommended requirements and start all servers at 512 MB of RAM, then go up from there. Use RAMBUS technology since it is a lot faster than EDO, DDR, and SDRAM and is becoming more comparable in pricing.

  Some server functions are RAM-intensive, such as Terminal Services or Application Servers. These will require more than the minimum you set. In addition, RAM size affects the paging file. The best practice here is to start the paging file at double the size of your RAM and set its maximum size to four times the size of RAM. This rule changes when you're dealing with massive amounts of RAM such as 4 GB configurations, but at first, it means that you'll need to reserve a minimum of 2 GB of disk space for the paging file.

- **Disk sizing**   The size and number of disks you put into each server will depend on a number of factors. How many partitions do you want to make? How much space do you want to reserve for the operating system, programs, and special elements such as the paging file? How much space for data storage? Most servers will end up with three partitions: one for the server utilities, one for the operating system and programs, and one for data. Windows Server 2003 uses only the last two partitions. The operating system partition should also store the paging file. Keep in mind that WS03 offers a better performance when it reads and writes to multiple disks, so you might want to reproduce the paging file on other disk drives. If that is the case, each drive will need to reserve the same amount of space for this file. System drives should be a minimum of 4 GB and should be more if you plan on having a lot of RAM in your server, because it will affect the size of the paging file.

  Data partitions should always be separate from system partitions and are most often significantly larger. Keep in mind that if you are preparing a file server to store user data, you'll have to offer a valid storage size on a per user basis. Many organizations don't have a consistent storage policy. They offer 50 MB of storage per user, something almost no one can live with today, and they insist that any data stored on the user's local PC is not protected by the organization. If you plan on storing user data, you'll have to consider allocating at least 200 MB per user and expect that it may well grow to 1 GB per person. It all depends on the type of activity they perform. But, worry not, disk space is a lot cheaper today and is always becoming more so.

- **Hardware protection**   All this data needs some level of protection. Local disk drives should be protected by a random array of inexpensive disks (RAID). Many people opt for a disk mirroring system (RAID 1) for the system drives and stripe sets with parity (RAID 5) for data partitions. There are differing opinions, but with today's fast-paced advances in disk technology, it is quite acceptable to opt for a single RAID 5 system and partition it into two for system and data drives. Don't forget the RAID overhead: 50 percent more disk space is required for RAID 1 and a minimum of 20 percent is required for RAID 5. This is 33 percent if you have the minimum number of drives to support RAID 5 (three drives).

  You can also use a random array of inexpensive network (RAIN) cards. They are similar to a RAID disk system in that they are composed of two network cards using the same resources. When one fails, the other automatically takes over using the same MAC address.

- **Storage strategy**   The hardware protection system you choose will also depend on your storage strategy. If you're building a multipurpose regional server, you'll probably want to focus on local storage. Thus, you'll design a suitable local RAID solution. But if you decide to centralize storage for single-purpose servers, you'll want to implement a storage area network (SAN). In this case, you'll need to consider storage requirements for all servers at once and change your strategy for operating system storage. In fact, WS03 servers can even boot from a SAN, letting you create diskless server configurations.

- **Physical location**   The physical location, the actual physical space the server will occupy, will help you determine whether you will choose a rack-mounted or tower server configuration. In most cases, multipurpose servers are tower servers and single-purpose servers are rack-mounted because they are concentrated in a single physical space. This physical location should be lockable and offer temperature controls, and all physical access to servers should be audited.

- **Backup method**   Once again, the physical location of the server will help determine the backup method selected. Regional servers often use tape drives for backup, but this depends on the speed and available bandwidth of your wide area network connection. Central servers use remote backup solutions such as tape or writable DVD robots. This solution can service regional servers as well if the appropriate network bandwidth is available.

  Time will also be a factor in this decision. If you choose a technology that cannot back up the system in the amount of time that is available, you'll be creating a problem, not solving it. Windows Server 2003 helps here since it has the ability to do backup snapshots—time-based images of the hard disk drives that are then used to create the backup, allowing the server to continue with other operations. More on this topic will be covered in Chapter 9.

- **Operating system**   Are there any special requirements for the operating system this server will host? For Windows Server 2003, it's easy. Everything—hardware and software—has to be certified. Microsoft has made great advances in stability with its operating systems, but these advances depend on products that follow strict guidelines. In an enterprise network, only certified products are allowed. If you have existing hardware that is not certified, you'll have to weigh the risk of using it on a critical component such as a server against the cost of buying replacement parts. If you're buying new hardware or software, make sure it is certified for Windows Server 2003.

- **Growth potential**   Finally, you don't want to be replacing this system six months after you put it in place, so make sure that it has a lot of capability for growth. All systems should have the ability to add more processors, more memory, and more disk space. As such, you'll need to consider the server life expectancy—when the server was introduced by the manufacturer, when it will be retired, its projected growth potential by the manufacturer, and so on. If you plan carefully, you'll be able to implement servers that will have a rich lifecycle that will meet your expectations. In some conditions, this lifecycle can last up to five years.

This exercise helps you identify the generic size of each server. Special functions such as domain controllers or Microsoft Exchange Servers will require different sizing parameters. Microsoft offers sizing tools for most of its .NET Enterprise Servers family. All are available on the Microsoft Servers Web site at http://www.microsoft.com/servers/. In addition, Dell, Hewlett-Packard, and IBM all offer sizing tools for their servers on the appropriate Web sites.

Upgrading Existing Systems

If you already have a network in place and you want to upgrade to WS03, you'll first want to check if your systems are going to be compatible to WS03. Like Windows 2000, the Windows Server setup includes a special feature that will verify if the existing system can be upgraded to WS03. Keep in mind that upgrades will only work with the Standard, Enterprise and Datacenter Editions of Windows Server 2003.

To perform a verification, insert the appropriate Windows Server 2003 CD and select Check system compatibility from the Startup menu. Next, click Check my system automatically. Windows Setup will offer to download the latest drivers and updates from the Windows Update site. If your system is connected to the Internet, it is a good idea to select this option. To do so, select Yes, Download the updated Setup files. If you do not have an Internet connection, click No, Skip this step and continue installing Windows.

▶ *NOTE*

The download of updated Setup files may take some time. It will depend on when you decide to migrate because Microsoft will continue to add new components after WS03 is released. Also, despite the message that is displayed in this process, you are not installing Windows; you are only verifying the compatibility of your system.

After a few minutes, Setup will display a dialog box about your system's compatibility. Each item includes additional information. To view the details for each item, select it and click Details. Setup will document the issue or the problem. The icons in the Report System Compatibility dialog box tell you whether the issue is significant, and the Details dialog box tells you how to solve the issue.

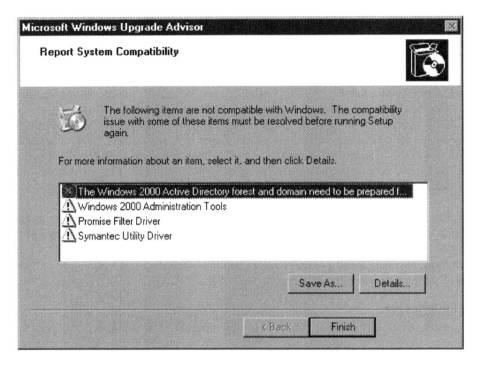

The compatibility report can be saved as a text file for further reference. In addition, you can automate this process by running the WINNT32 command with both the checkupgradeonly and unattend switches. The compatibility report will automatically be saved as UPGRADE.TXT in the %SYSTEMROOT% folder. Use the following syntax to do so:

```
WINNT32 /CHECKUPGRADEONLY /UNATTEND
```

You can write a simple script that will automate this process, rename the file to the system's computer name, and collect it to deposit it in a central share. In this way, you can quickly and easily verify the compatibility of all your servers.

You'll probably also want to verify compatibility information on the Microsoft Compatibility Web site. The simplest way to do so is to select the second option from the WS03 CD compatibility startup screen, "Visit the compatibility Web site" (http://www.microsoft.com/hcl/).

Dual-Boot Considerations

Many organizations have a tendency to create multiple boot partitions on a server. This only creates additional installation overhead with little benefit. Some argue that you can use a second bootable partition on a system for recovery purposes: if your drives use only the NTFS file format, as they should in an enterprise network, you may need a second bootable partition in case your system drive crashes.

While this may have been a good practice with Windows NT, it is not necessary with Windows Server 2003. Instead, organizations should install the Recovery Console. This command- line console is specifically designed to support the recovery or repair of a system. In addition, this console is more secure than a second bootable partition because it does not allow the copying of files *from* the system to an external source, but only allows the copying of information from an external source *to* the system. As such, you can use it to repair system drivers, start and stop services, and generally verify the state of your system, but it cannot be used to steal data.

A second bootable partition, on the other hand, will be difficult to manage because it is inactive when it isn't running. This means that to perform any updates or modifications to this partition, you must shut down your production system to reboot within this second partition. Since most organizations that have implemented this solution do not take the time to do this—servers after all, are designed to run 24/7—they end up having outdated passwords and unpatched systems in these partitions. It is conceivable that these partitions could eventually damage data if they are not kept up to date while the main system evolves. At the very least, they create a security flaw.

The best practice is to separate system and data drives. In this way, if your system drive does crash despite all of the precautions you take, you can reinstall it without affecting the data partition.

Using Virtual Machines

If a dual-boot system is required because a server must run incompatible software, the issue is different. If, for example, you need to design a dual-boot system to run Microsoft SQL Server version 7 in one partition and version 2000 in another, then you might consider using virtual machines instead. As you know, dual-boot systems can only run one partition at a time. As such, one system is always unavailable. Instead, use a technology such as VMware (see Chapter 1) to do this.

▶ *CAUTION*

If you intend to use virtual machines in your operating environment, you should do so with the collaboration of the manufacturer of the product the virtual machine will run. This will ensure that you are fully supported.

Network Planning

By default, Windows Server 2003 products install with a single network protocol, the TCP/IP protocol. Most organizations today use this protocol and most use *only* this protocol. WS03 installs the protocol with a dynamically updated configuration. While there are some considerations for using dynamic TCP/IP protocol configurations on servers, it is imperative that systems do not change names within the network because of all the connections that are linked to a server. In fact, all of the computer's names, NetBIOS for legacy applications, and host name should be identical.

If you want the best of both worlds—that is, to manage your server addresses centrally and ensure that they never change address—you can use address reservations for each system. You can then match an address to a specific server with the Dynamic Host Configuration Protocol (DHCP). To do so, you'll need to take note of the MAC address for each network interface card in each server. Using dynamically assigned network addresses is only recommended when you use RAIN network cards. Otherwise, use static addresses. More on this will be discussed in Chapter 4.

But whichever way you choose—address reservations with DHCP or manual address configuration—you'll need to plan for your server address pool *before* you begin installing systems. Add this planning sheet to the Server Sizing Exercise performed earlier. This way you can map server IP addresses to planned server locations. Make sure you provide a complete map to installers before they begin massive server installations.

BIOS Updates

Windows Server 2003 makes extensive use of a computer system's capabilities. Like Windows 2000, it is ACPI-aware. In fact, it uses the Advanced Configuration and Power Interface (http://www.acpi.info/) to enable several new features such as power management and remote management. Thus it is very important that the BIOS in all your systems be as up to date as possible. Make sure you check with your manufacturer and obtain all of the latest editions of the BIOS for all the systems you will upgrade. And when purchasing new systems, ensure they are up to date in terms of BIOS.

Using Installation Documentation

In an enterprise network, you want to ensure that everyone performs the same operations. As such, you need to prepare checklists and documentation for operators to follow. For installations, this documentation must cover three processes:

- Installation Preparation
- Server Installation
- Post-Installation Verification

Each requires a specific type of checklist.

The Installation Preparation Checklist

Figure 2-5 outlines the recommended steps for Installation Preparation. Remember that it is not recommended to perform an upgrade from any version of Windows NT to Windows Server 2003. Upgrades are only recommended from Windows 2000 if a new installation was performed for that system. This checklist takes these considerations into account.

Documenting Server Installations

In addition, you'll need to document every Server Installation. The best way to do this is to use a standard Server Data Sheet. As mentioned previously, you can obtain the Server Data Sheet from the companion Web site. It can be used either on paper or in electronic format. It can also be adapted to database format. In support of the Server Data Sheet, you will need a Kernel Data Sheet outlining the contents of the Server Kernel for this particular version of the kernel. Each sheet should provide detailed and up-to-date information.

> **QUICK TIP**
>
> *A Kernel Data Sheet can be found at http://www.Reso-Net.com/WindowsServer/.*

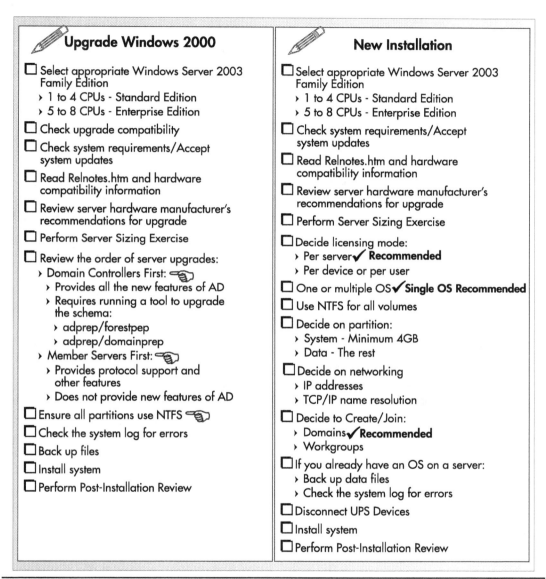

Figure 2-5   The Installation Preparation Checklist

The Post-Installation Checklist

Finally, when the installation is performed, you'll want to perform a post-installation customization and verification. Figure 2-6 illustrates the activities you would include here. Use this Post-Installation

---

Post-Installation Checklist

☐ Use Computer Management MMC to View/Repair device configurations
☐ Show the network adapter card icon on the taskbar
☐ Review activation (Enterprise Licenses - No Activation)
☐ Enable Theme Service and configure the Windows XP interface
☐ Configure Windows Explorer options
☐ Create shortcuts in the Quick Launch area of the taskbar
☐ Configure Event Viewer Log file size
☐ Rename the Local Administrator account
☐ Create a Backup Administrator account
☐ Tighten File and Folder permissions with Secedit
☐ Configure Time Service
☐ Set the OS menu display time to 5 seconds
☐ Set the Paging File size
☐ Configure Driver Signing
☐ Set Memory-dump and reboot options
☐ Customize the Command window
☐ Configure for Remote Administration
☐ Install Support Tools and Resource Kit
☐ Install the Recovery Console
☐ Install Emergency Management Services (if supported by appropriate
    hardware)
☐ Install additional server functions
☐ Apply appropriate Security Hot Fixes and Service Packs (if required)
☐ Update the Default User profile
☐ Defragment the hard disk

Figure 2-6   The Post-Installation Checklist

Checklist to customize your system and to perform a quality assurance verification of all systems. The activities outlined in this checklist are detailed in Customizing Your Server later in this chapter.

Massive Installation Processes

Now that you've reviewed installation prerequisites, you're ready for the Massive Installation Preparation Process. Here, you'll perform your initial installation, review the installation process, review default server configuration, and move on to determine the method you will use to automate the Massive Installation Process. This last stage is essential since it is focused not only on how you will perform the initial installation of all your servers, but also on how you will recover server installations should any untoward event occur during the server's operation.

This is a good place for a standard operating procedure since it is always the same no matter which version of Windows you want to install. It is basically outlined as follows:

1. Begin by choosing the Windows version to install.

2. Perform the initial installation.

3. Discover the new environment.

4. Document all configuration requirements (specifically).

5. Choose the massive installation method.

6. Automate the installation.

7. Deploy the new version of Windows.

▶ | **QUICK TIP**
|
| *A sample standard operating procedure for this process is available at http://www.Reso-Net.com/ WindowsServer/.*

As mentioned at the beginning of this chapter, Windows Server 2003 offers four installation procedures: interactive, unattended with an answer file, disk imaging with the System Preparation Tool and Remote Installation Services. Only the last three should be used for massive deployment in an enterprise network. Each of these has its benefits and disadvantages. All are based on the Windows deployment tools.

Figure 2-7 illustrates the Massive Installation Method Selection Process. Everything begins with the initial installation and discovery of the product.

The Initial Installation

The discovery process is important because this is where you'll find out what makes Windows Server 2003 tick. You'll also learn how the setup program works for this new version of Windows. Begin by choosing the Windows version to install; remember the Windows installation prerequisites. Next, perform the initial installation. If you're using new systems, insert the WS03 CD into a CD-ROM or DVD drive and boot the server. The installation process will begin immediately.

If you're upgrading from Windows 2000, insert the WS03 CD and select Install Windows Server 2003 from the autorun splash screen. Windows Server 2003 (either Standard or Enterprise) will automatically recommend an upgrade. Since this is the mode you will be working with, proceed with the upgrade.

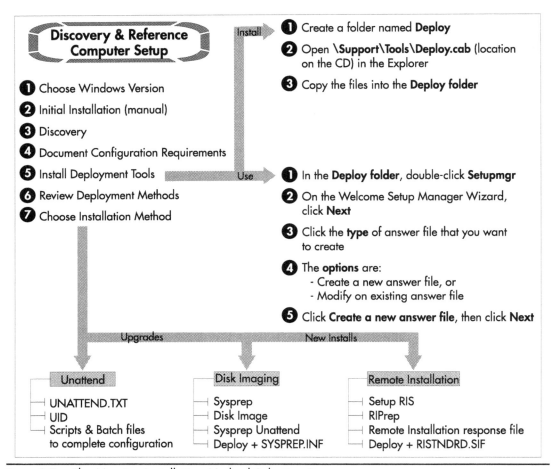

Figure 2-7   The Massive Installation Method Selection Process

This is an excellent place to use VMware Workstation since it allows you to create a WS03 virtual machine right on your desktop without affecting any of your applications. This means you can perform the discovery process from your own PC.

The WS03 setup process includes several steps, which can be divided into two major categories:

- **Character mode setup**   This mode is only used in a new installation. It allows you to define disk partitions and introduce special components such as a special hardware abstraction layer (HAL) driver or a massive storage device driver. You'll have to be careful here since you must press either F5 or F6, respectively, to install these components. If you miss these keys, you will need to start over. This mode is also used to copy setup files to the hard disk. Setup performs its first reboot at the end of this installation phase.

- **Graphic mode setup**   This is where you define how WS03 will be installed. It lets you choose configuration parameters such as computer name, network settings, regional settings, and so on. This process uses an installation wizard so you can usually go back to modify selections if you find you made a mistake.

Microsoft displays time-to-finish information, but it is only accurate on faster systems. An estimate of 39 minutes can easily become 59 or more if your system is not up to speed. The installation process covers five major steps:

- **Collecting information**   Identifying the target hardware environment.
- **Dynamic update**   Determining if relevant updates are available on the Windows Update Web site.
- **Preparing installation**   Copying appropriate files to the hard drive.
- **Installing Windows**   Performing the actual installation.
- **Finalizing installation**   Writing registry settings, removing temporary files, and restarting Windows.

WS03 includes a very powerful plug-and-play module that detects and installs hardware devices for you. Like Windows 2000, this greatly simplifies the installation process. The dynamic update portion of setup is also quite useful in this regard because it will automatically download new drivers before the installation begins, saving you from having to update drivers afterward.

By default, WS03 uses the warning mode for uncertified drivers. Uncertified drivers are not digitally signed and provide no guarantee that they will function properly on your hardware. If any uncertified drivers are used, Windows will display a warning. Accepting the installation of uncertified drivers can destabilize your installation. Refusing them can also cause your installation to crash since they may be critical for your hardware system. If you are using existing hardware, you may have to compromise and use unsigned drivers. All new hardware should include signed drivers for Windows Server 2003. It is also a good idea to reset the Signed Drivers option to refuse unsigned drivers when servers are shipped into the field, especially if they are going to regional offices. You can thus ensure that no one will install unsigned drivers and destabilize the system.

During installation, setup will request the Administrator account password. This password should include at least 8 characters (15 is preferred) and include complex characters such as numbers, uppercase and lowercase letters, and special characters. If you have difficulty remembering passwords, you can replace letters with special characters. For example, replace an *a* with @, replace an *o* with ¤, and so on. This makes passwords more difficult to crack. Even so, if an attacker has access to the system, they can use password cracking tools to display the text of the password (if it is 14 characters or less). If this is an issue, you can use a combination of ALT plus a four-number key code to enter characters into your password (for example, ALT 0149). The advantage of this method is that these characters often display as a blank square or rectangle when displayed as text by password-cracking software. All servers should require complex passwords. More on this topic will be covered in Chapter 8.

Once the installation is complete, Windows Server 2003 will reboot the system.

Customizing Your Server

Once the logon splash is displayed, open a session and begin the Windows Server 2003 discovery. WS03 begins with the Manage Your Server screen. You should take the time to thoroughly examine the contents of this screen before you move on to a massive installation.

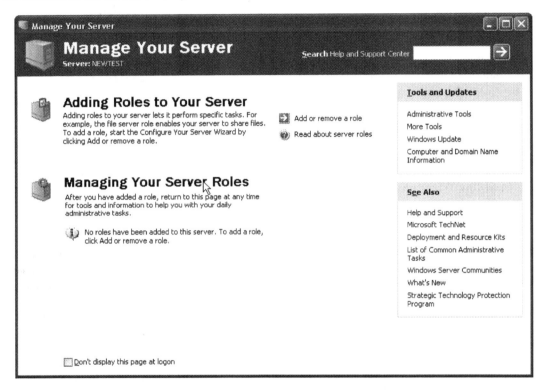

Next, WS03 will ask you for activation, but only if you are not using a corporate version of the operating system. If this is the case and you are only discovering the system, do not activate it—you have 30 days to do so. You can do a lot of discovery in 30 days and each activation requires a license.

Refer back to Figure 2-5 for the activities you will need to perform during the discovery. Be sure to document all configuration modifications you retain. This will be important for when you prepare your Reference Server for the Massive Deployment Staging Process. This documentation also forms the heart of the kernel for each server. You can use the Kernel Data Sheet to document kernel contents. This documentation must detail the steps you perform to modify the system's configuration. It should cover all the activities listed in Figure 2-6, but special attention should be paid to the following:

- Configuring devices with the Computer Management console
- Configuring Windows Explorer options

- Enabling the Theme service and configuring the Windows XP interface
- Configuring the event log
- Copying and renaming the Administrator account
- Using a Security Template to lock down the system
- Configuring paging file, driver signing and recovery settings
- Configuring for remote administration
- Installing Support and Resource Kit tools
- Installing the Recovery Console and Emergency Management Services
- Updating Default User settings

All of the operations in Figure 2-6 are important, but the ones listed here are significantly different from previous versions of Windows.

The first place to start is with the Computer Management console. This console is the one single Microsoft Management Console that can give you access to most everything configurable on the system. Begin by placing the console's shortcut on the Quick Launch area of the taskbar. You'll find the shortcut under Administration Tools in the Start Menu. To place the shortcut on the taskbar, right-click and drag the icon from the Start Menu to the Quick Launch area. Release it when you see a black insertion bar. Choose Copy Here from the context menu. You should do this with every icon you will need to operate the server. You might also find the Windows Explorer shortcut useful on this taskbar (it is located under Accessories). A well-prepared taskbar should include all of the most commonly-used shortcuts. You may even need to stretch it to two lines high.

Then use the Computer Management console to navigate to Devices to view any potential hardware problems or conflicts. Review any item that has either an exclamation mark or stop sign. You might have to install new drivers or update existing ones. This is where the notes you acquired from your hardware manufacturer's Web site will come in handy. Continue until there are either no conflicts or no critical conflicts left. A system where all the items are closed is what you're aiming for.

▶ **QUICK TIP**

Like Windows 2000, WS03 supports both basic and dynamic volumes. You may decide to convert your volumes to dynamic disks at this time, but do so only if you feel you will require the features dynamic disks offer. If you are using hardware RAID (as you should in an enterprise network), continue to use basic disks. See the Microsoft support article number Q329707 at http:// support.microsoft.com/ for more information.

Move on to configuring Windows Explorer options. Administrators and operators need to be able to see what is available in the file system. To do so, use the following procedure:

1. Start the Explorer and select the display mode you prefer—Details is a good view for administrators.

2. In the View menu, turn on the Status Bar. Also turn on the toolbars you find useful. Now you're ready to set your folder options.

3. Use the Tools menu to display Folder Options.

4. Select the View tab, then turn on Show hidden files and folders, but do not turn off Hide protected operating system files.

5. Click on Apply to All Folders. Close the dialog box.

Return to the Computer Management console to enable the Theme Service. This service is disabled by default because it uses system resources. If you're up to date and already using Windows XP on your desktops, you'll want this service activated. Otherwise, you'll always be moving from one interface to another (and so will your users). In fact, every server should have this service activated by default, especially if they are destined to provide Terminal Services (either for administration or for applications). This ensures that users and administrators have a consistent interface on both desktops and servers. It is also the only way you can configure the Windows XP interface on a server. The steps to enable this service are as follows:

1. Find the Theme Service in the service list, set its startup properties to Automatic and start the service now.

2. Minimize the console, right-click on the desktop, and choose Properties.

3. Choose the Windows XP theme and click OK. Your interface is set.

Return to the Computer Management console to configure the event logs. Set the size of the file for each event log and determine its looping mechanism. Don't forget that they are backed up every day so you only need the size that will be convenient without having to resort to a backup. Also, rename the Administrator account, as follows:

1. Again, in the console, select Local Users and Groups.

2. Under Users, right-click the Administrator account and choose Rename.

3. Next, create a new backup administrator account.

4. Make it a member of the Administrators group.

WS03 does not let you copy the Administrator account. Any backups must be created from scratch. Remember to set complex passwords for both these accounts.

This is a good time to use the Security Configuration Manager to apply a Security Template to the server. This procedure is explained in detail in Chapter 8.

Next, set the startup and recovery options:

1. Open the Explorer. Right-click on My Computer and select Properties.

2. Select the Advanced tab to set Startup and Recovery settings and Performance settings. Servers should perform a minimum memory dump when crashing. Because this is a dump of RAM, it can be of considerable size. Using the minimum setting reduces the amount of space required. Then, if you have a problem, you can reset it to Complete Memory Dump and use special tools to analyze the problem. Make sure you set the system to reboot automatically.

3. Paging files should be configured as discussed earlier: double the memory size for minimum and four times for maximum. While you may think that the paging file must be the same minimum and maximum size so that it is never fragmented, this is not necessary. Any temporary allocation to the paging file that may be done during operation and that may fall within fragmented space is automatically removed when the system restarts. So in the end, the paging file is very rarely fragmented.

4. Move to the Hardware tab and click on Driver Signing. Set it to Block - Never install unsigned driver software. This will protect the stability of the server.

5. You can take advantage of this opportunity to modify Remote Administration settings. To do so, select the Remote tab to activate the Remote Desktop. Windows warns you that if you use an account with a blank password for any reason, it will not be available for remote login. In fact, no connection can be performed through the network on WS03 if the account used does not have a password. Blank password accounts are only usable for local logons. You shouldn't use a blank password account in any case. You will also want to identify administrative groups that are allowed to connect to a remote desktop at this stage. Create a special Domain Local group (see Chapter 6) and add it to these settings. You can decide who will be in this group at a later stage.

Use the WS03 CD to install both the Support and Resource Kit tools. For the support tools, go to the Support\Tools folder to find SUPTOOLS.MSI. Double-click on it to begin installation. Use the Resource Kit CD to install the other tools you need.

You can also use the WS03 CD to install both the Recovery Console and Emergency Management Services. Use the Windows setup program, WINNT32, to install both components. To add the Recovery Console, use the cmdcons switch. This switch is only valid for 32-bit servers. Run the following command:

```
WINNT32 /CMDCONS
```

Next, if your hardware supports it, enable Emergency Management Services using the emsport switch. With Emergency Management Services, you can remotely manage a server in emergency situations that would typically require a local keyboard, mouse, and monitor, such as when the network is unavailable or the server is not functioning properly. Emergency Management Services have specific hardware requirements and are available only for products in the Windows Server 2003 family. Run the following command:

```
WINNT32 /EMSPORT:usebiossettings
```

The userbiossettings is the default setting. It uses the setting specified in the BIOS Serial Port Console Redirection (SPCR) table, or, in Itanium-based systems, through the Extensible Firmware Interface (EFI) console device path. If you specify usebiossettings and there is no SPCR table or appropriate EFI console device path, Emergency Management Services will not be enabled.

You can also use the System dialog box to update Default User settings, but you need to perform other operations first. Windows Server 2003 does not allow you to copy an open user profile to another because many of the open features are volatile. So to update your Default User, you must use the second administrative account created earlier, as follows:

1. Log out of Administrator.
2. Log into your backup administrator account. WS03 creates a new profile based on old settings.
3. Open Explorer and set Folder Options to view hidden files.
4. Right-click on My Computer and select Properties.
5. Choose User Profile Settings under the Advanced tab.
6. Copy the Administrator profile to Default User.

7. Browse to the Documents and Settings folder to find the Default User profile.
8. Click OK to replace existing files.
9. Close all dialog boxes and log out of the backup administrator account.
10. Log back into Administrator.
11. Open Explorer and return to the User Profile dialog box.

12. Delete the backup administrator's profile.

13. Close all dialog boxes and log out of the Administrator account.

14. Log back into the backup administrator's account to test the Default User. Note that you now have a copy of the Administrator profile.

15. Return to the Administrator profile.

► CAUTION

You'll have to be careful with this operation when dealing with servers running Terminal Services because the Default User will be used to create user, not administrator, profiles. Obviously, user profiles will require different settings than administrative ones.

You've documented each of these steps because they will need to be repeated every time you create a Reference Server. This Reference Server will be the model you use for your massive installation method.

► QUICK TIP

Carefully review the steps you use to create Reference Servers. You do not want to deploy machines created from an improperly prepared Reference Server. This is why a standard operating procedure for this process is available at http://www.Reso-Net.com/WindowsServer/.

Choosing the Massive Installation Method

The massive installation method you choose will depend on your migration method. If you are migrating from Windows 2000 to Windows Server 2003, you can use a scripted installation for in-place upgrades. Again, this is only if you performed new installations with Windows 2000. If you are migrating from Windows NT, you should decide whether to use disk imaging or remote OS installation. Remote Installation is the recommended method. It is new, it is faster than the scripted installation, and while it requires some expense, this expense is limited to the acquisition of preboot execution (PXE) enabled network cards. While they are not the cheapest component on your network, they will greatly add to your long-term support options because they can also be used to rebuild servers during recurring operations.

Disk imaging, on the other hand, requires the use of third-party software, which is a specific expense that is separate from the acquisition of server hardware and the new operating system. The Remote Installation Service (RIS) does not incur additional software costs, is quite complete, and can be used to rebuild systems in recurrent mode. This is also true for the other two automated setup methods, but RIS is by far the easiest to use and to manage.

To prepare for the automation of your Windows deployment, you'll need to install the deployment tools. Once this is done, you can launch the Setup Manager Wizard to create automated installation answer files.

Scripting Upgrades

In the case of Windows Server 2003, the unattended installation using an answer file is best left to the upgrade of a system from Windows 2000 to WS03. In fact, unattended installations are the only way to perform an automated upgrade because both of the other two methods replace the operating system. Using the Setup Manager Wizard, you can create UNATTEND.TXT files for different setup configurations. What is unfortunate is that the new version of the Setup Manager Wizard will no longer automatically create an answer file from an existing system. Answer files must always be created from scratch. This is regrettable because the purpose of a Reference Server is to prepare such items. Nevertheless, you can create the new one. Simply answer each of the questions posed by the wizard. This will create a generic answer file which you can customize through a variety of commands. These commands are rarely required when performing an upgrade.

> ▶ **QUICK TIP**
>
> *Like Windows 2000, WS03 supports slipstream service packs. This means you can apply the service pack to your original installation files and use them as the source for server installations. This saves you from having to apply the service pack after an installation.*

The advantage of the upgrade is that there are no reinstallations required for existing and compatible software. This means that your server should be up and running once you've finished the installation. You will most likely need to create a few scripts and/or batch files to complete the installation process, though. These can be inserted into the RunOnce, OEM Preinstall, or Additional Commands sections of your response file. Unattended installations present a couple of challenges because they do not reproduce an image of what is located on the hard disk of the Reference Server. Thus, you need to script a number of operations such as applying Security Templates, adding security hot fixes, or installing the Recovery Console. Make sure you fully test the configuration before deploying it.

Deployment can be performed through a number of manners. After all, the only thing you need to deploy is a command script running the WINNT32 command. These upgrades can be delivered through Microsoft System Management Server or through machine scripts that are remotely executed. Use the lab to ensure that all installation and deployment methods work in all situations. You don't want to be found with a dead server on Monday morning when 250 users are logging in.

If you insist on using unattended installation to prepare new machines, make sure you buy them in lots. This way, you can ask your dealer to provide a workable and well-documented UNATTEND.TXT file that includes all the particularities that are specific to their system. This will save you a lot of hard work and make the Unattended Installation Process much more profitable. All you'll have to do is customize the provided unattended answer file.

In short, unattended installations are a lot of work. While they may be acceptable for small organizations where fewer servers are required, they do not tend to provide adequate return on investment for medium to large organizations.

▶ **QUICK TIP**

You can and should use unattended installations for the initial installation of Reference Servers. This will save you a lot of time and help you become familiar with the content of the UNATTEND.TXT file.

▶ **NOTE**

If you are using a version of Windows 2000 in a language other than English, you can now transform to an English installation and use the Multilingual User Interface (MUI) to apply a language pack and view commands in your own language. This is useful for worldwide organizations that have multilingual system operators or for Terminal Services that are used by users from several different nationalities. Another advantage is that you can install service packs and hotfixes as soon as they are available because they are available in English first. To do so, you need to change the localized installation to support an upgrade to English and then apply the appropriate MUI language pack.

Disk Imaging

Disk image technologies have been mostly focused on PCs in the past. Since the coming of Windows 2000, IT departments can focus on the creation of one single disk image for all PCs because Windows 2000 supports plug and play. In addition, Windows 2000's System Preparation Tool for disk imaging can force every new system to automatically detect new hardware the first time it starts. Thus, a single disk image of a system based on Windows 2000 can seed every PC model in the enterprise (so long as the PC's hardware meets the requirements of the physical layer and uses the same hardware abstraction layer).

In addition, disk images can capture much more than just the operating system installation. Any imaging process not only includes the operating system but also customization, additional software installations, and much more. Everything, in fact, you do to the reference system will be captured. That's right, everything. That's why reference systems must be prepared with care.

Windows Server 2003 now officially supports the disk imaging of server systems as long as they are prepared first with the System Preparation Tool. The first roadblock to disk imaging is the fact that you need to acquire third-party software. If you don't have the liberty to do this, or if you don't have corporate licenses of such software already, then move on immediately to remote installations. If you're willing to work with disk imaging, you'll also have to get hold of Windows PE (Pre-execution Environment).

Windows PE is a stripped-down version of Windows XP Professional. It fits on a single CD and/or LS-120 floppy disk. It takes 120 MB for Pentium systems and 220 MB for Itanium systems (64-bit).

It is a version of Windows that runs exclusively off of its own media, meaning that it does not require a hard disk. It runs in protected mode and provides a 32-bit console that offers the following features:

- It is independent of the hardware it runs on and requires minimum RAM.
- It automatically detects network cards and provides TCP/IP connectivity.
- It can work with all massive storage drivers that are enabled for Windows XP, 2000 or Windows Server 2003.
- It can create, modify, and destroy NTFS partitions.
- It includes diagnostic tools.
- It supports PXE.

It does have limitations, though. It will only run for a period of 24 hours, requiring reboots if it is run for longer periods. It will only support a maximum of four network connections. It will connect to other servers on your network, but you cannot remotely connect to a computer running Windows PE. It is designed to work mainly with the TCP/IP protocol. And it only supports standard VGA graphics.

Windows PE is designed to replace DOS. For disk imaging, especially disk imaging with servers, it is a godsend because it lets you boot a server with absolutely nothing on it and download a server image to install it. Without Windows PE, using disk images for servers was very difficult, if not impossible. PowerQuest Corporation (http://www.powerquest.com/) was the first manufacturer to create a Windows PE version of their disk imaging software: Power Deploy Suite. This version is strictly a command-line program that does not have a graphical interface, thus it can be scripted to create and restore disk images. As Windows PE becomes more popular, other manufacturers will definitely create 32-bit versions of their disk imaging software.

▶ **QUICK TIP**

Whether or not you decide to use disk imaging for deployment, it is highly recommended to use it with disk imaging software to create a disk image backup of your Reference Server or servers. Windows PE is a great tool for this. But remember, you will need a 32-bit version of your disk imaging software because Windows PE does not support DOS applications.

The System Preparation Process is illustrated in Figure 2-8. It begins, of course, with the Reference Server Preparation. Then you need to prepare and run the System Preparation Wizard. The Sysprep folder you create must be on your system drive. It must contain five files: four executables from DEPLOY.CAB and the SYSPREP.INF file you prepare with the Setup Manager. Then, use SYSPREP.EXE to prepare the server. Close the warning dialog box and use default settings before clicking on the Reseal button. Sysprep will warn you again and then modify the server's security identifier (SID). The server is ready for imaging once it has been shut down. Be sure to test the server image before deployment.

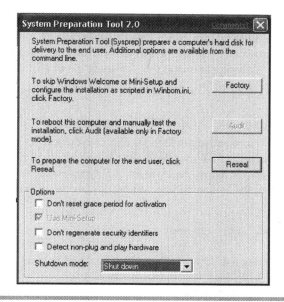

QUICK TIP

If you can, you should create a disk image of the Reference Server just before running the Sysprep command because it will destroy the server's SID. This image is useful if you find out that something was missed and you need to start from the beginning. This image saves you from having to reinstall the Reference Server from scratch.

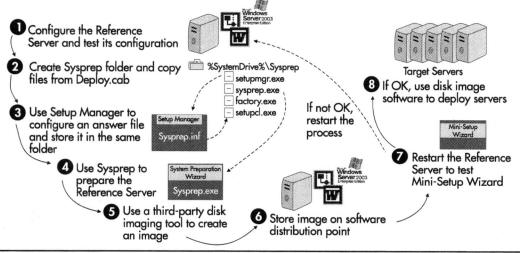

Figure 2-8   The System Preparation and Disk Imaging Process

The System Preparation Tool can be used to simply generate a reusable computer image or to prepare systems for massive reproduction. Since many system manufacturers use Sysprep to prepare the systems they resell, Microsoft has enhanced it to include the ability to audit a system or add additional drivers. Use the following command to know more about switches for the SYSPREP.EXE command:

```
C:\DEPLOY\SYSPREP.EXE /?
```

You should run Sysprep in interactive mode to familiarize yourself with its features. If you have been very rigorous in the preparation of your Reference Server, you will not need to perform system auditing. Instead, you can perform a post-deployment quality assurance test in the lab to test a deployed system. In this case, the command line you need to use to prepare your system for imaging is the following:

```
Sysprep -quiet -reseal -pnp -reboot
```

This will automatically generate a disk image that will reboot and prepare itself once it has been installed on a target system.

One great advantage of disk imaging is that most products support image multicasting. This means that you can use a multicast to send a single copy of the image over the network to a number of target systems. Multicasting greatly reduces the amount of network traffic when performing server or PC staging.

► **QUICK TIP**

Some disk imaging software provides a special RIS driver that helps combine RIS and Sysprep. It allows you to use RIS to send a disk image to a server or PC which speeds up the installation. This is similar to Microsoft Automated Deployment Services (out just before the final release of WS03), a system that combines both disk imaging and the deployment capabilities of RIS. See http://www.microsoft.com/windowsserver2003/techinfo/overview/ads.mspx for more information.

Remote Installation

Remote Installation is the most promising automated installation method for medium to large organizations because it provides the ability to repair a system as well as install it and captures a disk image of the installation. Unlike the System Preparation disk image though, it does not store the image in a single-special format file, it simply copies required files to a special shared folder located on a remote installation server. Since Windows Server 2003 supports not only the hosting of Remote Installation Service (RIS), but also the installation of servers through RIS, it is highly recommended that if you have PXE-enabled network cards, you should focus on RIS almost exclusively. In addition, WS03 includes a Single Instance Store (SIS) service that will eliminate duplicate files from a RIS or other servers. This service significantly reduces the amount of space required to store RIS images. Finally, RIS can also work with Emergency Management Services. This means that you can reboot a server remotely, use EMS to activate the RIS installation process and repair a server with a RIS image, all without having to leave the comfort of your desk.

▶ **NOTE**

Remote installation is quite acceptable for small organizations as well, though there are more costs involved than with unattended installations. The benefits quickly outweigh the costs when you find you can reuse RIS images for server or PC repairs.

RIS is faster than unattended installations because it is smart enough to copy only the files it specifically requires to the server it is installing. While unattended installations need every WS03 installation file, RIS only needs those that were retained in the disk image. This serves to considerably accelerate the installation process. Thus, RIS provides gains in speed as well as providing an installation method that duplicates a Reference Server. If you updated your Default User, or if you installed software such as support tools or recovery consoles on your Reference Server, your final system will have them as well. This means there is significantly less scripting required to install systems using RIS.

Remote OS installations require the implementation of Active Directory, the DHCP service, and the Remote Installation Service. DHCP is covered in Chapter 4, Active Directory in Chapters 3 and 4, and Remote Installation in Chapter 7. Once this infrastructure is in place, you can deploy your servers using RIS.

The RIS process is made up of four major stages:

- Preparing for the use of RIS (see Chapter 7)
- Preparing the image on the RIS Server using the appropriate WS03 CD
- Capturing the image of a Reference Server
- Deploying the RIS image

Once RIS is in place, you can begin working with RIS images. In fact, the place to start is to use the Remote Installation Preparation Wizard to create installation images on your RIS server. RIS first requires the distribution files for Windows Server 2003 in order to be able to deploy server installations. Once these files are copied to the server, custom images can be generated from your Reference Server. If you plan on installing more than one version of WS03, you will need to generate a server image for each one.

Image Preparation at the RIS Server

1. To add a new server-based image, open Active Directory Users and Computers.
2. Find your RIS Server (it may be in a special organizational unit).
3. Right-click on the server name and select Properties.

4. Choose the Remote Install tab. This displays the general RIS properties for this server.

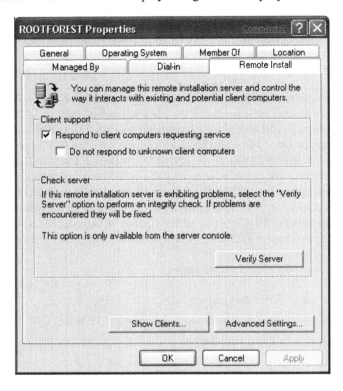

5. Click the Advanced Settings button to display the RIS properties for this server.

6. Select the Images tab and click Add. This starts the Remote Installation Preparation Wizard.

7. Follow the prompts provided by the wizard. Once you have given a name to your image and indicated the source and destination for the distribution files, the wizard starts the installation. It performs five tasks:

   • Copies the Windows installation files

   • Updates the Client Installation Wizard screen files

   • Creates Unattended Setup answer files

   • Starts the required Remote Installation Services

   • Authorizes the RIS server in DHCP

8. Permissions can be set on each image. For example, regional installers can be allowed to access only regional images. To apply permissions, use the Permissions button in the Image Properties dialog box.

Finally, you will have to determine how to name servers as you deploy them. Several options are available to you. You can use variables to automatically generate the names, but you can also prestage server names in Active Directory. Names are then automatically assigned as servers are built and deployed. This naming strategy is part of the RIS Server Preparation Process.

Now you're ready to proceed to the next step: capturing the image of a Reference Server.

Image Preparation at the Reference Server

Make sure your Reference Server is ready. One thing you will need to pay special attention to is the removal of extra user profiles from the server. The Remote Installation Preparation Wizard (RIPrep.exe) has specific constraints, one of which is the lack of support for migrating profiles. If you want to retain the extra profiles you created on the server, you should use the User State Migration Tool (USMT), located in the support folder of the WS03 CD. When you intend to use RIS, you should ensure that once you've updated the Default User profile on your Reference Server, you destroy everything but the Administrator profile. In addition, RIPrep will stop a number of server services before it performs the disk image copy. This is because only the core set of networking services are required for the copying process.

To create the image from the Reference Server, you'll need to use the Remote Installation Preparation Wizard, as follows:

1. When you created your RIS server, it created a distribution folder to store and publish remote installations. Navigate to this shared folder now from the Reference Server.

2. Locate the Admin\I386 folder and open it. This folder contains all of the client preparation tools.

3. Locate and launch RIPrep.exe. This launches the Remote Installation Preparation Wizard. This wizard helps you make the required choices for the preparation of your image.

4. Name the image and select a shared folder to store it in.

5. Next, the wizard will stop all extraneous services. This makes it easier to copy service state information. Only bare networking services are required to connect to the RIS server and copy the disk image.

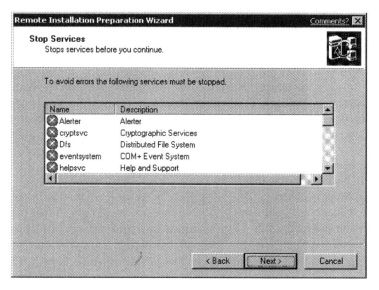

6. Once you've answered all its questions, the wizard will:

- Verify the Windows version
- Analyze disk partitions
- Copy partition information to the server
- Copy system files to the server
- Copy and update registry information
- Shut down the system

One of the great advantages of this method is that it is not destructive to the Reference Server. Unlike the System Preparation procedure, you do not have to depersonalize the Reference Server, because the RIS process is similar to the Unattended process. It actually performs a new installation based on Reference Server settings. As such, it generates a new computer security identifier each time it is used. It is the best of both worlds because it offers complete personalization of the system and image distribution.

You will also need to edit and customize the Unattended setup file used for installation. This file is located in the I386 folder of your image on the RIS server. It ends in .sif (for setup information file). The default RIS Unattended answer file is named RISTNDRD.SIF.

Now you're ready to deploy the images you have created.

▶ *NOTE*

RIS can now be used for either PCs or servers. Either one requires exactly the same steps as outlined here.

Deploying a RIS Image

As mentioned earlier, the best way to use RIS is with a PXE network card. It will work for non-PXE cards, but to do so, it requires a boot floppy disk. That means someone needs to be physically present at the server to perform its installation or rebuild. The boot floppy disk supports the network cards listed in Table 2-3. But you should always check the supported adapters by clicking the Adapters button in the Remote Boot Floppy Generator (RBFG.exe). Microsoft continually updates this list as new cards become available. RBFG is pretty much the only source of information on this supported list of NICs.

Make sure you fully test the images in every possible situation. Perform complete quality assurance verifications on all images. Then, to perform massive installation of your servers, you'll need to set up a staging center where servers can be prepared "en masse." Depending on the staging infrastructure you use—network speed and RIS server capacity—you can stage at least 20 servers per installer per day.

Installations are launched through the F12 key at PXE card boot to activate the Remote Installation Process on the destination servers. Installers choose the appropriate installation and let the RIS server perform its work.

▶ **QUICK TIP**

You can find a standard operating procedure for the Remote Installation Preparation Process at http://www.Reso-Net.com/WindowsServer/. You can customize it to fit your own environment.

Manufacturer	Card Models
3Com	3c90x Family 3c90xB Family FE575C PC Card FEM656C PC Card
AMD	AMD PCNet Adapters
Compaq	Netflex Cards
Digital Equipment Corporation (DEC)	DE 450 DE 500
Intel	Intel Pro Family
Generic	NE2000 PCI
RealTek	RealTek 8139
SMC	1211 TX EZCard 10/100 8432 EtherPower 10 9332 EtherPower 10/100 9432 EtherPower II 10/100

Table 2-3   Remote Installation Services Boot Disks: Supported NICs

Putting the Server in Place

Special care and attention will be needed when you put staged servers in place. If you are putting a new server in place, you can take your time because no user is currently using it. But if you are replacing an existing server, you will need to ensure that you have a complete inventory of all network-related services and dependencies on that server. Replacing each of these dependencies is at the core of the process for putting a server in place. Chapters 7 and 10 will cover this element in detail when they discuss the replacement of File and Print Servers.

In addition, now that you have a Server Kernel in place, you will need to begin assigning roles and functions to your servers. These assignations and the processes that must be associated with them begin in Chapter 4.

Best Practice Summary

This chapter recommends the following best practices:

- Perform new installation to take full advantage of WS03 functionalities.
- Use the Parallel Network Migration Approach.
- Migrate Identity Servers first instead of Member Servers.
- Determine your Member Server timelines, then apply them.

- Perform detailed inventories in two phases: at the beginning of the project and when you migrate the server.
- Know your servers!
- Don't install servers that only meet minimum hardware requirements.
- Double Microsoft's recommendations and perform a formal Server Sizing Exercise.
- Check system compatibility before the installation.
- Check the number of processors before choosing the WS03 version to install.
- Use virtual machines to test new technologies and in replacement of dual-boot.
- Plan your network addresses and network names before you install new servers.
- Document every server installation.
- Perform a post-installation customization and verification.
- Use unattended answer files to upgrade from Windows 2000 to Windows Server 2003, but only if you performed new installations of Windows 2000.
- Use Remote Installation in medium to large organizations.
- Document, document, document... and test, test, test... everything! To use a well-known proverb, "A good carpenter measures twice and cuts once." Having to try again because a test failed is a measure of your discipline, not a failure.

Chapter Roadmap

Use the illustration in Figure 2-9 to review the contents of this chapter.

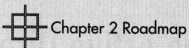 Chapter 2 Roadmap
Preparing for Massive Installations of Windows Server 2003

 Decisions to Make Before Installing
Choosing the Migration Approach
> The Parallel Network Migration Approach **(Figure 2-1)**
Choosing What to Migrate First **(Figure 2-2, 2-3)**
> Identity Servers
> Member Servers **(Figure 2-4)**
Detailed Inventories
Security Considerations
Licensing Considerations

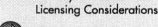 **Installing and Configuring Servers**
Preparing for Massive Installations
> Server Sizing Exercise
> Upgrading Existing Systems
> Dual-boot Considerations
> Using Virtual Machines
> Network Planning
> BIOS Updates
Using Installation Documentation
> The Installation Preparation Checklist **(Figure 2-5)**
> Documenting Server Installations
> Post-Installation Checklist **(Figure 2-6)**

Tools on the Companion Web Site
- Server Sizing Exercise
- Windows Server and Kernel Data Sheet
- Installation Preparation Checklist
- Post-Installation Checklist
- SOP: Preparing for Installation Automation

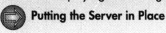 **Massive Installation Processes (Figure 2-7)**
The Initial Installation
> Customize Your Server
> The Reference Server Preparation Process

Tools on the Companion Web Site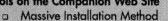
- Massive Installation Method Selection Process

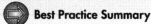 **Choosing the Massive Installation Method**
Scripting Upgrades
Disk Imaging
Remote Installation
> Image Preparation at the RIS Server
> Image Preparation at the Reference Server
> Deploying a RIS Image

Tools on the Companion Web Site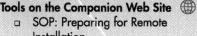
- SOP: Preparing for Remote Installation

 Putting the Server in Place

Best Practice Summary

Figure 2-9 Chapter Roadmap

CHAPTER 3

Designing the Active Directory

IN THIS CHAPTER

Active Directory is the core of the Windows Server 2003 network. It is the central component that not only serves to provide authentication and authorization, but also administration, information sharing, and information availability. It can be defined as follows:

"A secure virtual environment where users can interact either with each other or with network components, all according to the business rules of the enterprise."

Quite a change from Windows NT, isn't it? It's no wonder people have not accepted Active Directory (AD) at a neck-breaking pace. It is a paradigm shift that is even more complex than moving from character-based computing to the graphical interface. Understanding the breadth of possibilities Active Directory brings is the biggest challenge of the enterprise network with WS03.

The first rule you must set for yourself when working to design your Active Directory is "Use best practices everywhere!" Don't try to change the way Active Directory is designed to work no matter what you might think at first. Active Directory provides a wealth of opportunities that you will discover as you implement, use, and operate it. Changes that might make sense according to IT concepts today may well have a negative impact on the operation of your Active Directory tomorrow.

The first step toward the implementation of the enterprise network—you could say the major step toward this implementation—is the design and implementation of your Active Directory. Even if you have already implemented Active Directory and are using it with Windows 2000, a quick review of how you design and plan to use directory services in your network can't hurt, unless you are completely satisfied with the way your directory delivers service. In that case, you can move on to Chapter 4 to review your communications infrastructure and begin installing the enterprise network. *If, on the other hand, you are using Windows NT and want to move to WS03, the following section is a must and cannot be overlooked under any circumstances.*

Introducing Active Directory

Countless books, articles, and presentations have been written on the subject of Active Directory, and it is not the intention of this book to repeat them. However, it is important to review a few basic terms and concepts inherent in Active Directory. Figure 3-1 illustrates the concepts that make up an Active Directory.

Active Directory is first and foremost a database. As such it contains a *schema*—a database structure. This schema applies to every instance of Active Directory. An instance is defined as an Active Directory *forest*. The forest is the largest single partition for any given database structure. Every person and every device that participates in the forest will share a given set of attributes and object types. That's not to say that information sharing in Active Directory is limited to a single forest. Forests can be linked together to exchange certain information, especially with Windows Server 2003. WS03 introduces the concept of *forest trusts* which allow forests to share portions of their entire Active Directory database with others and vice versa.

If you compare the WS03 forest to Windows NT, you can easily see that while NT also included an identity management database—the domain—its scope was seriously limited compared to Active Directory. NT could basically store the user or computer name along with passwords and a few rules affecting all objects. The basic WS03 AD database includes more than 200 object types and more than 1,000 attributes by default. You can, of course, add more object types or attributes to this database. Software products that take advantage of information stored in the Active Directory will

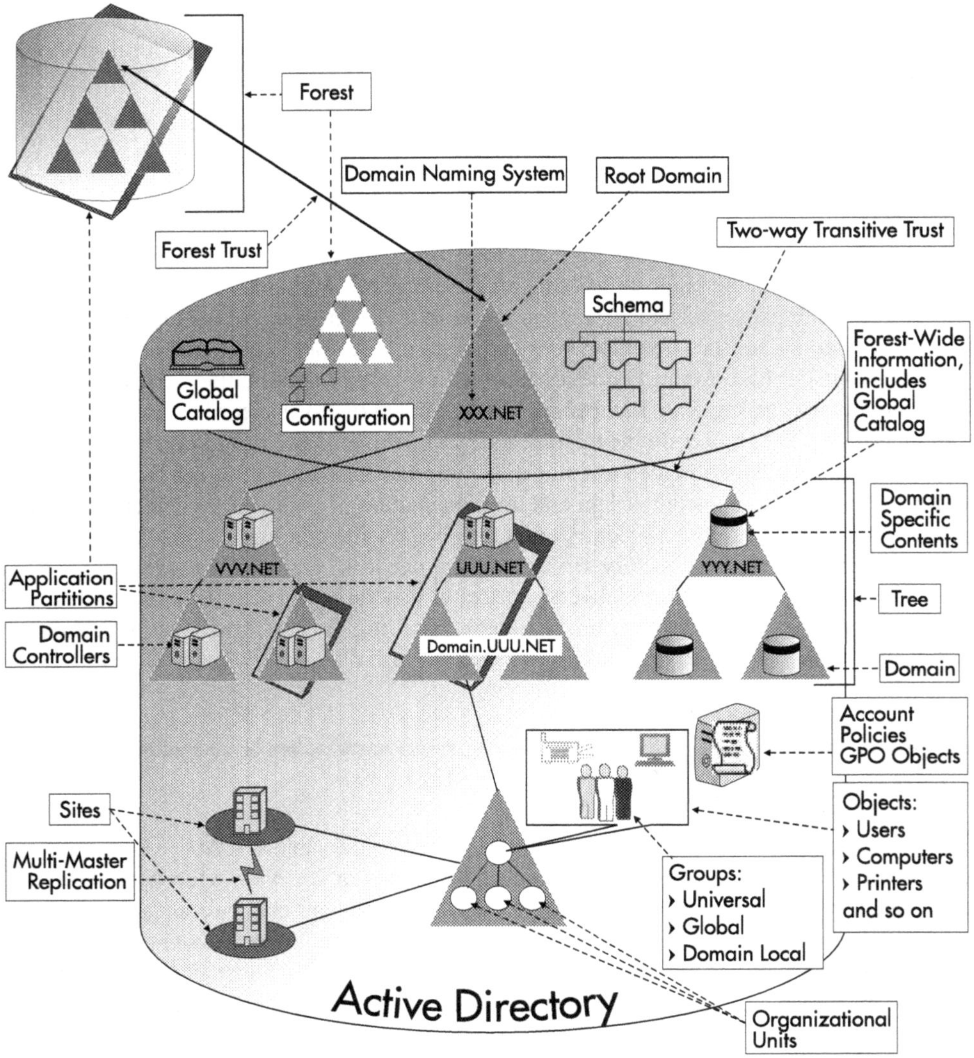

Forest

Domain Naming System

Root Domain

Two-way Transitive Trust

Forest Trust

Schema

Forest-Wide Information, includes Global Catalog

Global Catalog

Configuration

XXX.NET

Domain Specific Contents

Application Partitions

VVV.NET

UUU.NET

YYY.NET

Tree

Domain Controllers

Domain.UUU.NET

Domain

Account Policies GPO Objects

Objects:
› Users
› Computers
› Printers
and so on

Sites

Multi-Master Replication

Groups:
› Universal
› Global
› Domain Local

Active Directory

Organizational Units

Figure 3-1 The Active Directory database

also extend the AD schema. Microsoft Exchange, for example, practically doubles the number of objects and attributes in a forest because it is integrated to the directory.

Like any database, AD categorizes the objects it contains, but unlike relational databases, Active Directory's database structure is hierarchical. This is because it is based on the structure of the Domain Naming System (DNS), used on the World Wide Web. On the Web, everything is hierarchical. For example, the root of Microsoft's Web site is www.microsoft.com. Everything spans from this page.

Moving to any other section, such as TechNet or MSDN, sends you to pages whose names are based on the microsoft.com root.

Forests act in the same way except that in a forest, the root point (analogous to the home page) is the root domain. Every AD forest must have at least one domain. Domains act as discrete object containers in the forest. Domains can be regrouped into *trees*. Trees are segregated from each other through their DNS name. For example, Microsoft has a multitree forest. Its namespace, the DNS element that defines the boundaries of the forest, is microsoft.com. As such, all domains in this tree have names similar to domain.microsoft.com. Microsoft created a second tree when it incorporated MSN.com in its forest. The MSN.com namespace automatically created a tree and all domains under it are named domain.MSN.com.

Every forest will include at least one tree and at least one domain. The domain is both a security policy and an administration boundary. It is required to contain objects such as users, computers, servers, domain controllers, printers, file shares, applications, and much more. If you have more than one domain in the forest, it will automatically be linked to all others through automatic transitive two-way trusts. The domain is defined as a security policy boundary because it contains rules that apply to the objects stored in it. These rules can be in the form of security policies or Group Policy Objects (GPOs). Security policies are global domain rules. GPOs tend to be more discrete and are applied to specific container objects. While domains are discrete security policy boundaries, the ultimate security boundary will always be the forest.

Domain contents can be further categorized through grouping object types such as *Organizational Units* (OUs) or *groups*. Organizational Units provide groupings that can be used for administrative or delegation purposes. Groups are used mainly for the application of security rights. WS03 groups include Universal, which can span an entire forest, Global, which can span domains, or Domain Local, which are contained in a single domain. OUs are usually used to segregate objects vertically. Objects such as users and computers can only reside inside a single OU, but groups can span OUs. Thus they tend to contain horizontal collections of objects. An object such as a user can be included in several groups, but only in a single OU.

Users also have it easier with Active Directory. Working in a distributed forest composed of several different trees and subdomains can become very confusing to the user. AD supports the notion of user principal name (UPN). The UPN is often composed of the username along with the global forest root name. This root name can be the name of the forest or a special alias you assign. For example, in an internal forest named TandT.net, you might use name.surname@tandt.com as the UPN, making it simpler for your users by using your *external* DNS name for the UPN. Users can log on to any domain or forest they are allowed to by using their UPN. In their local domain, they can just use their username if they prefer.

Forests, Trees, Domains, Organizational Units, Groups, Users, and Computers are all objects stored in the Active Directory database. As such, they can be manipulated globally or discretely. The single major difference between Active Directory and a standard database is that in addition to being hierarchical, it is completely decentralized. Most Active Directory databases are also distributed geographically because they represent the true nature of an enterprise or an organization.

Managing a completely distributed database is considerably more challenging than managing a database that is located in a single area. To simplify distributed database issues, Active Directory introduces the concept of *multimaster replication*. This means that even though the entire forest database is comprised of distributed deposits—deposits that, depending on their location in the logical hierarchy of the forest, may or may not contain the same information as others—database consistency will be maintained. Through the multimaster structure, AD can accept local changes and ensure consistency by relaying the information or the changes to all of the other deposits in the domain or the forest. This is one of the functions of the Domain Controller object in the directory.

The only deposits that have exactly the same information in the AD database are two domain controllers in the same domain. Each of these data deposits contains information about its own domain as well as whatever information has been determined to be of forest-wide interest by forest administrators. At the forest level, you can determine the information to make available to the entire forest by selecting the objects and the attributes from the database schema whose properties you want to share among all trees and domains. In addition, other forest-wide information includes the database schema and the forest configuration, or the location of all forest services. Published information is stored in the Global Catalog. AD publishes some items by default, such as the contents of Universal groups, but you can also add or subtract published items to your taste. For example, you might decide to include your employees' photos in the directory and make them available forest-wide.

▶ **NOTE**

Not all items are unpublishable; some items are prerequisites for the proper operation of Active Directory Services.

Whatever is published in the Global Catalog is shared by all domain controllers who play this role in the forest. Whatever is not published remains within the domain. This data segregation controls the individuality of domains. Whatever is not published can contain discrete information that may be of the same nature, even use the same values, as what is contained in another domain. Properties that are published in the Global Catalog of a forest must be unique just as in any other database. For example, you can have two John Smiths in a forest so long as they are both in different domains. Since the name of the object includes the name of its container (in this case, the domain), Active Directory will see each John Smith as a discrete object.

Figure 3-2 illustrates the contents of the directory store, or the NTDS.DIT database, that is located on every domain controller in the forest. Three items are in every directory store—the schema, the configuration and the domain data—and two are optional—the Global Catalog and the application partition (defined later).

The Global Catalog, schema, and configuration are information that is replicated throughout the forest. Domain data is information that is replicated only within the domain. Replication over local and distant networks is controlled through regional database partitions. Organizations may decide to create these partitions based on a number of factors. Since the domain is a security policy boundary, authoritative organizations—organizations that span a number of geographic locations they control—may want to create a single domain that spans these locations. To segregate each region, and control the amount and timing of database replication between regions, the domain would be divided into *sites*. Sites are physical partitions that control replication by creating boundaries based on Internet Protocol (IP) addressing.

Organizations that are not authoritative, have independent administrations, do not control their regional locations, or have slow links between each location, may want to further control replication through the creation of regional domains. Regional domains greatly reduce replication since only

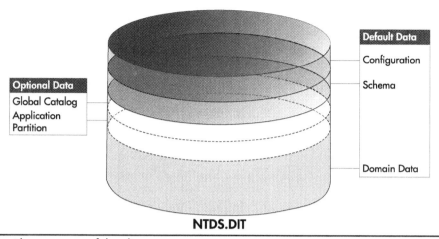

NTDS.DIT

Figure 3-2   The structure of the directory store

forest-wide information is replicated from location to location. Forest-wide information rarely exceeds 20 percent of global forest data. In addition, organizations that only have the control of a portion of the forest namespace will be owners of the trees in the forest. Organizations that cannot guarantee a minimum level of consensus or authority between groups will always create separate forests.

There is one more replication partition in the Active Directory. This partition is new to Windows Server 2003. It is the *application partition*. This partition has several features such as the ability to host several instances of the same application and COM+ components on the same physical machine, but for the purposes of replication, this partition can be defined as a specific group of domain Controller IP addresses or DNS names. For example, WS03 automatically creates a forest-wide application partition for forest-wide DNS data so this information will be available on all domain controllers with the DNS role in the forest.

That's it. That's the basis of Active Directory. What's truly impressive about this database is that once it's in place, it can let you do some amazing things. You can manage an entire network from a central location. All management interfaces are the same throughout the forest, even across forests. Since everything is hierarchic, you can implement forest-wide standards for naming conventions, operations, database structure, and especially, security policy implementations. If you do it right, you can implement these standards automatically. This must be done before you create anything below the root domain. Though simple to understand, Active Directory is indeed quite powerful.

New Features for Active Directory

Windows Server 2003 boasts several improvements in regards to Active Directory. While this technology was introduced in Windows 2000, it has been refined and enhanced in WS03. Table 3-1

> **QUICK TIP**
>
> *A complete glossary of Active Directory terms is available at http://www.Reso-Net.com/ WindowsServer/.*

lists the new features found in WS03 for Active Directory since Windows 2000. This table first identifies new features that can operate within a mixed Windows 2000 and WS03 forest, and then identifies features that can only operate in a native WS03 forest.

Feature	Description
Multiple selection of directory objects	Modify common attributes of multiple users at one time.
Drag-and-drop functionality	Move directory objects from container to container in the domain hierarchy. Add objects to group membership lists.
Improved search capabilities	Search functionality is object-oriented and provides an efficient browse-less search that minimizes network traffic associated with browsing objects because it focuses on the local directory store.
Saved queries	Save commonly used search parameters for reuse in Active Directory Users and Computers.
Active Directory command-line tools	Run new directory service commands for administration scenarios.
InetOrgPerson class	This class has been added to the base schema as a security principal and can be used in the same manner as the user class. The userPassword attribute can also be used to set the account password.
Application directory partitions	Configure the replication scope for application-specific data among domain controllers running WS03S, WS03E, and WS03D. The Web Edition does not support the Domain Controller role.
Add additional domain controllers to existing domains using backup media	Reduce the time it takes to add an additional DC in an existing domain by using backup media instead of replication.
Universal group membership caching	Prevent the need to locate a Global Catalog across a WAN during logon by caching user Universal group memberships on an authenticating domain controller.
New domain- and forest-wide Active Directory features (in a Windows Server 2003 native domain or forest mode)	
Domain controller rename	Rename domain controllers without first demoting them.
Domain rename	Rename any domain running Windows Server 2003 domain controllers. This applies to NetBIOS or DNS names of any child, parent, tree-, or forest-root domain.
Forest trusts	Create a forest trust to extend two-way transitivity beyond the scope of a single forest to a second forest.
Forest restructuring	Move existing domains to other locations in the domain hierarchy.
Defunct schema objects	Deactivate unnecessary classes or attributes from the schema.
Selective class creation	Create instances of specified classes in the base schema of Windows Server 2003 forest, such as country, person, organizationalPerson, groupOfNames, device, and certificationAuthority.

Table 3-1   New Active Directory Features

Feature	Description
Dynamic auxiliary classes	Provide support for dynamically linking auxiliary classes to individual objects, and not just to entire classes of objects. Auxiliary classes that have been attached to an object instance can subsequently be removed from the instance.
Global Catalog replication tuning	Preserve the synchronization state of the Global Catalog by replicating only what has been changed.
Replication enhancements	Linked value replication allows individual group members to be replicated across the network instead of treating the entire group membership as a single unit of replication.
Reduced directory store	In native WS03 forest mode, the directory store is 60 percent smaller than in Windows 2000 because it can take advantage of the Single Instance Store feature, which does not duplicate redundant information on a disk.
Unlimited site management	In a native WS03 forest, the Knowledge Consistency Checker (KCC)—the service that automatically manages replication topology—can manage the topology for an unlimited number of sites. In Windows 2000, this service had to be turned off if your directory had more than 200 sites.

Table 3-1   New Active Directory Features *(continued)*

You can see from Table 3-1 that WS03 supports several functional modes for Active Directory. You can run AD domains in Windows NT mixed mode, which limits the functionality of AD to Windows NT capabilities; you can run domains in Windows 2000 native mode, which limits WS03 functionality to Windows 2000 AD capabilities; or you can run them in WS03 native mode. This last mode precludes the inclusion of any domain controllers other than WS03 within a domain. WS03 includes a second native mode: the WS03 native forest mode. While a WS03 forest can still include domains that operate in any of the three modes, a native WS03 forest can only include native WS03 domains. Table 3-2 identifies the differences between domain modes: Windows NT mixed mode, Windows 2000 native mode, and WS03 native mode. It serves to identify the limitations of Windows NT and Windows 2000 domain modes. It also includes the features of a native WS03 forest.

Both Tables 3-1 and 3-2 will be useful for the next step, designing your enterprise Active Directory.

The Nature of Active Directory

One final key element to understand before you move on to the creation of your Active Directory design is the nature of the directory. You already understand that a directory is a distributed database and as such must be viewed as distributed data deposits. But databases and data deposits include two basic components:

- **The database service**   The engine that allows the database to operate
- **Data**   The data contained in the database

Feature	Windows 2000 Mixed	Windows 2000 Native	Windows Server 2003 Native
Domain-wide Features			
Number of objects in domain	40,000	1,000,000	Same as Win2K
Domain controller rename	Disabled	Disabled	Enabled
Update logon timestamp	Disabled	Disabled	Enabled
Kerberos KDC key version numbers	Disabled	Disabled	Enabled
User password on InetOrgPerson object	Disabled	Disabled	Enabled
Universal groups	Disabled (security groups). Allows distribution groups.	Enabled. Allows security and distribution groups.	Same as Win2K
Group nesting	Disabled (for security groups, allows only group nesting for groups with domain local scope that have groups with global scope "Windows NT 4.0 rule" as members). For distribution groups, allows full group nesting.	Enabled. Allows full group nesting.	Same as Win2K
Converting groups	Disabled. No group conversions allowed.	Enabled. Allows conversion between security groups and distribution groups.	Same as Win2K
SID history	Disabled (security groups). Allows universal scope for distribution groups.	Enabled. Allows universal scope for security and distribution groups.	Same as Win2K
Forest-wide Features			
Global Catalog replication tuning	N/A	Disabled	Enabled
Defunct schema objects	N/A	Disabled	Enabled
Forest trust	N/A	Disabled	Enabled
Linked value replication	N/A	Disabled	Enabled
Domain rename	N/A	Disabled	Enabled
Improved replication	N/A	Disabled	Enabled
Dynamic auxiliary classes	N/A	Disabled	Enabled
InetOrgPerson object class	N/A	Disabled	Enabled
Reduced NTDS.DIT size	N/A	Disabled	Enabled
Unlimited site management	N/A	Disabled	Enabled

Table 3-2   Windows NT Mixed, Windows 2000 Native, and WS03 Native Domains

The WS03 directory is the same as any other database. Active Directory management is divided into two activities: service management and data management. AD management is comparable to intranet Web site management. Technicians and technical staff are required to manage the service behind AD just like the Web service for the intranet site, but users and user departments must be responsible for and administer the data contained in the AD as they would for information contained in the intranet pages.

For AD, the management of the data contained in the database can and should be delegated. Users should be responsible for their own information—telephone number, location, and other personal information—and departments should be responsible for information that is department-wide—organization structure, authority structure, and so on. Of course, user and departmental information should be validated before it is stored in the directory. Often, the best way to manage and delegate this information is through the use of a Web form located on the intranet. This allows the concentration of all delegated data in a single place. In addition, the Web form can support a content approval process before being put into the directory. For example, this content approval process could be delegated to the Human Resources department.

Service management—management of domains, Operation Masters, domain controllers, directory configuration, and replication operations—must be maintained and operated by IT. Delegating data management tasks takes the pressure off IT staff and allows them to focus on IT-related operations within the directory such as database service management.

Designing the Solution: Using the Active Directory Blueprint

Like the Enterprise Network Architecture Blueprint presented in Chapter 1 (refer back to Figure 1-5), the Active Directory Design Blueprint emerges from the structure of the Microsoft Certification Exam number 70-219, "Designing a Microsoft Windows 2000 Directory Services Infrastructure." It also includes the same prerequisites: business and technical requirements analyses. The advantage of using the same blueprint structure for both operations is that you should already have most of this information in hand. If not, now's the time to complete it. Without this information, you can go no further. You simply cannot achieve a sound Active Directory design without fully understanding your organization, its purpose, its objectives, its market, its growth potential, its upcoming challenges, and without involving the right stakeholders.

Your Active Directory design must be flexible and adaptive. It must be ready to respond to organizational situations that you haven't even anticipated yet. Remember, Active Directory creates a "virtual space" where you will perform and manage networked operations. Being virtual, it is always adaptable at a later date, but if adaptability is what you're looking for, you need to take it into account at the very beginning of the design.

Once you have the information you need, you can proceed to the actual design. This will focus on three phases: partitioning, service positioning, and the implementation plan.

> ▶ **QUICK TIP**
>
> *To help simplify the AD Design Process for you, sample working tools are available at http:// www.Reso-Net.com/WindowsServer/. The first is a glossary of Active Directory terms. You can use it along with Figure 3-1 to ensure that everyone has a common understanding of each feature. There is also an AD Design Blueprint Support Checklist that follows the steps outlined in Figure 3-3. It is a working process control form that lets you follow the AD Design Process stage by stage and check off completed tasks. In addition, there is an OU documentation table that will support your OU creation process. These tools will help you design the AD that best suits your organization's requirements.*

AD Partitioning

Partitioning is the art of determining the number of Active Directory databases you want to manage and segregating objects within each one. This means you will need to determine the number of forests your organization will create, remembering that each is a separate database that will require maintenance and management resources. Within each forest, you will need to identify the number of trees, the number of domains in each tree, and the organizational unit structure in each domain. Overall, you'll need to identify if your Active Directory database will share its information with other, non-AD databases. This will be done either through integration of the two database structures (if the other database is compatible to the Active Directory format) or information exchange. In this case, you will need to identify the information exchange strategy.

To control data replication, you will identify and structure sites, design replication rules, and identify replication methodology. This is *Site Topology* Design. Microsoft provides an excellent tool to support you in this process, the Active Directory Sizer. It is found at http://www.microsoft.com/ windows2000/downloads/tools/sizer/.

Since you intend to fully exploit the AD database (after all, why go through all this trouble if you're not going to use it?), you'll have to put in place a Schema Modification Strategy. Since every schema modification is replicated to every domain controller in the forest, you'll want to ensure you maintain a tight control over these. You might even decide to separate application from network-based schema modifications. Of course, all schema modifications will go through lab testing before making it to the production network.

AD Service Positioning

Site Topology Design is closely related to Service Positioning. Each Active Directory domain controller performs important operations that support the proper functioning of the database. In fact, the object of Site Topology Design is to determine how each of these database containers will be linked to the others. Since AD is a distributed database, domain controllers should be positioned as close as possible to the user. These points of service should be convenient without becoming overabundant.

Operation Masters are special domain controllers that manage global forest or global domain operations. Global Catalog (GC) servers are domain controllers that maintain copies of information that is published throughout the forest. But since WS03 domain controllers can cache frequently requested global information, GC servers do not need to be as widely spread as domain controllers. Finally, DNS servers are a must since they provide namespace management functionality to the directory. They should be seen as subsidiary functions for directory support and married to every domain controller. Proper positioning of each of these services can vastly improve directory performance.

Implementation Plan

The last step of the blueprint is the AD Implementation Plan—the actual procedure you will use to put your Active Directory design in place. Indeed, this is where the Parallel Network Strategy comes in handy. It gives you the freedom to implement a brand new Active Directory without any limitations. This directory can immediately operate in native mode since it does not have to share database space with previous technologies. The limitations of Windows NT can be contained in specific domains or can even be excluded entirely from your Windows Server 2003 enterprise forest. In this way, you can obtain immediate benefits from native-mode Active Directory functionalities. The blueprint for AD design is illustrated in Figure 3-3.

Putting the Blueprint into Action

While the information collected for business requirements is the same as the information collected for the Enterprise Network Architecture Blueprint, your view of the information collected for technical requirements has to be slightly different. In particular, the second section, "Impact of the Enterprise Network," is changed to "Impact of Active Directory." Here you need to see how existing systems and applications will be affected by the arrival of a central database containing primary information such as usernames and user identity. You also need to see how these systems and applications can be integrated with this new central data repository.

You need to review planned upgrades and rollouts to make sure they will be compatible with Active Directory and that these projects will not negatively affect the rollout of an enterprise AD. In terms of IP infrastructure, your focus needs to be the internal network Domain Naming System since this function becomes integrated with the directory itself. You need to identify how the technological support structure functions in your organization in order to determine who has authority over what. This will allow you to determine where your authoritative AD boundaries (Forests, Trees, and Domains) will lie and where you will be able to perform delegation (through Organizational Units). You also need to review your system management structure (both current and planned) to see which functions you will want to delegate or integrate to Active Directory. Finally, you need to review your current identity management deposits, either Windows NT or Windows 2000 domains or other deposits such as Novell Directory Services or even UNIX systems to see how they will be integrated or how they will interact with the WS03 directory.

Once this is complete, you can proceed to the third step of the blueprint, the partitioning design. The directory partitioning exercise allows you to determine the scope, naming strategy, Organizational Unit strategy, integration model, position for core services, topology, and Schema Modification Strategy for each forest in your enterprise.

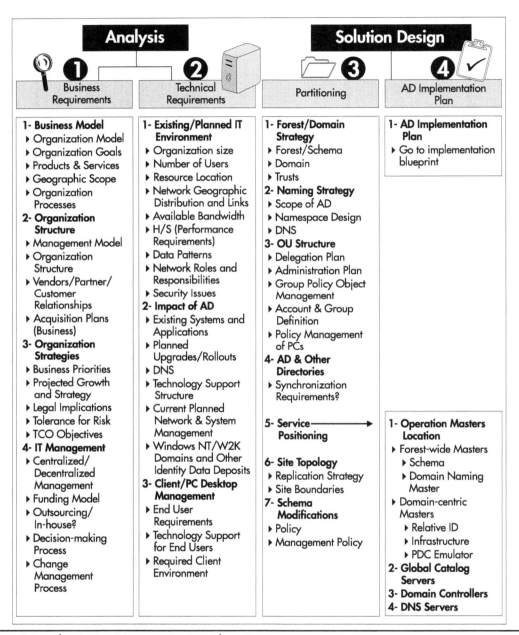

Figure 3-3   The Active Directory Design Blueprint

▶ *NOTE*

Microsoft produced an excellent partitioning guide, "Best Practice Active Directory Design for Managing Windows Networks." It can be found at www.microsoft.com/windows2000/techinfo/ planning/activedirectory/bpaddsgn.asp.

Forest/Tree/Domain Strategy

The first step in the partitioning exercise is to determine the number of forests, the nature of the trees in each forest, and the nature of the domains in each of the trees your enterprise will require. Forests are the partitions that contain:

- **Database schema** Only one database structure can be stored in a single forest. If someone in your organization needs to modify the schema and does not want to share this modification with others in the organization, they should be placed in their own forest. Obviously, this would not be departments that share physical locations, but it could be a subsidiary or a partner organization. Commercial and/or corporate applications will also personalize the schema. With the advent of forest trusts, you might decide to use an *application forest* to store an application with its own schema inside a different forest and link it to your enterprise network Active Directory through a trust. This strategy keeps the two schemas completely separate.

▶ *QUICK TIP*

You could also use Active Directory in Application Mode (AD/AM) for this purpose. AD/AM is a special directory service that is an add-on to WS03 and that is designed to run as a pure lightweight application protocol (LDAP) directory. Its schema is much smaller than AD's, though—it contains 30 objects and 160 attributes. More information is available at http:// www.microsoft.com/windowsserver2003/techinfo/overview/adam.mspx.

- **Configuration data** The structure of the forest, the number of trees it contains, and the domains in each tree as well as the structure of replication sites make up the configuration data for the forest.
- **Global Catalog** The Global Catalog includes all of the searchable objects for the forest. It contains the values and properties for all of the objects you deem important to users in the entire forest.
- **Trust relationships** Trust relationships between the domains in a forest are also forest-wide information. This is because of the transitive nature of Windows Server 2003 intra-forest or inter-domain trusts. Every domain in a forest will automatically be linked to its parent domain. The parent domain will be linked to its parent and so on. Since all domains of a forest include two-way transitive trusts, all domains trust all other domains of the forest.

In Windows NT, you needed to create specific trusts between each domain if you wanted domains in a group to trust each other. Trusts were not transitive. That means that Domain A would not trust Domain C even if they both trusted Domain B. For Domain A to trust Domain C, you had to create an explicit trust. You do not need to create direct trusts between domains in a forest. If Domain A and Domain C both trust Domain B in a forest, Domain A will automatically trust Domain C without an explicit trust. You can create shortcut trusts if the hierarchical path between two domains that share a lot of information is too long or too complex. This is illustrated in Figure 3-4.

Forests can contain millions of objects, so most small, medium, and even large organizations will usually require a single production forest. The main reason for the creation of separate forests within the same organization is to protect the database schema. Schema modifications are complex and must be tightly controlled if you want to minimize their impact on production environments. If you need to play or experiment with the schema, you need to create a forest that is separate from your production forest. Most medium to large organizations have development and test forests as well as at least one production forest.

A second reason for the segregation of forests is the level of authority of the central organization. You can only include organizations, divisions, or departments over which you have political and economic control in your forest. This is because of the hierarchical nature of the forest and the inheritance model that is derived from it. The organization at the root of the forest has influence and even authoritative control over all of the organizations or departments that are grouped into its trees and subdomains. For example, the Ford Motor Company and Volvo would have had separate forests before the acquisition of Volvo by Ford. But once Ford bought Volvo, it established financial authority over Volvo. In an Active Directory, Volvo could then become a tree under the Ford production forest. Much depends on how well the Volvo and Ford IT staffs get along and whether Ford will impose the joining even if the Volvo staff does not agree.

As you can see, no matter the size of your production forest—whether it is in a small enterprise located within a single site or a multinational spanning the world, the role of the forest owner is an important one. Forest owners manage forest-wide services. This means they are:

- **Forest-wide operation masters administrators**   The forest owner is the administrator of the domain controllers that execute the Schema and Domain Naming Master services and thus can impact the entire forest.

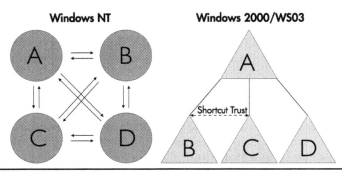

Figure 3-4   Windows NT trusts versus Active Directory trusts

- **Root domain administrators**   Every forest, even if it only has a single tree and a single domain, includes a root domain. The first domain in a forest is the root domain because all other domains in the forest are created as subdomains of the root domain. The operation of the root domain is critical if the forest is to run properly.

- **Root domain data owner**   Since the root domain is the basis of the forest, the forest owner is also the root domain data owner.

- **Schema and configuration owner**   Since the forest operation is based on the structure of its schema and configuration containers, the forest owner is responsible for their integrity.

- **Forest-wide security group owner**   The forest owner is also responsible for forest-wide security groups. These groups reside in the root domain. Active Directory creates two management forest-wide groups: Enterprise Administrators and Schema Administrators. Membership in these groups is limited because they can affect the operation of the entire forest.

- **Root domain security group owner**   In addition to the two universal administration groups, the root domain contains its own administrative group, Domain Administrators. The forest owner is also owner of this security group.

If there is more than one domain in the forest, the forest owner will have to communicate frequently with subdomain owners to coordinate forest-wide efforts.

In fact, determining the number of forests in your organization can be summarized as the identification of all forest owners. These will be the highest level of IT administration in the organization for any given network. Once this is done, you will be able to proceed to identifying the forest content.

Forests share a lot of elements. Many are required elements; others are recommended elements based on common sense. Forests require the sharing of:

- **Security**   Only include people you trust in a forest. This would include employees as well as administrative staff. Since a forest is made up of distributed database containers, domain controllers, you need to trust the people who will be responsible for all domain controllers that will be placed outside your office site.

▶ *CAUTION*

This point is extremely important. Even though you can secure domain controllers by locking down the system and placing the servers in locked rooms, you should be absolutely sure that any DCs that will be in distributed locations are under the responsibility of people in whom you have absolute trust. Because of the multimaster replication model of Active Directory, a rogue domain administrator who has physical access to a DC can do a lot of damage in a forest. For example, they can take the DC offline and edit the directory store in debug mode, adding special access rights for themselves. Once the DC is back on line, these access rights are replicated throughout the forest. There are ways to control this remotely, and they will be covered in Chapter 8. For now, include remote offices in your forest only if you can trust that your DCs will be safe from tampering.

- **Administration**   Everyone who participates in a forest is willing to use the same schema and configuration.

- **Name resolution**   Everyone who participates in a forest will use the same Domain Name System to resolve names throughout the forest.

In addition to the required elements, you might decide to share the following:

- **Network**   If all organizations in a forest trust each other, they may have put a private network in place. Though it is not impossible to separate forest sites with firewalls, it is recommended to minimize the exposure of your Active Directory information to the outside world. If forest members must use public network links to transport replication traffic, they may opt for separate forests.
- **Collaboration**   If you work with other organizations and have implemented domain trusts with them, they may well be candidates for joining your new AD forest.
- **IT groups**   If organizations share IT groups, it is a good idea to create single forests to simplify network administration.

You must also keep in mind that creating more than one forest will have administrative impacts:

- Forests do not share transitive trusts. In WS03, these trusts must be created manually, but once created will allow two entire forests to trust each other. If forests need to interact at a specific domain level, you can still use explicit domain trusts between the two specific domains limiting the trust relationship between the forests. Both forest and domain trusts can either be one- or two-way trusts.
- The Kerberos security protocol (the native Windows Server 2003 authorization protocol) will only work between forests that have implemented forest trusts.
- Using an email-like logon name (*name@domain*), the UPN, will also only work if a forest trust is in place.
- Global Catalog replication is limited to a single forest unless there is a forest trust in place.

Forest Design Example

Now that you're comfortable with the forest concept, you can identify the number of forests you need. Use the following examples to review the forest creation process.

The first design example focuses on the identification of the number of forests for a medium-sized organization with 5,000 users. It is distributed geographically into ten regions, but each region is administered from a central location. The organization operates under a single public name and delivers the same services in each region. Since the organization has a "buy, don't build" policy, it tries to make use of commercial software whenever possible, but even with this policy, it still needs to create custom code or adapt existing applications. Thus it requires a separate development environment.

In addition, it has had a lot of growing pains in the past because of friction between IT and IS. In fact, IS was seriously disappointed when IT created a single master domain network with Windows NT.

In their forest design, this organization would create at least two, possibly three or more, permanent forests:

- A production forest that replaces the single master Windows NT domain.
- A staging forest to test, analyze, and prepare new products for integration, especially those that may integrate with Active Directory and modify its basic database schema.
- A development forest to allow the testing and development of corporate applications that take advantage of schema customizations.
- A separate forest will also be created for the extranet. Because this forest is exposed through the security perimeter of the network, it is separate from the production forest.

No trust would be established between three of these forests: production, staging, and development. In an illustrated model, this is represented by solid lines separating each Active Directory database. There may, however, be a trust established between the perimeter forest and the production forest, but since the nature of this trust (one-way, explicit, domain-to-domain) is not completely precise at this time, its boundary with the production forest is displayed as a dotted line.

Production Forest Design

In the production forest design you will determine the structure of the forest you use to run your network. Once again, authority boundaries will determine the structure you create. Here you need to determine the number of trees and the number of domains your forest will contain.

Begin with the trees. Does your organization operate with a single public name? If not, these are good candidates for different trees. Even though the tree structure is completely internal and will rarely be exposed to the external world, its structure should reflect the names your organization uses publicly. Good candidates for trees are organizations that rely on others for service completion; organizations that form a partnership and want to collaborate closely; enterprises that merge with each other; and organizations that share IT management resources.

The second design example covers a tree design for a worldwide organization that has four subsidiaries. The organization is a single enterprise, but each of its business units is known under a different public name. It understands the complexity of interbusiness administration, but wants to implement operational and security standards throughout the corporation. IT budgets are controlled centrally, but most of the administrative work is performed by large IT groups from each of the business units.

After a series of discussions, the different IT groups decided on a single production forest with multiple trees. The forest owner identified and began ongoing discussions with each tree owner. As a group, they determined the level of integration for each tree and the level of authority the forest root domain would be allowed.

This model uses the same number of forests as before, but now trees are created in the production forest. It allows the organization to set standards while supporting regional diversity.

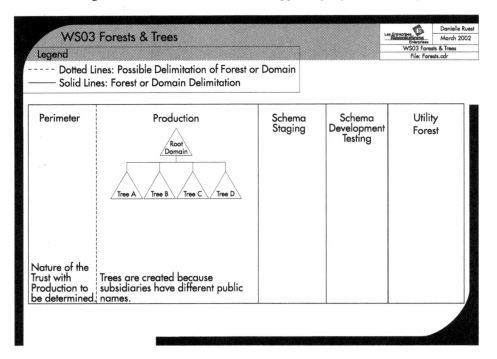

Had the different IT groups not been able to agree, they would have created multiple production forests. In this case, the organization would not have met its goals for standardization because there is no technical way to ensure forests use the same standards. These goals could only have been obtained through political enforcement measures and not through the operational infrastructure of Active Directory.

Using forest trusts, an organization can interact through multiple forests, and thus gain benefits such as single sign-on and global interforest searches, but cannot enforce standards through AD.

Domain Strategy Design

The first thing to remember when working with Windows Server 2003 domains is that they are *not* like Windows NT domains. In Windows NT, the largest identity database boundary was the domain. If you wanted multiple domains to work with each other in either a master/master or a master/resource relationship, you had to enable trusts between each of the domains. In WS03, domain trusts in a forest are transitive. Here the domain must be viewed as what it is—a security policy boundary that can contain:

- **Authentication rules**   Domains form the boundary for the rules used to authenticate users and computers since they are the container into which these objects are created.

- **Group Policies**   Policies are limited by domain boundaries because they are objects that reside within the domain container.

- **Security policies for user accounts**   Security policies applying to user accounts are stored in the domain. These can be different from one domain to another.

- **Publication services for shared resources**   All of the resources that can be shared in a domain are published through Active Directory. By default, these resources—shared printers and folders—are published only to members of the domain.

Your domain design will depend on a number of factors: for example, the number of users in a forest and the available bandwidth for replication from remote sites. Even though domains can contain one million objects each, it doesn't mean you need to fill them up. You might decide to create multiple domains to regroup objects into smaller portions. If you find that you are applying the same policies to two different domains and it's not for replication control, you've got one too many. In fact, you may consider upgrading wide area network links to eliminate the need for multiple domains.

In addition, you can use several domain models just as in Windows NT. WS03 forests support the unique domain model, the multiple domain model, and the mixed model. Because of the hierarchical nature of the forest, these models are not like their Windows NT predecessors. Few organizations today opt for the unique domain model. Small businesses with fewer than 500 employees may decide to use this model, but it is very rare in larger organizations.

Most large organizations will decide to create a *Protected Forest Root Domain* (PFRD). There are several advantages to this approach. A Protected Forest Root Domain is often much smaller than production domains because it only contains forest management groups and users. As such, it has a minimum amount of data to replicate, which makes it easier to rebuild in case of disasters. It contains a small group of forest-wide administrators, which reduces the possibility of mistakes that may affect the entire forest. It is never retired since it does not contain production data. Because domains are created below the forest root domain, organizational restructuring is easier to accomplish. Because it is small and compact, it is easier to secure. And should transfer of ownership be required, it is easier to transfer an empty domain than to transfer your entire production domain which contains all of your hundreds of users.

▶ **CAUTION**

The Protected Forest Root Domain is the most commonly overlooked feature of an AD design. If your organization has more than a few hundred users and you can afford the domain controllers the PFRD requires, it is highly recommended that you implement a PFRD in your AD design, as it gives you the most flexibility in AD.

Production domains are created under the Protected Forest Root Domain. Any medium to large organization that has a single master domain in Windows NT should create a Single Global Child Domain. This Single Global Child Domain (SGCD) has the same purpose of the single NT domain: regroup all of the users of your network into a single production environment. The only users that are not in this child domain are the forest root domain users.

Now that you have a parent and child domain structure, you can expand forest contents to include other security policy boundaries. The main requirement of a Single Global Child Domain is that users be identifiable and that their actions be traceable within the network. As such, you will definitely want to exclude generic user accounts from the production domain. Generic accounts—accounts that are named according to function rather than individual—are most often used for three activities: testing, development, and training. You can use security policy boundaries—domains—to segregate these accounts from the production domain. In this manner, you can create other domain containers where rules can either be more or less stringent than in the production domain to enclose testing, development, and training. In fact, not all tests or development will require schema modification. In most organizations, 95 percent of all tests and/or development will *not* require schema modifications. The creation of both testing (or rather, staging) and development subdomains becomes quite easy since the parent/child structure is already in place. The same applies to a training domain. This is the *functional domain* design model. This model does not include multiple trees, but rather, multiple child domains.

Domains can be required in other situations as well. For example, an organization whose operations span several countries will often require multiple subdomains because of the legal restrictions in some of these countries. If there are legal requirements that differ from country to country and that may even require special security settings, you will need to create additional domain boundaries.

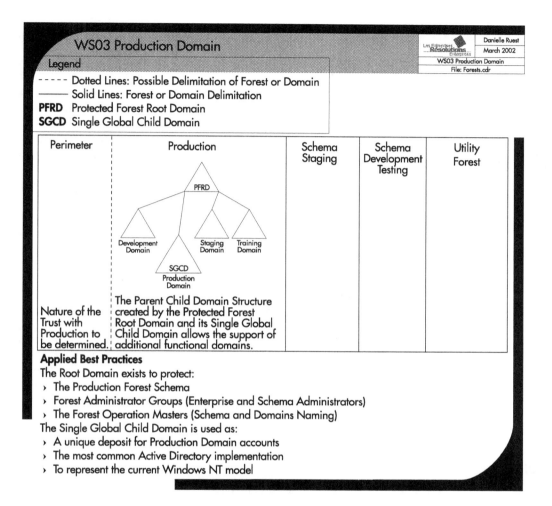

The final reason for domain segregation is WAN bandwidth. If your *available* bandwidth is inappropriate to support intra-domain replication, you will need to create regional domains. Specific information on bandwidth requirements is detailed later in this chapter, in the section "Site Topology Design."

Keep in mind that every domain you create will require an administration team. In addition, each new domain requires at least two domain Controllers for redundancy and reliability. The hardware costs may become prohibitive if too many domains are created. In addition, each new domain means new trust relationships. While they are transitive and automatic, they still need to be monitored. Finally, the more domains you create, the more it is likely that you will need to move resources and objects between domains.

Other Forest Domain Designs

Now that you have determined the domain structure to implement in your production forest, you can use it to derive the structure for the other forests you created. The staging forest is simple. It should represent the same structure as the production forest. As such, it requires a parent and a child domain. Since it is designed to represent only the production environment, it does not require additional domains for training, development, or other purposes.

The development and utilitarian forests require a single combined root and production domain since schema development testing is not dependent on the parent/child naming structure found in the production forest. Finally, the perimeter (extranet) forest is made of a single domain because this structure reduces the complexity of its management. Since it is exposed to the outside world (through a firewall, of course), its structure is also kept as simple as possible.

There you go! Your forest design is complete. It should resemble the illustration in Figure 3-7.

> ### QUICK TIP
>
> *Development forests are created when organizations want to integrate their applications with the Active Directory they will use to manage their network. Because they must change the schema to integrate applications, developers working on these projects must be located in a separate forest. There are costs, of course, associated with this approach. You may decide that your AD production forest will be used only for network management (remember Figure 3-1—a network operating system directory can be complex). If so, you can use AD/AM to perform application integration with Active Directory. Using AD/AM eliminates the need for a development forest because it is a service that can reside either on a member server or even a Windows XP workstation. This can greatly reduce your AD development costs. More on this strategy is discussed later when you prepare your Schema Modification Strategy.*

Forest Design Best Practices

The forest design process includes the following best practices:

- Identify the number of forests and write a justification for each one.
- Identify the number of trees and write a justification for each one.
- Wherever possible, create a Protected Forest Root Domain.
- Wherever possible, create a Single Global Child Domain for production in each tree.
- Identify the number of additional domains required in each tree.
- Identify the scope and contents of each domain.
- Justify each domain.
- Choose the generic name for each domain.
- Once the domain structure for the production forest is complete, design the domain structure for the other forests you created.

Designing the Naming Strategy

The next step is defining the Active Directory namespace. The namespace defines the scope of the Active Directory. It is based on the hierarchical nature of the Domain Naming System. Not only does it define the naming boundaries of the Active Directory database, but it also defines the structure of the database and the relationships between its objects. The actual object naming convention for Active Directory is not DNS. It is based on an X.500 naming scheme that identifies containers when naming objects. This allows for the creation of duplicate objects so long as they are located in different containers. For example, dc=com/dc=root/ou=IT/cn=User/cn=Mike Smith means that Mike Smith's user account is contained within the IT organizational unit in the root.com domain.

As you can see, the X.500 naming scheme is not practical for everyday use. But most everyone is familiar today with the Domain Naming System, so it is the naming scheme presented to users and administrators. Since it is hierarchical, DNS can be used to subdivide the forest into trees. This is done through the modification of the DNS root name. For example, MSN.com is a root name change from Microsoft.com, thus it is a second tree that is created in the Microsoft.com forest.

Since the domain name of your forest is a DNS name, you should use only registered DNS names. When you register a name, you ensure that you have complete ownership over it. For instance, if you use Microsoft.com as your external name, you might use Microsoft.net as your internal network name. By buying the rights to the Microsoft.net name, you ensure that no outside event will ever affect your internal network. You are also segregating your internal namespace from your external namespace. This allows you to identify the source of all traffic more easily and track intruders more effectively. Domain names can be registered with Internic. A complete list of domain name registrars by location can be found at http://www.internic.net/origin.html.

If, for some reason, you choose to use a name you do not own, be sure you verify that it does not exist on the Internet before creating your first domain controller. Organizations that do not perform this step often find themselves using an internal name that is used externally by a different organization. This will cause problems that range from having to rename your forest to being unable to reach the external domain from inside the network. Even though renaming an entire forest is possible with Windows Server 2003, it doesn't mean that you'll find it pleasant to have to change your internal name because someone outside your organization forces you to do so. Use a real DNS name with standard DNS naming conventions; with the .gov, .com, .org, .net, .edu, .biz, .info, .name, .cc, .tv, .ws, or .museum name extension and register it. That way, you'll control your namespace.

Never use the same forest name twice even if the networks are not interconnected. If you know that your sister organization has named their development testing forest DEVTEST, name yours something else. You'll also have to worry about NetBIOS names. NetBIOS names are composed of 15 characters with a reserved 16th character. They must be unique within a domain. The first part of the DNS names you choose should be the same as the NetBIOS name. Since DNS names can contain 255 characters per fully qualified domain name (FQDN), you will have to limit the size of the DNS names you use (in fact, you have 254 characters to choose from; DNS places a final dot in the name, the 255th character). Use short, distinct, and meaningful names, and distinguish between domain and machine names.

You should also identify your object naming scheme at this stage. All objects such as servers and PCs will have a distinct DNS name (or host name). This name, like the universal principal name for users, will have a DNS structure and use the domain and forest root names to complete its own. You can use the naming scheme illustrated in Figure 3-5. In this scheme, every object uses TandT.net, a registered DNS name, as a forest root. Next, it uses either a geographic naming scheme for child domains (single letter code for region and three-digit number code for each region), or a functional scheme (function name such as Intranet.TandT.net). Finally, servers and PCs can use up to five letters for the function code along with three digits to identify the number of machines offering this function. An example would be ADDC001.Intranet.TandT.net for an Active Directory DC in the Intranet child domain of the TandT.net forest.

Forest, tree, and domain names should be considered static. You should try to find a name you will not need to change, even if you know you can later. The domain and domain controller renaming process in Windows Server 2003 is complex and can cause service outages. Geographic names are often the best. In most cases, it takes a lot of momentum to change a geographic name, so they are considered quite stable. Don't use organizational structure to name domains unless you are confident that it is and will remain stable.

Table 3-3 lists the type of objects that you could place within domains and the holding domain for each object. Each object will require naming.

Naming Best Practices

Use the following best practices to name your AD forests:

- Use standard Internet characters. If they work on the Internet, they will definitely work in your network. Avoid accents and solely numeric names.

- Use 15 characters or less for each name.

- For the root name, use a simple, short name that is representative of the identity of the organization.

- Follow all DNS standards and make sure the internal DNS name is different from your external name.

- Finally, before proceeding, buy the name.

DNS is a cornerstone of Active Directory. Since it is designed to manage the AD namespace, Microsoft has vastly enhanced the Windows DNS service. It can now be completely integrated with Active Directory. In fact, it should be because proper AD operation depends on DNS since DNS is

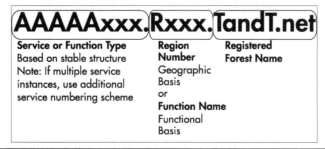

Figure 3-5   An object naming scheme

Objects	Production	Development	Training
Internal regular PCs	✓	✓	
Internal portables	✓	✓	
External PCs for development		✓	
Managed external PCs	✓	✓	
Unmanaged external PCs	✓	✓	
Multimedia PCs	✓	✓	
Member Servers (Services: HIS, SMS, SQL, and so on)	✓	✓	
Domain Controllers	✓	✓	✓
Quotas (shared folders)	✓	✓	
Printers and printer queues	✓	✓	✓
Meeting rooms	✓		
Projectors, shared PCs	✓		
Service accounts	✓	✓	✓
Users	✓	✓	
Administrators	✓	✓	✓
Technicians/installers	✓	✓	
Groups	✓	✓	✓
Generic accounts		✓	✓
Organizational Units	✓	✓	✓
Group Policy objects	✓	✓	✓
Domain administrators	✓	✓	✓
Applications	✓	✓	✓

Table 3-3   Domain Objects

used to locate domain controllers at logon. For this reason, you should avoid using third-party DNS servers with Windows, especially if they are non-Windows based. WS03 brings several enhancements to the DNS service so long as it is integrated with AD. With WS03, the DNS service has moved from being simply a network infrastructure service to become an Active Directory and Windows base service. More on this topic will be covered in Chapter 4.

The forest design can now be named. The production forest belongs to the T&T Corporation. Their Internet name is TandT.com. They have researched and bought TandT.net. It will be the name for their forest root. Subdomains are named after their function. The production domain is named with something more meaningful to users, such as Intranet.TandT.net. Development, training, and staging domains are named as such. The external forest found in the perimeter is named TandT.com. The staging forest is named TandTLab. This forest does not require a registered DNS name since it is not a production environment. The impact of recreating or renaming a staging forest is always much smaller than for the production forest. Volatile or utility forests can be named when needed. The development forest will not be retained because T&T Corporation has decided to use AD/AM for application integration and will reserve its production Active Directory for NOS operations only. This model is illustrated in Figure 3-7.

Designing the Production Domain OU Structure

What's truly amazing with Active Directory is how a simple database can be used to manage objects and events in the real world. That's right, the objective of Active Directory is to manage the elements you store inside its database. But to manage objects, you must first structure them. Forests, trees, and domains begin to provide structure by providing a rough positioning for objects throughout the Active Directory database. This rough positioning needs to be vastly refined, especially when you know that a single domain can contain more than a million objects.

The tool you use to refine the structure of objects is the organizational unit (OU). An OU is a container that, like the domain, is designed as an object repository. OUs must be contained within a domain, however. But since they can act as object repositories, they can and should be used to identify your network administration structure. Remember also that OUs can store other OUs, so you can create an administrative structure that reflects reality.

A second advantage of an OU is the ability to delegate its management to someone else. This means that when you design the structure of the Organizational Units within the domains of your Active Directory, you design the way the objects in your network will be managed. In addition, you identify who will manage which components of your network.

For example, you might decide that users in a given business unit are the responsibility of the business unit, delegating the management and administration of this group of users to a local business unit administrator. In this way, the OU in Active Directory is comparable to the domain in Windows NT. Whereas in Windows NT you needed to give "Domain Administrator" rights to anyone responsible for groups of users, in Active Directory you delegate ownership of an organizational unit, thus limiting access rights to the contents of the OU and nothing else.

In short, the OU is designed to help support the data/service concept of Active Directory. Since OUs contain AD objects and their properties, they contain data. By controlling access to OUs through security settings, in much the same way you would for a folder on an NTFS volume, you can give someone ownership of the data contained in the OU. This frees domain administrators to manage AD services. Making sure that all AD services are healthy and operating properly is the new role of the domain administrator. In a well-rounded Active Directory, you have a series of new interaction roles such as the OU administrator, the domain operator, the service administrator—roles that have significantly less authority in a domain than their Windows NT counterparts. You can now limit the Domain Administrator group to a small, select group of people.

The OU Design Process

In this design process, administrators must create a custom OU structure that reflects the needs of their organization and proceed to the delegation of its contents where appropriate. The best place to start the design process is with the Single Global Child Domain. Since this is the production domain, it will be the domain with the most complex OU structure. Once this domain's structure is complete, it will be simple to design the structure for other domains both within and outside the production forest since they are all derived from the production forest's requirements.

There are four reasons to create an Organizational Unit:

- It is required to regroup AD object types.

- It is required to administer AD objects.

- It is required to delegate the administration of AD objects.

- It may be required to hide objects.

Because OUs can include objects, you should first use them to regroup the different types of objects your network contains. There are three basic object types: People, PCs, and Services. These should create your first level of custom OUs.

Second, objects are regrouped for administrative purposes. You manage objects in AD through the application of Group Policy objects (GPOs). More on this is covered in Chapters 5, 6, and 7, but what is important to understand here is that the way you design your Organizational Unit structure will directly affect the way you apply Group Policy objects.

WS03 applies two policies by default to each domain: the Default Domain Policy and the Default Domain Controller Policy. You should review the contents of these policies to ensure that they conform to your security requirements. More on security is discussed in Chapter 8. WS03 also creates a number of default containers such as Users, Computers, and Domain Controllers. The only one of the three that is an OU is Domain Controllers. The other two are *not* OUs and cannot contain either GPOs or other OUs. If you want to control users and computers, you need to create a custom OU structure to regroup these types of objects.

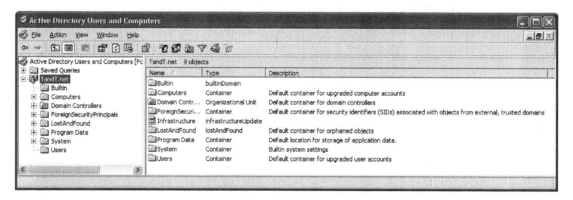

The third reason for OU creation is delegation. Delegation should be considered hand in hand with administration to create the sublayer structure of OUs. For each type of OU, you must identify potential object subtypes and determine if they are significantly different. Each significantly different object, either at the administrative or delegation level, will require a separate OU. WS03 will support a hierarchy of more than ten levels of OUs, but you should try for as flat an OU structure as you can. Objects buried in multiple layers of Organizational Units will be very demanding to index and locate when you need to find them in the directory. Aim for a five-layer OU structure as much as possible.

Keep in mind that if you control only the top layers of the structure and you need to delegate its finalization, you should leave at least two untapped layers for local departments to use.

The final reason is to hide objects. Since OUs contain access control lists, it is possible to hide sensitive objects in the directory. These objects are placed in special OUs that have very tightly controlled access control lists. Thus the objects become "invisible" to non-administrative users of the directory.

The administration design process begins when you create the three different object type OUs—People, PCs, and Services—and regroup objects under them. To do so, you need to identify every manageable object in your network and use a questioning process for each. As an example, Table 3-4 lists a series of objects that require management within the directory. In addition, it defines a classification and expected contents for each object. Two questions need to be answered for each object: Will I ever delegate this object? Do I need to manage this object through Group Policy objects? Each "Yes" answer means that a custom OU needs to be created.

Objects	Classification	Contents	Delegation?	GPO?
Workstations	Resource OU	Users with elevated rights Generic users Multimedia PCs		✓
Portables	Resource OU	Users with elevated rights Generic users		✓
External PCs	Resource OU	PCs for development projects (managed)		✓
External PCs	Resource OU	Consultant PCs (managed)		✓
External PCs and Portables	Resource OU	Consultant PCs (unmanaged)		
Member Servers	Resource OU	Services: HIS, SMS, SQL, Exchange	✓	✓
Domain Controllers	Service OU	Services: Authentication, identity management, security		✓
Quotas (shared folders)	Resource OU	Information sharing		✓
Printers	Service OU	Delegate printer queues	✓	✓
Meeting rooms	Resource OU	Reservation system	✓	
Projectors, shared PCs	Resource OU	Reservation system	✓	
Service accounts	Service OU	System process tracking		✓
Users	Data OU	(Similar to organizational structure)	✓	✓
Administrators	Data OU	Master OU in a delegated OU		✓
Domain administrators	Service OU	Located in default OU		✓
Technicians/ installers	Service OU	Global objects, but with limited delegation rights	✓	✓
Groups	Service OU	Universal, Global, Domain Local	✓	✓

Table 3-4   Manageable Objects in AD

Objects	Classification	Contents	Delegation?	GPO?
Generic accounts	Data OU	Domains other than production	✓	✓
Applications	Service OU	COM+ objects, MSMQ	✓	✓

Table 3-4   Manageable Objects in AD *(continued)*

Though the OU design process begins with object categorization, it is not complete until you have also designed the following plans:

- Group Policy Object Management Strategy (Chapter 5)
- PC Management Strategy (Chapter 5)
- Account and Group Definition (Chapter 6)
- Service Management Strategy (Chapter 7)
- Security Design (Chapter 8)
- Delegation Plan (Chapters 5, 6, 7, and 8)
- Service Resilience Plan (Chapter 9)
- Administration Plan (Chapter 10)

Though you begin the OU design here, its design will not be complete until you consider each of the elements in the remaining chapters of this book. Each of these items has some impact on your OU design.

The PCs Object OU Structure Design

You'll begin by categorizing PCs. Table 3-4 identified six possible types of PCs in the organization. The organization has its own PCs and includes PCs from external sources as well. They are first divided into two categories: internally owned and external PCs. The former are all managed PCs, but have a few differences. Mobile computers have different policies than desktops. Among the desktops are basic PCs as well as multimedia and shared workstations. Among external PCs are managed and unmanaged systems. External PCs that are onsite for the development of code must be tightly controlled and must be the image of the internal PC build in order to ensure code quality. Other consulting PCs may be for productivity purposes only. PCs that are used only to produce documentation should not be the organization's responsibility. Therefore they need to be segregated within the OU structure. Of course, this structure assumes that PCs are managed centrally. If not, the PCs OU structure may resemble the People OU structure outlined later.

The Services Object OU Structure Design

Next, organize the services in your network. This means creating OUs to delegate application servers such as those from the Microsoft .NET Enterprise family: SQL Server, Exchange, Systems Management Server, and Host Integration Server. By placing the server objects within these OUs, you can delegate their management and administration without having to give global administrative rights. Each of these servers should be a member server. Windows Server 2003 no longer requires services to be installed on domain controllers. Even Microsoft Message Queuing services, which required domain controllers in Windows 2000, now operate on Member Servers. You should always beware in WS03 when someone wants to install an application on a domain controller. Each of these services should be created under the Services root OU. In this way, if you need to apply a policy to all member server objects, such as a security policy, you only need to apply it to the root OU.

In addition to application servers, this OU should include services such as File and Print Servers. In fact, every server type identified in Chapter 1 and reviewed in Chapter 2 (except for Identity Management Servers) should be placed within an OU in this structure. This OU should also include all of the service accounts—special administrative accounts that are used to run services in a Windows Server 2003 network. These accounts are all data objects of the same type, so they can be managed through a single container. Finally, operational groups such as support technicians or system installers can be located in an Installer/Technician OU, making it easier to give them rights to other objects in the domain. The additional advantage of the Services OU is that it is much easier to locate objects of the service category.

The People Object OU Structure Design

The last OU structure to populate is the People OU. These OUs will contain either user accounts and/ or groups. This is also the OU structure that will most resemble the organizational chart. In fact, the organizational chart is a good information source for the regrouping of the people in your enterprise in the directory. Few people know the organization's structure as well as the Human Resources group. This is a good place to enlist their assistance.

Like the organizational chart, the People OU structure defines a hierarchy of distinctiveness. The difference is that the two are inversed. The organizational chart defines a hierarchy of authority (who controls whom), whereas the People OU structure goes from the most common to the most distinctive. In the organizational chart, the employee mass is at the bottom. In the People OU structure, it is at the top.

When you want to manage all of the People object types, you can do so by applying a Group Policy to the root OU. The second level of this OU structure should reflect the business unit structure of the organization. Though the organizational chart is a source of information, it should not be used in its exact form because organization charts tend to change too often. You need to create as stable an OU structure as possible to minimize change in the directory. Because of this, many organizations only use lines of business (LOB) at the second level of OUs for the People object.

This OU level may also include special team groupings—business units whose purpose is to support all other business units across the enterprise on an administrative basis. It will also contain regional groupings if your organization spans a large geographic territory. In this case, regional groupings are essential since you must delegate ownership of regional objects to regional administrative representatives.

In most cases, you will generate three general levels of OU within this OU structure:

- **Root level**   Used to manage all People objects (user accounts and groups). This level contains only other OUs and administrative groups for the structure.

- **Line of business level**   Used to manage all user accounts that are within defined segments or lines of business within the corporation and located at headquarters or central offices, as well as all groups for the entire line of business. The groups to whom this level is delegated are all located in the root OU.

- **Regional level**   Used to manage regional offices. This includes user accounts for every line of business located in the regional office as well as regional groups. The parent OU for the regional OUs contains every regional administrative group.

The third OU level may also represent groups or administrative services within the line of business level. For example, IT and IS will be found within the organization's administrative line of business, but you can be sure that they will not have the same policies and rights, so they are segregated at the third OU level. IT especially will most probably be segregated into further sublevels as well, but this will most likely be done through a process internal to the IT department. The final structure for IT will be delegated to the IT group.

The complete OU structure is illustrated in Figure 3-6. Here the OU shape identifies the purpose and contents of each OU.

Replicating the OU Structure to Other Domains

Now that you have a solid and complete OU structure, you can replicate it to other domains. Table 3-5 identifies the OU structure in other domains.

The completed Forest, Tree, Domain, and OU structure is illustrated in Figure 3-7.

Production OU Design Best Practices

Keep the following rules in mind when you create OU structures:

- Think in terms of equipment and objects in the directory.
- Determine how you will implement the administrative delegation process.
- Identify standards for all administrative categories in the organization.
- Use the administrative service or function or the line of business to name OUs. These tend to be more stable than organizational structure.
- Limit your structure to five levels, three if you are not responsible for the finalization of the structure. Recommend a maximum of five levels even though ten are possible. This gives you some breathing room.
- Remember the four reasons for the creation of OUs: categorization, administration, delegation, and segregation.
- Each OU you create must add value to the system.
- Never create an OU that does not contain any objects.
- Never create an OU that does not have a specific purpose.
- If an OU reaches an empty state, consider removing it. This may not be necessary because it may only be temporarily empty. If not, remove it.
- Identify an OU owner for each one you create. If no owner can be identified, remove the OU.

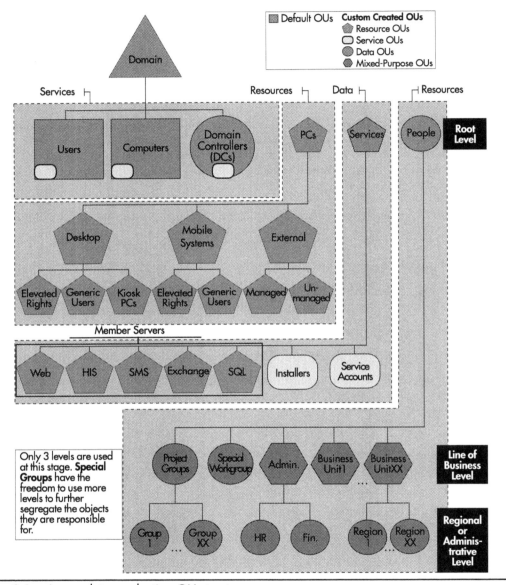

Figure 3-6 A complete production OU structure

- Justify all OUs you create.
- If you find that two OUs have the same purpose, merge them. This means that the combination of owner plus GPO plus delegation strategy is the same for both OUs.

Forest	Domain	PCs OU	Services OU	People OU
Production	Training	One level only, all objects in root	Same basic structure as production	Same as first two levels as in production
	Staging	One level only, all objects in root	Same basic structure as production	One level only, all objects in root
	Development	Same as first two levels as in production	Same basic structure as production	Same as first two levels as in production
	Protected Forest Root	Default OUs only	Default OUs only	Default OUs only
Perimeter	Perimeter	Default OUs only	Default OUs only	Default OUs only
Staging	Protected Forest Root	Default OUs only	Default OUs only	Default OUs only
	Production	Same as production	Same as production	Same as production
Development testing (if required)	Forest root	Default OUs only	Default OUs only	Default OUs only or may require same as production OU for testing
Utility forests	Forest root	Defined as required	Defined as required	Defined as required

Table 3-5   OU Structure in Other Domains

- Use default OUs to administer the whole domain. Domain controllers should be kept in the DC OU. Domain Administrator accounts and groups should be kept in the Users OU. Domain Administrator PCs should be kept in the Computers OU.

- Use the production domain OU strategy to define the OU strategy for other domains and forests.

- Don't forget to define and put in place standards for the recurring creation and deletion of OUs. These will help control the proliferation of OUs in your directory.

Your OU strategy should be based on the information in Table 3-4. While its categorization may differ with the final results of your own Object Categorization Exercise, those differences will be minor. They will vary due to factors such as political situation, business strategy, and IT management approach, rather than because of fundamental differences. Keep in mind that your OU design will not be the answer to every management process in the directory. It is only a first level of object management.

The OU design process should result in the following deliverables:

- An OU hierarchy diagram
- A list of all OUs
- A description of the contents of each OU
- The purpose of each OU
- The identification of each OU owner

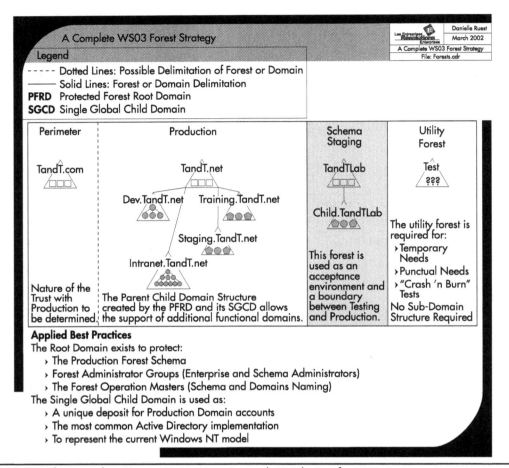

Figure 3-7 The complete Forest, Tree, Domain, and OU design for T&T Corporation

- A list of groups that have control over each OU
- A list of the object types each group can control in each OU
- The rules for the creation and deletion of OUs in regular operations

AD and Other Directories

As you have seen so far, Active Directory is much more than a simple authentication and authorization system. It is a central identity management system. As such, it will interact with other systems on your network, some of which may already hold identity data. Since AD is a central identity management system, new systems you develop can integrate with AD and should not require identity management components. Microsoft Exchange is an excellent example of this level of integration. In version 5.5, Exchange required its own complete identity management infrastructure. In current versions, it integrates completely with Active Directory and uses AD's functions to manage all identity components.

In this manner, Active Directory is comparable to Windows itself. When programmers prepare software for Windows, they do not need to be concerned with how the application will print or how it will interact with a display device; Windows manages all of these components. The developer only needs to make sure the new code will work with Windows and concentrate on the functions to be built in the application itself. AD provides the same integration features to applications. Application developers no longer need to worry about identity and security management, as AD provides all of these functions. They can now concentrate on richer product-specific features. In addition, they can use AD/AM to integration object extensions. For example, if you want to include a fingerprint hash in your authentication scheme but don't want to modify your NOS directory, you can add it to an AD/AM directory and link it to the NOS directory. This avoids custom schema extensions that must be replicated throughout the enterprise.

In addition, you may already have systems that may not integrate directly with Active Directory, such as human resource systems, custom corporate applications, or third-party software. For each of these systems, you will need to determine which data deposit, the original system or Active Directory, is the primary source for specific data records. For example, if AD can store the entire organizational structure through the information properties you can add to each user account (location, role, manager, and so on), shouldn't AD be the primary source for this information since it is also the primary source for authentication?

These are the types of decisions you need to make when determining how your Active Directory will interact with other directories. Will it be the primary information source? If so, you need to ensure that information is fed into and maintained in the directory. This information feed must be part of your initial AD deployment process. You will also need to consider the changes you must make to your corporate systems so they will obtain primary data from AD, otherwise you will need to maintain several authoritative sources for the same data. If this is the case, you should consider using Microsoft MetaDirectory Services 2003 (MMS).

Microsoft MetaDirectory Services

MMS is a special application that is designed to oversee multiple directory services. MMS manages the operations of several directories to ensure data integrity. If you install MMS over AD and you identify AD as the primary source of information, MMS will automatically modify the values in other directory services when you modify values in AD.

The Standard Edition of MMS is available for free (http://www.microsoft.com/mms/) and is designed to support the integration of data between AD, AD/AM, and Exchange. The Enterprise Edition is designed to integrate heterogeneous data sources. Both run as services on Member Servers and both include simplified deployments. It is important to keep in mind that MMS implementations are additional and separate from AD implementations. But the advantages are clear. If you need to integrate several directories such as in-house databases, third-party software applications, and even other forests, or if you need to integrate AD and AD/AM, MMS is the best way to ensure that data is populated from one information source to all others or automatically synchronize data in multiple deposits. It will also help you manage the employee move, add, and change process since it provides

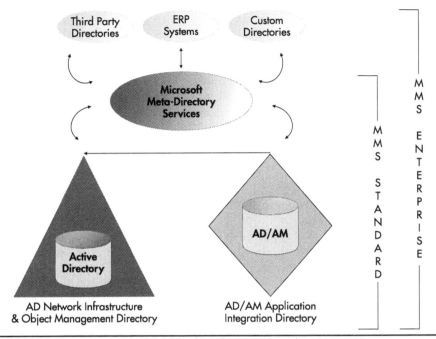

Figure 3-8   Integrating AD, AD/AM, and other directories with MMS 2003

a single, integrated view of all employee data. The integrated operation of MMS, AD, and AD/AM is illustrated in Figure 3-8.

> ### NOTE
>
> *For more information on the integration of WS03's directory services, search for "A New Roadmap to Directory Services" at http://www.thedotnetmag.com.*

Integrated Applications for NOS Directories

Microsoft has outlined a new application certification program with Windows 2000, the Windows Logo program. This program continues with Windows Server 2003. Logo-approved applications will integrate with Active Directory to use its identity management and authentication capabilities. Today, several applications fall in this category. For a complete and up-to-date list of Logo-certified applications for Windows Server 2003, go to http://www.veritest.com/certified/win2000server/.

Integrating a few applications with the directory is inevitable, especially management or directory extension applications. A good example is the .NET Enterprise Server family. Several of these integrate directly to Active Directory and through this integration bring modifications or extensions to AD database schema. These extensions are necessary because each application adds functionality which is not usually required in a base Active Directory. Among these applications, you will find:

- **Exchange Server**   Exchange in fact doubles the size of the AD schema, adding twice the object classes and twice the properties.

- **Internet Security and Acceleration Server**   ISA modifies the schema to add special ISA objects. This integration streamlines the security, authentication, and management processes for ISA.

- **Host Integration Server**   If you require integrated access between a legacy environment and Windows Server 2003, you will require HIS. HIS also extends the AD schema to streamline HIS management and authentication.

- **Systems Management Server**   Version 2003 of Microsoft's enterprise management tool, SMS integrates with AD to extend its network and infrastructure management capabilities.

The reason why it is important to identify how your Active Directory will integrate with other applications or information sources is because of schema extensions. If this is your first implementation of an Active Directory, you should install all schema modifications when you install your forest root domain. In this way, you will limit the amount of replication on your production network. That's right, every time you make a schema modification, it will be replicated to every domain controller in the forest. If you have regional domain controllers that replicate over WAN lines, massive modifications may incur service outages. Extending the schema in the forest root domain, before installing child domains, will contain replication and limit it to the installation process for each server.

In fact, WS03 supports the population of a domain controller from backup media at installation. This means that while you had to build all domain controllers while they were connected to a high-speed network with Windows 2000, in WS03, you will be able to rebuild and repair DCs remotely so long as you have created an offline copy of the directory with the Windows (or another) Backup tool. Domain controllers should still be built in a staging area using a high-speed network during AD deployment if possible.

AD Integration Best Practices

Five activities need to be performed at the AD integration stage:

- Position the Active Directory as the core directory service in the organization.

- Position the role of AD in Application Mode, if required, in your organization.

- Position the relationship other corporate directories will have with AD.

- Identify the interaction model between directory services and position the role Microsoft MetaDirectory Services will play in your organization.

- Determine which operational applications will be integrated in your directory.

Use the following best practices during this process:

- Active Directory should be the core directory service. AD can be modified through a graphical interface. You can also use scripts to perform massive modifications with AD. AD also supports a powerful delegation model. Finally, it supports PC management, something few directory services can perform.

- Use AD as your single point of interaction. AD provides a single point of interaction because it is a distributed database that uses a multimaster replication process. Users can modify data in any regional office and it will automatically be updated through the directory.

- If you need to maintain data integrity between multiple directories, use Microsoft MetaDirectory Services with Active Directory as your primary data source.

- If you need to install NOS-related applications that modify the schema, add them to the forest root domain *before* creating the child domains.

- If you need to integrate in-house applications to the directory, use AD in Application Mode. This will have no impact on your NOS directory.

- Integrate NOS-related and other applications to AD only if it is absolutely required. Schema modifications can be retired and reused, but only through a complex process that will involve replication throughout your distributed NOS directory.

- Maintain your Active Directory as a NOS directory first and foremost. This will limit the amount of replication in the forest and will make it easier to upgrade to future versions of Windows server operating systems.

Service Positioning

Now that you have identified the number of Forests, Trees, and Domains in your Active Directory, designed your OU structure, and identified how the directory service will act in your organization, you can move on to Service Positioning. Service Positioning relates to the position and role domain controllers will have in each forest and each domain. Domain controllers are the core service provider for Active Directory. They provide multimaster replication throughout the entire forest. Some types of information cannot be maintained in a multimaster format. To store and manage this information, some domain controllers have a special role, the Operation Master. Another special role is the Global Catalog; this server supports the research and indexing of forest-wide information. Core Active Directory services fall into three categories: Operation Masters, Global Catalogs, and generic domain controllers. A fourth category must also be considered if the Active Directory is to stay healthy: the DNS server.

Operation Masters Positioning

Operation Masters are AD services that manage requests for specific information changes at either the forest or the domain level. Without these services, AD cannot operate. They fall into two groups: forest-wide and domain-centric Operation Master roles. Operation Master roles are sometimes called flexible single master of operations (FSMO) because even though only a single instance in the forest or the domain can exist, this instance is not rooted to a given server; it can be transferred from one domain controller to another. Thus, it is flexible, and it is single because it must be unique in its scope of influence.

Forest-wide Operation Master roles are:

- **Schema Master**   The master service that maintains the structure of the forest database and authorizes schema changes.

- **Domain Naming Master**   The master service that controls and authorizes domain naming in the forest.

Only a single instance of these services can exist in the forest at a given time. Both services can be located on the same domain controller if required. In large forests, these services are distributed on two separate domain controllers.

In addition to forest-wide Operation Master roles, there are domain-centric Operation Master roles. If you only have one domain in your forest, you will have a single instance of each of these roles, but if you have more than one domain, every domain will have one instance of each. These include:

- **Relative ID (RID) Master**   The master service that is responsible for the assignation of relative IDs to other domain controllers in the domain. Whenever a new object—user, computer, server, group—is created in a domain, the domain controller who is performing the creation will assign a unique ID number. This ID number consists of a domain identification number followed by a relative identification number that is assigned at object creation. When a domain controller runs out of its pool of relative IDs, it requests an additional pool from the RID Master. The relative ID role is also the placeholder for the domain. If you need to move objects between domains in the same forest, you need to initiate the move from the RID Master.

- **Primary Domain Controller (PDC) Emulator**   The master service that provides backward compatibility for Windows NT. If there are Windows NT domain controllers or Windows NT network clients in the domain, this server acts as the Primary Domain Controller for the domain. It manages all replication to Backup Domain Controllers (in NT, of course).

  If there are no non-Windows 2000 or XP clients or Windows NT DCs, the forest can operate in native mode. In this case, the PDC Emulator focuses on its two other roles: Time Synchronization on all DCs and Preferential Account Modification Replication to other DCs. All domain controllers in the domain will set their clock according to the PDC Emulator. In addition, any account modification that is critical, such as password modification or account deactivation, will be immediately replicated to the PDC Emulator from the originating server. If a logon attempt fails on a given DC, it checks with the PDC Emulator before rejecting the attempt because it may not have received recent password changes. The PDC Emulator supports two authentication protocols: Kerberos V5 (Windows 2000 and more) and NTLM (Windows NT).

- **Infrastructure Master**   The master service that manages two critical tasks:

  - The update of references from objects in its domain to objects in other domains. This is how the forest knows to which domain an object belongs. The Infrastructure Master has a close relationship to the Global Catalog. If it finds that some of its objects are out of date compared to the GC, it will request an update from the GC and send the updated information to other DCs in the domain.

> ## CAUTION

The Global Catalog service and the Infrastructure Master service should not be stored on the same DC unless there is only one server in the forest or the domain is very small (for example, the forest root domain). Problems can arise if they are on the same computer because the Infrastructure Master will share the same database as the Global Catalog. It will not be able to tell if it is out of date or not. It will never request updates. In a large forest, this can cause other DCs to be out of synch with GC contents.

- The update and modification of group members in the domain. If a group includes objects from another domain and these objects are renamed or moved, the Infrastructure Master will maintain the consistency of the group and replicate it to all other domain controllers. This ensures that users maintain access rights even though you perform maintenance operations on their accounts.

These domain-centric master roles should be separated if possible. This depends on the size of each domain. Whatever its size, each domain should have at least two domain controllers for redundancy, load balancing, and availability.

Global Catalog Server Positioning

The Global Catalog server is also a special domain controller role. Any domain controller can operate as a Global Catalog server. The GC is the server that holds a copy of the forest-wide database in each domain. By default, it includes about 20 percent of forest data; everything that has been marked in the forest database schema as having forest-wide interest is published in the GC. A forest with a single DC will automatically include the Global Catalog server role.

The GC has three functions:

- **Find objects**   The GC holds information about the users and other objects in your domain. User queries about objects are automatically sent to TCP port number 3268 and routed to the GC server.
- **Allow UPN logons**   Users can log onto other domains across the forest by using their user principal name (UPN). If the domain controller validating the user does not know the user, it will refer to the Global Catalog server. Because the GC holds information about every user in the forest, it will complete the logon process if it is allowed by the user's rights. UPN logons are also supported across forests when a forest trust exists.
- **Support Universal groups**   All Universal groups are stored in the Global Catalog so they can be available forest-wide.

Native WS03 forests have enhanced GC functionality. For example, they can replicate only Universal group modifications instead of the entire Universal group when changes are made. In addition, native WS03 DCs can cache user's universal membership data, removing the need to constantly consult the GC, so the GC service does not need to be as widespread as in Windows 2000 networks.

The GC service should be widely available, however. If your network spans several regions, you should place at least one GC server per region. In addition, you should enable Universal Group Membership (UGM) Caching for all DCs in the region. Placing the GC server in the region will ensure that Universal group logon requests are not sent over the WAN. The WAN is required for the first logon attempt if no GC is present in the region even if UGM Caching is enabled because the logon DC must locate a GC server from which to cache data. Local GC servers are also useful for applications using port 3268 for authentication requests. Consider potential cross-domain logons when determining where to place GC servers.

Domain Controller Positioning

Positioning both Operation Master roles and Global Catalog servers is positioning domain controllers because each of these services will only operate on a domain controller. As mentioned before, in a single domain forest, all of the FSMO roles and the GC could run on a single DC. But in a medium to large network, these roles are usually distributed among several domain controllers. In addition to performing these roles, Domain controllers support authentication and multimaster replication. This means that the more users you have, the more DCs you will need if you want to keep your login time short. Large multiprocessing servers running the DC service can handle millions of requests a day. Regional servers tend to have several additional functions. Regional servers are often multipurpose servers and they tend to be smaller in capacity than centralized servers. If they are multipurpose servers as well, consider adding additional DCs whenever the user load exceeds 50 users per server.

If some of your regional sites have fewer than ten users, don't place a domain controller in the site. Instead use Terminal Services to create terminal sessions for the users in the closest site containing a DC. All logons will be performed at the remote site. But if you can afford it, place a DC in each site that has more than ten users.

The best way to determine how many DCs to position across your network is to evaluate network performance. In many cases, it is a matter of judgment. Define a rule of thumb based on your network performance and stick to it. You can also predict the number of DCs during the site topology exercise.

DNS Server Positioning

Network performance is exactly the reason why the DNS service is the fourth Active Directory service that needs positioning for optimal directory operations. Since part of the AD structure is based on the Domain Naming System and since all logons must resolve the name and location of a domain controller before being validated, the DNS service has become a core Active Directory service. When positioning services for AD, you will quickly learn that you should marry the DNS service with the domain controller service.

In Windows Server 2003, as in Windows 2000, every domain controller in every domain in every forest should also be a Domain Name Server because AD uses DNS to locate objects in the network and because DNS data can be integrated to the directory. If DNS is configured to integrate with AD, it can also become completely secured. You can ensure that only trusted network objects and sources will update information in the DNS partition of Active Directory. Finally, directory integration means secure replication. Since DNS data is integrated to the directory, it is replicated with other directory information.

DNS data can also be stored in application partitions, directory partitions that can designate which domain controllers are to store the information. For example, in a multidomain forest, WS03 automatically creates a DNS data application partition that spans the entire forest. This means that since the data is replicated to every domain controller in the forest, global forest name resolution will always work everywhere.

Windows 2000 and Windows Server 2003 bring many new concepts to the Domain Naming System. This is why it changes from a simple IP service to become an integrated AD service.

Service Positioning Best Practices

Use the following rules to design your Service Positioning scenario:

- In large AD structures, place the forest-wide Operation Masters in a Protect Forest Root Domain.
- If your forest spans multiple sites, place the Schema Master in one site and the Domain Naming Master in another.
- Carefully protect the access to the Schema Master role.
- Place the RID Master and the PDC Emulator roles on the same DC.
- Create a dedicated PDC Emulator role in domains that have more than 50,000 users.
- Separate Global Catalogs and Infrastructure Masters if you can.
- Place at least two domain controllers per domain.
- If a small domain spans two sites, use at least two domain controllers, one for each site.
- Place a Global Catalog server in each geographic site that contains at least one domain controller.
- Enable Universal group membership caching in each geographic site.
- Place a domain controller wherever there are more than ten users unless the WAN link speed will adequately support remote logon attempts.
- Add a regional domain controller whenever there are more than 50 users per DC, especially if it is a multipurpose server.
- Install the Domain Naming Service on every domain controller.
- Use application partitions to designate DNS replication scopes.

Server Positioning Scenario

The best way to learn how to perform server positioning is to use scenarios. In this scenario, the T&T Corporation endeavors to create and populate its Active Directory. It has more than 10,000 users. It has decided to use a multidomain production forest as displayed in Figure 3-7. Its headquarters are in a single city, but in separate buildings. Both buildings are linked together through a metropolitan area network operating at high speed. In addition, it has fifteen regional offices, some in other metropolitan areas that are of considerable size. In these metropolitan areas, satellite offices use local links to "hop" into the wide area network.

T&T needs to position its domain controllers, Global Catalogs, DNS, and Operation Master roles. Table 3-6 describes the position of each domain in each region. The regional distribution of the organization's offices is illustrated in Figure 3-9.

	Region	Domain	Number of Users
1	HQ Main	Dedicated Root	7
2	HQ Main	Production	3000
3	HQ Main	Development	200
4	HQ Main	Training	300
5	HQ Main	Staging	20
6	HQ Site 2	Production	2200
7	HQ Site 2	Development	250
8	HQ Site 2	Training	200
9	Region 1	Production	250
10	Region 2	Production	300
11	Region 3	Production	100
12	Region 4	Production	125
13	Region 5	Production	2100
14	Region 6	Production	75
15	Region 7	Production	80
16	Region 8	Production	140
17	Region 9	Production	80
18	Region 10	Production	150
19	Region 11	Production	575
20	Region 12	Production	250
21	Region 13	Production	90
22	Region 14	Production	110
23	Region 15	Production	40
24	Satellite 1 (Region 2)	Production	10
25	Satellite 2 (Region 5)	Production	5
26	Satellite 3 (Region 5)	Production	8
27	Satellite 4 (Region 11)	Production	50
28	Satellite 5 (Region 12)	Production	35
Total			**10750**

Table 3-6   Production Forest Server Positioning Scenario Information

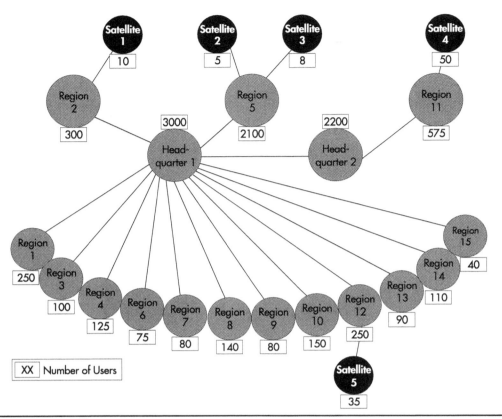

Figure 3-9 T&T Office Locations Map

▶ **NOTE**

In Table 3-6, development users include the developers themselves as well as test accounts, while users in the training domain only represent generic accounts.

As you can see, the first step for T&T in this phase is to identify the geographical layout of its offices. Once this is identified, T&T can proceed to server positioning. Using the rules outlined earlier, T&T will begin the positioning process. It needs to proceed systematically, thus it will place servers in the following order:

1. The first servers to position are the forest-wide Operation Master roles. These will be in the Protected Forest Root Domain (PFRD): Schema Master and Domain Naming Master.

2. Next will be the PFRD's domain-centric Operation Master roles: RID Master, PDC Emulator, and Infrastructure Master. These should be positioned according to the best practices outlined earlier.

3. The size (number of users) and location of the PFRD will help determine the number of domain controllers required to operate the PFRD.

4. If PFRD DCs are separated physically, the Global Catalog service should be added in each location that includes at least one DC.

5. Next are the child domain DCs. Begin with the production domain because it is the most complex. The first services to position are the domain-centric Operation Master roles: RID Master, PDC Emulator, and Infrastructure Master.

6. Now that the core roles are positioned, position domain controllers. A DC should be positioned in each region with at least 50 users. Regions with more than 50 users should have more than one DC. Regions with less than 50 users should be gauged on an as-needed basis. Also set a rule of thumb for DC positioning in large sites: one DC per 1,000 users (remember, central DCs tend to be more powerful servers than regional DCs).

> **NOTE**
>
> *The AD Sizer will tell you that you can manage more than 40,000 users per DC. This may be optimistic because DCs have other roles than simply to manage user logons. Test performance and determine if 1,000 users per DC is appropriate or not in your network.*

7. Each region that has at least one DC also hosts at least one Global Catalog service.

8. Next, position Operation Master roles, GCs, and DCs for the other three domains: development, training, and staging. Staging is easy since it is located in a single geographic site; two servers are more than adequate. Training can also perform with two DCs, one in each HQ office. The positioning of development DCs will depend on its level of activity. It is not unusual for development DCs to be used for stress testing analysis. In such situations, the development DC needs to host as many users as the entire production domain.

9. The easiest is kept for the end. Position the DNS service wherever there is a DC.

10. Use application partitions to determine how DNS information should be shared from domain to domain. The result is described in Table 3-7. Keep in mind that the DNS strategy is described in more detail in Chapter 4.

Region	Domain	Users	Servers	Role
HQ Main	Dedicated Root	7	1	1st DC in the forest
				Forest FSMO: Schema Master
				Domain FSMO: PDC and RID
				Global Catalog
				Integrated DDNS

Table 3-7   T&T Server Positioning Results

Region	Domain	Users	Servers	Role
HQ Site 2	Dedicated Root	7	1	2nd DC in the forest
				Forest FSMO: Domain Naming Master
				Domain FSMO: Infrastructure
				Global Catalog (placing the GC with the Infrastructure Master is okay because of the small number of objects in this domain)
				Integrated DDNS
HQ Main	Production	3000	3	1st Domain DC
				Domain FSMO: PDC
				Global Catalog
				Integrated DDNS
				2nd Domain DC
				Domain FSMO: RID
				Integrated DDNS
				Other DCs
				DC role only
				Integrated DDNS
HQ Site 2	Production	2200	3	FSMO Domain DC
				Domain FSMO: Infrastructure
				Integrated DDNS
				GC Domain DC
				Global Catalog
				Integrated DDNS
				Other DCs
				DC role only
				Integrated DDNS
Region 1	Production	250	2	GC Domain DC
Region 2		300	3	Global Catalog
Region 3		100	2	Integrated DDNS
Region 4		125	2	Other DCs
Region 5		2100	2	DC role only
Region 6		75	2	Integrated DDNS
Region 7		80	2	
Region 8		140	2	
Region 9		80	2	
Region 10		150	2	
Region 11		575	1	
Region 12		250	2	
Region 13		90	2	
Region 14		110	2	
Region 15		40	1	

Table 3-7 T&T Server Positioning Results *(continued)*

Region	Domain	Users	Servers	Role
Satellite 1 (Region 2)	Production	10	0	N/A
Satellite 2 (Region 5)		5		
Satellite 3 (Region 5)		8		
Satellite 4 (Region 11)	Production	50	1	GC Domain DC
				Global Catalog
Satellite 5 (Region 12)		35	1	Integrated DDNS
HQ Main	Development	200	1	1st Domain DC
				Domain FSMO: PDC and RID
				Global Catalog
				Integrated DDNS
HQ Site 2	Development	250	1	2nd Domain DC
				Domain FSMO: Infrastructure
				Global Catalog
				Integrated DDNS
HQ Main	Training	300	1	1st Domain DC
				Domain FSMO: PDC and RID
				Global Catalog
				Integrated DDNS
HQ Site 2	Training	200	1	2nd Domain DC
				Domain FSMO: Infrastructure
				Global Catalog
				Integrated DDNS
HQ Main	Staging	20	2	1st Domain DC
				Domain FSMO: PDC and RID
				Global Catalog
				Integrated DDNS
				2nd Domain DC
				Domain FSMO: Infrastructure
				Global Catalog
				Integrated DDNS
Total		**10750**	**54**	

Table 3-7   T&T Server Positioning Results *(continued)*

As you can see, the server positioning stage requires the application of a set of rules to the data you have collected on your organization to produce a working result. T&T Corporation, for example, will implement the servers and the roles identified in Table 3-7. They will have two server models, one for regions (multipurpose) and one for large offices (dedicated DC). But they will also need to monitor performance on these servers to ensure that service response times run as expected. If not, they will need to refine their model. If that is the case, they will need to update their own version of Table 3-7 to ensure that it always reflects reality. The Server Positioning Strategy for T&T Corporation is illustrated in Figure 3-10. For simplicity's sake, this figure only includes the root and production domains.

Another factor that will affect this evaluation is the network speed at which each office is linked with others. Analyzing network speeds and adjusting directory replication is what the next stage, Site Topology Design, is all about.

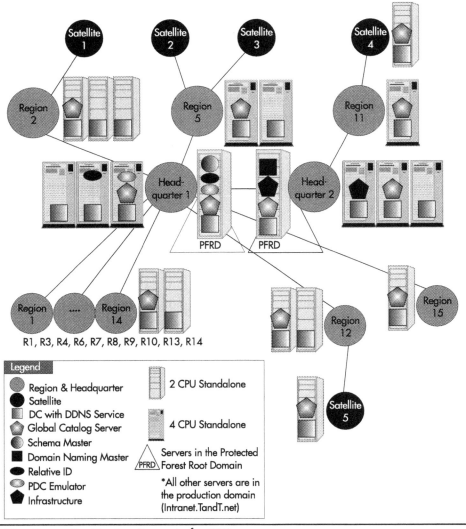

Figure 3-10   Server Positioning Scenario for T&T

Site Topology

The Active Directory design is almost complete; only two further stages are required: Site Topology Design and Schema Modification Strategy. Site Topology Design relates to the analysis of the speed of all WAN links that bind the forest together and the identification of the forest replication strategy. A site is a physical replication partition. Replication is key to proper AD operation.

Windows Server 2003 DCs replicate information on an ongoing basis because they are all authoritative for certain portions of forest information. This multimaster environment requires constant replication if the distributed forest DCs are to be kept up to date. WS03 can perform two types of replication: intra-site and inter-site. Intra-site replication is at high speed because it uses the local area network. Local servers are also often on very high speed links to ensure faster information transfer between them. Intra-site replication occurs constantly because the link speed can support it. Because it is constant and because the link speed can support it, no intra-site replication is compressed.

Inter-site replication is at lower speeds because it must cross a WAN link to other offices. Inter-site replication must be scheduled and compressed, otherwise it will use more than the available bandwidth. The process of creating Active Directory sites is based on the identification of the replication mode between servers. Is it intra- or inter-site replication? A site is also a physical regrouping of servers. A site is usually defined as a TCP/IP subnet. It can be a virtual local area network (VLAN)—a set of network nodes that are grouped together in a single subnet in a geographic location—or a regional subnet. Inter-site replication can occur at 15-minute intervals (it is set at 180 minutes by default). Two transport modes are supported: Internet Protocol (IP) and Simple Mail Transfer Protocol (SMTP). *Never* consider SMTP for inter-site replication! It is more complicated to set up than IP, and it is an asynchronous replication method because changes are sent in discrete messages. It is possible for changes to arrive out of order. Who hasn't sent an email message to someone only to have it come back a week later telling you the person never received it? You can't take the chance that this will happen with directory replication data.

IP uses the Remote Procedure Call (RPC) to send changes to other DCs. It uses the Knowledge Consistency Checker (KCC) service to determine automatic routes between replication partners. For this to occur between sites, a Site Link must be created between each site that contains a domain controller. This Site Link includes costing information. The KCC can use this information when determining when to replicate, how to replicate, and the number of servers to replicate with. Special values such as password changes or account deactivations are replicated immediately to the PDC Emulator in the domain despite site-specific schedules. Inter-site replication data is also compressed. AD compresses replication data through a compression algorithm. Data is automatically compressed whenever it reaches a certain threshold. Usually anything greater than 50 KB will automatically be compressed when replicated between sites.

In a native WS03 forest, you should enable linked value replication. This option greatly reduces replication by sending only the values that have changed for any multivalued attribute such as groups. Whenever a change is made to a group member such as a new member addition, only the changed value (the new member) is replicated instead of the entire attribute.

Site Topology Design

To perform Site Topology Design, you need the following elements:

- A map of all site locations.
- The WAN topology and link speeds for each location. Router configuration is also important. TCP/IP ports that are required for replication are often closed by default. These ports are identified in Chapter 4.
- The number of DCs in each site.

Site design is simple: it should follow the enterprise TCP/IP network design. Sites are IP subnets, thus they are the same as structures you already have in place for TCP/IP. When you proceed with the design, it will result in the creation of:

- Site boundaries for each geographic location
- Site replication links
- Backup replication links
- Costing scheme for each link

Sites are independent of the domain structure. This means that you could have multiple domains in a site, multiple sites in a domain, as well as multiple sites and multiple domains in a wide area network.

Forest replication is divided into three categories: forest-wide, application partition, and domain-centric replication. Both forest-wide and application partition replication span domains. Fortunately, the data replicated through these partitions is relatively small. This is not the same for domains. Production domains especially contain vast amounts of information. This is the core reason for Site Topology Design: data availability between separate domain sites.

Production domains should be split if they must replicate over link speeds of 56 kilobits per second or lower. Very large production domains require high speed WAN links if they are to span regional offices even though data is compressed and replication is scheduled. If vast amounts of data must be sent, the "pipeline" sending it must be big enough for the time allowed. In very large sites with low-speed links, it is possible to have a situation where replication never completes because the replication window opens at intervals that are shorter than the time it takes to replicate all changed data. This is a good opportunity to use the AD Sizer.

Site Link routes should resemble the basic IP structure of your WAN. The cost of each link should reflect the link speed; the lower the cost, the higher the speed. Lower costs also mean faster replication. Table 3-8 identifies sample link costs for given bandwidths.

Creating Site Link Bridges

In some cases, it is necessary to bridge replication. If you create Site Links that overlap, you should create a Site Link Bridge. This will allow the replication to use the bridging site to create a direct connection to the destination site. If you want to further control inter-site replication in given sites, you can designate Preferred Bridgehead Servers at the site. The Bridgehead Server manages all

Available Bandwidth	Suggested Cost for Prime Link	Suggested Cost for BU Link
56	Separate domain	N/A
64	750	1000
128	500	750
256	400	500
512	300	400
1024	150	300
T1	100	150

Table 3-8   Recommended Link Cost per Available Bandwidth

inter-site replication in a site. All updates are received and sent through the Bridgehead Server. Thus no other DCs in the site need dedicate resources to inter-site replication. On the other hand, if you designate Bridgehead Servers, the Knowledge Consistency Checker will no longer be able to calculate replication routes automatically. You will have to monitor replication closely to ensure that all sites are up to date.

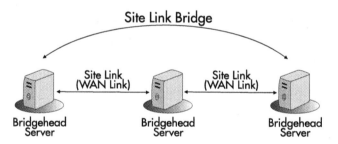

It is a good idea to calculate replication latency—the time between a modification on a DC and the reception of the modification on all other DCs—in the site topology. This will allow you to identify what the longest possible replication delay can be within your network. Replication latency is calculated with the replication interval, the time it can take to replicate data, and the number of hops required to perform replication. For example, if your site topology includes two hops, your replication interval is set at 180 minutes, and it takes 30 minutes to complete a replication change, your replication latency is 420 minutes (180 times 2, plus 30 minutes times 2). Also, remember to base all your replication calculations on available bandwidth, not global bandwidth. If only 10 percent of bandwidth is available for AD replication, it will affect your calculations.

Finally, as mentioned before, the Univeral Group Membership Caching option is assigned to sites in a native WS03 AD forest. This option should be set for all sites. DCs will be able to cache requesting users' universal group memberships, reducing the amount of communications with central Global Catalog servers.

Best Practices for Site Topology Design

Use the following best practices to design your site topology:

- Use the default configuration for inter-site replication.
- Do not disable the Knowledge Consistency Checker.
- Do not disable transitive trusts.
- Do not specify Bridgehead Servers.
- Calculate replication latency between sites.
- Create sites according to network topology; Site Links and WAN links should correspond.
- Make sure that no single site is connected to more than 20 other sites.
- Each site must host at least one DC.
- Do not use SMTP for domain-centric replication.
- Do not use SMTP replication if at all possible.
- Use 128 Kbps as the minimum WAN circuit for a Site Link.
- Associate every site with at least one subnet and one Site Link, otherwise it will be unusable.
- Create backup Site Links for each site. Assign higher costs to backup Site Links.
- Create Site Link Bridges wherever there are two hops between sites to reduce replication latency.
- If your available network bandwidth can afford it, ignore replication schedules in all sites. Replication will be performed when required with this option, but it will be more demanding on WAN bandwidth.
- Enable Universal Group Membership Caching in all sites.
- Use Preferred Bridgehead Servers only if replication must cross a firewall.
- Size your DCs accordingly.
- Monitor replication once your forest is in place to determine the impact on your WAN links.

T&T Corporation's Site Topology Scenario

T&T's site topology is based on the information displayed previously in Figure 3-9 as well as the WAN Link Speed for each site. Using this information, T&T produced the grid outlined in Table 3-9.

▶ **NOTE**

The perimeter forest is also identified in Table 3-9 and in Figure 3-11 to demonstrate the potential use of Bridgehead Servers.

T&T used some global settings in their Site Topology Design. These include:

- Open schedules for all sites.
- KCC on by default in all sites.

- All Site Link costs decrease as they get closer to HQ1, so HQ1 replication is prioritized.
- Replication is only performed with the RPC through IP.
- Default schedules are enabled in all sites (replication every 180 minutes).
- High priority replication can occur immediately.
- Every site has a backup replication route at a higher cost.

Site Link Name	Link Speed to HQ	Site Link Type	Site Link Cost	Options
HQ Main	LAN	VLAN	1	Site Link available (VLAN for server connections) KCC on (setting for all sites) Site Links with all sites Site Link Bridge with S5 and R11
HQ Main to Security Perimeter Security Perimeter to HQ Main	LAN with Firewall	VLAN	50	Preferred Bridgehead Server
HQ Site 2 Region 5	T1	VLAN	100	Site Links with HQ1 and R11 BU Site Links with all sites Site Link Bridge with S4
Region 1 Region 3 Region 4 Region 6 Region 7 Region 8 Region 9 Region 10 Region 13 Region 14	256	Regional	400	Site Link with HQ1 BU Site Link with HQ2
Region 2 Region 12	512	Regional	300	Site Link with HQ1 BU Site Link with HQ2
Region 11	T1	VLAN	150	Site Link with HQ2 Site Link Bridge with HQ1 BU Site Link with HQ1
Region 15	128	Regional	500	Site Link with HQ1 BU Site Link with HQ2
Satellite 1 (Region 2) Satellite 2 (Region 5) Satellite 3 (Region 5)	64	N/A	N/A	N/A
Satellite 4 (Region 11) Satellite 5 (Region 12)	128	Regional	500	Site Link with R11 Site Link Bridge with HQ2 BU Site Link with HQ2

Table 3-9 T&T Site Topology

- Everything is based on calculated available bandwidth.
- Every site is set to cache universal group memberships.
- Firewall replication is controlled through preferred Bridgehead Servers.

Of course, T&T will need to monitor AD replication performance during the operation of the directory to ensure that the values in this table are appropriate to meet service levels. If not, both the table and the Site Links will need to be updated. This Site Topology Design for T&T Corporation is illustrated in Figure 3-11.

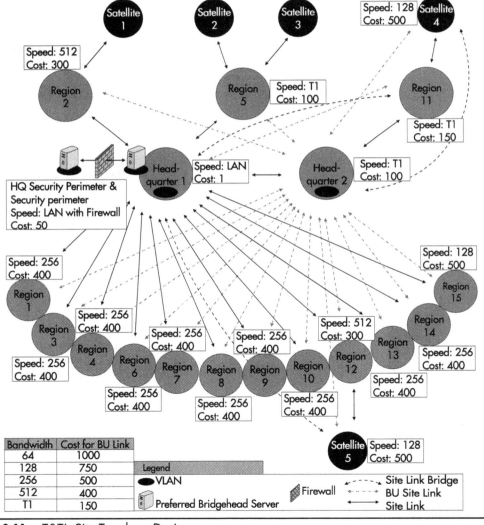

Figure 3-11 T&T's Site Topology Design

Schema Modification Strategy

Now that your forest design is done, you can put it in place. The final process you need to complete is the outline of your Schema Modification Strategy. Operating an Active Directory is managing a distributed database. Modifying the structure of that database has an impact on every service provider in the forest. Adding object classes or object class attributes must be done with care and in a controlled manner. Adding components always implies added replication at the time of the modification. It may also mean added replication on a recurring basis. Retiring components also implies added replication at the time of modification, though it may also mean reduced ongoing replication. Native Windows Server 2003 forests support the reuse of certain types of deactivated object classes or attributes.

Expect your AD database schema to be modified. Even simple tools such as enterprise backup software will modify the schema to create backup objects within the directory. Without a doubt, some of the commercial server tools you acquire—be they only Microsoft Exchange—will modify your production AD schema.

In addition, you may also want to take advantage of schema extensions for your own purposes. You will definitely shorten application development timelines if you choose to use the directory to store frequently requested information. AD will automatically replicate information throughout your enterprise if it is part of the directory. Be careful what information you include in the directory. Because of its multimaster and hierarchical models, AD is not designed to provide immediate data consistency. There is always replication latency when more than a single DC is involved. Use the directory to store static information that is required in every site, but is unlikely to change very often. You may also decide that you do not want to modify the schema for your own purposes. The arrival of AD/AM with WS03 means that AD can now be solely used as a NOS directory. This is the recommended approach. It will make it simpler to upgrade your directory when the next version of Windows comes out.

However you decide to use your directory, one thing is sure, you must always be careful with schema modifications within the production directory. The best way to do so is to form a Schema Modification Policy. This policy is upheld by a Schema Change Policy Holder (SCPH) to whom all schema changes are presented for approval. The policy will outline not only who holds the SCPH role, but also how schema modifications are to be tested, prepared, and deployed. Assigning the SCPH role to manage the schema ensures that modifications will not be performed on an ad hoc basis by groups that do not communicate with each other.

In addition, the X.500 structure of the AD database is based on an object numbering scheme that is globally unique. A central authority, the International Standards Organization (ISO), has the ability to generate object identifiers for new X.500 objects. Numbers can also be obtained from the American National Standards Institute (ANSI). X.500 numbering can be obtained at http://www.iso.org/ or http://www.ansi.org/. Microsoft also offers X.500 numbering in an object class tree it acquired for the purpose of supporting Active Directory. You can receive object IDs from Microsoft by sending email to oids@microsoft.com. In your email, include your organization's naming prefix and the contact name, address, and telephone number. To obtain your organization's naming prefix, read the Active Directory portion of the Logo standards at http://www.microsoft.com/winlogo/downloads/software.asp.

Object identifiers are strings in a dot notation similar to IP addresses. Issuing authorities can give an object identifier on a sublevel to other authorities. The ISO is the root authority. The ISO has a number of 1. When it assigns a number to another organization, that number is used to identify that organization. If it assigned T&T the number 488077, and T&T issued 1 to a developer, and that developer assigned 10 to an application, the number of the application would be 1.488077.1.10.

To create your Schema Modification Strategy, you need to perform three steps:

- Identify the elements of the Schema Modification Policy.
- Identify the owner and the charter for the Schema Change Policy Holder role.
- Identify the Schema Change Management Process.

The Schema Modification Policy includes several elements:

- List of the members of the Universal Enterprise Administrators group.
- Security and management strategy for the Universal Schema Administrators group. This group should be kept empty until modifications are required. Members are removed as soon as the modification is complete.
- Creation of the SCPH role.
- Schema Change Management Strategy documentation including:
  - Change request supporting documentation preparation with modification description and justification.
  - Impact analysis for the change. Short term and long term replication impacts. Costs for the requested change. Short term and long term benefits for the change.
  - Globally unique object identifier for the new class or attribute, obtained from a valid source.
  - Official class description including class type and location in the hierarchy.
  - System stability and security test results. Design standard set of tests for all modifications.
  - Modification recovery method. Make sure every modification proposal includes a rollback strategy.
  - Schema write-enabling process. By default, the schema is read-only and should stay so during ongoing production cycles. It should be reset to read-only after every modification.
- Modification Authorization Process; meeting structure for modification recommendation.
- Modification Implementation Process outlining when the change should be performed (off production hours), how it should be performed, and by whom.
- Modification report documentation. Did the modification reach all DCs? Is replication back to expected levels?

This process should be documented at the very beginning of your implementation to ensure the continuing integrity of your production schema. If this is done well, you will rarely find your staff performing midnight restores of the schema you had in production yesterday.

Schema Modification Strategy Best Practices

Use the following schema modification best practices:

- Don't make your own modifications to the schema unless they are absolutely necessary.
- Use AD primarily as a NOS directory.
- Use AD/AM to integrate applications.
- Use MMS 2003, Standard Edition to synchronize AD and AD/AM directories.
- Make sure all commercial products that will modify the schema are Windows Server 2003 Logo approved.
- Limit your initial modifications to modifications by commercial software.
- Create a Schema Change Policy Holder role early in the AD Implementation Process.
- Document the Schema Modification Policy and Process.

AD Implementation Plan

The first stage of AD preparation is complete. You have designed your AD strategy. Now you need to implement the design. To do so, you require an AD Implementation Plan. This plan outlines the AD migration process. Basically, this plan identifies the same steps as the design process, but is focused only on those that deal with implementation. It is reduced to four major steps:

- Forest, Tree, and Domain Installation
- OU and Group Design
- Service Positioning
- Site Topology Implementation

Once these four steps are complete, your AD will be in place. These four steps are outlined in Figure 3-12 through the AD Implementation Blueprint.

This blueprint is designed to cover all the major steps in a new AD implementation. It uses the parallel network concept outlined in Chapter 2 to create a separate new network that can accept users as they are migrated from the existing production network. Because the AD Implementation Process is closely tied to the design of the IP network, the deployment of a new Active Directory and the IP network infrastructure are covered together in Chapter 4. If you already have a Windows 2000 AD in place, however, you are more likely to use the upgrade process outlined at the end of Chapter 4.

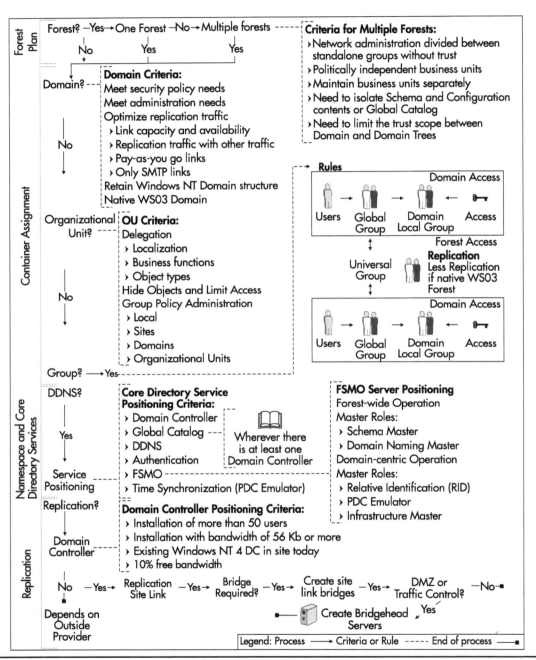

Figure 3-12 The AD Implementation Blueprint

The Ongoing AD Design Process

In summary, the AD Design Process is complex only because it includes a lot more stages than the Windows NT design. One of the things you need to remember is that creating a production AD is creating a virtual space. Since it is virtual, you can manipulate and reshape it as your needs and comprehension of Active Directory evolve. WS03 makes this even easier by supporting drag and drop functionality in the AD Management Consoles: Active Directory Users and Computers, Active Directory Domains and Trusts, and Active Directory Sites and Servers. WS03 also supports multiple object attribute changes—for example, if you need to change the same attribute on several objects.

Also, a tool that is very useful in the Active Directory Design Process is Microsoft Visio Professional, especially the version for Enterprise Architect. In fact, you can actually draw and document your entire forest using Visio. Once the design is complete, it can be exported and then imported into Active Directory. Microsoft offers a complete step-by-step guide to this task at http://www.microsoft.com/technet/treeview/default.asp?url=/TechNet/prodtechnol/visio/visio2002/deploy/vsaddiag.asp.

These tools can only *assist* you in the design process. The success or failure of the Active Directory Design Process you will complete will depend entirely on what your organization invests in it. Remember, AD is the core of your network. Its design must respond to organizational needs. The only way to ensure this is to gather all of the AD stakeholders and get them to participate in the design process. In other words, the quality of the team you gather to create your AD design will greatly influence the quality of the output you produce.

Best Practice Summary

This chapter is chock-full of best practices. It would be pointless to repeat them here. One final best practice or recommendation can be made: Whatever you do in your Windows Server 2003 migration, make sure you get the Active Directory part right! It must be designed properly if you want to meet all of the objectives of a migration to WS03.

Chapter Roadmap

Use the illustration in Figure 3-13 to review the contents of this chapter.

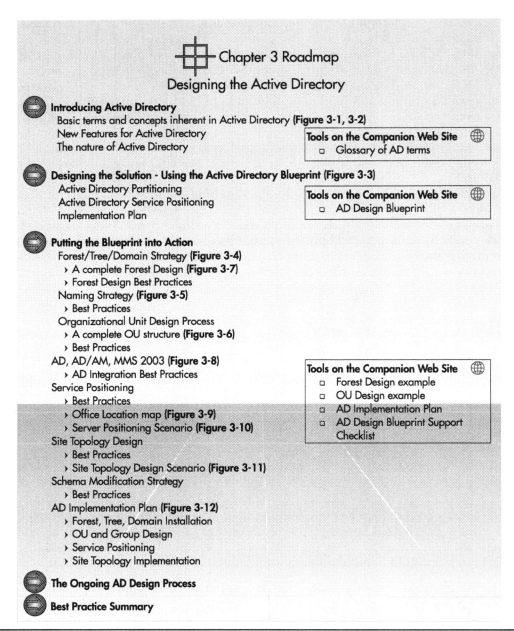

Figure 3-13   Chapter Roadmap

CHAPTER 4

Designing the Enterprise Network IP Infrastructure

The basis of an enterprise network is the concept of communication. The competitive advantage an information technology network gives to an organization is one that no organization today can afford to be without. Few organizations do not use the TCP/IP protocol for network communications. Even fewer haven't standardized on this protocol, and only this protocol.

The principle behind this protocol is simple: each network component is given a specific identifier. In version 4 of the implementations of the TCP/IP protocol (IPv4), this identifier is a 32-bit number, with four sections of eight binary values each. This addressing scheme generates a total of more than 4 billion IP addresses. Given the number of addresses, you would think that IPv4 can serve the Internet requirements of the entire world, but this is not the case. This is due to the structure of IPv4 addressing. Since every address is subdivided into a class and organizations are given the opportunity to acquire classes for private use even if they don't actually require all of the addresses within this class, the networking world has had to come up with innovative ways to use IPv4 to fulfill the networking needs and requirements of the wired world.

One of these solutions is the use of Network Address Translation (NAT). NAT is a great tool since it allows an organization to use an internal address scheme that is different from the external address scheme it exposes to the world. As such, three address ranges have been reserved for internal use:

- **Class A**   10.0.0.0 to 10.255.255.255 (Mask 255.0.0.0)
- **Class B**   172.16.0.0 to 172.31.255.255 (Mask 255.255.0.0)
- **Class C**   192.168.0.0 to 192.168.255.255 (Mask 255.255.255.0)

Organizations choose the class that best fits their needs based on the number of hosts that are required inside the internal network. Class A supports more than 16 million hosts per subnet, class B more than 65,000, and class C only 254. When communicating on the Internet, NAT translates the internal address to an external address, one that is often provided by an Internet service provider (ISP). NAT uses TCP ports when more than one internal address needs translation, greatly multiplying the number of addresses organizations can use even with the limitations of IPv4.

▶ *NOTE*

With Windows 2000, Microsoft has begun to use classless inter-domain routing notation (CIDR). It is more compact and easier to express because it only indicates the number of bits that are hidden by the subnet mask. For example, 255.0.0.0 is /8, 255.255.0.0 is /16, 255.255.255 is /24, and so on.

In addition, IPv4 cannot automatically assign host addresses without external help. If your internal network includes several thousand hosts, you'll definitely want to take advantage of automatic addressing mechanisms. In IPv4, this is done through the Dynamic Host Configuration Protocol (DHCP). Finally, even though all of the hosts on your network have a specific address, using this 32-bit number to communicate between hosts is not practical for human beings. Thus, we need to resolve these numbers to names we can more easily remember. The Domain Naming System (DNS) is the process we use to resolve an Internet address to a more manageable name. But if you use legacy technologies within your Windows network, you'll also require legacy name resolution. This is performed through the Windows Internet Naming System (WINS).

Despite these temporary solutions, IPv4 use is becoming increasingly more difficult, especially in terms of routing. Internet routers using version 4 of TCP/IP are having more and more trouble storing routing tables, the path a host must use to reach a given destination. Eventually, a permanent solution will be required if the entire world is to have access to the Internet, especially emerging nations.

The Internet Engineering Task Force (IETF) has been working for some time on a complete solution to the IPv4 situation. This solution is embedded into version 6 of the TCP/IP protocol: IPv6. Version 6 uses a 128-bit addressing scheme. This addressing scheme results in 340,282,366,920,938,463,463, 374,607,431,768,211,456 unique entities on the Internet, quite enough for the time being. This means that when fully implemented, IPv6 will support true point-to-point communications between hosts and destinations without the use of schemes such as address translation. In addition, IPv6 includes numerous other improvements. For example, an IPv6 host does not require DHCP since it will generate its own address from the unique number assigned to its network interface card, the Media Access Control (MAC) number. If the host needs to communicate externally, its IPv6 address will be generated from both the MAC address and the address of the router it is connected to, greatly simplifying both addressing and communications since the router address becomes part of the host's address.

There are issues with using IPv6, though. For example, routers will need to support IPv6 for the protocol to work. Most router manufacturers have implemented software solutions for IPv6 support for existing routers. Cisco Systems and others have downloadable software revisions for their operating systems which include IPv6 support. Future router products will have hardware solutions for IPv6 support. But router support is not the only requirement. Applications that are based on IPv4 today will not automatically function with IPv6 since the core operation of the TCP/IP protocol is different. Organizations wishing to move to IPv6 will have to carefully plan their implementation before proceeding.

TCP/IP in Windows Server 2003

Windows Server 2003 supports both IPv4 and IPv6, though IPv4 is installed by default and cannot be removed even in a pure IPv6 network. Thus, the IPv4 network is still required.

Most organizations using Windows networks already have a complex network addressing scheme in place to support the use of IPv4 within their internal networks. These organizations will continue to use this scheme with Windows Server 2003. This addressing scheme includes the following elements:

- Centralized IP addressing including both virtual and physical LAN planning
- Name resolution, both Internet and legacy
- Alert management

- Service load balancing
- Multicasting

When ready for a full IPv6 implementation, organizations will benefit from a simplified addressing scheme which will remove the need for centralized IP addressing management through technologies such as DHCP since all IPv6 addresses are generated automatically.

New IP Features in WS03

Windows Server 2003 is completely based on the TCP/IP protocol. In fact, the entire functioning of the WS03 Active Directory, the core of the WS03 network, is based on TCP/IP addressing and name resolution. As such, the TCP/IP protocol in WS03 becomes a core component of the WS03 enterprise network.

Since WS03 relies so heavily on TCP/IP, Microsoft has enhanced the protocol and improved it over and above the many improvements included in Windows 2000. These improvements include:

- Alternate configuration
- Automatic determination of the interface metric
- Internet Group Management Protocol (IGMP) version 3 support
- IPv6 support

In addition, the WS03 version of TCP/IP includes special configuration features such as large TCP windows, better round-trip time estimation, and DNS caching.

Alternate Configuration

Windows 2000 introduced the concept of Automatic Private IP Addressing (APIPA). This process automatically assigns a private IP address in the nonroutable range of 169.254.0.1 through 169.254.255.254 when a DHCP server cannot be located by a host. This ensures that the TCP/IP protocol continues to work even in the case of a DHCP server failure. APIPA begins by assigning a private address and then tries to communicate with a DHCP server to renew the dynamic address properly. APIPA will try to reach the DHCP server ten times every five minutes before giving up.

But in a server environment, you simply cannot afford to have an IP configuration that is dynamic. It can be dynamically managed, but it cannot be dynamically allocated because servers should always keep and maintain the same address. If you decide to use DHCP to centrally manage server address allocation through address reservations in your DHCP system, you should also take advantage of the Alternate Configuration feature of WS03.

This Alternate Configuration allows you to statically set the server's address as a backup in case the DHCP server cannot be reached. You should use this function for all servers even if you use RAIN network interface cards (NIC) as discussed in Chapter 2.

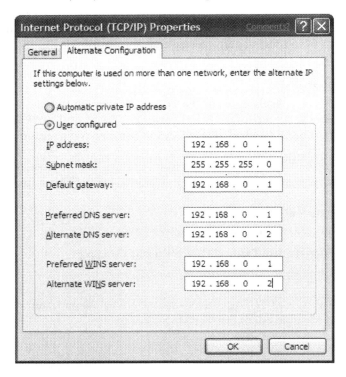

Automatic Determination of the Interface Metric

WS03 has the ability to automatically determine the best route to a given point. For example, if you have several network interface cards on a system, WS03 will automatically determine interface metrics for each card. This calculation is based on interface speed as well as binding order. If the interfaces have varying speeds, WS03 will select the interface with the highest speed and assign it the lowest metric, ensuring that this interface is always the first to be used to communicate to a given point. If, however, the interface cards all have the same speed, WS03 will assign metrics according to binding order. By default, interface binding order is determined through the network card detection process during the installation of the operating system. Thus the first card detected during installation is assigned the lowest metric.

Binding order can be controlled through the Advanced Settings option in the Advanced menu in Network Connections. But even so, it is always best to ensure that the first card you place in a system will be the card with the fastest connection because of the Windows binding mechanism.

Automatic determination of the routing metric is enabled by default and can be overridden by deselecting the checkbox on the IP Settings tab of the Advanced TCP/IP Settings dialog box for any network connection.

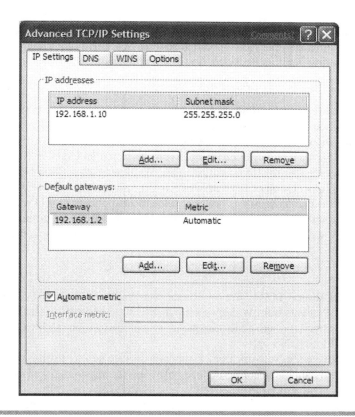

QUICK TIP

The NIC binding order is extremely important in Windows even though it can be controlled and modified after system installation. If, for example, you intend to set up a domain controller with two network cards, one for internal communications and one for external communications (such as in the case of a regional office or small office/home office installation), ensure that the internal NIC is the first one detected at installation. By default, Active Directory binds all services to the first card in the binding order, or in other words, the first card detected at installation. This will avoid many binding management headaches.

The best way to do this, though it requires more work at installation, is to perform the installation with only one NIC in the server, then add the second NIC once the operating system is installed. (This does not apply to RAIN cards since they appear as the same NIC to the operating system.)

IGMP Version 3 Support

Like Windows 2000, WS03 can make extensive use of IP multicasting. IP multicasting consists of information sent to a single address but processed by multiple hosts. In version 1 and 2 of IGMP, it was possible for a multicast to be sent to a network without listening hosts, thus sending the information for nothing to this network. With IGMP version 3 support, WS03 allows the host to request to receive a multicast either from specified sources or from all but a specific set of sources. This allows network administrators better control of the multicast traffic on their network.

IPv6 Support

WS03 boasts enhanced support for IPv6. In fact, a WS03 server can act as a translator between IPv4 and IPv6 networks. Since IPv6 addresses are always autoconfigured, using IPv6 greatly reduces the addressing workload. In addition, installing IPv6 on a WS03 server automatically installs the 6To4 service. This service manages communications between version 4 and version 6 networks. It also serves to automatically register the IPv6 address in the Windows Server 2003 Domain Naming Server service. While the implementation of IPv6 in WS03 is very powerful, it will still be some time before organizations begin widespread use of this protocol since most applications will require rewrites to operate properly on this protocol. Now is the time, though, to begin the migration process to IPv6. Windows Server 2003, with its compatibility modes between IPv6 and IPv4, is the perfect tool to support this migration.

Other New Features

Finally, WS03 includes several TCP/IP improvements over Windows 2000 and especially Windows NT. For example, all TCP/IP clients from Windows 2000 on can automatically cache DNS information. This information can be managed through added functionality included within the IPCONFIG command-line tool, especially the /FLUSHDNS option.

WS03 servers also have the Network Load Balancing service automatically installed on all servers. This means that it is fairly simple to configure load balancing for mission-critical network services such as Web, firewall, proxy and Virtual Private Networking (VPN) servers.

NetBIOS over TCP/IP (NetBT) can also be disabled more easily on network interface cards, reducing the level of risk involved with servers connecting to networks no longer requiring NetBIOS name resolution. Internet connections, for example, are connections where this service should be disabled at all times. Internal networks will still require this service in many cases. Microsoft themselves are providers of a lot of technologies which require the use of NetBIOS name resolution.

> ▶ **QUICK TIP**
>
> *A complete listing of the most common TCP/IP port mappings for Windows networks can be found at http://www.Reso-Net.com/WindowsServer/.*

WS03 also includes enhanced Simple Network Management Protocol (SNMP) security settings. Since SNMP is an excellent tool for systems and event management, these enhanced security features are a boon for its use. By default, SNMP is set to communicate with the *public* community and accept SNMP packets from any hosts. If you intend to use SNMP, you should change the community name to one that is private and specific to your organization (use a complex name that is difficult to guess) and you should identify specific hosts on your network from which systems can accept SNMP packets.

All of these features will help you design and configure a secure enterprise network IP configuration.

Implementing a New Enterprise Network

Chapter 2 introduced the concept of a parallel network for Active Directory implementation. The opportunities presented by the parallel network are quite bountiful and beneficial. For one thing, you get to recreate your production network from scratch using a design that capitalizes on the new operating system's core features. It's an ideal opportunity to revise every network concept and detail to see how it can be improved upon to further meet its basic objective, information service delivery and intra-organization communications support.

Of course, every part of the Parallel Network Implementation Process must be fully tested in a laboratory before being implemented in actual fact. The parallel network also gives you the opportunity to restructure domains if you feel that your Windows NT or Windows 2000 domain structure needs to be modified, especially in light of the information provided in Chapter 3 and the Active Directory Implementation Blueprint outlined in Figure 3-12. Restructuring can be done in three ways:

- Everything can be created from scratch. This means that there is nothing to be recovered from the existing network.

- The existing production network can be used as an information source for the new network. During this transfer process, administrators can perform additional data filtering to clean up information such as the identity database for the organization. If the existing domain is a Windows NT domain, two options are available to recover information. The first option involves integrating the existing Windows NT domain(s) into a Windows Server 2003 forest as a subdomain, creating a new production domain in native WS03 mode, and then performing an intra-forest transfer. The movetree command is used to perform this information transfer from domain to domain. Movetree can also be used at this time to filter information from one domain to the other. When emptied, the Windows NT domain is decommissioned and removed from the forest.

- The second option is to perform an inter-forest transfer. This means that a new WS03 forest is created within the parallel network while the Windows NT domain structure remains as is. Inter-forest data migration tools are used to perform the transfer. This can be performed with the Active Directory Migration Tool (ADMT) version 2. ADMT v2 can transfer data objects such as user accounts from the Windows NT domain to the WS03 forest, including passwords. Commercial data migration tools are also available, such as NetIQ's Domain Migration Administrator (DMA). While ADMT offers limited filtering capabilities, DMA offers very sophisticated filtering and reporting tools as well as complete rollback capabilities. ADMT performs well for migrations of a few thousand objects or less. But if you have tens of thousands of objects and dozens of Windows NT domains to consolidate, you would be well advised to obtain a copy of NetIQ's Domain Migration Suite (or any other commercial migration tool). This suite includes the following products:

  - Domain Migration Administrator for domain consolidation and data migration. DMA can perform both intra-forest and inter-forest migrations.

  - Server Consolidator for consolidation and migration of file and print services.

- Configuration Assessor to report information from all domain sources before, during, and after a migration.
- Exchange Migrator for migration of Microsoft Exchange-specific objects.
- NetIQ NetWare Migrator to migrate objects from NetWare directories to Windows directories.

Of the three restructuring options, few are likely to perform the first since it is extremely rare to find a network from which there is nothing to recover. The second limits the growth of the Windows Server 2003 network for the duration of the migration. Remember, a WS03 forest cannot operate in native forest mode until all domains are in native domain mode. Including an upgraded Windows NT domain in the forest will limit its growth potential until the migration is complete. Migrations take time, time that is evaluated in a proportional manner based on the number of users in the network and on the deployment strategy, whether parallel deployments (several deployments in several regions at the same time) or sequential deployments (one after the other).

The recommended migration strategy is the third one. It applies whether you are migrating from Windows NT or Windows 2000 (to integrate a Windows 2000 domain within a WS03 forest, you must upgrade the entire Windows 2000 forest) and you need to restructure the forest. Its great advantage is that the forest can immediately operate in native mode, profiting from full WS03 forest functionality from day one. You can also filter all data input into the new forest. This means you can start your new WS03 enterprise network with a squeaky clean environment. And keeping the existing network separate gives you a clear rollback strategy in case you need it.

Implementing a parallel network and designing a new forest is based on the Active Directory Implementation Blueprint (Figure 3-12), but implementing this blueprint is a complex process that must be taken a step at a time. The first stages of this implementation are begun here, but the implementation will not be complete until the Data Migration Process is complete. This will be done in future chapters.

To implement the parallel network and perform the restructuring exercise, you must begin with the following activities:

- Prepare for the parallel network
- Create the production Active Directory
- Connect the parallel enterprise network

The details of each procedure are outlined in this chapter. They follow the steps outlined in the Parallel Network Blueprint illustrated in Figure 4-1. If on the other hand, you simply need to upgrade your existing Windows 2000 forest to WS03, you can use the procedure at the end of this chapter. It is still a good idea though to review the contents of the Parallel Network Creation Process to ensure that your upgraded forest uses the latest WS03 concepts and features.

Preparing the Parallel Network

Chapter 1 outlined eight different enterprise network server roles (including the Failsafe Server). These roles are illustrated in Figure 4-2. Two of these are required for the initial implementation of the parallel network: Network Infrastructure and Identity Management Servers. You will need to

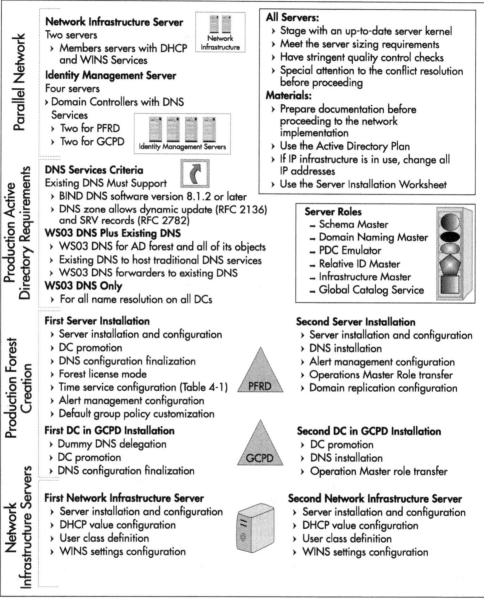

Parallel Network

Network Infrastructure Server
Two servers
> Members servers with DHCP and WINS Services

Identity Management Server
Four servers
> Domain Controllers with DNS Services
  > Two for PFRD
  > Two for GCPD

Identity Management Servers

DNS Services Criteria
Existing DNS Must Support
> BIND DNS software version 8.1.2 or later
> DNS zone allows dynamic update (RFC 2136) and SRV records (RFC 2782)

WS03 DNS Plus Existing DNS
> WS03 DNS for AD forest and all of its objects
> Existing DNS to host traditional DNS services
> WS03 DNS forwarders to existing DNS

WS03 DNS Only
> For all name resolution on all DCs

All Servers:
> Stage with an up-to-date server kernel
> Meet the server sizing requirements
> Have stringent quality control checks
> Special attention to the conflict resolution before proceeding

Materials:
> Prepare documentation before proceeding to the network implementation
> Use the Active Directory Plan
> If IP infrastructure is in use, change all IP addresses
> Use the Server Installation Worksheet

Server Roles
- Schema Master
- Domain Naming Master
- PDC Emulator
- Relative ID Master
- Infrastructure Master
- Global Catalog Service

Production Active Directory Requirements

Production Forest Creation

First Server Installation
> Server installation and configuration
> DC promotion
> DNS configuration finalization
> Forest license mode
> Time service configuration (Table 4-1)
> Alert management configuration
> Default group policy customization

PFRD

Second Server Installation
> Server installation and configuration
> DNS installation
> Alert management configuration
> Operations Master Role transfer
> Domain replication configuration

First DC in GCPD Installation
> Dummy DNS delegation
> DC promotion
> DNS configuration finalization

GCPD

Second DC in GCPD Installation
> DC promotion
> DNS installation
> Operation Master role transfer

Network Infrastructure Servers

First Network Infrastructure Server
> Server installation and configuration
> DHCP value configuration
> User class definition
> WINS settings configuration

Second Network Infrastructure Server
> Server installation and configuration
> DHCP value configuration
> User class definition
> WINS settings configuration

Figure 4-1   The Parallel Network Blueprint

ensure that you have enough new servers to create the basic network infrastructure. This will include at least two Network Infrastructure Servers and at least four Identity Management Servers, two for

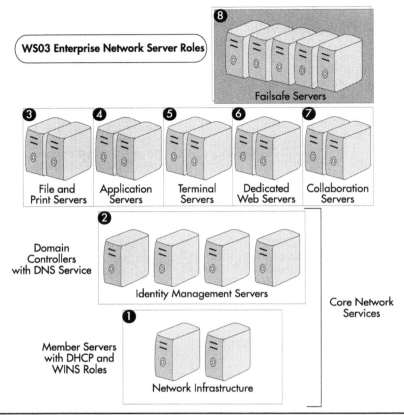

Figure 4-2 WS03 Enterprise Network Server roles

the Protected Forest Root Domain and two for the creation of the Global Child Production Domain (GCPD). Two servers are required for each role in the initial parallel network in order to provide complete service redundancy right from the start.

Network Infrastructure Servers will run services such as DHCP and WINS, while Identity Management Servers will be domain controllers with an integrated DNS service. There is absolutely no requirement for the Network Infrastructure Servers to be domain controllers; they should be Member Servers only. For economy's sake, you might decide to combine the root domain controller roles with the network infrastructure roles. This is acceptable in smaller networks, but it is not recommended in larger environments even though the server load on the root forest DCs is quite light. Several issues arise when you try to integrate the DHCP service for the production domain with the domain controllers for the root domain. These include security as well as configuration issues. If at all possible, keep these roles on different physical servers.

All parallel network servers should be staged with an up-to-date Server Kernel according to staging practices outlined in Chapter 2. Each server should meet the server sizing requirements outlined in the same chapter. In addition, each server should have stringent quality control checks to ensure that it is ready for production. These checks should ensure that everything on the server is running smoothly. Since several of these servers will be domain controllers, special attention should be paid to hardware conflict resolution before proceeding.

If you have several large sites within your organization, you'll most likely want to separate each double server role physically by putting a server for each role in each of two physical sites. This provides network redundancy and creates an automatic service backup in case of disasters.

You'll also need prepared documentation before proceeding with the network implementation. Your existing IP infrastructure design will most likely be adequate for the implementation of the parallel network. You will, however, need to change all IP addresses since the new network and the old network will need to coexist for some time. You should have this information in hand before proceeding with network creation.

In addition, you will also require your Active Directory plan. For this, you must have performed the planning exercise outlined in Chapter 3. This plan will serve as a directory map for you to follow during the implementation of the WS03 Active Directory. With these documents in hand, you can prepare the parallel network. Remember, everything is done in a laboratory first. Here you can specifically document every step that is required for the actual creation of the production enterprise network. The more documentation you have, the less likely you are to commit errors when creating the new network. This is not a time when errors are allowed.

Once your parallel network is up and running, you'll be able to create a trust relationship between the new production domain and your legacy Windows NT domain(s). This trust relationship will last for the duration of the migration to provide cross-forest services to all users. Then you can migrate users, computers, and services at will using either ADMT version 2 or a commercial migration tool. This process is illustrated in Figure 4-3.

You are now ready to proceed to the first stage, implementing the production Active Directory.

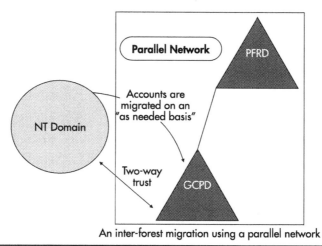

An inter-forest migration using a parallel network

Figure 4-3   Using a parallel network to migrate data between forests

Creating the Production Active Directory

Creating a brand new Active Directory is a very straightforward process. It involves the creation of at least four different domain controllers according to the Server Positioning Strategy identified in Figure 3-10 in Chapter 3. Two of these domain controllers belong to the Protected Forest Root Domain. Each will host a forest-wide Operation Master role: Schema or Domain Naming Master. These two DCs will also host the domain-centric Operation Master roles: PDC Emulator, Relative ID and Infrastructure Masters. In addition, these DCs will host the Global Catalog Service.

There are additional tasks that must be performed during the creation of these servers. Since the very first DC is the first server in the enterprise network, it must host a few additional functions. These functions include:

- **Time Service Hosting**   You may require that your entire network be synchronized with an external time source such as an atomic clock. Whether you do so or not, you must ensure that time synchronization is implemented in your network. Time synchronization is essential since Kerberos, the preferred authentication protocol in Windows Server 2003, is time-sensitive.

- **Licensing Mode Hosting**   The WS03 enterprise network must use a consistent licensing mode. Thus the first server in the network is the best server to configure and control licensing.

- **Alert Management**   The initial alert management community must be configured on this server as well.

Name resolution will also be required. The first DC in a network requires a Domain Naming System server to function properly. You could use an existing DNS server for this purpose, but Windows Server 2003 has particular requirements for the DNS service. If you choose to use a DNS server other than the WS03 DNS server, this DNS server must support the following criteria:

- BIND DNS servers must be version 8.1.2 or later of the BIND software to meet the DNS requirements for Active Directory support.

- The DNS zone must allow dynamic updates (RFC 2136).

- The DNS server hosting that zone must support the SRV resource records (RFC 2782) to advertise the directory service.

If there are issues and you cannot move existing DNS services to WS03, then compromise. Use WS03 DNS for the AD forest and all of its objects and use the other DNS service (UNIX, for example) to host traditional DNS services. Include forwarders in your WS03 DNS servers to perform name resolution of non-AD objects through your legacy DNS servers.

You will also need to identify whether client resolution will be performed through root hints or through forwarders. This will define the name resolution mechanism for clients.

If there are no issues, use the WS03 DNS service for all name resolution. WS03 uses DNS for directory operation. One of the critical operations supported by DNS is the logon process. When a user logon is initiated from a Windows 2000 or Windows XP client, the Net Logon service collects the required logon information for the domain to which the user is attempting to log on and sends a DNS query to its configured DNS servers. This query includes the following characteristics:

- Query type: SRV (Service locator resource record)
- Query name: _ldap._tcp.domain_name

The DNS server responds with the name of the domain controller that is closest to the client. The logon request is sent to the DC and if the username and password are valid for that domain, the user is logged onto the domain. This process is illustrated in Figure 4-4.

In addition, WS03 can store DNS zones within the Active Directory, simplifying replication and ensuring the security of these records. Security is important here since Windows 2000 and Windows XP clients using DHCP will also use the dynamic feature of the DNS service to update their own records within the DNS service. If your network includes non-Windows objects that require name resolution, you will need to enter static canonical names for these objects within your WS03 DNS server, unless, of course, their IP addresses are assigned through the Windows DHCP server. Finally, when the DNS service is integrated into the directory, WS03 no longer requires the use of secondary zones to provide information from one DNS domain to another. WS03 now includes the concept of application data partitions. These replication partitions can span several domains to ensure that data is available to everyone within the forest. These partitions are automatically created when you integrate DNS with Active Directory.

The WS03 DNS service should thus be married to the DC service in Windows Server 2003. This ensures that the name service is always available in the same place as the domain controller and logon service. This also ensures that all DNS zones are secured and replicated through the directory replication mechanism. This is the approach that is recommended and used throughout this book.

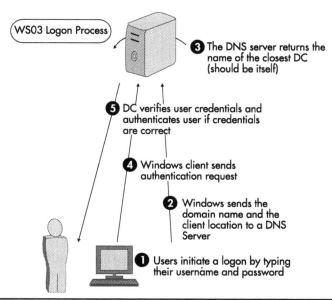

Figure 4-4   The WS03 Logon Process

Forest Staging Activities

Staging the new forest requires a given set of activities, each of which include several steps. These activities are listed in the Production Forest Creation Checklist illustrated in Figure 4-5. As you can see, this checklist is divided into four great activities: creation of the forest and root domain, creation of the production domain, creation of the IP infrastructure, and system finalization.

> **NOTE**
>
> *All of the servers installed here should use at least the Enterprise Edition of WS03 because they will be located in large offices and may need to scale with time. Using a lower edition could cause you to have to reinstall the server. The machine size should also be designed for scaling in mind. Remember the Server Sizing Exercise from Chapter 2.*

> **QUICK TIP**
>
> *The list of activities for server preparation is comprehensive. To simplify the Parallel Network Server Creation Process, Server Preparation Worksheets for each required server role are available at http://www.Reso-Net.com/WindowsServer/. These worksheets include space to write the server administration password. It is a best practice to encrypt this password, to protect the worksheets electronically, or to locate passwords elsewhere to ensure that these passwords are not leaked to the wrong personnel.*

Installing the First Server in a Forest

The place to start is with the very first server in the forest. This server will have several characteristics: it will be a DC with integrated DNS service, it is the Schema Master for the forest, it is also the PDC Emulator and the RID Master for the forest root domain, it hosts the Global Catalog service, it synchronizes time for the forest, and it is the forest License Manager.

Server Installation and Configuration

Begin with the Server Kernel Installation per the procedures outlined in Chapter 2. This installation, since it is unique, can be performed interactively, but if you recall the complexity of the creation process for the Reference Server, you might prefer to use an automated kernel installation. If not, make sure you perform all the steps required for a reference computer when creating this server.

Next, configure the TCP/IP client for this server. Since there are no DHCP servers in this network yet, you can't expect DHCP to assign an address to this server. But since WS03 includes the capability to assign an alternate address, you can configure the server to use a DHCP address provided there are no rogue DHCP servers on the network which could assign an incorrect address to the server and provided you have correctly entered the server's parameters within the Alternate Configuration tab of the server's TCP/IP properties.

Production Forest Creation Checklist

❶ Root Forest Creation
Install and name the first server in the network - Install this server in a workgroup at first

☐ Promote the first server to Active Directory creating the forest root domain

☐ Configure Server Licensing Modes for the forest

☐ Configure the Time Service for this server

☐ Configure Alert Management for this server

Install and name the second server for the forest root domain - This server can be a member of the forest root domain

☐ Promote the second server to Active Directory within the forest root domain

☐ Install and configure the DNS service

☐ Transfer Operation Master roles to this server

☐ Verify that the domain is operating properly

❷ Production Domain Creation
Install and name the first server for the Global Child Production Domain (GCPD) - Install this server in a workgroup at first

☐ Create dummy DNS delegation

☐ Promote this server to AD creating the Global Child Production Domain

☐ Include the DNS service during this promotion

☐ Finalize the configuration of the DNS service

Install and name the three other servers for the core operation of the parallel network -
Install each server as a member of the production domain

☐ Promote one of the servers to AD within the production domain

☐ Install and configure the DNS service

☐ Transfer Operation Master roles to this server

☐ Update DNS delegation

❸ IP Infrastructure Creation
Proceed to the configuration of the Network Infrastructure Servers

❹ System Finalization
Move servers to their final site and then configure domain replication

☐ Verify that all domains are operating properly

Figure 4-5   The Production Forest Creation Checklist

▶ *NOTE*

If you must use dynamic addressing for your servers, you need to take a couple of precautions at this stage. Dynamic server addresses must be based on an address reservation since DC and DNS server addresses should never change. It is also important to ensure that there are no rogue DHCP servers on the network because they will assign an inappropriate IP address to the server (since the reservation does not exist yet). If this happens, you'll need to start over again.

For the client DNS configuration for this server, you should set the server to first point to itself. The second DNS server address should be one of the servers you intend to use as a forwarder, if forwarders are what you intend to use. If you do so and you choose to install the DNS service during the domain controller promotion, WS03 will *automatically* install the DNS server to use forwarders and automatically insert this DNS address as the first forwarder.

Finally, this server should belong to a workgroup that uses the same NetBIOS name you will use for your forest. For example, if you intend to use TandT.net as your root forest name, your workgroup name should be TANDT. This will simplify the communication process between this server and the next server you create.

Performing DC Promotion

The best way to perform this first DC promotion is through the Manage Your Server Web page. This page is launched automatically at system startup. If not, you can start this page with the Manage Your Server shortcut located in the Administrative Tools of the Start Menu. Once this Web page is activated, use the following procedure to create your first forest domain controller.

1. Click Add or remove a role. This will launch the Configure Your Server Wizard.
2. Review the configuration requirements, and then click Next.
3. Windows Server 2003 will verify the existing roles on the server and produce a selection of installation options.
4. Select Domain Controller (Active Directory), and then click Next.

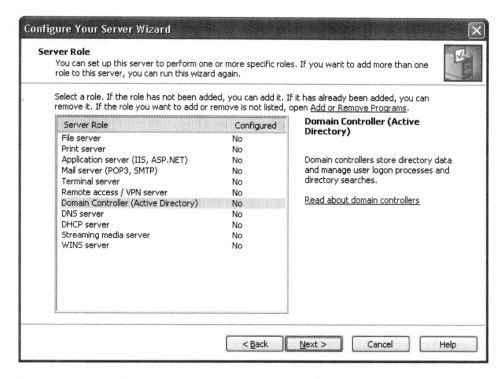

5. Confirm your selection by clicking Next. This launches the Active Directory Installation Wizard. Click Next.

6. Select Domain Controller For A New Domain, and then click Next.

7. Select Domain in a new forest, and then click Next.

8. Name your forest, and then click Next.

9. Select the NetBIOS name for the forest, and then click Next.

10. Select the location of the database and log folders, and then click Next. Since this domain will not contain very much data, database and logs can reside on the same disk.

11. Select the location of the SYSVOL folder (replication folder), and then click Next. Once again, default values are acceptable for this folder.

▶ **NOTE**

Remember, every WS03 Enterprise server is built using NTFS partitions only. This is important because every advanced feature requires this type of disk format to operate.

12. Next, the DC Promotion service tries to find a DNS record for the domain you are creating. Since no such record exists anywhere, it returns an error code. Select Install and configure the DNS server, and then click Next. This will launch the DNS installation process.

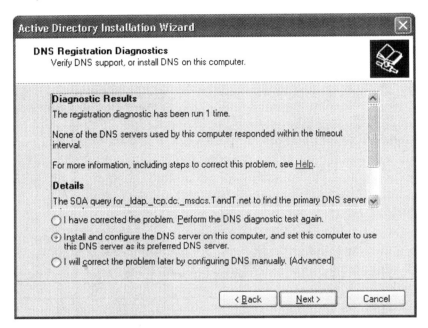

13. The next question relates to the default permission level for users and groups. If you intend to run pre-Windows 2000 operating systems within this network, you need to set these permissions now. Since this is a parallel network that will only contain WS03 and Windows XP servers and computers (there may be Windows 2000 machines as well though they are not recommended), select the second option (Permissions compatible with only Windows 2000 or Windows Server 2003 operating systems), and then click Next.

14. Set the Directory Service Restore Mode Administrator Password, and then click Next. This password is extremely important since it is used to perform authoritative restores or restores that overwrite existing directory information during system recovery. Guard it carefully.

15. The DC Promotion service will outline your choices. Review them carefully and when ready to proceed, click Next. If you see errors in your choices, use the Back button to return and correct them. Clicking Next will launch the Active Directory Installation Wizard. It will perform a series of tasks, including the reapplication of security parameters on the server's disks, and it will launch the DNS service installation.

16. The WSE installation files will be required at this stage. Either insert the CD or identify a network location for the installation files.

17. The Active Directory Installation Process completes once the DNS server is installed. When complete, the AD Installation Wizard displays a completion report. Click Finish. The system will require a restart to finalize the AD Installation Operation.

18. Once the system has restarted and initialized the Active Directory, the Configure Your Server Wizard displays a completion page after you log on. Here you can view the next steps Microsoft recommends for domain controllers.

In actual fact, you will want to proceed to the completion of the First Server Creation Process as follows.

DNS Configuration Finalization

The Active Directory DNS service installation prepares the DNS server to operate with Active Directory, but it does not complete a full DNS configuration. Several elements are required to complete the configuration:

- Set Aging/Scavenging for all zones.
- Verify application partitions for DNS replication.
- Finalize DNS Forward Lookup name resolution configuration.
- Finalize Reverse Lookup name resolution configuration.

DNS server configuration is performed through the Computer Management Microsoft Management Console (MMC) found in Administrative Tools. Use the following procedure to configure your server.

1. Locate and expand the Services and Applications item in the left pane of the console.
2. Locate and expand the DNS item in the left pane.
3. Begin with the Aging and Scavenging settings. To do so, right-click on the server name and select Set Aging/Scavenging for all zones from the context menu.
4. Click Scavenge stale resource records to turn the feature on. Accept the default refresh intervals (seven days) and click OK. This will ensure that your DNS database will not contain outdated records.
5. This will also give you the opportunity to set the scavenging mode for all future new Active Directory integrated zones. Make sure you set Apply these settings to the existing Active Directory-integrated zones and then click OK.

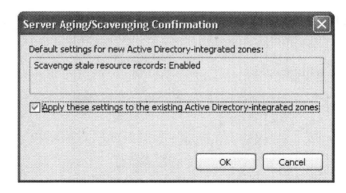

6. Verify the application partitions for the forest and the root domain DNS information. Windows Server 2003 separates forest DNS information from the root domain DNS information. It automatically sets the application partition scope for each set of DNS data. Application partitions are special replication partitions that can store any information that is not related to security principals. These partitions are composed of a set of IP addresses or DNS names defining the scope of the application partition. Using an application partition to store DNS information saves you from having to create copies of DNS zones within child domains as read-only secondary DNS zones. This ensures that all DNS replication is secured and controlled through Active Directory.

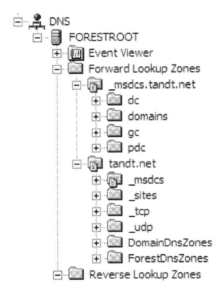

7. To verify that appropriate application partitions have been created for DNS data, right-click on the forward lookup zone name and select Properties from the context menu. WS03 includes a new Replication section under the Zone Type section of the General tab in Zone Properties. This replication section controls the scope of the application partition. WS03 automatically sets the forest DNS data (_msdcs.*forestname*) to use a forest-wide application partition. It sets domain-specific data to use a domain-only application partition. Click OK or Cancel when done.

8. Verify that your forward name resolution settings are appropriate. To do so, right-click on the server name and select Properties.

▶ **QUICK TIP**

DNS is odd in AD. First, you must always begin by left-clicking on an item in the left pane. This updates the view in the right pane. Once this is done, you can right-click on the item to view the object's context menu.

9. Use either Root Hints or Forwarders. If you use Forwarders and you properly configured the client DNS settings earlier, you will see that at least one forwarder address has been entered by the DNS setup process. Add additional DNS servers as required, and then click OK to close the dialog box.

10. To configure your reverse lookup zone, right-click on the Reverse Lookup Zone item in the left pane and select New Zone. This launches the New Zone Wizard. Click Next to begin the zone creation process.

11. Select the zone type, in this case a Primary Zone, and make sure you select to store the zone in Active Directory. Click Next.

12. Define the Application partition for replication of zone data. Since this is information that is domain specific, select To all DNS servers in the Active Directory domain *domainname*. Selecting this option is the same as selecting the To all domain controllers in the Active Directory domain *domainname* option since all domain controllers in this forest will host the DNS service. Click Next.

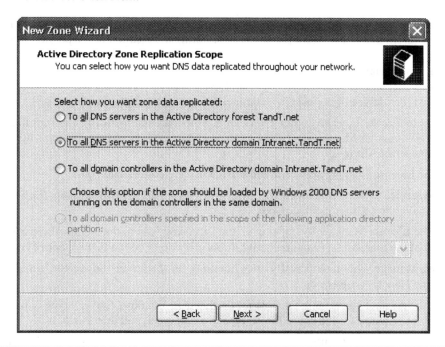

▶ **QUICK TIP**

To have the New Zone Wizard automatically insert the name of the Reverse Zone, select Network ID and type in the network address for the zone, for example, 192.168.1. The New Zone Wizard will automatically insert the value for the Reverse Lookup Zone even though it is not selected. To clear the Network ID box, select the Reverse Lookup Zone Name radio button.

13. Identify the parameters for the Reverse Lookup Zone you want to create, and then click Next.

14. Select Allow only secure dynamic updates, and then click Next.

15. Click Finish to create the zone.

That's it; your DNS server is ready. You can move on to the next stage.

> ### QUICK TIP
>
> *For more information on WS03 DNS, go to http://www.microsoft.com/windows2000/techinfo/ howitworks/communications/nameadrmgmt/w2kdns.asp and http://www.microsoft.com/ windows2000/en/server/help/default.asp?url=/windows2000/en/server/help/ sag_DNS_imp_BestPractices.htm?id=1847.*

Forest License Modes

Next, you need to configure the License Mode for the forest. By configuring this properly now, you won't need to return to this configuration at any time during the creation of the parallel forest.

1. Begin by verifying that you are using the proper license mode on this server. Move to the Control Panel and open the Licensing icon. Ensure that you are using the licensing mode you need. Per device or per user is recommended. Close the dialog box.

2. Make sure that the License Logging Service is set to start automatically and start it. To do so, open the Computer Management console, expand the Services and Applications item in the left pane and select Services.

3. Find the License Logging service in the service list and double-click on it.

4. Set the service to start automatically. Click Apply, then start the service using the Start button in the dialog box. Close the dialog box.

5. Open the License Manager by clicking on the Licensing icon in the Administrative Tools section of the Start Menu (Administrative Tools can also be found in the Control Panel).

6. License Manager will automatically open licensing for the server you are configuring. Click the New License button.

7. Select the product you require licenses for (in this case Windows Server), type in the number of licenses required for the entire forest, type in a comment, and then click OK.

8. WS03 will create the licenses and replicate them throughout the forest. You'll note that since you are using per device or per user licensing, the New License dialog box does not give you the licensing mode choice, but you must select the I agree checkbox, then click OK to close the license agreement dialog box.

In the case of organizations that have a different number of computers and users, WS03 supports the creation of Licensing Groups. In a per device or per user license mode, each client computer requires a client access license, but WS03 tracks licenses on a per user basis. So, if you have more users than computers, you need to create license groups that identify the users who can use the more limited number of computer client access licenses. This ensures that you do not need to purchase more licenses than required and that you are always legally up to date.

Time Service Configuration

Enterprise networks are very sensitive to time synchronization. That's why WS03 includes a built-in time synchronization system. In a WS03 forest, the Windows Time Service configures itself automatically, taking advantage of the time service that is available on domain controllers. A special domain controller, the PDC Emulator, serves as the authoritative source for time within a domain. In a forest, PDC Emulators synchronize with time sources in parent domains. Ultimately, only one server needs manual time synchronization. This is usually the first domain controller in the forest.

You need to decide whether you will synchronize your AD forest with an external time source, use an internal time source, or let the forest synchronize on this server even though its time setting may not be accurate. Each choice has its own issues. Table 4-1 lists a series of accurate time sources provided by the U.S. Naval Observatory Master Clocks in Washington, D.C., and Colorado Springs, Colorado. Use the appropriate setting according to the time zone your source server belongs to. Not setting the time source will create ID 12 events in the System Event Log.

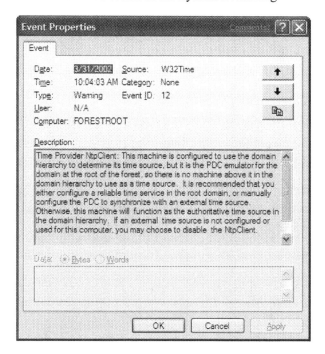

To set a time source server, use the w32tm command line tool. For example, the command to use to set an Eastern time zone clock with three time servers would be:

```
w32tm /config /syncfromflags:manual /manualpeerlist:"ntp2.usno.navy.mil,
tock.usno.navy.mil, tick.usno.navy.mil"
```

U.S. Time Zone	Available Addresses
Eastern	ntp2.usno.navy.mil tock.usno.navy.mil tick.usno.navy.mil ntp-s1.cise.ufl.edu ntp.colby.edu navobs1.oar.net gnomon.cc.columbia.edu tick.gatech.edu navobs1.mit.edu
Central	ntp0.mcs.anl.gov navobs1.wustl.edu tick.uh.edu
Mountain	navobs1.usnogps.navy.mil navobs2.usnogps.navy.mil
Pacific	montpelier.caltech.edu bigben.cac.washington.edu tick.ucla.edu usno.pa-x.dec.com
Alaska	ntp.alaska.edu
Hawaii	tick.mhpcc.edu
Note: More information can be found at http://tycho.usno.navy.mil/ntp.html.	

Table 4-1   U.S. Naval Observatory Master Time Servers

This will set the first DC to synchronize time with one of the three computer systems listed. Remember, to do this, you will have to open the UDP port (123) in your firewall to allow SNTP traffic.

Alert Management Configuration

Most enterprise networks use a system-wide alert management tool. This is performed through the Simple Network Management Protocol (SNMP). This protocol must be installed on all servers and computers if the alert management system is to work. Because there are security risks in running this service without a rigid configuration, its configuration must be customized.

1. Begin by installing the SNMP service on your server. Use the Add/Remove Programs item in the Control Panel and click Add/Remove Windows Components. This will launch the Windows Components Wizard.

2. Select the Management and Monitoring Tools item in the list (but don't check the box), and then click Details.

3. Select the Simple Network Management Protocol and if your alert management tool supports it, select the WMI SNMP Provider, and then click OK. The WMI SNMP Provider will provide much richer information to the SNMP agent.

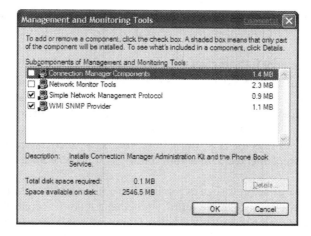

4. Click Next once you're back to the Windows Component Wizard. The installation process will begin. You will require either the installation CD or access to a network share containing the WSE installation files.

5. Once SNMP is installed, proceed to its security configuration. To do so, you need to find the SNMP Service in the Computer Management Console. Double-click on it when you locate it.

6. Three items need configuration here: Agent Information, Trap Destinations, and SNMP Security Properties. Select the Agent tab and type in the operator's name and physical location.

7. Select the Trap tab and identify the community name and valid trap destinations.

8. Select the Security tab and set the Accepted Community Names. Delete the public community and type in your organization's community. Your community name should be complex and not easy to guess. Select Accept SNMP Packets from these hosts and add the valid hostnames. Click OK when done.

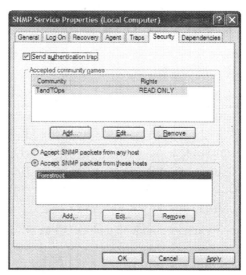

There you are. The first server in your network is almost ready. One final operation needs to be performed.

Default Group Policy and Security Customization

The first DC in a forest includes two default Group Policy objects (GPO): the Default Domain Policy and the Default Domain Controller Policy. While there is no such thing as recurring group policy inheritance between the domains in a forest, there is a one-time GPO inheritance process during domain controller installation. This means that every subsequent domain controller you create in any part of the forest will inherit the settings for these two GPOs. This is an excellent opportunity to ensure that a given set of standards is implemented within your forest. To do so, you must customize both of these default GPOs.

You might want to change settings such as forcing the renaming of the administrator account, enforcing strong passwords throughout the forest, strengthening domain controller security settings, and much more. The suggested parameters for both of these policies are outlined in Chapter 8, which covers Enterprise Security. Be sure to review these settings and modify the ones you deem appropriate for your environment.

In addition, this is the time to raise domain and forest functional levels. Since there is only one domain controller, you will not have to wait for replication to complete while performing this task. Replication will occur, however, when you install additional domain controllers. Remember, you need to raise the functional level of the domain first, then the forest.

1. To raise domain functional level, open Active Directory Domains and Trusts from the Administrative Tools in the Start Menu.

2. Right-click on the domain name and select Raise Domain Functional Level from the context menu.

3. Two domain functional levels are available since WS03 is automatically installed in Windows NT Mixed Mode: Windows 2000 and WS03 functional levels. Select Windows Server (version 2003), and then click Raise.

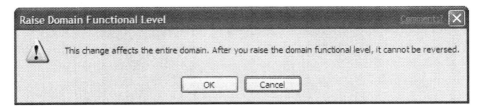

4. WS03 will warn you that this action cannot be undone. Click OK to continue.

5. Click OK when WS03 indicates that the domain functional level has been raised.

6. To raise the level of the forest, right-click on Active Directory Domains and Trusts just above the domain name, and select Raise Forest Functional Level from the context menu.

7. A single functional level is available for forests. Click Raise.

8. WS03 will warn you that this action cannot be undone. Click OK to continue.

9. Click OK when WS03 indicates that the forest functional level has been raised.

10. You can now view the properties of the domain to see that both functional levels are raised.

Next, you should proceed to the creation and the customization of your accounts. The first thing to do is to rename the administrator's account.

1. Launch Active Directory Users and Computers from the Administrative Tools in the Start Menu.

2. To view all of the objects in this console, open the View menu and select Advanced Features. WS03 will display all of the hidden objects in this console.

3. Move to the Users container and right-click on the Administrator account to select Rename.

4. Rename the Administrator account to a complex name that is hard to guess.

5. Create a backup administrator account by right-clicking on the Administrator account and choosing Copy.

6. Name the new account and assign it a password. Click OK when done.

7. You can fill in the properties for both administrative accounts by right-clicking on the account and selecting Properties.

Once this is complete, your first server will be ready. Make sure you verify every aspect of this server's configuration before moving on. You will then be ready to proceed to the creation of the second domain controller for the forest root domain.

Creation of the Second DC in the Forest Root Domain

The second domain controller in the forest root domain is much simpler to create than the first. You need to perform the installation of the server, install Active Directory with DNS, review the configuration of the DNS Server, install SNMP, and migrate two of the Operation Master roles. Once this is complete, you will need to configure and verify the proper operation of the AD replication system. Then you'll be ready to move on to the creation of the Global Child Production Domain.

Server Installation and Configuration

Proceed with the standard Server Installation Process. Make sure the Server Kernel is up to date and perform a quality control on the server. This server can be configured to be a Member Server of the TandT.net domain since it is destined to become a domain controller for this domain. If you decide to install it in a workgroup, ensure that at the very least, it is part of the TANDT workgroup. This will facilitate the communication process with the TandT.net domain because it uses the same NetBIOS name.

Also, remember to configure TCP/IP client properties in the same way that you configured the first server in the network. There is one variation here, though: you can configure the DNS addresses to be itself as the first address, and the first DC as the second address.

DC Promotion

Next, promote this server to a domain controller. Use the same procedure as with the first domain controller in the forest root domain with the following variations:

1. In the first screen of the Active Directory Installation Wizard, select Additional Domain Controller in an existing domain.

2. Type in appropriate credentials to create the DC in the existing domain. This account must be a member of the Domain Administrators group.

3. Type the name of the domain to join.

4. Locate the Database and Logs as well as the System Volume in the same places as the first DC.

Use the AD consoles to verify the proper operation of the DC after it reboots.

DNS Installation and Configuration

The interactive DC Promotion Wizard does not automatically install the DNS service on the domain controller as it performs the installation of Active Directory. However, this installation can be scripted when mounting massive numbers of domain controllers.

To install the DNS service, return to the Manage Your Server Web page.

1. Click Add or remove a role. This will launch the Configure Your Server Wizard.

2. Review the configuration requirements, and then click Next.

3. Windows Server 2003 will verify the existing roles on the server and produce a selection of installation options.

4. Select DNS Server, and then click Next.

5. Confirm your selection by clicking Next. This launches the DNS Installation Wizard. Click Next.

6. Since you only want to install the DNS service (all zones have been created already), you do not need to configure any forward or reverse lookup zones. But, since the wizard is designed to configure zones during service installation, you will need to select Create a forward and reverse lookup zone from the next screen. When it requests if you want to configure a zone, select No, don't create a forward lookup zone now.

7. Finish the DNS installation. Active Directory replication will automatically replicate information from the first DC you created earlier.

Verify the proper operation of the DNS service by launching the Computer Management console and scrolling down to the DNS service. DNS parameters should be the same as in the first DC for the forest. In addition, no reverse lookup zone needs to be created here since it was created earlier on the first DC. All zones should have been replicated by Active Directory.

Alert Management Configuration

Perform the same operations on this server as were done on the first DC to install and configure the SNMP service. Make sure that proper community names have been entered, that the Public community name has been removed, and that messages are received and sent to approved sources. This will ensure a secure SNMP installation and Alert Management configuration.

Operation Master Role Transfers

Next, transfer the appropriate Operation Master roles to this server. Transferring Operation Master roles is a very delicate procedure. Some roles are extremely sensitive. The Schema Master in particular must be transferred with care since only one Schema Master can exist per forest and the forest schema can be corrupted by the simultaneous existence of two Schema Masters. Operation Master role transfers occur in two situations: during the installation of a forest or domain and during service failures. You must be extremely careful in both cases.

Take the following situation, for example. The Schema Master server fails. It is turned off for repairs. An administrator seizes the Schema Master role and applies it to another DC in the forest. The original server is repaired and reinserted in the network without removing its Schema Master role. The consequence: two Schema Masters in the forest and a corrupt schema. The AD database must be reloaded from backups. As you can see, you must be as careful with the Schema Master role as with the schema itself. Only stringent processes and procedures can help ensure the proper operation of the enterprise network.

Several different tools are required to migrate Operation Master roles:

- **Schema Master**   Use the Active Directory Schema MMC
- **Domain Naming Master**   Use the Active Directory Domains and Trusts MMC
- **PDC Emulator, RID Master, Infrastructure Master**   Use the Active Directory Users and Computers MMC

Since you need to transfer both the Domain Naming and Infrastructure Masters, you will need to use two AD consoles to perform the task. The operation can also be performed from the command line using the NTDSUtil command. But since it only has to be done once, use the consoles. It is easier and will familiarize you with the contents of AD.

Begin with the Domain Naming Master.

1. Open the Active Directory Domains and Trusts console on the target DC.

2. Right-click on Active Directory Domains and Trusts, just above the domain name, and select Operation Master from the context menu.

3. Click Change to select the name of the DC to which you want to transfer the role.

4. Click Close when done.

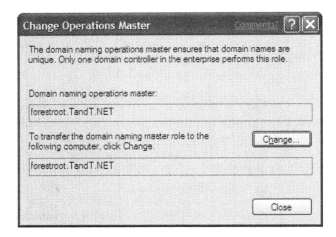

5. Move to Active Directory Users and Computers.

6. Right-click on the name of the domain and select Operation Master from the context menu.

7. Select the Infrastructure tab and click Change to select the target DC.

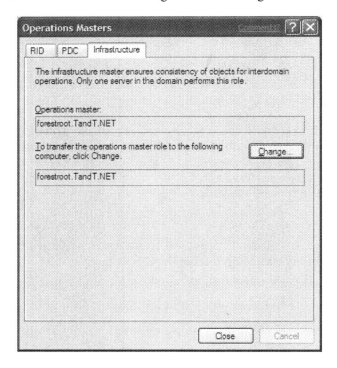

8. Click Close when done.

The operation is complete. Your second DC has now been created and configured. Perform a quality check to ensure that everything is operating normally within both DCs. Once everything has passed quality control, proceed to the creation of the global child production domain.

Creation of the First DC in the Global Child Production Domain

The production domain DCs are slightly different from the forest root and other domain controllers because the production domain is where massive domain information will be stored. Thus one of the configuration differences you should make is to create a special disk on the server to store AD database logs. It is a standard database server practice to store transaction logs and databases on separate disks when database volume is high. This practice needs to be applied to domain controllers that will store massive amounts of data. This is the case for production domain controllers.

Otherwise, the installation of this DC is very similar to the installation of the preceding DCs. In fact, every operation is the same except for the following:

- **Server disk structure**   An additional 2 GB drive should be created in the RAID partition (drive E).
- **Client TCP/IP configuration**   The DNS servers should be set to this server, then one of the root domain servers.
- **Dummy DNS delegation creation**   You need to delegate the name of this domain in the forest root DNS server. This is a "dummy" delegation because the server to which you need to delegate it does not exist yet.
- **DC promotion**   This will be the first DC in a new domain. This will also install the DNS service.
- **DNS configuration finalization**   The DNS service configuration needs to be finalized.
- **Account creation**   The Administrator account needs to be renamed and a backup account should be created. You'll also need a special account for the DHCP service to be installed later.

The following procedures will highlight these differences. It will still be necessary to apply all of the modifications outlined in the server configuration worksheet.

▶ NOTE

It may be possible that your parallel network needs to host two child domains as soon as it is ready. If your corporate applications do not run on Windows Server 2003 and need to be converted, you may have to create the Development domain as soon as possible to support the redevelopment process. If this is the case, simply use exactly the same creation procedure for the Development domain that is outlined for the Production domain. Keep in mind that it may contain less data, though.

Creating the Dummy DNS Delegation

Return to the forest root server and use the Computer Management console to create a DNS delegation. Use the following procedure:

1. Right-click on the TandT.net Forward Lookup Zone to select New Delegation from the context menu. This launches the New Delegation Wizard. Click Next.

2. Type in the name of the domain you want to delegate, in this case Intranet. Click Next.

3. Click Add. Type in the fully qualified domain name of the first domain controller in the child domain (for example, ChildDomainOne.Intranet.TandT.net) and type in its IP address. Click Add and then click OK. The server is added to the delegation list. Click Next. Click Finish to complete the delegation.

This delegation is required to force the DC promotion process to install the DNS service and create the proper application partition.

▶ **NOTE**

You must type in the name of the first domain controller of the child domain and its IP address even if it doesn't actually exist yet. This fools DC Promo into thinking that the DNS service for this zone doesn't work right and forces it to launch the DNS service installation.

Performing DC Promotion

On the first DC for the child domain, use the same procedure as with the first DC in the forest with the following modifications:

1. In the first screen of the Active Directory Installation Wizard, select Domain Controller for a new domain.

2. In the next screen, select Child domain in an existing domain tree.

3. Type in appropriate credentials to create the DC in the existing forest. This account must be a member of the Enterprise Administrators group.

4. Type the name of the forest to join and the name of the new domain.

5. Locate the Database and Logs as well as the System Volume. Note that the AD database Logs should be located on drive E.

6. The wizard will try to locate an appropriate DNS record for the domain. It will fail because of the dummy DNS delegation you created earlier. Install and configure DNS in the same manner as you did for the first DC in the forest.

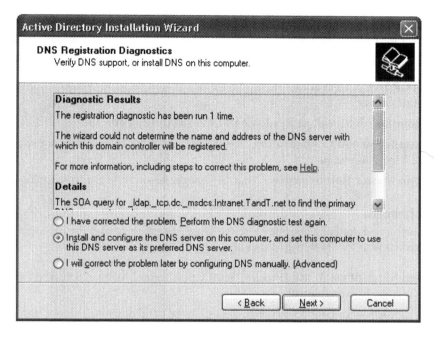

Use the AD consoles to verify the proper operation of the DC after it reboots. You can proceed to the next operation, finalizing DNS configuration.

Finalizing the DNS Configuration

Since the DNS service is installed, all you need to do here is finalize its configuration. Perform the same steps outlined in the DNS configuration finalization section described earlier during the creation of the first DC in the forest. Once the DNS service configuration is complete, you can proceed to the modification of the Administrator account and the creation of a backup administrative account for this domain. You will require an additional account in this domain. This account will be used as credentials for DHCP/DNS interaction. It should be a service account with domain administration privileges. Use a complex name and password; ensure that the user cannot change passwords and that passwords never expire. Make note of this account because it will be required when configuring the DHCP service on Member Servers.

You will not need to raise the functionality level for this domain since you performed this action for the forest during the creation of the first DC. Native WS03 forests will only allow native WS03 child domains to be created. You are now ready to complete the child domain preparation.

Creating the Second DC in the Global Child Production Domain

This installation will be very similar to the installation of the second DC in the forest root domain. The major difference is the migration of the domain's Operation Master roles. Since this is a child domain, it does not include any forest-wide Operation Master roles.

In addition, the remaining three servers, this DC and the two Network Infrastructure Servers will all belong to the production domain; therefore all three can be staged at the same time and installed as Member Servers for this domain. Once these servers are staged, set the two Network Infrastructure Servers aside for the time being while you complete the configuration of the second DC for this domain. This DC will be the same as the first DC in this domain, with the following differences:

- **Client TCP/IP Configuration**   The DNS servers should be set to this server, then the other DC for this domain.
- **DC Promotion**   This will be an additional DC in an existing domain.
- **DNS Installation and Configuration**   Once again, only the DNS service is required. AD will replicate zone information.
- **Operation Master Role Transfer**   Migrate the Infrastructure Master role to this server.

Performing DC Promotion

Promote this server to a domain controller. Use the same procedure as with the first domain controller in the child domain with the following variations:

1. In the first screen of the Active Directory Installation Wizard, select Additional Domain Controller in an existing domain.
2. Type in appropriate credentials to create the DC in the child domain. This account must be a member of the Domain Administrators group.
3. Type the name of the domain to join.
4. Locate the Database and Logs as well as the System Volume in the same places as the first DC.

Use the AD consoles to verify the proper operation of the DC after it reboots.

Proceed to the installation of the DNS service using exactly the same procedure as with the second DC for the forest root domain (install the service only).

Operation Master Role Transfers

Use the Active Directory Users and Computers console to seize the Infrastructure Master role for this server. It is the same procedure as for the second DC in the forest root domain.

You do not need to move any other Operation Master roles at this time, but you may once this domain grows to its intended size. If you expect to have more than 50,000 users in your production domain, you will need to create a dedicated PDC Emulator. But this is not necessary at this time since directory objects have not been created yet. And since you are performing a migration of objects from Windows NT or Windows 2000 domains to the new WS03 forest, you will not require this until enough objects have been migrated.

Two strategies can be used for data migration:

- **Create all DCs first.**   Deploy DCs once the parallel network is up and running, then migrate users and other objects. For this strategy to work, you need enough new computers to create all of the DCs.
- **Migrate users and create DCs as you go.**   In this case, use your judgment, but you might decide to add new DCs at every 500 users migrated (depending on whether it is a central or

regional DC). Of course, you will need to add at least a DC in each remote region that has more than a given number of users (10 or more if you can afford the server hardware).

In addition, the second DC does not need to be a Global Catalog server since you will be adding more DCs to this domain as it grows. Thus you can be guaranteed that the site that holds this DC will have at least one more which can act as the Global Catalog server for the site. In this manner, you will not be faced with potential problems that might incur from the cohabitation of a GC and the Infrastructure Master.

Finally, when you create massive numbers of domain controllers, you will most likely want to automate the process. Like the setup of the operating system, DC promotion can be scripted with unattended text files. This scripted installation can also automatically include the DNS service. Use the following command to perform automated DC promotion:

```
dcpromo /answer:filename
```

where *filename* is the name and location of the unattended installation text file.

In addition, you can repair DCs and avoid network replication with WS03. To do so, you require an AD backup. This can be done to CD, to tape, or even to a network share. Then, if you need to rebuild a remote DC, you can use the following command:

```
dcpromo /adv
```

This will display an additional data source screen which lets you input AD data from the backup copy, reducing the amount of replication required. Once the DC is rebuilt, normal AD multimaster replication will take over and update this DC's contents. Even if you choose a network location for backup data, you can discard extra information and limit the data transfer to the new DC during its creation. This method is impractical for DC staging since most DCs will be staged in a central area with high-speed connections.

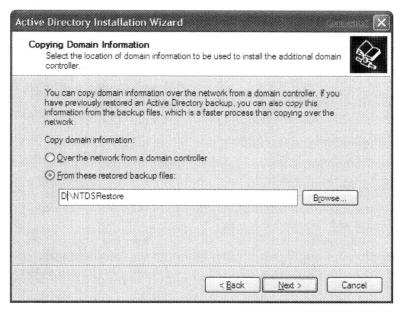

As for the DC you are currently installing, proceed with all of the operations outlined in the second child domain DC worksheet. Once you are finished, you will be ready to proceed to the preparation of the two Network Infrastructure Servers.

> ▶ **QUICK TIP**
>
> *Don't forget to go back to the root domain DNS service and add this DC to the records in the DNS delegation for the Intranet.TandT.net DNS zone. You will need to add records to this delegation each time you add a DC in the Intranet domain.*

Connecting the Enterprise Network

Your parallel network is almost ready. Two more services need to be prepared in order for the parallel network to be able to accept client computers and users. These two services are part of the Network Infrastructure Server role:

- Centralized IP addressing
- Legacy name resolution, since Internet name resolution is performed by the directory service

Both of these roles will be played by a minimum of two servers located in different sites if possible. The configuration of both servers will be almost identical, but of course, each will have some slight modifications because they are in different physical locations.

Network Infrastructure Staging Activities

The activities that must be performed to install both Network Infrastructure Servers are detailed in the Network Infrastructure Server Configuration Checklist illustrated in Figure 4-6. They include four activities: server preparation, DHCP configuration, WINS configuration, and system verification. The first three activities are repeated for each of the two servers.

Server Installation and Configuration

Both of the Network Infrastructure Servers should be Member Servers only. Both should belong to the production domain since this is where their services will be needed most. Few legacy operations will occur in the forest root domain so legacy name resolution is rarely required. The forest root domain will also have very few objects such as users and computers, therefore it will not be necessary to dynamically assign IP addresses to these objects.

Both of these servers use the basic Server Kernel and can have been staged at the same time as the last domain controller previously. If not, perform a basic staging operation for each of these servers and join them to the production domain. Also perform a quality control check on the servers themselves before proceeding to the next step.

Network Infrastructure Server Configuration Checklist

Server Preparation
☐ Install and name the two servers as Member Servers of the production domain
☐ Install and configure the DHCP and WINS services on the first Member Server
DHCP Configuration
☐ Configure DHCP Global Options
☐ Configure DHCP Scopes and Scope Options
☐ Configure User Class IDs if required
☐ Configure Address Reservations for each scope on this server
☐ Activate the DHCP scopes and Authorize the DHCP server
WINS Configuration
☐ Configure the WINS service
☐ Activate WINS backups
☐ Configure WINS replication
Server Preparation
☐ Install and configure the DHCP and WINS services on the second Member Server
DHCP Configuration
☐ Configure DHCP Global Options
☐ Configure DHCP Scopes and Scope Options
☐ Configure User Class IDs if required
☐ Configure Address Reservations for each scope on this server
☐ Activate the DHCP scopes and Authorize the DHCP server
WINS Configuration
☐ Configure the WINS service
☐ Activate WINS backups
☐ Configure WINS replication
System Verification
☐ Verify the operation of both DHCP and WINS Services in the network

Figure 4-6   The Network Infrastructure Server Configuration Checklist

Configuring the First Network Infrastructure Server

Once your servers are ready, you can proceed to the service installation. The two services that are required to perform network infrastructure management are DHCP and WINS. Both will coexist on the same machines.

WS03 does not include very many improvements or new features for DHCP. Most features that were delivered with Windows 2000 have not required major improvements. The most significant change is the Alternate Client Configuration for clients using DHCP and an improved Backup and Restore function for the DHCP database. You can now back up and restore a DHCP database directly from the DHCP console.

Since Windows 2000, the DHCP service is closely integrated to the DNS service. The DHCP service can enable dynamic updates to the DNS namespace for any clients that support these updates. For clients that do not support the updates, DHCP can perform the update for them. In addition, the DHCP server must now be authorized in Active Directory, ensuring that only official DHCP servers can operate on any given enterprise network.

If you already have a DHCP and WINS strategy in place, there is probably no need to modify it unless you feel you need to. Remember, a WS03 DHCP server can easily manage 1,000 scopes and 10,000 clients, given the proper hardware capabilities. In addition, though WINS is still required in WS03 networks, its use has been greatly diminished. So depending on the size of your network, you may determine that two WINS servers for redundancy are more than enough for your production network.

▶ *NOTE*

DHCP is disk intensive. DHCP servers should have high-performance hard disks and a lot of RAM. Paging files should also be set to maximum values (see Chapter 2).

Service Installation and Configuration

Once again, you will use the Manage Your Server Web page to add the two services, DHCP and WINS, to your server.

1. Launch the Configure Your Server Wizard by clicking Add Or Remove A Role. Click Next to continue.

2. In the Server Role page, select DHCP Server, and then click Next.

3. Review your selections, and then click Next. WS03 will begin the DHCP service installation process. This process will require access to the WSE installation files.

4. Once the installation process is complete, the Configure Your Server Wizard will launch the Create New Scope Wizard. Cancel this operation. It is not required at this time since you will require more than a single scope for the enterprise network. Click Finish on the Configure Your Server Wizard.

5. Once again, click Add or remove a role in Manage Your Server. Click Next to proceed.

6. Select WINS Server in the Server Role page and click Next. WS03 will begin the WINS service installation process. This process will also require access to the WSE installation files.

7. Click Finish to close the Configure Your Server Wizard when done.

The Manage Your Server Web page should now include both new server roles. You can use this page to view the next steps for each service or begin using the service immediately.

Configuring DHCP Values

There are a number of steps required to configure DHCP properly. First, as in Windows NT, you begin by configuring global scope options. Global scope options include the same as Windows NT, but local scope options will now include the DNS server since DNS is now integrated to Active Directory and each client will most likely find a DNS server that is local to its network (especially in regions).

You'll also want to configure user class options if you need to use them. One example of a useful user class is a special class for mobile users. This allows you to differentiate mobile users and set their lease duration to a shorter time period than those of the PC workstations in your network. Thus, when a mobile user goes from one site to another, addresses are automatically released when they leave the site.

Next, you configure DHCP scopes and scope-specific options. If you use the 80/20 rule for scope redundancy (creating a scope on two servers and enabling 80 percent of the scope on one and 20 percent on the other), you will need to create each scope and exclude the appropriate range on each server. Once all scopes are created, you must join them into a superscope. Superscopes are scope groupings that allow the DHCP server to service more than one subnet. They are required whenever multinetting is used, thus they are required in an enterprise network. Use the superscope to include all of the scopes in a set of server ranges. Superscopes should be the same on both the servers you create.

Each of the two servers you configure should include the same address reservations, especially if these reservations are for servers such as domain controllers. In this way, the reservation will stand no matter which DHCP server responds to the DHCP request. Servers using dynamic address allocation should also have their Alternate Configuration set to the same values as the reservation.

In Windows Server 2003, DHCP services must be authorized and scopes must be activated. This is quite useful since you can configure your server, review all scopes, and correct potential errors before putting the server into service. In addition, scope activation can act as a failsafe mechanism where spare scopes are prepared before they are actually required and activated only as needed.

▶ | **QUICK TIP**

It is very important to fully document your DHCP information. An excellent DHCP address worksheet is available from the TechRepublic Web site at http://www.techrepublic.com/download_ item.jhtml?id=r00220020409van01.htm&src=search. You must be a member to access this worksheet.

The best place to work with both the DHCP and the WINS services is the Computer Management console. All system services are listed under Services and Applications.

1. To begin configuring the DHCP server, launch the Computer Management console.

2. Locate the DHCP service and begin by setting the Server Properties. This is done by right-clicking on DHCP and selecting Properties. Move to the DNS tab and set the DNS update settings you require. Since this is a parallel network that should only host Windows 2000, XP, or WS03 systems, the default settings are fine. If you must allow down-level clients, choose to have the DHCP server update A and PTR records for them. Next, move to the Advanced tab

and click Credentials. This will allow you to input the account you created earlier to ensure that you can always track DHCP operations within DNS servers. Click OK when done.

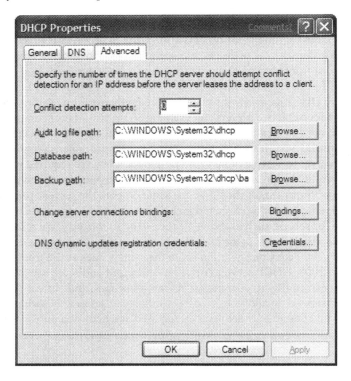

3. This is an ideal time to set up user classes if you wish to use them. They can then be assigned as server options. The procedure for creating and using user-defined classes is outlined in the next section.

4. To input your server options, right-click on Server Options and choose Configure Options from the context menu.

5. Configure the following options as a minimum: Router, DNS Servers, DNS Domain Name, WINS/NBNS Name Servers, and WINS/NBT Node Type. Click OK when done. This will set the global options for all scopes on this server. DNS servers are set globally even though they will be overridden by local scope values. In this way, a DNS server is always available for all clients. WINS/NBT Node Type should be set to H-node. H-node resolution is best even in wide-area networks because it greatly reduces the amount of broadcasting on each network.

6. To create your first DHCP scope, right-click on the DHCP item and select New Scope from the context menu. DHCP will launch the New Scope Wizard. This wizard allows you to input all of the values for the scope: starting address, end address, exclusions and even scope-specific options. Even though the wizard displays options that are not required locally, such as WINS servers, simply skip these screens by clicking Next. You can choose to activate the scope or not at the end. It is best to skip activation at this stage. This lets you review all of your settings before activation.

7. Repeat this procedure for each scope you require. Remember to exclude 80 or 20 percent of the scope depending on where you want the main portion of the scope to be hosted.

▶ **NOTE**

Superscopes cannot be created until at least one scope has been created on a DHCP server.

8. Once all scopes have been created, right-click on DHCP again and select New Superscope. This will launch the New Superscope Wizard. Click Next to proceed. Name the superscope, then select the scopes that will be part of this superscope. Close the dialog box when done. Once a superscope is created, new scopes can be added to it in one of two ways: the scope can be created within the superscope by right-clicking on the superscope name and selecting New Scope, or the scope can be created outside the superscope and added to the superscope once created. This is done by right-clicking on the scope and selecting Add To Superscope.

9. You now want to select the appropriate scope to create reservations within it. Click Reservations in the left pane, then right-click on Reservations and choose New Reservation from the context menu. Fill in the reservation details. You will need the MAC address for each of the network cards for which you want to reserve an IP address. MAC addresses can be displayed by typing ipconfig /all at the command prompt of the system for which the reservation is required. Close the dialog box by clicking Add. Repeat as necessary.

10. After you have reviewed your DHCP settings, you can activate the scopes and authorize the server. One advantage of using superscopes is that you can activate the entire superscope in one fell swoop. Right-click on the superscope name and select Activate from the context menu. Now that all scopes are activated, authorize the server. Make sure you are using a domain administrator account, then right-click on DHCP and select Authorize from the context menu.

Your first DHCP server is now ready. You can move on to configuring the WINS service. As you'll see, this service is very easy to configure.

▶ **NOTE**

Remember to include regional DNS server addresses when you configure regional DHCP scopes. The specific addresses you add to the regional scope will override the generic addresses provided by global DHCP defaults, making sure regional users use their local DNS server instead of central DNS servers.

Defining User Classes

As mentioned previously, user classes are quite useful when you want to designate special DHCP assignments to specific classes of machines in your network. For example, you can use a user class to define mobile computers and, once defined, ensure that their lease duration is shorter than that of workstations. You can also ensure that whenever the mobile computer is shut down, it releases the IP address lease it was granted. This makes it more effective for users who frequently move from one site to another.

User classes are defined within DHCP.

1. Right-click on DHCP in the Computer Management console and select Define User Classes.
2. Click Add in the User Class dialog box.
3. In the New Class dialog box, type the class Display Name and Description, and then place your cursor directly below the word ASCII. Type in the class name. You will note that the New Class dialog box inputs the ASCII values as you type characters. Do not modify these characters! Remember class names are case sensitive. You'll need to make note of how you spelled the class name. Repeat the process for each class you need to add.

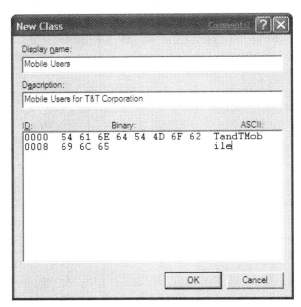

4. Make sure your classes have been added, then click the Close button to close the User Class dialog box.

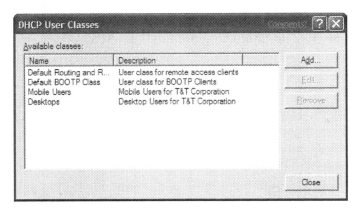

5. Back in the Computer Management console, right-click on the Server Options item and select Configure Options. Move to the Advanced tab and select Microsoft Windows 2000 Options as the Vendor Class and Mobile Users as the User Class. Set the value for option 002, Microsoft Release DHCP Lease On Shutdown Operating System by clicking the checkbox.

6. Change the Vendor Class to DHCP Standard Options to set option 51, Lease. The value is in the form 0x*seconds*, where *seconds* is the number of seconds for lease duration. For example, 0x86400 means 24 hours.

7. You will need to set this user class on mobile systems. To do so, you need to use the ipconfig command on each computer. This setting can be performed at PC staging. The command structure is as follows:

```
ipconfig /setclassid adapter_name class_id
```

For example, if your class ID is TandTMobile, your command would be:

```
ipconfig /setclassid Local Area Connection TandTMobile
```

Remember, class IDs are case sensitive. You must type in the exact class ID wording for it to work properly.

User-defined class options can be assigned to either server or scope options depending on whether they apply to systems in all scopes or only to systems in specific scopes.

User-defined classes are also useful for the assignation of domain names to systems that are located in the same physical locations. For example, if you have users in the same physical location that use different domains such as the Intranet and Development domains, you can use a user-defined class to ensure that systems register DNS values in the proper DNS domain controller. Be sure that you use the user-defined class for the smallest number of systems. This will make it easier to stage and manage the systems.

Configuring WINS Settings

WINS hasn't changed much since Windows 2000 and even then it didn't change much from Windows NT. It can now accept replication partners, though, giving you more control over replication sources. Two great features were also added in Windows 2000: persistent connections and record verification. Persistent connections ensure that a link is always open between push replication partners. This provides real-time replication capabilities for WINS servers. Record verification performs a consistency check on registered names, replicating only valid records from the database. Otherwise, the configuration you used with WINS in your current network should work with WINS in Windows Server 2003.

To configure WINS settings for this server, open the Computer Management console and move to the WINS service.

1. Right-click on the WINS item and select Properties from the context menu.

2. Review the WINS server properties and ensure they are modified if required.

3. To set automatic WINS Backups, simply type the location of the backup file. You can also check the Back up database during server shutdown option. Click OK to close the dialog box when done.

4. Now, add a replication partner. This partner is the second server you will prepare afterwards. Right-click on Replication Partners and select New Replication Partner. Type in the name of the other server. If it isn't available, you will get another dialog box stating the server name cannot be validated. If so, type in the server's IP address and click OK.

5. Right-click on Replication Partners to set replication Properties. Make sure the option to Replicate only with partners is set under the General tab, then move to the Push Replication tab. Select all the options on this tab. This will turn on real-time replication.

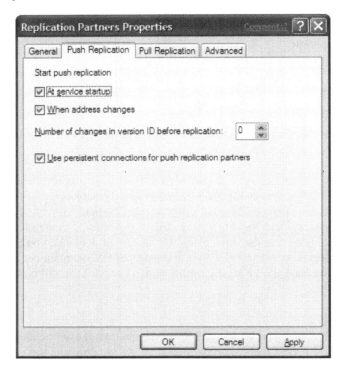

6. Configure Pull Replication settings on the appropriate tab, and then turn on the Enable automatic partner configuration option in the Advanced tab. WINS uses multicasting to provide configuration parameters to its replication partners. This ensures consistent configurations.

7. Click OK to close the dialog box.

That's it; your first Network Infrastructure Server configuration is complete.

▶ **NOTE**

More information on WINS is available at http://www.microsoft.com/technet/treeview/ default.asp?url=/TechNet/prodtechnol/windows2000serv/evaluate/featfunc/nt5wins.asp and in the TechNet articles Q185786 and Q239950.

Configuring the Second Network Infrastructure Server

The configuration of the second Network Infrastructure Server is the same as the first, but in reverse. You need to install and configure both DHCP and WINS. Create all of the DHCP scopes in the DHCP server, make sure that these scopes are the reverse of the 80/20 configuration you performed on the first server, activate all scopes, and authorize the DHCP server. Don't forget to set DHCP server credentials to ensure secure DNS updates.

When you are finished with DHCP, configure WINS properties and create the WINS replication partner. Now that the first server exists, you should not face any error messages during this configuration. Refer to the server configuration worksheets for complete server configuration steps.

WINS Connectivity and DNS Settings

Depending on your migration strategy, you may need to temporarily configure your Windows Server 2003 WINS servers to share information with the legacy network you are replacing. If this is the case, create only one-way replication partnerships: from the WS03 network to the legacy network. You do not want your new WINS databases to fill up with objects that have nothing to do with your new network.

In addition, DNS can be linked to WINS for additional name resolution support. If you have done your homework and have convinced the organization to move to a complete Windows 2000, XP, or WS03 network, this connection should not be necessary. Even though most Microsoft networks still require NetBIOS name resolution to some degree, failures of DNS name resolutions, especially failures that could be solved with WINS, should be very rare.

Moving Servers and Configuring Domain Replication

Now that all your servers are ready, you can move them to a new physical site. When you move DCs to another site, you need to ensure that Active Directory replication operates properly. For this, you need to work with the Active Directory Sites and Services console. Chances are that you'll also have to modify some of the properties of the DCs and Network Infrastructure Server you move. As you know, it is preferable not to modify a DC's IP address. Thus, your staging center would ideally include a router that supports the assignation of multiple subnets. In this way, you can actually give the appropriate addresses to these two DCs right from the start (as well as the DHCP/WINS server). Then, when you move them, you won't need to change addresses.

However, if you need to do so, it isn't the end of the world. Just make sure that everything continues to operate properly once you've changed addresses. Now that you have DCs located in a different physical location, you need to configure domain replication. The activities you need to perform include the following:

1. Create a new site and enable Universal Group Membership Caching.
2. Add subnet(s) to the site.
3. Create a Site Link for the site.
4. Create a backup Site Link for this site.
5. Modify properties for each Site Link.
6. Install or move DCs into the site.
7. Select the licensing computer for the site.

As you can see, the first five steps are preparatory steps. It is only when you reach the sixth step, placing the DC in the site, that replication actually begins. To configure replication, you will require the site topology report from the site topology planning exercise you performed during your Active Directory design exercise. An example of the contents of this report can be found in Table 3-9 in Chapter 3. You can configure site replication before moving the DCs physically into the site location, but if you do so, the Knowledge Consistency Checker (KCC) service will generate errors within the Directory Service portion of the Event Log. It is best to move the servers first, and then configure replication.

Replication configuration is done through the Sites and Services console.

1. Open Active Directory Sites and Services.

2. Right-click on Sites and select New Site from the context menu.

3. Name the site and select the transport mechanism, in this case IP.

4. Click OK to close the dialog box and create the site.

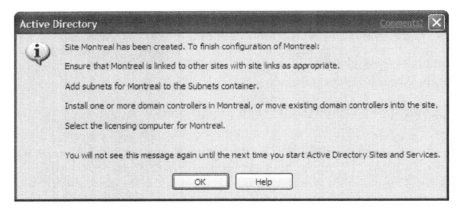

5. View the Properties for the site and check Enable Universal Group Membership Caching. Click OK to close the dialog box.

6. Add a subnet to the site by right-clicking on the Subnets and selecting New Subnet from the context menu.

7. Type in the IP address and the subnet mask to use. Select the site to associate to this subnet. Click OK to create the subnet.

8. Now you want to create the site link for this site. A site link always includes at least two sites. Move to Inter-site Transports and right-click on the IP transport. Select New Site Link from the context menu.

9. Name the site link and identify the two sites in the link. Click OK to create the site link.

10. Repeat the procedure to create the backup site link.

11. As you can see, WS03 automatically assigns a cost and a replication interval to each site link. The default cost is 100 (a value that is appropriate for T1 links). The default replication interval

is 180 minutes. If your physical link is a T1, you don't need to change the site link cost for your main replication link. If not, see Table 3-8 for the recommended values for site link costs. As you'll remember, you don't want to modify either the site replication interval or the site link schedule in order to let the KCC perform its work in optimal fashion.

12. However, you will want to add a description for the main site link you just created. To do so, right-click on the site link and select Properties. Type in the description and change the site link cost if you need to do so. Click OK when done.

13. Type in a description and change the site cost for the backup link as well.

14. Now you need to move the DCs into the new site. Move to the Default-First-Site-Name and right-click on the server you want to move. Select Move from the context menu.

15. Select the destination site and click OK.

16. The final step is to identify the licensing server for the new site. Click the site name and double-click on Licensing Site Settings in the right pane. Click Change to locate a server. Type in the first part of the server name and click Locate. Click OK to use this server as the licensing server. You should use your forest root domain DC as the licensing server in this case. Click OK to close the License Site Settings dialog box.

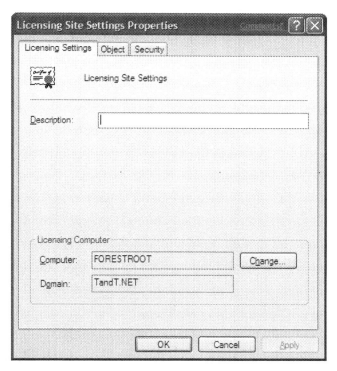

Your replication is now configured.

Two activities remain: designating a Global Catalog server in the new site and enabling the site for Global Catalog caching. The first is a function of the NTDS settings for the server you want to use as a GC and the second is a function of the NTDS settings for the site itself.

1. Expand the site information in the left pane until you see the server names in the site. Select the server you want to make a GC, in this case, the forest root domain server.

2. Double-click on NTDS settings in the right pane.

3. Select the Global Catalog Server checkbox and click OK.

4. To enable the site for GC caching, select the site name in the left pane. In the right pane, double-click on NTDS Site Settings.

5. Select the Enable Universal Group Membership Caching checkbox. Click OK to close the dialog box. Perform this for each site you create.

▶ **QUICK TIP**

You might consider configuring Printer Location Tracking at this time since it is done in this console and must be prepared on DCs. To do so, proceed to the section "Integration with Active Directory" in Chapter 7 and review the steps required to configure this option.

You're all done. Now you need to verify that replication works properly. To test inter-site replication, perform some AD modifications in the AD Users and Computers console and test them from the remote DC. You can use Terminal Services in Administrative mode to do so. Also verify the Directory Service portion of the Event Log to make sure there are no errors.

▶ *CAUTION*

Your parallel network is now ready for prime time. The remaining chapters will show you how to populate this network and ensure its resiliency. Before moving on, though, be sure that you fully test every part of this network. It is the basis of your new enterprise network infrastructure. You want to ensure that everything is running smoothly. It is not too late at this stage to start over and repeat the Parallel Network Creation Process. It will be too late once you have begun populating this network.

Upgrading Active Directory from Windows 2000 to WS03

Upgrading to a native WS03 forest from Windows 2000 is much less complex a process than migrating from Windows NT to Windows Server 2003. The advantage of having a Windows 2000 network is that everything is already in place. You may not need to plan for a new or parallel IP infrastructure. You may not need to perform an AD design, though it is necessary to review the design in light of new WS03 features. Even though this review might indicate a forest restructure, it is a task that is much less complex than creating an entirely new WS03 forest.

▶ *CAUTION*

Only perform a Windows 2000 upgrade to Windows Server 2003 if you performed a clean installation of Windows 2000 when you migrated from Windows NT. If you performed an upgrade from NT to Windows 2000, this might be the right time to review your needs and use the parallel network to move to a native WS03 enterprise network.

Even if you feel you are ready for the upgrade, make sure you review the information presented previously in this chapter to enable new WS03 features in your forest.

Upgrading a production network to Windows Server 2003 is a major undertaking that will affect the entire network. This is why you should proceed with care. It is especially at this stage that you discover the usefulness of the testing and staging processes outlined in Chapter 1. Make sure you thoroughly test your upgrade procedure before you proceed.

The Upgrade Process

The recommended steps for an upgrade from Windows 2000 to WS03 are detailed in the forest staging activities checklist illustrated in Figure 4-7. It is divided into four stages: preparing for the upgrade, performing the upgrade, post-upgrade tasks, and ongoing forest management. Several

Forest Staging Activities Checklist

❶ Preparing for the Upgrade
- ☐ Performing a Forest consistency check
- ☐ Running DC compatibility check
- ☐ Preparing the Upgrade task List
- ☐ Obtaining the Schema modifications authorization

❷ Performing the Upgrade
- ☐ Preparing the forest   ☐ Upgrading DCs
- ☐ Preparing domains   ☐ Automating the upgrade

❸ Post Upgrade Tasks
- ☐ Verifying native WS03 compatibility
- ☐ Migrating domains to native WS03 mode
- ☐ Migrating the Forest to native WS03 mode
- ☐ Updating Forest server roles
  - ☐ Modify DC role (Add/Delete from Global Catalog)
  - ☐ Modify Operation Master roles
- ☐ DNS strategy review
  - ☐ Add DNS service on all DCs
  - ☐ Create/Modify application partitions
- ☐ Reviewing Active Directory replication
  - ☐ Replication within sites
  - ☐ Replication between sites
  - ☐ Create/Modify AD site
  - ☐ Create/Modify replication rules between DCs
- ☐ Restructuring Domains (if required)
  - ☐ Updating Domain structure (movetree command)
  - ☐ Create/Modify OUs
  - ☐ Create/Modify OU structure
- ☐ Implement Forest trusts
  - ☐ Create/Modify trust

❹ Ongoing Forest Management
- ☐ Site coverage monitoring   ☐ Schema modifications
- ☐ Directory replication   ☐ AD operations follow-up and maintenance

Figure 4-7   Windows 2000 Upgrade Checklist

subtasks are derived from each stage. Make sure everything is tested and documented before proceeding in your production network.

Preparing for the Upgrade

The first thing to do to prepare for the upgrade is to perform a *forest consistency check*. This activity basically involves a review of the choices that were performed when planning your Windows 2000 Active Directory. Are they still valid in light of what you have learned from Active Directory and new Windows Server 2003 features? Don't make light of this step. There's never a better time than an infrastructure project to implement structural changes. Since you will be performing a systemwide upgrade, you may as well take the time to check how things are running and see if there are any possible improvements you could make.

The second step is to run Windows Server 2003 Setup with the /checkupgradeonly switch to verify compatibility of every domain controller. This process was outlined in Chapter 2. Retrieve all of the output files and check the status of each of the domain controllers.

Three steps need to be performed before you can move on to the WS03 upgrade:

• Performing an Active Directory Preparation for the forest

• Performing an Active Directory Preparation for every domain

• In addition, if you used a Server Kernel concept as described in Chapter 2 and you installed the Windows 2000 Administration Tools on every DC, you will need to remove them before proceeding.

This should bring your DCs to WS03 compatible levels. One last thing to check is free space. Depending on the size of your directory, you will require a minimum of 1.5 GB of free space on each DC to perform the upgrade.

Next, prepare an *upgrade task list*. This list should detail, step by step, every activity you need to perform to upgrade your Active Directory from Windows 2000 to Windows Server 2003. Set it up as a checklist and check off each item as you proceed with your upgrade. This list should include all of the steps identified in Figure 4-7.

The last step for preparation is to obtain the *schema modification authorization*. Since you are using Windows 2000, you have taken the time to put a schema change management committee in place. You should get its authorization to perform both a forest and a domain preparation. This authorization should include a time window outlining when the upgrade will be possible.

Upgrading to WS03

You're ready to proceed. Remember, test and retest in a laboratory first. Preparing the forest means moving to the Schema Operation Master and executing the adprep /forestprep command. The adprep executable can be found in the I386 folder of the WS03 CDs. Ensure that you are using the proper version of WS03 (refer to Table 1-2 in Chapter 1 for upgrade paths) and execute the following command:

```
D:\i386\>adprep /forestprep
```

where *D* represents your CD/DVD drive letter. Once you consent to the upgrade by typing **C** and pressing ENTER, this will launch the forest preparation process. In fact, this process consists of importing a number of different commands to extend the forest's schema. This process is fairly quick, but by default, it doesn't give you a lot of feedback while executing. Have patience. Don't stop it in the middle because it seems to be hung. Once the preparation is complete, you need to wait until the changes have been replicated to the entire forest. If you performed a forest replication latency calculation during your migration to Windows 2000, you will know exactly how long you need to wait because replication latency is the longest possible time of completion for a forest replication process.

```
C:\WINNT\System32\cmd.exe - adprep /forestprep                          _ □ ×
ADPREP WARNING:

Before running adprep, all Windows 2000 domain controllers in the forest should
be upgraded to Windows 2000 Service Pack 1 (SP1) with QFE 265089, or to Windows
2000 SP2 (or later).

QFE 265089 (included in Windows 2000 SP2 and later) is required to prevent poten
tial domain controller corruption.

For more information about preparing your forest and domain see KB article Q3311
61 at http://support.microsoft.com.

[User Action]
If ALL your existing Windows 2000 domain controllers meet this requirement, type
 C and then press ENTER to continue. Otherwise, type any other key and press ENT
ER to quit.


c
Opened Connection to DOMAINA
SSPI Bind succeeded
Current Schema Version is 13
Upgrading schema to version 30
Connecting to "DOMAINA"
Logging in as current user using SSPI
Importing directory from file "C:\WINNT\System32\sch14.ldf"
Loading entries...................
```

Once the forest change is complete, you can perform the domain preparation on each domain of the forest. This command needs to be performed on the Infrastructure Master for each domain. Execute the following command:

```
D:\i386\>adprep /domainprep
```

where *D* represents your CD/DVD drive letter. If you only want to test the upgrade process for both the forest and the domain, add the /analyze switch to either command. As before, you need to wait for domain replication to complete.

Now you can upgrade each DC to WS03. It is always wise to perform another upgrade compatibility check to ensure that everything is okay. Then proceed with the Windows Server 2003 installation. WS03 will automatically propose an upgrade.

The upgrade process is very simple. No answers need to be given during the upgrade, unless you need to provide special massive storage system drivers. The entire process can be automated as outlined in Chapter 2. Simply create a network share to store the installation source files, share it, and use scripts to perform the DC preparation, the domain preparation, and the Windows Server 2003 upgrade. These scripts can all be executed automatically through Terminal Services Administrative mode.

Post-Upgrade Tasks

Once all DCs have been upgraded, you can migrate your forest to native WS03 mode. But before you do so, you need to verify that every domain in the forest supports native WS03 compatibility. Windows Server 2003 offers two native modes: domain and forest. The native domain mode requires that all services in the domain be compatible to WS03. The forest mode requires every domain in the forest to run compatible applications. Native domains cannot have either Windows NT or Windows 2000 DCs in them, and native forests can only have WS03 DCs.

To migrate your domains and forest to WS03 native mode, first make sure that they meet all of the prerequisite conditions, and then use the following procedure:

1. Open the Active Directories Domains and Trusts console.
2. Right-click on the Console Root.
3. From the context menu, select Raise domain functional level.
4. Click Raise. Agree to all the warning messages.
5. Wait for domain replication to occur. If the forest has more than one domain, raise the functional level of each domain in turn.
6. Once all domains are raised to WS03 functionality, return to the Active Directories Domains and Trusts console.
7. Right-click on the Console Root.
8. From the context menu, select Raise forest functional level.
9. Click Raise. Agree to all the warning messages.
10. You will need to wait for replication to occur to all DCs within the forest before using WS03 native forest functions.

Other operations you might consider at this stage are updating forest server roles and performing a DNS strategy review. If you decide to modify DC roles, you'll find that operations are much the same as they were in Windows 2000. There are great new functionalities such as drag and drop editing within AD MMC consoles that make life a lot easier with AD. Operations you might perform at this stage are:

- Modify DC role (Add/Remove Global Catalog service)
- Modify DC role (Enable Universal Group Membership Caching)
- Modify Operation Master roles

DNS should be on every DC, and if it isn't, you should add it. It doesn't generate a lot of overhead and it makes DC location a lot easier. Next, you can create or modify application partitions to hold DNS data. The DNS Wizard will automatically create these partitions for you. These can be forest-wide or domain-centric. The advantage of application partitions in this case is that you no longer need to create secondary DNS zones anywhere in your network. The DNS infrastructure process is outlined in a previous section titled "DNS Configuration Finalization" for the first server in the parallel network.

Your final migration tasks should cover a review of Active Directory replication. Make sure that all replication works properly. This should include replication within a site and replication between sites. You may need to create or modify AD sites or modify your replication rules to match WS03 best practices.

You may also be interested in restructuring domains. If you find that your original Windows 2000 forest and domain structure does not meet all your needs, you can restructure domains. WS03 offers several tools for this step. The movetree command allows you to move computers and users from domain to domain. This command must be performed on the Infrastructure Master. WS03 also offers the Active Directory Migration Tool. Version 2 of this tool is more advanced than its predecessor. It can migrate users and passwords from one domain or forest to another. You can also use third-party migration tools. Remember that to restructure domains, you will first need to update your domain structure, then create or modify its OU structure, then migrate users and computers.

The final upgrade operation is the implementation of forest trusts. Now that you have WS03 forests, you can decide to implement global forest trusts. These will link multiple forests together. Beware, though! You can easily find the same difficulties in forest trusts that you found in Windows NT domains. Forests are designed to protect schemas. Unless there are significant requirements for forest trust implementations, you should avoid creating them.

Ongoing Forest Management

Ongoing forest management will not be much different with WS03 as it was with Windows 2000. You still use the same tools you used before: Active Directory Sites and Services, Active Directory Domains and Trusts, and Active Directory Users and Computers. But all have increased functionality. Each will be examined in turn as you progress through the WS03 implementation outlined through the Enterprise Network Architecture Blueprint in Chapter 1's Figure 1-5.

Best Practice Summary

This chapter recommends the following best practices:

- Use a parallel network to implement the new enterprise network (unless you already have Windows 2000 and it qualifies for an upgrade).
- Test the implementation process in a laboratory.
- Prepare documentation before proceeding with the network implementation.
- In large environment, do not combine root domain controller roles with the network infrastructure roles.
- Stage all parallel network servers with an up-to-date Server Kernel (see Chapter 2).
- Each server should meet the server sizing requirements.
- If you do not use an automated kernel installation, be sure you perform all steps required for a reference computer.
- Each server should have stringent quality control after staging.
- For DCs, pay special attention to hardware conflict resolution before proceeding with the DC promotion.

- If you have several large sites, separate each double server role physically.

- If you use your existing IP infrastructure in the parallel network, change all IP addresses.

- Use your Active Directory plan (see Chapter 3).

- Raise the domain and forest functionality when you create the first DC in the forest. This ensures that all other domains will be created in native mode.

- Create license groups to manage different numbers of users and computers.

- Use the appropriate settings according to the time zone (see Table 4-1) for time synchronization.

- If the alert management system is to work, install SNMP on all servers and computers (if required). Secure the SNMP service.

- Verify every aspect of the server's configuration before moving on to configure another server.

- If you ever need to do so, transfer the Schema Master with care.

- For better performance, create a special disk on DCs in the GCPD to store AD database logs.

- Create a dedicated PDC Emulator if you expect to have more the 50,000 users in the production domain.

- Create an application data partition before you create the child domain DNS zone partition.

- It is recommended to create both domain and forest-wide application partitions for the production domain DNS data because users from most every other domain will require access to intranet resources.

- DHCP servers should have high-performance hard disks and a lot of RAM, and set the paging files to maximum values.

- Use superscopes to include all of the scopes in a set of server ranges.

- Use user classes to distribute special DHCP values to specific classes of machines in the network.

- Set DHCP server credentials to ensure secure DNS updates.

- For the DHCP service account, use a complex name and password, make sure the user cannot change the password and that the password never expires.

- If you need to interact with the legacy network in terms of WINS name resolution, create only one-way replication with it.

- If you use DHCP for server addresses, especially DCs, use the Alternate Configuration tab as a backup.

- Set at least one DC in each site as a Global Catalog server and enable Universal Group Membership Caching in all sites.

Chapter Roadmap

Use the illustration in Figure 4-8 to review the contents of this chapter.

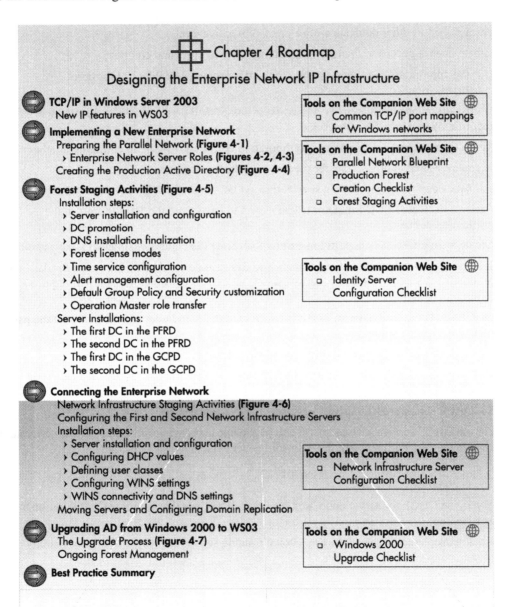

Figure 4-8   Chapter Roadmap

CHAPTER 5

Building the PC Organizational Unit Infrastructure

IN THIS CHAPTER

C hapter 4 described how to put the parallel network in place. Eventually this network will offer complete enterprise services as you migrate users from your existing network to the new infrastructure. But, before you can begin this migration, you need to finalize the network infrastructure you have begun to put in place. Several different activities must be completed before you can claim that your new network is ready to accept users. One of these is the finalization of your organizational unit (OU) infrastructure.

Chapter 3 identified that there were three object types that should be managed through the OU infrastructure: PCs, People, and Services. This chapter begins the finalization of the OU infrastructure with the PC container. To do this, you must finalize three key PC-related elements:

- The PC Group Policy Management Strategy
- The PC Delegation Strategy
- The Enterprise PC Management Strategy

The first of these activities is the design of a PC management infrastructure within the new network. This begins the design of your overall management infrastructure for every object contained in the directory. This design should be complete by the end of Chapter 8 with the design of your Enterprise Security Strategy. Your enterprise network will then be ready to host new objects of every type and offer a complete set of services.

Managing Objects with Active Directory

One of the main purposes of Active Directory is to manage objects. As mentioned before, AD provides a single infrastructure for the integration of the objects people interact with when using an IT infrastructure. In addition, AD provides a centralized infrastructure for the management of these objects. This infrastructure is based on Group Policy objects (GPO). A GPO is a directory object that is designed to define the way a user's computing environment appears and behaves. This includes items such as the contents of the Start Menu, icons on the desktop, ability to modify the desktop, ability to run various software products and more. GPOs can be used to manage PCs, servers, and users.

Group Policy Concepts

GPOs were first introduced with Windows 2000 and were designed to replace the cumbersome system policies used in Windows NT. A GPO can manage the following elements:

- **User and Computer Settings**   Windows Server 2003 includes administrative templates that allow GPOs to write specific settings to user (HKEY_CURRENT_USER—HKCU) and computer (HKEY_LOCAL_MACHINE—HKLM) registry hives.
- **Scripts**   Windows 2000, XP, and Server 2003 can run startup and shutdown scripts as well as logon and logoff scripts. These are normally managed through GPOs.

- **Data Management**   WS03 can redirect user folders from the desktop to a central server location allowing full availability of these folders from any PC as well as centralized backup of user information.
- **Software Lifecycles**   WS03 can deploy software to both desktops and servers so long as the software product is integrated with the Windows Installer service.
- **Security Settings**   WS03 can centrally manage Security Settings for PCs, servers, and users through GPOs. WS03 can also restrict access to software applications through Software Restriction Policies.

Every computer running Windows 2000, XP, or Windows Server 2003 includes a local GPO by default. The settings in this file are applied each time the computer starts up. An organization that wants to standardize certain elements of the desktop and other computer behavior should configure this policy object with default organizational settings and make sure this file is part of the installation set for each computer. Since these GPOs are local, they can be different on each computer. To make the best of local GPOs, you should define a set of parameters for each computer type (PCs, servers, and domain controllers) and change them as little as possible.

The local GPO is located in the %Systemroot%\System32\Group Policy folder. To view this folder, you must enable two settings in the Folder view options (Windows Explorer, Tools menu, Folder Options, View tab):

- Show hidden files and folders
- Hide protected operating system files (Recommended)

Disabling the latter will generate a warning dialog box. The best practice in this regard is to enable the setting to capture a copy of the local GPO you want to deploy, then disable the setting afterward.

Computers running Windows NT, Me, or 9x versions of Windows do not contain local GPOs and will not be affected by Global GPOs deployed by Active Directory. The parallel network should include only up-to-date versions of Windows for all client computers.

▶ **NOTE**

To make the most of your parallel network, make sure you deploy only Windows 2000 or Windows XP PCs, and Windows 2000 or 2003 servers. Ideally, you will deploy only Windows XP and Windows Server 2003 in your new infrastructure. This will ensure that you make the most of this new network and provide the best return on investment because every WS03 feature will be available on your network.

In addition to local Group Policy objects, networks running Active Directory will have centralized GPOs. Compared to local GPOs, centralized GPOs are *management GPOs* because you can modify them in a central location and have them affect any group of objects. Every Active Directory network includes two default policies:

- The Default Domain Policy
- The Default Domain Controller Policy

A specific default domain policy is applied to every domain in an enterprise Windows Server 2003 network. In the example used in Chapters 3 and 4, the T&T enterprise network will have several default domain policies because it has several domains. In the case of your parallel network, you will have two different versions of the policy since only the root and the production domains have been created at this point. The same applies for the Default DC Policy, except that instead of being applied at the domain level, this policy is applied specifically to the Domain Controllers organizational unit.

Policies do not follow the hierarchical path of your AD forest. If you design a new policy in the forest root domain, it will not automatically be applied to child domains that are below the root domain in the hierarchy. This is because policies are domain-specific. If you define a custom policy that you want to apply to every domain in your forest, you will have to copy it from domain to domain. You can also link policies from domain to domain, but this is not a recommended approach because the client must traverse the inter-domain trust to read it. There is one exception that was mentioned in Chapter 4: at the creation of any child domain, it automatically copies the contents of the two default policies from the parent domain. So, in the same manner that you would adjust the local GPO before deploying systems, you should adjust the default GPOs in the forest root domain before you create any of the child domains. This will ensure that a basic set of standards will be applied to both domains and DCs as soon as they are created. The recommended modifications for these two default policies are covered in Chapter 8.

Group Policy Processing

Group Policies are applied in the following order:

1. Computer settings are applied first.
2. User settings are applied second.

It makes sense since the computer starts before a user can log on. In a WS03 network, the computer has its own Active Directory account and must negotiate a logon within the directory before it allows users to log on and open a session.

In addition, local and central GPOs have a specific application order:

1. The local GPO is applied at computer startup.
2. If available, site GPOs are applied next.
3. Domain GPOs are applied after site GPOs.
4. Organizational unit GPOs are applied last. If the object (either computer or user) is located within a child OU and the child OU contains an additional GPO, this GPO is applied last.

This process is often called the *L-S-D-OU* process for local-site-domain-OU application order. Figure 5-1 illustrates the GPO application order. If there are conflicts between policies, the last policy provides the applied setting. For example, if you deny access to an item in the Start Menu in the domain policy, but it is allowed in an OU policy, the result will be that access will be allowed.

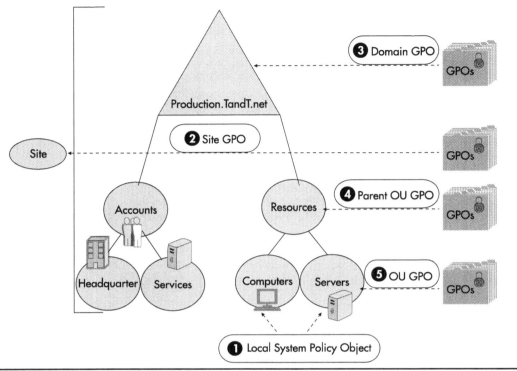

Figure 5-1 The GPO application order

GPO Inheritance (and Blocking)

In addition to the application order, you can control the inheritance settings for GPOs. This means that if you assign a setting at the domain level or any other higher level, you can ensure that your setting is the one that is propagated to the object whether or not there are conflicting settings lower down in the application hierarchy. This is done by forcing GPO inheritance.

Normally, GPOs are inherited automatically throughout the GPO application order. If a setting is enabled at the domain level and it is not configured at the OU level, the domain setting is applied. If a setting is not configured at the domain level and is disabled at the OU level, the OU setting is applied. If a setting is disabled at a parent OU and disabled at the child OU, the setting is not applied. To force GPO inheritance, you can assign the No Override attribute to the GPO. This means that even if the settings are conflicting at the lower end of the hierarchy, the setting with the No Override attribute will be applied.

GPOs are managed in either AD Users and Computers or AD Sites and Services. Since both domains and organizational units are managed in the first of the two consoles, you'll tend to use this console most often to work with GPOs. To set a GPO to No Override, select the properties of the object to which the GPO is attached. This can be a domain, a site (in AD Sites and Services), or an

OU. In the Properties dialog box, select the Group Policy tab. Select the GPO you want to set to No Override and click the Options button in the lower part of the dialog box.

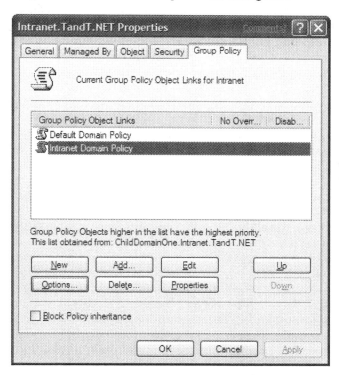

A second dialog box appears. Here you can either set the GPO to No Override or disable it completely. Disabling GPOs is useful as well since it means that you can set up a GPO in a disabled mode and wait until you are ready to activate it before doing so. Select the option you require and click OK when done.

▶ **QUICK TIP**

You can also edit GPOs with the Group Policy Management Console. This free console is available for download from the Microsoft WS03 Web site and provides a single interface for GPO management. It is covered at the end of this chapter. There are also commercial tools such as FAZAM 2000 from Full Armor Corporation (http://www.fullarmor.com/) or NetIQ's Group Policy Administrator (http://www.netiq.com/) that can provide much more comprehensive GPO management capabilities, such as extensive reporting and complex GPO debugging.

In addition to enforcing inheritance, OU administrators can determine when they want to block inheritance. Blocking inheritance is useful when you want to store objects in your directory and give them different settings than those that are set globally. For example, in the PCs OU design illustrated in Figure 3-6 in Chapter 3, there is an external container at the second level. This container is designed to store computers that do not belong to your organization, such as consultants' PCs. In some cases, you want to manage some parameters on consultant systems, especially in the case of developers who are working on long-term projects and who will be creating code that will be deployed in your network. But there are other cases where you do not want to manage the external systems. This is why there are two OUs at the third level of the External OU: Managed and Unmanaged.

The Unmanaged OU is an excellent example of where you would apply the Block Policy Inheritance setting. To block inheritance, right-click on the object where you want inheritance blocked and then select Properties. Move to the Group Policy tab and click the Block Policy Inheritance checkbox at the bottom of the dialog box. Click OK when done.

You have to be very careful with both the No Override and the Block Policy inheritance settings. Between the two, No Override always wins, but if both are applied with abandon, you'll find it really hard to determine the final settings that have been applied to any given object.

It is easily possible to apply any number of GPOs to objects. It is also easy to become confused with GPOs. The organizational unit structure has a direct impact on how GPOs are applied by default. The final result of GPO application is called the *resultant set of policies* (RSoP). Windows Server 2003 includes an RSoP tool that allows you to debug policy application so that you can identify the result of multiple policy application on a specific object.

Policy application begins as soon as the computer is powered on. It uses a ten-step process that is illustrated in Figure 5-2. As you can see, this process relies on several technologies: DNS, ping, the Lightweight Directory Access Protocol (LDAP), and client-side extensions. Also, slow links can affect GPO processing; WS03 considers anything less than 500 Kbps to be a slow link, though this setting can be changed through a GPO. The process is also linked to the Group Policy Container (GPC) which is used to identify the path to each of the Group Policy Templates (GPT) that must be applied. These are located in the domain controller's Sysvol share. To view the GPC, you must enable the advanced features of the AD Users and Computer console.

The GPO application process relies on the GPT.INI file located in the GPT folder for each GPO. This file lists the GPT's current version number. This number is incremented every time you make a change to a GPO. By default, this number change forces objects to reapply the changed settings of the GPO. If the number is the same as it was the last time it was applied, the object does not reapply the GPO, though this behavior can be changed through a Group Policy setting. Once GPOs are applied, all applicable startup scripts are run. Since these scripts are run without a user interface, they are set to run for a maximum amount of time—600 seconds by default—in case the script hangs while running. After the scripts are run, the computer will allow logons and display the logon splash. Everything from steps 4 to 10 is reapplied during user logon.

Windows XP uses an asynchronous policy application process, while Windows Server 2003 and Windows 2000 use a synchronous process. This means that for servers and Windows 2000 systems, the computer session won't open until the entire list of GPOs are processed, including any scripts that are referenced in the GPO. On Windows XP systems, though, GPO processing is delayed to speed up the session opening process. This is called fast logon optimization. This delay will have an impact on the way policies are applied to XP systems. More on this subject will be covered later.

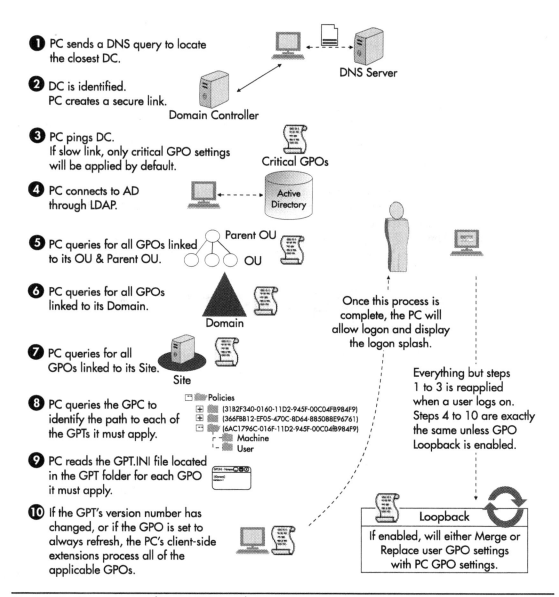

① PC sends a DNS query to locate the closest DC.

② DC is identified. PC creates a secure link.

DNS Server

Domain Controller

③ PC pings DC. If slow link, only critical GPO settings will be applied by default.

Critical GPOs

④ PC connects to AD through LDAP.

Active Directory

⑤ PC queries for all GPOs linked to its OU & Parent OU.

Parent OU

OU

⑥ PC queries for all GPOs linked to its Domain.

Domain

Once this process is complete, the PC will allow logon and display the logon splash.

⑦ PC queries for all GPOs linked to its Site.

Site

Everything but steps 1 to 3 is reapplied when a user logs on. Steps 4 to 10 are exactly the same unless GPO Loopback is enabled.

⑧ PC queries the GPC to identify the path to each of the GPTs it must apply.

Policies
(31B2F340-0160-11D2-945F-00C04FB984F9)
(366FBB12-EF05-470C-8D64-885088E96761)
(6AC1796C-016F-11D2-945F-00C04FB984F9)
Machine
User

⑨ PC reads the GPT.INI file located in the GPT folder for each GPO it must apply.

⑩ If the GPT's version number has changed, or if the GPO is set to always refresh, the PC's client-side extensions process all of the applicable GPOs.

Loopback

If enabled, will either Merge or Replace user GPO settings with PC GPO settings.

Figure 5-2   Computer and User GPO application process

Policy Loopback

There is one more option for GPO application. Loopback is an option that can be used in special computer scenarios such as for kiosks, schools, reception areas, or other zones where it is important that no matter who logs on, the computer settings always remain in the same secured state. Since user settings are applied after computer settings in the application order, GPOs allow you to enable a Loopback setting to ensure that computer settings are reapplied instead of or with user settings.

Loopback can be set to two modes:

- **Merge**   This option appends computer settings to user settings during the application of GPOs at user logon. They are aggregated. In this process computer settings override conflicting user settings.

- **Replace**   This option effectively replaces a user's settings in a GPO with computer settings. At logon, the computer settings are applied instead of the user's.

Loopback is set in the GPO under Computer Configuration | Administrative Templates | System | Group Policy. Double-clicking on the policy setting allows you to configure it. Enabling the Loopback setting allows you to choose between the Merge and Replace options. Click Apply or OK. The advantage of using Apply is that if you have a lot of settings to change, you don't need to close the dialog box until you're done. You can use the Next Setting or Previous Setting buttons to move through all the settings without having to close the dialog box.

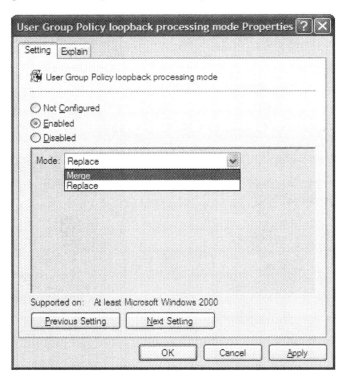

If you do use the Loopback setting, limit its impact by creating a special GPO linked to a special OU that will be used to contain the computers this GPO will be applied to.

Policy Filtering

As mentioned before, the OU design is closely tied to the GPO strategy you intend to use. One of the factors you must remember at all times during this design stage is that objects can only be placed inside a single OU. In addition, you want to make sure that you keep your OU design as simple as possible. Therefore, you may find yourself in a situation where you want to choose to either create a complex OU design with too many OUs just because you want to assign different GPOs to specific objects.

Don't. You will not have to because Windows Server 2003 also includes the concept of policy filtering. Policy filtering means applying basic read and execute rights to the policy itself. By using filtering, you can apply any number of policies to a specific container and ensure that only the appropriate policy will affect the objects it is designed to manage. WS03 supports two types of policy filtering: Security Policy filtering and Windows Management Instrumentation (WMI) filtering.

Security Policy Filtering

Filtering through Security Settings is done by assigning access rights or permissions to a Group Policy object. To do so, you need to create security groups and assign the objects each policy is to manage to these groups. Then you assign the policy object to the appropriate groups.

For example, say you have two groups of users within the same container—common users and power users—and you need to apply different policy objects to each group. You simply create two policy objects and set one to read and apply for the common users, while setting it to deny read and apply to the power users group. You reverse the settings on the GPO you wish to apply to power users.

Applying security GPO filtering is fairly straightforward. In Active Directory Users and Computers, right-click the container to which the GPO is applied, and select Properties. Move to the Group Policy tab, select the GPO you want to filter and click the Properties button. Move to the Security tab and click Add to find the groups you want to use to filter the policy. You can find both groups at the same time if you want to. Next, select the group to which you want to apply the GPO. Click both the Allow Read and Allow Apply Group Policy checkboxes. Click Apply. Next, select the group to which you want to deny permissions. Click the Deny Read and Deny Apply Group Policy checkboxes.

Click Apply or OK if you're done. You will notice that WS03 presents a warning dialog box. Since you have decided to deny permissions to the GPO object, WS03 warns you that the cumulative result for anyone belonging to several groups will be denial since denials always take precedence over allows. Click OK to close the warning dialog box. Close the container's property dialog box when done.

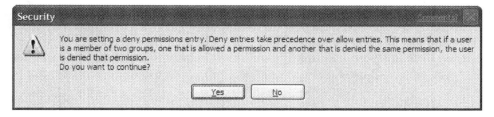

Be careful how you use Security Policy filtering. Remember that denies always take precedence.

WMI Filtering

Windows Management Instrumentation is a management infrastructure in Windows that allows the monitoring and controlling of system resources through a common set of interfaces and provides a logically organized, consistent model of Windows operation, configuration, and status. WMI is Microsoft's answer to the Desktop Management Task Force's (http://www.dtmf.org/) Desktop Management Interface (DMI). The DMTF designed DMI to allow organizations to remotely manage computer system aspects such as system settings within the BIOS, BIOS replacement or upgrades, and system power on or off. But since no single standard management tool is available for all computer brands (each manufacturer tends to create their own tools to manage their own systems), a generic interface was required. Microsoft has attempted to provide this generic interface through WMI.

In the case of GPO filtering, WMI can be used to identify specific machine aspects before applying a GPO. Several example applications are available in the WS03 help files. Take for example a system monitoring policy that should be applied only to systems that run Windows Server 2003, Enterprise Edition. To do so, you can create the following filter:

```
Root\CimV2; Select * from Win32_OperatingSystem where Caption = "Microsoft
Windows Server 2003 Enterprise Edition"
```

Then you can apply this filter to the Group Policy object you create for the monitoring policy.

Another example is when you need to apply a policy to a specific set of computer systems. If you have a series of computer systems that do not have the capacity to host specific policies, you can create a WMI filter that identifies them and deny policy application to that group of machines. For example, if the machines were Toshiba Satellite Pros, such a filter would include the following instructions:

```
Root\CimV2; Select * from Win32_ComputerSystem where manufacturer =
"Toshiba" and Model = "Satellite Pro 4200" OR Model = "Satellite Pro 4100"
```

WMI filters can also be saved to special files, making them easier to manage. WMI filters are basically text files that have a special structure and use the .mof file extension.

Applying WMI filters is done in much the same way as security filters. In Active Directory Users and Computers, right-click the container to which the GPO is applied, and select Properties. Move to the Group Policy tab, select the GPO you want to filter, and click the Properties button. Move to the WMI Filter tab and click the This Filter button. Type in the name of the filter if it has already been prepared, or if you need to locate or create it, click Browse/Manage.

A second dialog box appears. If the filter has already been imported into the directory, it will already be listed. Simply select the required filter and click OK to close the dialog box. If you need to create a new filter or import an existing filter, click Advanced. The bottom part of the dialog box opens. Here you can click New to create a new filter, name it, attach a filter description, type in the filter instructions, and save it, or you can import an existing filter. If you create a new filter, it is a good idea to export it and save it in a management folder with all other .mof instruction files. Click OK when you're done. This returns you to the WMI Filter tab. Click OK when done.

> ## CAUTION

Be careful how you use WMI policy filtering and be especially careful when you delete WMI filters. Deleting a filter will not disassociate the filter from all of the GPOs it has been assigned to. You must disassociate the filter from each of the policies it has been applied to. Otherwise, the policies will not be processed since the filter does not exist, but it is a condition for application.

Make sure you fully document all GPOs and all of their properties at all times.

Fast Logon Optimization

As mentioned previously, Windows XP provides Fast Logon Optimization to speed the process of opening a user session on a corporate PC. Fast Logon Optimization refers to a feature in XP that supports the asynchronous application of some policy settings. These settings are related to three specific policy categories:

- Software Installation
- Folder Redirection
- Roaming User Profiles

All other policy settings are applied synchronously. Remember also that GPOs are only applied if they have changed unless otherwise specified in your Group Policy application settings. This also speeds up the logon process.

Software Installation

Since it is impossible to install or, rather, uninstall software in an asynchronous manner because the user may be using the application as the uninstall begins, it will take up to two logons before software that is delivered through the directory will install on XP machines using Fast Logon Optimization. The first time a user logs on, the machine identifies that a software package is ready for delivery. It then sets a flag for software installation at next logon. This means that when the user logs on a second time, GPOs will be applied in a synchronous manner to allow the software installation to proceed. Once the software product is installed, GPOs are reset to asynchronous application.

Folder Redirection

Folder Redirection refers to the redirection of user folders such as My Documents, My Pictures, Application Data, Start Menu, and Desktop to shared network folders. This replaces the older Home Directory settings found in Windows NT. Folder Redirection supports two modes: Basic and Advanced. Basic redirection sends everyone's folders to the same location and creates special subfolders for each user. Advanced allows you to set Folder Redirection paths for specific security groups.

It is obvious that if you redirect a user's My Documents folder, you cannot do so while the user is using it. Thus, if you use advanced Folder Redirection, it can take up to three logons before the policy is applied because advanced redirection is based on policy filtering. The first logon is required to update the user security group memberships. The second detects the change in the policy and sets the flag for synchronous GPO application at the next logon. The third applies the change and resets the GPO processing mode to asynchronous.

Roaming User Profiles

Fast Logon Optimization speeds up the logon process by caching all user logons. This means that if you make a change to a user's properties such as changing their profile from local to roaming, it won't be applied until after two logons. The first is required to update the cached user object and the second is required to apply the change. If a user has a roaming profile, Fast Logon Optimization is automatically disabled for that user.

Deactivating Fast Logon Optimization

Some administrators may decide to deactivate Fast Logon Optimization (FLO) because they are concerned that GPOs are not applied properly or that it may take a few logons for specific GPO settings to be applied. *It is not recommended to deactivate this feature.* Deactivating this feature will make all logons take longer on all XP machines when, in fact, only two or three aspects of Group Policy are affected by it. Follow these recommendations for FLO:

- If you do not use directory-enabled software installations, do not deactivate FLO.
- If you intend to redirect folders, make your users perform a triple logon before beginning to work with their systems. This can be included in their training program or their migration activity sheet.
- If you use roaming profiles, FLO is deactivated automatically.

As you can see, there is little justification for changing Windows XP's default behavior.

Policy Design

The policy application process outlines a clear division between both computer and user settings. This is by design. Policies are also divided into two parts: computer configuration and user configuration. Since both portions are designed to address specific settings for either a machine or a user, you can and should disable unused portions of GPOs. You can open a GPO's properties and disable either the computer or the user portion of a GPO. Disabling both computer and user settings has the effect of disabling the entire GPO.

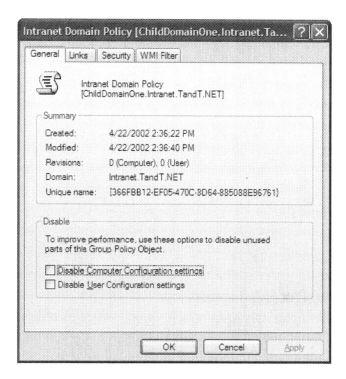

Since policies have a natural separation between user and computer configurations, you can use them to define how you will manage both types of objects. There are, however, certain GPO settings that are applied at the domain level and that cannot be overridden by lower-level GPOs such as those found in organizational units. Policies that can only be defined at the domain level focus on *Account Policies* and include:

- **Password Policy**   Including settings such as password history, maximum and minimum password age, minimum password length and password complexity requirements as well as reversible encryption for passwords.

- **Account Lockout Policy**   Including lockout duration, lockout threshold (the number of failed logon attempts before lockout), and the lockout reset timer.

- **Kerberos Policy**   Including enforcing user logon restrictions such as account lockout, maximum lifetime for service and user tickets, maximum lifetime for user ticket renewal, and maximum tolerance for computer clock synchronization. Kerberos authentication functions through the issuing of access tickets to services and users. These tickets are time-based so clock synchronization is important within a domain.

There are other policies you might decide to set at the domain level in order to ensure that they are applied globally, but the three mentioned above can only be set at the domain level. It is impossible to have multiple versions of these policies within the same domain. The settings you should use for your Default Domain Policy are outlined in Chapter 8.

Designing a GPO Strategy

You can see that the policy management structure you want to apply within your production domain will affect the way you design your OU structure. Even though you can disable computer or user settings in a GPO, you still don't want a user object to read computer-related GPOs while logging on in order to speed up the logon and GPO application process. This is one reason for the OU strategy outlined in Chapter 3.

Computer-related GPOs will be applied in both the PCs and the Services OUs as well as the Domain Controllers default OU, and user-related GPOs will be applied to the People OU. (Remember, the User and Computer default containers in AD are not organizational units and therefore do not support the application of Group Policy objects except as objects within the domain.) In addition, your GPO strategy should include domain and site-level GPOs. You will most certainly use domain-level GPOs, but site-level GPOs are more unusual. They are useful in some circumstances since a site can host more than one domain. If you want a default set of parameters to apply to objects within a site even if they are from different domains, you can create a site-level GPO to enforce standards. The GPO scoping strategy is outlined in Figure 5-3.

GPO Application and Processing Speed

Be careful how you design your GPO strategy. Many organizations choose to create regional OU designs. In such a design, each region is created as a top-level OU. Then inside each region, two OUs

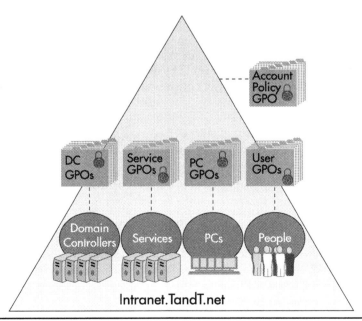

Figure 5-3 An enterprise GPO strategy

are created, one for PCs and one for People. The problem with this strategy is that when you need to apply a GPO to all PCs, you have to use one of three strategies:

- Create the first GPO and link it to each PCs OU.
- Create a separate GPO for each PCs OU.
- Create a Global PC GPO, assign it to the domain, and filter it with a special PC security group.

These strategies are illustrated in Figure 5-4.

The last option, applying the GPO at the domain level with filtering, is by far the easiest one to implement in this situation and, especially, manage afterwards. But it does cause issues since by assigning it to the domain level every PC, server, DC, and user will attempt to read the GPO, even if it is only to discover that according to the access control list for the GPO, they are denied rights. If your domain includes several GPOs that every object must review, it will impact the speed of GPO processing on your systems.

▶ **NOTE**

By creating object type OUs at the top level, you can ensure that your GPOs are only applied to and read by the object type for which they are designed. Thus, PC GPOs are only read by PCs, user GPOs by user objects, DC GPOs by DCs, and server GPOs by servers. The only GPO that is read by all is the account GPO that is set at the domain level. This eases the GPO management and administration process and it also speeds up the GPO application process at computer startup or user logon.

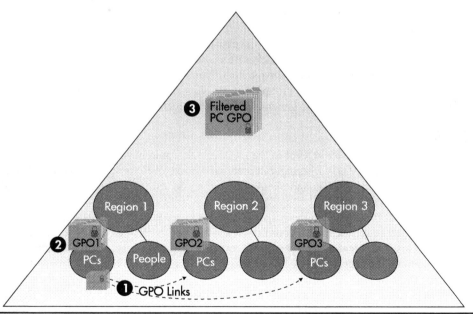

Figure 5-4   A regional OU design

Creating an OU Design for PC Management Purposes

Since user and computer management do not focus on the same activities, they are treated in different chapters. PC management is outlined here. User management will be outlined in Chapter 6. Server management is outlined in Chapter 7, and domain controller management is outlined in Chapter 8 since they are considered part of the security strategy for the enterprise. PC management includes the configuration of GPOs for three different types of machines:

- Desktop PCs
- Mobile devices (includes portable computers and handheld devices)
- External PCs

The OU design you use for these types of machines will depend on a lot of factors—size of the organization, number of PCs to manage, differentiation among your PCs, and especially, your administrative strategy (centralized or decentralized).

Centralized PC Administration

The PCs OU design in Chapter 3 is an example of a centralized PC administration strategy. In the example scenario, T&T Corporation has a decentralized user administration, but a centralized PC Management Strategy. If this is the case in your organization, it will greatly simplify your OU strategy for PCs.

Three levels of OUs were used in this scenario. Each is used to further segregate the PC object type. Level one is used to regroup all PCs. This is where Global PC GPOs are applied. Level two begins object segregation. If a Global GPO is required for all desktops or all portables or even all external PCs, it is applied at this level. Finally, level three is used to apply GPOs to specific types of PCs within each grouping. For example, desktop PCs whose users have elevated local rights will still require some management, but a lighter management than PCs whose users are more generic. Thus, you may require a special GPO for this group of users. No special GPO is required for generic users because they should be covered by the general GPOs set at level one and two.

The Desktop OU

The segregation applied at the child level of the Desktop OU could have been performed directly at the Desktop OU itself using GPO filtering, but creating a child level also gives you the advantage of being able to categorize objects. Thus as an administrator, you will be able to find each type of PC more easily.

In addition, the Desktop OU includes a special OU for kiosk PCs. These systems are placed in public zones and give people access to your network. Thus you need to ensure that they are always highly secured. This is an ideal place to use the Loopback feature to ensure that no matter who logs onto these computers, the secure GPO you apply to these PCs is always in effect. In addition, you need to manage these systems. In some specific cases, you will need to be able to unlock the secure environment to perform updates and system fixes. To do so, you can store a special security group within this OU and apply GPO denial to this group. To work on a system, you simply need to add the PC account to the denial group, perform the work, and then remove the PC's account from the group.

The Mobile Systems OU

The Mobile Systems OU is designed to help apply special GPOs for mobile devices. For example, since portables are computer systems that often leave the secure network your organization provides, you will want to ensure that certain policies are always applied to these systems. These could include the enforcing of file encryption on the portable and the use of a personal firewall whenever the PC connects to any system through its modem, wireless network connection, or infrared port. In addition, if the mobile device is wireless, it will require the application of a Public Key Infrastructure (PKI) certificate for authentication as well as a virtual private network connection to secure the wireless link. These policies are applied directly to the Mobile Systems OU.

There is a second level of segregation for mobile devices: common users and users with elevated rights. The same types of policies applied to these child OUs in the Desktop OU are applied here. This can be done through the use of a separate GPO object or through the linkage of the appropriate Desktop GPOs to these OUs.

The External OU

An External OU is created to ensure that external PCs are always regrouped. Policies that apply specifically to all external PCs are applied at the top level of this OU. Once again, a child level is included to help categorize systems that are managed versus systems that are unmanaged. If the unmanaged systems are completely so, you can set the Unmanaged OU to block policy inheritance. If not, you can filter policies in this OU.

Managed external systems are often not quite the same as your own managed systems. It is very difficult for you to ensure that consultant systems are exactly the same as your own. Consulting firms often tend to buy clone systems that are less expensive than corporate systems and that do not fully support your managed systems environment. Some of the settings you apply to your own systems will be different from the settings you need to apply to this group of heterogeneous machines (especially if you have more than one consulting firm on site).

Managed systems tend to be mostly desktops, while unmanaged systems are often portables. This is because the consultants that use managed systems are often programmers, and programmers prefer to have desktops because for the same price you can get a lot more speed and power on the system. Thus, you have a natural segregation between desktops and portables in the External OU structure. Table 5-1 outlines the use of each of the OUs in this PC administrative strategy.

OU	Level	Objective	GPO	Notes
PCs	One	Grouping of all PCs in the organization	Global PC GPO	Applies to all PCs
Desktops	Two	Grouping of all desktops in the organization	Global Desktop GPO	Includes differences from Global PC GPO only
Elevated Rights	Three	Grouping of desktops whose users have elevated local rights		Policy filtering to allow elevated local rights
Generic Users	Three	Grouping of desktops with common user rights		Categorization only

Table 5-1   A Centralized PC Administration OU Structure

OU	Level	Objective	GPO	Notes
Kiosks	Three	Grouping of special high-risk PCs	Special Kiosk GPO	Loopback enabled Special exclusion group for repairs (deny read to Kiosk GPO)
Mobile Systems	Two	Grouping of all mobile devices in the organization	Global Mobile GPO	Includes differences from Global PC GPO only
Elevated Rights	Three	Grouping of mobile devices whose users have elevated local rights		Policy filtering to allow elevated local rights
Generic Users	Three	Grouping of desktops with common user rights		Categorization only
External	Two	Grouping of all external PCs in the organization	Global External GPO	Includes differences from Global PC GPO only
Managed	Three	Grouping of all managed external PCs in the organization		Categorization only
Unmanaged	Three	Grouping of all unmanaged external PCs in the organization		Block Policy Inheritance

Table 5-1   A Centralized PC Administration OU Structure *(continued)*

The results of this table are graphically represented in Figure 5-5.

▶ **CAUTION**

You may not want to block policy inheritance in the unmanaged External OU. You will have to negotiate with consultants to define your own enterprise policy for unmanaged consultant PCs.

Computer Policy Contents

As mentioned above, Group Policy objects are composed of two categories of settings: Computer and User configurations. Since the GPOs that you will be designing for the PCs OU structure are all related to computers, the first thing you should do when creating a GPO for this organizational unit structure is disable the User Configuration portion of the GPO.

Now that your GPO is structured only for computers, you can begin to examine the settings you can manage with this GPO. The Computer Configuration section is divided into several subcategories. Table 5-2 lists these categories and their possible application.

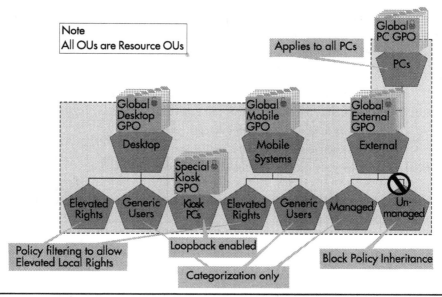

Figure 5-5   GPO application in a centrally managed PCs OU structure

GPO Section	Comment	Applicable
Software Settings	This section deals with software installations. If you want to assign a software product to a computer instead of a user using Windows Server 2003 software delivery, you set the parameters here.	See management strategy below
Windows Settings	This section deals with general Windows settings and includes elements such as scripts and Security Settings.	Some
Scripts	Controls access to startup and shutdown scripts.	If required
Security Settings	Includes account policies, local policies, event logs, and more.	Some
Account Policy	Controls all account policies. Set at the domain level.	N/A
Local Policy	Specific to each computer or to the domain. Includes audit policy, user rights assignments, security options. Most user rights assignments are set at the domain level, but some such as Modify firmware environment values and Perform volume maintenance tasks should be assigned at the PC level to allow technical groups the rights required to maintain PCs.	Audit policy and some user rights
Event Log	Controls size of each event log.	Yes

Table 5-2   Computer Policy Categories and Contents

GPO Section	Comment	Applicable
Restricted Groups	Controls who belongs to high security groups such as Domain Administrators. Set at the domain level for high level administrative groups (Domain and Enterprise Administrators). Set at the PC level for local administrators such as technician groups.	Partially
System Services	Determines how given services will behave on a computer.	Yes
Registry	Allows you to set access rights to registry hives.	No
File System	Allows you to set access rights to files and folders.	No
Wireless Network	Allows you to set policies for wireless network connections.	For mobile devices
Public Key Policies	Controls all PKI settings, including the Encrypting File System.	For mobile devices
Software Restriction Policies	Allows you to determine which applications are allowed to run in your network.	At the domain level
IP Security Policy	Allows you to set the PC behavior when using IPSec.	For mobile devices
Administrative Templates	Administrative Templates are scriptable GPO components that can be used to control a wide variety of settings such as Windows Components, System, Network, and Printers.	Yes
Windows Components	Controls settings such as NetMeeting (for the remote desktop), Internet Explorer, Task Scheduler, Terminal Services, Windows Installer, Windows Messenger, and Windows Update. Several settings are of use here. Terminal Services determines how the TS session is established between the local and the remote systems. Windows Update in particular allows you to assign an internal server location for update collection.	Yes
System	Controls system-wide settings such as User Profiles, Scripts, Logon, Disk Quotas, Net Logon, Group Policy (Loopback, for example), Remote Assistance, System Restore, Error Reporting, Windows File Protection, Remote Procedure Call, and Windows Time Service. This section controls the behavior of each listed feature. The Scripts section, for example, determines the behavior for scripts, not the script names. Remote Assistance should be set to facilitate Help Desk tasks, especially the Offer Remote Assistance setting. Error Reporting should be set for critical applications. This will enable these applications to send any error reports to a corporate share without telling users. It also controls device driver signing. This should be turned on for all deployed PCs.	Yes

Table 5-2 Computer Policy Categories and Contents *(continued)*

GPO Section	Comment	Applicable
Network	Controls network related settings such as DNS Client, Offline Files, Network Connections, QoS Packet Scheduler, SNMP, and the BITS protocol. Offline Files settings should be set so that users cannot configure them for themselves. Network connections should be set so that wireless connections should use machine authentication. SNMP is not normally configured for PCs.	Yes
Printers	Mainly controls how printers are used with the Active Directory.	At the Domain level

Table 5-2   Computer Policy Categories and Contents *(continued)*

▶ *NOTE*

Registry keys and files and folder access rights should not be set with Group Policy. They should be set using the Secedit command along with Security Templates. More on this will be discussed in Chapter 8.

▶ | **QUICK TIP**
|
| *A GPO documentation spreadsheet is available at http://www.Reso-Net.com/WindowsServer/. You can use it to document GPOs.* |

You should document all of the GPOs you create. You should also use a standard naming strategy for all GPOs and ensure you maintain a complete GPO registry.

Decentralized PC Administration

The OU structure defined previously is useful if all PC operations are centralized even if your organization includes regional offices. But if your regional offices include a vast number of computer systems, you'll probably find that you need to allow regional technicians to perform some degree of operations on regional PCs. If this is the case, you'll have to design an OU structure that will support *delegation of administration*. To do so, you must create geographic containers for all PCs.

Once again, it remains useful to segregate your object type at the first OU level. The difference lies in the second level OU structure. Here, you will need to create a geographic structure to store PCs. Since you will most likely still have external PCs in this structure, you will need to create an External OU as well. Most organizations that hire consultants will do so in central or large offices. This means that your External OU does not necessarily need to be divided into regions. Your desktop and mobile computers, however, will require regional distribution.

Even if you create regional units, you will still require some form of segregation for the two types of machines. Since you know that creating a regional structure followed by Desktop and Mobile child OUs will only complicate the application of GPOs by either requiring individual GPOs for each container or having to link GPOs from one container to another, you'll need to use a different strategy. In this case, the best strategy is to use Group Policy filtering.

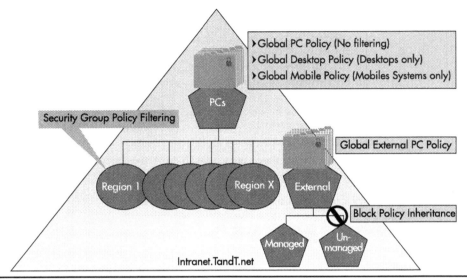

Figure 5-6   A decentralized PCs OU strategy

Create two principal OU levels, the PCs and then the Regional child OUs. Then create Global Security groups for each type of PC: desktop and mobile. Apply all Group Policy objects to the PCs OU and filter them through the use of your security groups. In this way, all PC objects will receive the GPOs, even the PCs located in the regional child OUs. Since GPO filtering is enabled, policies that apply to desktops will only apply to desktops and policies that apply to mobile computers will only apply to mobile computers.

In most cases, the PCs OU will contain the following policies:

- **Global PC Policy**   Applicable to all PCs; no filtering applied.
- **Global Desktop Policy**   Filtered with the desktop Global Security group.
- **Global Mobile Policy**   Filtered with the mobile Global Security group.
- **Global Kiosk Policy**   Filtered with a kiosk Global Security group.

This policy structure is a little more difficult to manage than the centralized PC management structure since it must be managed through group memberships, but it allows you to design a strategy that maintains central control as well as allowing delegation to regional technicians. Figure 5-6 illustrates the decentralized PCs OU strategy.

 # Designing for Delegation

The decentralized OU strategy outlines the need for delegation of administration. In this case, it means that regional technicians must be allowed to perform specific activities related to PC and user management and administration within the directory. These activities can range from resetting user passwords to much more comprehensive administrative tasks. Users of Windows NT will not be very familiar with the concept of delegation since in this operating system, to delegate authority, you pretty well had to give someone domain administration rights. There were, of course, third-party products that allowed some form of delegation within Windows NT, but they were costly and took time to implement.

This is not the case in Windows Server 2003. In fact, since Windows 2000, the concept of delegation is embedded into the operating system. Active Directory offers delegation rights and permissions by default. This is because each object in the directory can hold security properties. Thus, you can assign user rights to any object: user, computer, site, domain, organizational units, and so on. Delegation is inherent to an Active Directory design.

In terms of Group Policy objects, you can delegate administration, creation, linkage, modification, and much more. You'll soon learn to be careful what you delegate in terms of GPOs, because the more you delegate, the more complex your GPO administration will become. For example, if all GPO creation and administration is centralized, there is never any requirement for the No Override option to be applied to a GPO since you are in control of everything and no one will try to block the application of a GPO to replace it with another. If you delegate GPO rights, then you'll definitely want to use the No Override option since you'll want to make sure that Global GPO settings are always applied.

Delegation in Active Directory

Delegation in Active Directory is performed through the use of a wizard. The tool you use to perform delegation depends on the object you want to delegate. If it is a site, you need to use the AD Sites and Services console. If it is a domain or an OU, use the AD Users and Computers console. Delegation is simple: right-click on the object you want to delegate and choose Delegate Control to launch the Delegation Wizard.

WS03 includes a series of preassigned tasks you can delegate. These include:

- Create, delete, and manage user accounts
- Reset user passwords and force password change at next logon
- Read all user information
- Create, delete, and manage groups
- Modify the membership of a group
- Manage Group Policy links
- Generate Resultant Set of Policy (Planning)
- Generate Resultant Set of Policy (Logging)
- Create, delete, and manage inetOrgPerson accounts
- Reset inetOrgPerson passwords and force password change at next logon
- Read inetOrgPerson user information

On the other hand, you may decide that you wish to delegate a specific operation which is not included in the default list. To do so, you need to choose Create a custom task to delegate in the Tasks to delegate window. There are more than 60 different objects or combinations of objects you can choose to delegate under the Active Directory Objects to delegate window. You can assign a variety of permissions to the custom objects. Everything from full control to read or write all objects can be assigned at the general, property specific, and/or creation/deletion of specific child objects level.

▶ **QUICK TIP**

The Microsoft TechNet Web site (http://support.microsoft.com/default.aspx) lists several Q articles on the subject. Some examples are: Q308404 for customizing a task list, Q221577 to delegate authority for editing a GPO, Q320044 to show how to give enough permissions to people maintaining remote servers, and Q315676 to delegate administrative authority.

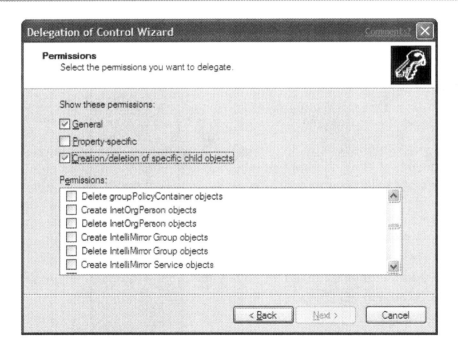

Delegation Through Group Membership

In addition, some global delegation rights can be assigned in a more traditional manner: through group memberships. Special groups such as the Group Policy Creator Owners, DnsAdmins, Print Operators, Server Operators, or Backup Operators allow the delegation of certain tasks at the domain level simply through their group memberships. You have to be more careful with this type of delegation, though, since it gives domain-wide delegation rights. This may be more authority than what you originally wanted to grant.

Creating Custom Microsoft Management Consoles

One of the impacts of delegation within Active Directory is the need for custom consoles to allow access to delegated objects for groups with delegated rights and permissions. This means that you can create a custom version of a Microsoft Management Console (MMC) containing only the objects you have delegated access to and distribute this console to members of the group with delegation rights.

1. To create custom consoles, you need to start the console program in authoring mode. To do so, run the following command (the /a parameter is only required if you are not logged in as an administrator):

```
mmc /a
```

2. This launches an empty MMC. You then need to add the appropriate snap-in to the console. To do so, move to the File menu and select Add/Remove Snap-in. In the Snap-in dialog box, click Add. Select the snap-in you require, for example, Active Directory Users and Computers. Many snap-ins include extensions. You should view the extensions to see if they are required for the group to which you intend to delegate this console. If not, deselect all of the extensions that are not required.

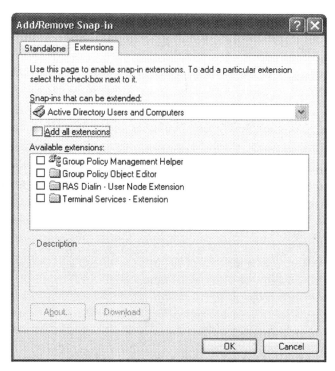

3. Click OK when done. Save your console and give it an appropriate name.

4. You need to create a Taskpad view for the console. This allows you to modify the way information is presented to console users. To do so, move to the Action menu to choose New Taskpad View.

This launches the Taskpad Wizard, which will allow you to choose the presentation mode of the console.

5. Continue with the wizard to select the way you want to present information.

6. You need to set the focus for this console. To do so, select the object you want to delegate, such as an organizational unit. Right-click on this object and select New Window From Here. This will create a new window that displays only the appropriate information for console users.

7. You need to set the view options for this window. Since the console users will not require the ability to create consoles, you can remove a number of items, such as the console tree, standard menu, standard toolbar, and so on. To do so, move to the View menu and select Customize. Deselect all of the items you do not deem necessary for console users. This dialog box is live—when you deselect an item, you immediately see the result in the console behind the dialog box. Click OK when done.

8. You need to customize the console. Move to the File menu and select Options. Here you can type in a console description, assign a new icon (the Shell32.dll file contains several icons that can be used to customize MMCs), and determine the console operation mode. There are four console operation modes:

   - **Author mode**   Provides full control of all console settings.

   - **User mode, full access**   The same as author mode, but users cannot add snap-ins, change options, and create Favorites or Taskpads.

   - **User mode, limited access, multiple windows**   Gives access only to the selected items when the console was saved. Users can create new windows, but cannot close any previously saved windows.

   - **User mode, limited access, single window**   Same as above, but users cannot create new windows.

For single-purpose consoles, the last setting is appropriate. Save the console again when done. Test the console to ensure it operates as designed. To do so, close it and reopen it by double-clicking on its icon.

You can save the console and distribute it to users through Group Policy using software distribution. To do so, you will need to package consoles, including any snap-ins that are required for it to operate. Remember that snap-ins must be registered on the target computer for the console to work. The best way to distribute consoles is to package them as Windows Installer executables. You can use a repackaging tool to do so. More on this is covered in "Enterprise Software Assets" later in this chapter.

Another way to distribute consoles is through Terminal Services. The advantage of using Terminal Services to distribute consoles is that only one installation of the snap-in is required, on the hosting server. In addition, since all users access the same console on the same computer, global modifications are simple: change a single console in a single place. Remember to assign read and execute permissions to appropriate groups to the console folder on the Terminal Server. Finally, distribution is simple; all you need to do is send the link to the console icon to the users requiring it. More on Terminal Services is covered in Chapter 7.

Custom consoles are an important part of a Windows Server 2003 delegation strategy.

Designing a Delegation Strategy

The delegation strategy you require will have a direct impact on your organizational unit strategy. This design will also have to take into account the Group Policy object strategy you outlined above. When designing for delegation, you need to take several factors into account. Begin by identifying the business needs that influence delegation. Many of these will have been inventoried at the very beginning of your project. You also need to have a good understanding of your IT organizational structure. You'll have to review how you can change your administrative practices now that you have access to a technology that fully supports delegation. More on this is covered in Chapter 8.

If you decide to delegate, you will need to formalize the delegation process. This includes a series of activities such as:

- Identifying all delegated officers
- Identifying the role for each officer
- Identifying the responsibilities for each officer
- Identifying the name of the backup delegated officer for each officer
- Listing any special consoles you may have created for each delegation level
- Specifically identifying all rights and permissions that have been delegated
- Preparing and delivering a delegation training program to ensure all delegated officers are completely familiar with their responsibilities

Another required aspect is the identification of object owners and the addition of object managers within the properties of each object in the directory. This will allow you to use the directory to support the documentation of your delegation program. Figure 5-7 illustrates the assignment of object ownership.

▶ **NOTE**

Figure 5-7 displays a generic user name. Chapter 3 outlined that generic account names are not allowed in the Production domain, and they shouldn't be. A generic name is used here for the purpose of illustrating the type of user you would identify as owner of an OU.

Finally, your Delegation Plan will most likely require the creation of a new position within your administrative activities: the delegation manager. This role concentrates all delegation activities within a centralized function. The delegation manager is responsible for overseeing all delegation and making sure that all information that is related to delegation is maintained and up to date.

Enterprise PC Management

The last part of your organizational unit design strategy for PCs is the Enterprise PC Management Strategy you intend to use. PC management in an enterprise deals with a lot of activities which include (but are not limited to) hardware inventory, software inventory, remote control and remote

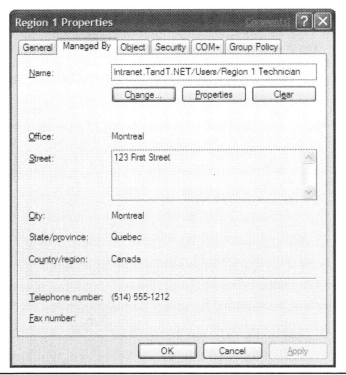

Figure 5-7   Assigning object ownership in the directory

assistance, software lifecycle management, and software usage metering. By default, Windows Server 2003 offers several of these capabilities. Both remote assistance and software lifecycle management are features that are now built into both Windows XP and Windows Server 2003. Software lifecycle management first appeared in Windows 2000.

Software Installations with WS03

Windows Server 2003 includes a set of Group Policy objects that can be used to deliver software to both users and computers. These GPOs are closely tied to the Windows Installer service which is available for both PCs and servers. Windows Installer is a service that has been designed to help take control of the software lifecycle. This does not only mean remote installation of software, but more specifically it means software upgrades, patches, maintenance fixes, and something which is more often than not overlooked, software removal. Figure 5-8 displays the different aspects of software lifecycle that are managed through the Windows Installer service.

Policy-based software installations will usually only work with installation files that are supported by Windows Installer. These files have .msi extensions. A Windows Installer executable is in fact an installation database that is copied to the computer system along with the program it installs. This is one reason why Windows Installer supports both software self-healing as well as clean software

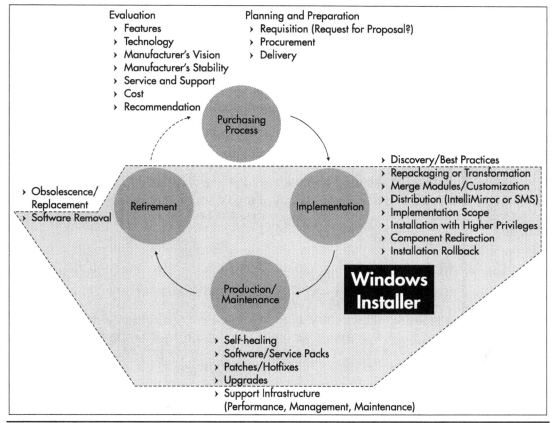

Figure 5-8   Software Lifecycle Management with Windows Installer

removal. Once a program is installed on a system, Windows Installer will perform a program consistency check every time the software program is launched. If there are inconsistencies between the actual program state and the contents of the installation database, Windows Installer will automatically launch a software repair phase.

During this repair phase, Windows Installer will connect to the original installation source of the software program and reinstall missing or damaged components. This means that if self-healing is to work, installation source files must be maintained permanently. This is a significant change from traditional approaches which focused on deploying software and then removing installation source files once deployment was complete. Organizations that want to use the self-healing capabilities of Windows Installer must maintain permanent software installation depots.

In addition, the Windows Installer consistency database is used to perform clean removals of software from a system. Anyone who has had any experience with software removal in versions of Windows previous to Windows 2000 (or older systems that have the Windows Installer service installed) will know that for those systems, the concept of a clean uninstall is nothing more than a myth. This is not the case with Windows Installer-enabled software. In fact, one of Windows Installer's main functions is to manage software conflicts and ensure that shared system components are not damaged by software installations. If conflicting components are added during a software product installation, Windows Installer will automatically ensure that these components are installed in a special directory called %Systemroot%\WinSxS, or side by side, to avoid potential conflicts. This is a simplistic definition of this function, but it is sufficient to help you understand that any application installed through Windows Installer will cleanly uninstall because its components are isolated by this service. At last, uninstalling software has little or no impact on the rest of a computer system.

In addition, since the Windows Installer installation file is in fact a database, it can be modified at will for different installation types. These are called *transform* files and have the .msp extension. For example, you can create a global MSI file that includes all of the Microsoft Office program files and use custom transform files to install only Access, or install only Word, Excel, PowerPoint, and Outlook, or install only FrontPage, or FrontPage and Access, and so on. Finally, MSI files also support *patching*. Patch files have an .msp extension and allow the application of hot fixes and service packs to installed software.

Enterprise Software Assets

Given that Windows Server 2003 software installations through Group Policy require Windows Installer-enabled programs, and given the major advantages you can gain from using these types of installations just by integrating them to the Windows Installer service, you should seriously consider migrating all of your software programs and applications to versions that are integrated with this service. Of course, most corporations will not be able to achieve this through upgrades for several reasons. First, some programs, especially internally developed programs, may not be so easily upgraded. Second, the average corporation (more than 1,000 users) has about 300 different software applications within its network. Upgrading all of these products would be cost-prohibitive and often unnecessary. Third, some applications simply do not offer upgrades. Fourth, some manufacturers, unfortunately, still do not integrate their software products to the Windows Installer service.

In most cases, you will have to consider repackaging software installations in order to take advantage of the many features of the Windows Installer service. Several tools are available on the market for this repackaging process. One is available on the Windows 2000 Professional CD. It is free for 60-day use and is called WinInstall Lite from Veritas (http://www.veritas.com/). This product is no longer on the Windows XP CDs. One of the best repackaging tools is Wise for Windows Installer from Wise Corporation (http://www.wise.com/), but if you are really serious about installation packaging, you should consider Package Studio, Enterprise Edition, from the same company. This is a comprehensive enterprise-level packaging solution. Another excellent tool is AdminStudio from InstallShield Corporation, the makers of InstallShield Setup (http://www.installshield.com/). These aren't the only products on the market, as you'll find when you search for Windows Installer repackaging on the Internet, but one of the prerequisites for an enterprise solution is a tool that will provide the same functionality for both repackaging commercial software and packaging corporate applications that you develop in-house. The last two products mentioned above provide this functionality.

Most likely your software assets will fall into several categories:

- **Native Windows Installer software** This software includes any product that bears the Designed for Windows Server 2003, Designed for Windows XP, or Designed for Windows

2000 logos. Part of the requirement for the logo program is integration with the Windows Installer service. You will most likely upgrade a portion of your network's software to this level. This should include the most popular software on your network.

- **MSI-integrated corporate applications**   New versions of your corporate applications should be integrated to the Windows Installer service.

- **Repackaged commercial software**   All products that are not upgraded should be repackaged. In most organizations undertaking this repackaging process, 99 percent of software has been repackaged to take advantage of Windows Installer. Only products such as device drivers or applications which install device drivers will resist Windows Installer integration.

- **Repackaged corporate applications**   Corporate applications that do not require recoding or upgrades can be repackaged in the same way as commercial software.

This undertaking will take considerable effort, but it is one of the migration processes that provide the best and most immediate return on investment.

Software Delivery in the Enterprise

The collection of Windows 2000 services known as IntelliMirror includes software installation services. It integrates the capability to install software through Group Policy. But software installation in the enterprise requires much more than Group Policy can provide. A comprehensive software installation program must include features such as:

- **Delivery guarantee**   To guarantee that a software installation has occurred before a given time. This is useful in corporate deployments when versions of software applications must match central data deposits.

- **Scheduling**   To control delivery times for non-working hours.

- **Bandwidth control**   To control bandwidth usage and compress data when sent over the WAN.

- **Inventory**   To ascertain that target systems have the required resources to install and operate the software and to keep abreast of where software has been installed.

- **Status**   To be able to determine the status of a software delivery job across the WAN to multiple geographic locations.

- **Reporting**   To be able to generate comprehensive activity reports.

- **Software metering**   To be able to determine if users you send software to actually require it.

None of these features are available with policy-based software delivery.

Enterprise Software Deployment Concepts

Since GPOs do not support these features and since an enterprise will not want to use multiple software delivery procedures (not if you use standard operating procedures), you will have to integrate a comprehensive software management system with your Active Directory. In the Microsoft world, this means using Systems Management Server. Two versions of SMS work with Windows Server 2003: SMS version 2.0 with Service Pack 4 or more and SMS 2003. Version 2.0 of SMS uses features compatible to Windows NT to integrate to the directory along with special scripts which help synchronize information between its own database and the directory. Version 2003 modifies the AD schema to integrate more directly with the directory. Both support enterprise software management processes.

Enterprise software delivery means being able to ensure that a process is repeatable and always gives the same result. In a standard operating environment, the software delivery process includes the steps outlined in Figure 5-9. New software packages are prepared and integrated into the corporate software asset repository. This repository is the single source listing of all authorized software (in MSI format). Software packages are assigned to groups that can be either users or computers. Most often, you will assign software to computers (especially if your organization promotes assigned PCs to users). Assigning software to users, especially in environments where users move from PC to PC, will constantly enable software installations and removals. If at all possible, assign software to users' primary systems.

▶ **QUICK TIP**

Windows XP and Windows Server 2003 promote the assignation of PCs to users much more than any other Windows operating system to date. This is because both support the Remote Desktop. Making extensive use of the Remote Desktop greatly reduces the software deployment workload because you only need to install software on a user's principal machine. Then, if the user needs to use another system, instead of delivering the same software product to this system, you can enable Remote Desktop on the user's primary PC. The user can remotely connect to their primary system from the other system. Remote Desktop gives the user access to everything on their principal system, uses little bandwidth since it is the same as Terminal Services, and greatly reduces the need for multiple installations of the same product. In Windows XP, Remote Desktop only supports a single user logged on at a time. If the user accesses their system through the remote desktop while someone else uses the system, it will log off the current user.

Software delivery is a good place to use the Distributed File System (DFS) since it allows you to use a single alias for all deposits wherever they are. More on this will be covered in Chapter 7, but the use of a single alias makes software packaging easier. In addition, the MSI file format supports multiple source listings, which helps ensure that self-healing will work no matter where the source file is located: either on the local system, on a local server, or on a remote server. As can be seen in Figure 5-9, this Software Delivery Process fulfills all of the requirements of enterprise software management.

Software Assignation

In the enterprise, you must manage software through assignations to computers (preferably). SMS has the ability to collect group information from Active Directory using the Group Discovery method. This method gathers Global Security group information from the directory and inserts it into the SMS database. Since discovery methods are dynamic, any changes to Global groups performed in Active Directory will be automatically reflected within the SMS database.

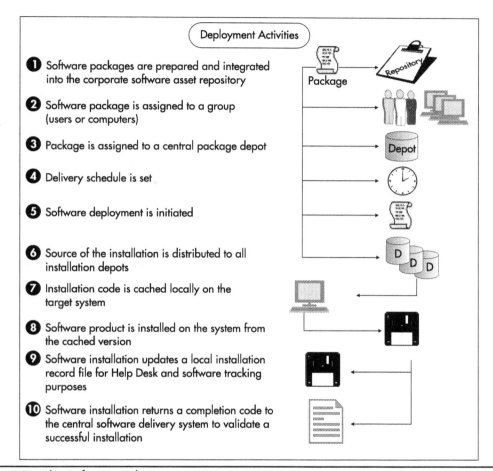

Figure 5-9   The Software Delivery Process

In addition, Windows Server 2003 allows you to treat machine accounts in many of the same ways you can treat user accounts. One of these is the assignation of membership in certain groups, notably Global Security groups. Thus you can use a combination of both features to manage software on your PCs. To do so, you need to perform a few activities beforehand. These include the following:

- Inventory all software in your network.
- Use the software kernel concept outlined in Chapter 1 for PC construction (the PASS model).
- Identify all non-kernel software.
- Regroup non-kernel software into role-based categories—groupings of software that are the same for given IT roles within the enterprise. For example, Web developers will always require tools such as FrontPage, Visio, Corel Draw, and Adobe Acrobat as well as the kernel. These

four products would be included in a Web Developer category, but not in the PC kernel. Perform this for all IT user roles within your enterprise.

- Create Global Security groups for each role within Active Directory (the production domain, of course). In SMS 2003, you can use Global Distribution groups since it has the ability to discover this group type. SMS 2.0 will only discover Global Security groups. By using distribution groups, you do not need to delegate rights to security group management. Machine accounts in Active Directory will need to be assigned to the appropriate groups when they are integrated to the directory.

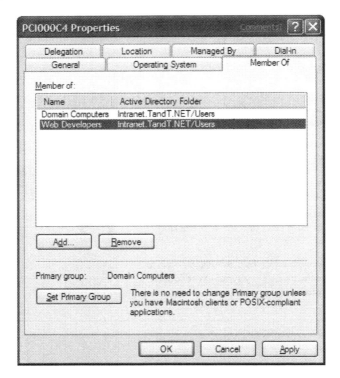

- Assign principal machines to each user.
- Create an inventory tying together user, principal machine, and software category for each user. You can even link this inventory to AD through programming.
- Assign the machines in Active Directory to appropriate Global groups.

Now you're ready to manage deliveries through SMS.

 NOTE

The Advanced Security Mode of SMS 2003 also works through the use of AD computer accounts.

A critical factor for this process to work is the *uninstallation* instructions within the SMS software delivery package. This is vital. The purpose of this entire process is to ensure that you can maintain a legal status for all software you deploy. If you do not include uninstallation instructions in your software delivery packages (Package Definition Files in SMS), the software you deploy will not be automatically removed when a PC is removed from a group authorizing the installation and use of the software. In SMS version 2, this is done by including the uninstallation registry key (found under HKEY_Local_Machine\Software\Microsoft\Windows\Currentversion\Uninstall) for the software package and selecting "Remove software when it is no longer advertised" within the advanced features of a package's properties. Since Windows Installer files always uninstall cleanly, this process should always work.

▶
QUICK TIP

A detailed presentation outlining how this process works is available at the companion Web site at http://www.Reso-Net.com/WindowsServer/.

In SMS, you need to create dynamic collections which correspond to the Global groups you created in Active Directory. Then assign software installation packages to the appropriate collections. That's it. Your enterprise software management system is now ready. From now on, all you need to do to deliver the proper software to a system is ensure that it is a member of the appropriate group within Active Directory. Then if the PC's vocation changes, just change its group memberships. SMS will automatically uninstall software that is no longer needed and install software belonging to the new vocation. This process is illustrated in Figure 5-10.

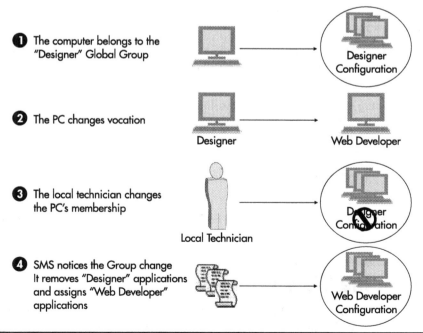

① The computer belongs to the "Designer" Global Group — Designer Configuration

② The PC changes vocation — Designer → Web Developer

③ The local technician changes the PC's membership — Local Technician → Designer Configuration

④ SMS notices the Group change It removes "Designer" applications and assigns "Web Developer" applications — Web Developer Configuration

Figure 5-10 Using Global groups to assign software

▶ *NOTE*

More information on this topic can be found by searching for "Set Strategies for Enterprise Software Management" at http://www.fawcette.com/dotnetmag/.

Legality and Regional PC Assignments

This strategy is very useful, especially if you have remote offices. In many organizations, the management of PC assignations in remote offices is very difficult because there is no official PC assignation process. For example, when a powerful new PC is delivered for use by an employee with little seniority, it often happens that this PC is "reassigned" by local staff to another staff member with more seniority. The employee for whom this PC was originally destined receives another PC that does not have appropriate software on it. While there are issues with this process, the major problem lies in the fact that neither PC has the appropriate software loaded on it. This is one of the reasons why organizations do not always conform to legal software usage guidelines.

The solution lies in the software management process outlined above. Linked with the AD delegation process, this system will ensure that even if PC vocations are changed, the proper software will always remain on each PC. To solve this issue, you need to implement an official PC assignment process. It should include a number of different elements, but mostly it should include:

- The implementation of the software management process based on role-based PC categorization groups.
- The creation of an OU structure which places regional PC objects within a regional organizational unit.
- The delegation of specific rights over PC objects to local technical staff. These rights should include the ability to modify a computer's group memberships.
- The documentation of the official PC assignation process.
- A formal training program to all regional technical staff.

Now that the process is official, there is no reason for copies of software products to be found on systems that have been reassigned.

▶ **QUICK TIP**

It is much easier to delegate AD consoles than it is to delegate SMS consoles, even in SMS 2003.

Completing the OU Strategy

Now you're ready to complete your OU design for PC management and administration. You have reviewed the requirements for Group Policy application. You have reviewed the requirements for delegation within your enterprise. And you have reviewed the requirements for PC management and administration. You should have everything in hand to go ahead and finalize your OU design for PC management. Once it is finalized, you can put it in place. The next section gives an example based on a centralized PC Management Strategy.

Putting the PCs OU Infrastructure in Place

T&T Corporation is ready to implement their PCs organizational unit infrastructure. They have determined that they need to use a centralized management strategy with delegation only to central technicians for specific tasks such as assigning PC group memberships for software delivery. They will implement the PCs OU design that was outlined previously in Figure 5-5. To do this, they will need to perform the following activities:

- Create and document the entire OU/GPO/delegation/management strategy for PCs
- Create the OU structure using AD Users and Computers
- Create and document the appropriate GPOs for each container
- Assign the Block Policy inheritance property to appropriate OUs (if required)
- Delegate the proper level of authority to technical staff
- Create the groups required for software delivery through SMS

Once each of these tasks is complete, the infrastructure to receive new PCs within the parallel network will be in place.

For the first activity, you must use information grids. These will help you document your entire OU/GPO/delegation/management strategy for PCs. For your own network, do not proceed with the other steps until you have completed these grids. You should not begin to use any of these features until your strategy has been fully planned and documented.

▶ **NOTE**

Information grids for the documentation of an OU/GPO/delegation/management strategy are available at http://www.Reso-Net.com/WindowsServer/.

For the second activity, make sure you are within the Intranet.TandT.net domain and open AD Users and Computers. Place the cursor's focus on the domain, then either right-click to create a new organizational unit from the context menu, or use the console toolbar to click the New Organizational Unit button. Both will display the New Organizational Unit dialog box. Type in the OU's name and click OK. The OUs that need to be created have been listed previously in Table 5-1. Repeat the process until each OU has been created. Don't worry if you create an OU in the wrong place, all you need to do is drag it to the appropriate place once created since WS03 supports drag and drop. The resulting OU structure is illustrated in Figure 5-11.

Figure 5-11   A PC management OU structure

Five PC-related GPOs are required for T&T Corporation. Here's how to create them:

1. Begin by downloading the GPO spreadsheet from the companion Web site.

2. Identify all of the settings you require for each GPO using the information in Table 5-2.

3. Fully document each GPO.

4. When ready, move to AD Users and Computers, right-click on the PCs OU, and select Properties.

5. Under the Group Policy tab, click New.

6. Name the policy, using the information in Table 5-1. This policy is named Global PC GPO.

7. Once the GPO is named, click Edit. This launches the Group Policy Editor (GPE).

8. Right-click on the policy name and select Properties. In the properties dialog box, click the Disable User Configuration Settings checkbox. These settings need to be disabled since this GPO is for computers only.

9. WS03 displays a warning to tell you that none of the disabled settings will be applied. Click Yes to close it. Close the Properties dialog box by clicking OK.

10. In the Group Policy Editor, use the * key on your keypad to expand all of the subsections of the Group Policy object. Move through the policy to modify appropriate settings. For example, in this GPO you will want to set the Automatic Updates Properties for all PCs.

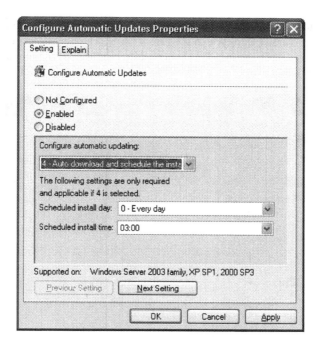

11. Close the GPE when done. You can also close the PCs OU Property dialog box since no other action needs to be performed on the GPO. (For example, No Override is not required since T&T will not delegate GPO creation to other users.)

12. Repeat this process for each GPO you need to create. This includes the Global Desktop GPO, the Global Mobile GPO (for EFS mostly), the Global External GPO, and the Global Kiosk GPO (for more security and to enable Loopback).

13. Move to the PCs/External/Unmanaged OU. Right-click on this OU and select Properties. Move to the Group Policy tab and click the Block Policy inheritance checkbox. T&T has decided to leave all external unmanaged systems without any significant GPO assignment.

Two more tasks are required to complete the PCs OU setup: delegating authority and creating software category groups. Both are relatively simple.

T&T has decided that the only tasks they will delegate to technicians are the ability to modify group memberships for PCs and the ability to manage PC location information. The latter is tied to the WS03 Printer Location Tracking Service which links the nearest printer to users' PCs. More on this subject is covered in Chapter 7. The former will ensure that they will be able to modify a PC's vocation when it is reassigned to a new user. Once again, this is done in AD Users and Computers.

1. The first thing you need to do is create a group to which you can delegate authority. It doesn't matter if you don't know who will be in this group yet, all you need is the group with the proper delegation rights. You can assign members to the group later. Since Windows Server 2003 uses Domain Local Groups for rights assignments (more in Chapter 6), you will create a Domain Local group called PC Technicians (Local). To do so, right-click on the Users object

in the directory and select New | Group. Click the Domain Local radio button, make sure that Security Group is selected, and type in the group name. The down-level (or pre-Windows 2000) group name is L_PC_Technicians. This is not really required since there are no down-level systems in the parallel network, but it pays to be structured anyway. Click OK to create the group.

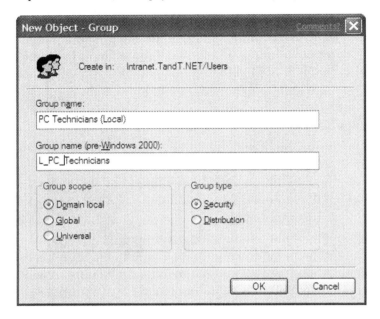

2. Right-click on the PCs OU (top-level) and select Delegate Control from the context menu.

3. Follow the steps provided by the wizard. Add the PC Technicians (Local) group, and then click Next.

4. Delegate a Custom task and then click Next.

5. In the Active Directory Object Type window, select Only the following objects in this folder. Click the Computer Objects checkbox, and then click Next.

6. Uncheck General and check Property-specific. Then scroll down the list to check appropriate values. The technicians require the right to read most object properties and the right to write group memberships as well as write PC location information. Use your judgment to apply appropriate rights. For example, it will be useful for technicians to be able to write descriptions for computers that change vocation, but it will not be a good idea to let them change the computer name. Make a note of each security property you assign.

7. Click Next when done. Click Finish once you have reviewed the wizard's task list.

Delegation is now complete, but you still need to create a delegation console for the technicians. Use the instructions outlined earlier in "Creating Custom Microsoft Management Consoles" for console creation and be sure that you set the focus for the console on the PCs OU. Store the console in the PCs OU as well. Finally, use Terminal Services to distribute the console to technicians.

The final activity for the PCs OU strategy is the creation of Global Security groups that correspond to the software categories in your organization. You can have several of these, but most organizations try to keep them to a bare minimum. If you have designed your PC kernel properly, you should be able to satisfy a very large clientele with it—all generic or common users, in fact. Then your software categories include only the systems that require additional software. This software should be grouped by common need. An organization that has more than 3,000 users, for example, only uses nine software categories over and above the kernel. Another with 12,500 users has 15 categories, mostly because they are distributed worldwide and special software products are required in different geographic regions.

The first thing you need to do is create the groups. It doesn't matter if you don't know which machines will be in this group yet; all you need is the group itself. You can assign members to the group later. If you are using SMS 2.0, you'll need to create Global Security groups.

To create your software category groups, use the following procedure:

1. Right-click on the PCs OU object in the directory and select New | Group. Make sure the Global radio button is selected, determine if you need a Security or a Distribution group, and then type in the group name. Use significant names for both the actual name and the down-level group name. Remember that down-level names are usually linked together since down-level systems do not like names with spaces. Click OK to create the group.

2. Repeat as many times as required.

Your PCs OU structure is now in place. Machine groups have been created directly in the PCs OU so that they will be subject to machine policies. You will also need to complete your software distribution strategy within SMS.

Now the only thing you need to do is ensure that machines are placed within the appropriate OU and the appropriate software category group when you integrate them into the parallel network.

Preparing the OU structure before integrating new machines into the network also ensures that they will be managed as soon as they join the network. Mistakes are minimized when you use this procedure because everything is ready *before* PCs are integrated into the network.

Chapter 7 will identify how you can coordinate this OU strategy with the use of RIS to install PCs. You can also script the addition of PC names into your directory before installing the actual machines.

Next, you'll begin to look at how you can use this same approach to prepare for users within your enterprise network.

 # Using the Group Policy Management Console

Microsoft has released the Group Policy Management Console (GPMC) as an add-on to WS03. This console can be downloaded from the Microsoft Windows Server 2003 Web site (http://www.microsoft.com/windowsserver2003/). The best feature of the GPMC is that it provides a single, integrated interface for the management of all GPO activities within the enterprise. As mentioned earlier, it is not as complete as commercial consoles, but for a free add-on, it provides a lot more functionality than the traditional GPO management approach.

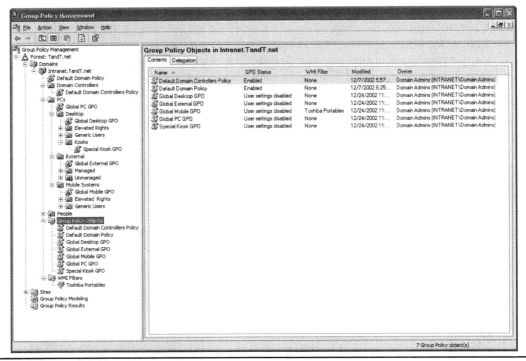

Figure 5-12 Using the GPMC to manage PC GPOs

The GPMC is a Windows Installer file that can be installed either on WS03 or Windows XP. If you install it on a server, you can use it through Terminal Services (this is the recommended approach). Once installed, the traditional GPO management method will no longer be available. The GPOs created in this chapter are illustrated in Figure 5-12. As you can see, the GPMC allows you to configure everything in a much more simple and straightforward manner.

▶ **NOTE**

The traditional approach to GPO management has been used throughout this chapter because it is important for you to understand how to manage GPOs without the GPMC. But from now on, all GPO-related activities will be managed through the GPMC.

Best Practice Summary

This chapter recommends the following best practices:

- Segregate by object type at the first OU level. This makes it easier to manage objects.
- Do not move domain controllers from their default OU.

- Integrate your PCs OU strategy with your GPO, delegation, and software management strategies.
- Minimize the use of the No Override and Block Policy Inheritance settings because they complicate the use of policies.
- Always document all of the GPOs you create and make sure your entire GPO/OU solution is completely documented.
- Use a standard naming strategy for all GPOs and maintain a complete GPO registry.
- Keep to the GPO KISS (Keep It Simple, Stupid) rule. Don't complicate matters if you can help it. For example, apply general settings at the top of the GPO application hierarchy, and then refine them further at each lower level.
- Adjust the default GPOs in the forest root domain before creating any of the child domains.
- Try to avoid linking policies between domains.
- Set local GPOs once and stabilize them. Since they are distributed (on each computer system), you'll want to modify them as little as possible.
- Modify GPOs to always refresh, but do not disable Fast Logon Optimization. This ensures that security settings are always applied but that logon speed is not impacted.
- Turn to GPO filtering if you find your OU design becomes too complex because of your GPO application strategy.
- Always make sure your kiosk PCs are highly secure.
- If you use the Loopback setting, make sure you create a special GPO and link it to a special OU that will be used to store the PCs the GPO applies to.
- Be thorough when you create your Delegation Plan.
- Make sure you assign the delegation manager role in your organization.
- Support your delegation strategy with appropriate custom MMCs.
- Custom consoles are an important part of a WS03 delegation strategy. Make sure your consoles are secure and well documented.
- Custom MMCs should be deployed through Terminal Services to maintain central control of all custom consoles.
- Integrate your software management system with your Active Directory and use AD as the source of enterprise software delivery.
- Manage Software Lifecycles by integrating all application installs to the Windows Installer service.
- To use the self-healing capabilities of Windows Installer, you must maintain a permanent software installation depot.
- Ensure the machines are placed within the appropriate OU and the appropriate software category group when they are integrated into the parallel network.
- Assign PCs to primary users and use the Remote Desktop to give them access to their software when they are away from their PC.
- Use the GPMC to manage all GPOs within the enterprise.

Chapter Roadmap

Use the illustration in Figure 5-13 to review the contents of this chapter.

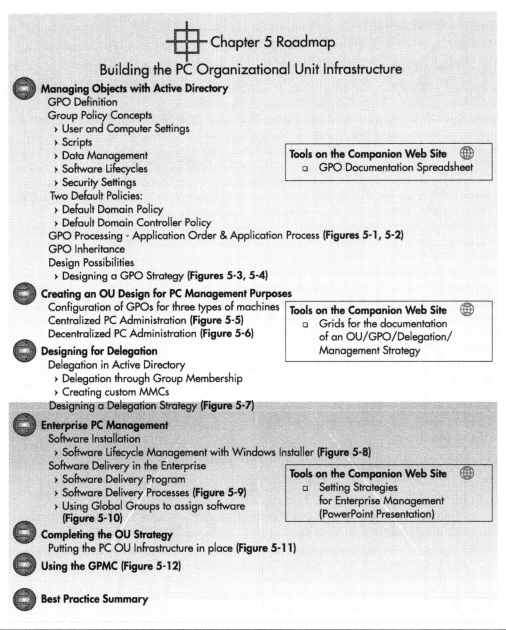

Figure 5-13   Chapter Roadmap

CHAPTER 6

Preparing the User Organizational Unit Infrastructure

Chapter 5 outlined how to prepare your management environment for PC objects. This chapter continues the Parallel Network Implementation Process by helping you identify how to create a user management environment within the Active Directory. When this infrastructure is in place, you will be able to migrate users from your existing network into the new parallel environment.

Three activities are required for the creation of a user organizational unit infrastructure:

- The User and Group Management Strategy
- The User Delegation Strategy
- The User Group Policy Management Strategy

The first forms the core of traditional user management strategies. The second identifies how your organization plans to use the decentralized management features of Windows Server 2003 to provide relief to central management and administration groups, and assign administrative activities where responsibility centers are located. The third activity is very similar to the same activity in Chapter 5. This time though, you will focus on the *user* portion of Group Policy objects.

Once these strategies are defined and in place, they'll form the basis of the different strategies you can use to massively migrate users from your existing network to the parallel environment.

Managing User Objects with Active Directory

User objects are special objects within the directory. After all, if it wasn't for users, there wouldn't be much need for enterprise networks. In traditional networks such as Windows NT, User objects are mostly managed through the groups they belong to. Groups are also present in Active Directory. In fact, it is essential to have a comprehensive group management strategy within your WS03 network if you want to be able to administer user-related events within it. But group management is not the only requirement anymore.

Like computers, users are also affected by Group Policy. The GPO strategy you design for users will complement the group strategy you intend to use. In addition, you will need to consider how and to whom you will delegate some administrative tasks, since user management is by far the heaviest workload in the directory. Each of these strategies serves as the input for the design of your User Organizational Unit infrastructure.

As outlined in Chapter 3, a User object can only be contained within a single OU. Chapter 5 illustrated how the location of this OU could affect the User object through the hierarchical application of Group Policy objects. It also illustrated how GPOs can be filtered through the use of security groups. Though the user account can only be within a single OU, it can be included within a multitude of groups. Thus, OUs are usually seen as a means to provide vertical user management while groups provide horizontal management. This cross-management structure is illustrated in Figure 6-1. This element will have a direct impact on the way you design your User Object Management Strategy.

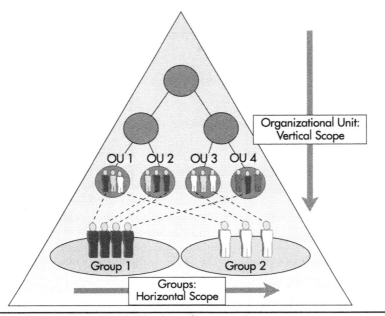

Figure 6-1   The cross-management relationship of OUs and groups

The Active Directory User Object

The Windows Server 2003 User object is much the same as its Windows 2000 counterpart, but quite different from its Windows NT counterpart. This is because of the nature of a directory service. One of the basic functions of a directory service is to store information in order to make it available to users, administrators, even applications. While the Windows NT User object basically stored the user's name, password, and account particularities, the WS03 User object can store more than 200 properties. Many of these are generated automatically. Nevertheless, there are almost 100 properties that can be set interactively for each user. This means that you must determine which properties you will manage and who will be responsible for each of these properties within your network.

Fortunately, you will be able to delegate quite a few of these properties to other personnel. Since many of a user's properties have to do with their localization within the organization, it makes sense to let users manage many of their own properties within the directory. You'll also probably have a number of other administrative levels within your organization. The system-related administrative levels will be covered in Chapter 7. The user-related administrative levels are covered in this chapter. Administrative tasks will be covered in Chapter 10.

User versus InetOrgPerson

Active Directory includes two User object classes: User and InetOrgPerson. The *User* class object is the traditional User object that organizations normally use when designing network infrastructures. In the intranet portion of the enterprise network, the User object is the one you will focus on. In addition, if you migrate User objects from an existing Windows NT or Windows 2000 network to a Windows Server 2003 network, the user accounts will be created with the User object class.

InetOrgPerson is a new addition to Active Directory. It is an object class found in standard Lightweight Directory Access Protocol (LDAP) implementations and has been added to Active Directory to provide better compatibility to these implementations. In LDAP, it is used to represent people who are associated with an organization in some way. In WS03, it is almost exactly the same as the user class object because it is derived from this class. In fact, in a native WS03 forest, the InetOrgPerson object becomes a complete security principal enabling the object to be associated with a password in the same manner as a standard User object. InetOrgPerson is used in several third-party LDAP and X.500 directory implementations and is provided in WS03 to facilitate migrations from these directories to Active Directory.

▶ **NOTE**

InetOrgPerson was available for Windows 2000, but as a patch to Active Directory.

Windows Server 2003 implementations will tend to focus on the User object rather than the InetOrgPerson object. But if you need to integrate a directory application that requires use of this object or if you intend to use Active Directory within your extranet with partners hosting other directory services, you will find the addition of this class object quite useful.

Both types of objects, user and InetOrgPerson, are created the same way. Interactively, they can be created through the use of either the New command in the context menu or the toolbar buttons within the Active Directory Users and Computers console.

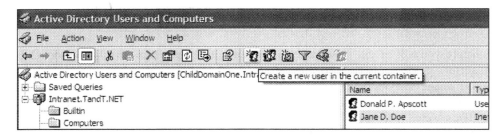

Since both object classes are quite similar, this chapter will focus on the User object class.

The Contact-Class Object

A third user-like object class exists within Active Directory. It is the *Contact* object class. This object is a subclass of the User object. It is not, however, a security principal. It is mostly used as an email address and can thus be used for communication purposes. The Contact object includes less than half of the properties of the User object.

Contacts can be included within groups in the directory, but since they are not security principals, you cannot assign permissions or user rights to them. Creating contacts is the same as creating user or InetOrgPerson objects.

Contacts are mostly used to store information about personnel outside your organization (since you require a means to contact them) who do not require access to internal resources. More than 30 settings can be managed for each contact. This task is often delegated to personnel in Human Resources since it does not require extensive training, but does require structure and control.

```
┌─────────────────────────────────────────────────────────────┐
│ Yoshi Akura Properties                              [?][X]    │
├───────────────────┬──────────────┬──────────────────────────┤
│   Member Of       │    Object    │      Security            │
│ General     Address      Telephones        Organization     │
│                                                               │
│  [=]    Yoshi Akura                                           │
│                                                               │
│  First name:      [Yoshi          ]   Initials: [        ]    │
│                                                               │
│  Last name:       [Akura                              ]       │
│                                                               │
│  Display name:    [Yoshi Akura                        ]       │
│                                                               │
│  Description:     [PR Manager for T&T Japan           ]       │
│                                                               │
│  Office:          [Hiroshima, Japan                   ]       │
│                                                               │
│                                                               │
│  Telephone number: [(555) 555-1212    ]    [ Other... ]       │
│                                                               │
│  E-mail:          [yoshi.akura@tandt.com              ]       │
│                                                               │
│  Web page:        [www.tandt.com/japan ]   [ Other... ]       │
│                                                               │
│                     [ OK ]   [ Cancel ]   [ Apply ]           │
└─────────────────────────────────────────────────────────────┘
```

User Object Property Sheets

One of the activities you will need to perform during the Planning Phase of your WS03 directory is to identify which User object properties you want to manage, who will be responsible for the administration of the values for each property, and how these properties will integrate with your other identity management databases within your organization. If you determine that Active Directory will be the host database for some user-related primary data values, you will need to ensure that these values are always up to date and always protected and recoverable.

In fact, it is quite possible that you will decide that AD is the primary source for user data within the organization since it is replicated on a constant basis and available to all members of the organization in all locations. Remember, though, that AD replication includes latency. This means that you shouldn't store data that is of a timely nature within the directory. For example, you can store a user's office phone number in the directory because chances are that other users within your network don't need it immediately. But you shouldn't store your company's price list in the directory, especially if your replication latency is significant, because it means that when you change a price, some users will have access to the old price (replication has not yet occurred) and some will have access to the new price (replication has occurred). At best, this would lead to very unhappy customers. At worse, it could lead to potential financial losses for the company.

In addition, you will probably decide that the directory is the proper place to store employee business addresses and phone numbers, but not employee home addresses and other personal information because users can search the directory. You yourself probably don't want other employees to phone you at home to bother you with office questions. On the other hand, your organization must have this information, but since it is of a private nature, it will most likely be stored within the Human Resources database. This database can have a link to AD to enable it to share information with and possibly update information in the directory. Similarly, asset management databases would have a link to AD to share information on computer resources.

▶ QUICK TIP

Before you decide which role AD will play in the user data management process, you need to gain a better understanding of each of the properties of the User object within the directory. A table providing a complete list of the default attributes and recommendations for attributes that should be considered as primary values within your organization can be found at http://www.Reso-Net.com/WindowsServer/. It is highly recommended that you download this table and become familiar with its contents before you finalize your AD User Object Management Strategy.

User-Managed Properties

By default, users can manage their own data within the directory. All they have to do is use their desktop to search for their own names within Active Directory. Once they have found their name, they need to view its properties. The Properties dialog box will automatically gray out the parts they cannot change and display in white the parts they have control over. Mostly, they control their own business information. The problem with this update method is that there is no quality control over data entry in Active Directory.

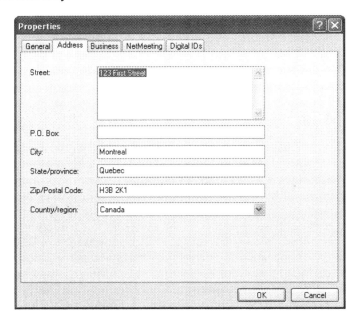

Users can enter phone numbers using dots, can forget to add their area code, can even enter more than one number in the field, and Active Directory will accept the entry. Supporting this type of modification does not lead to the type of standardized information input required at the enterprise level.

One of the best ways to let users manage their own data is to provide them with an intranet Web page that automatically locates their name in AD and lets them modify elements such as their address and phone number, additional phone numbers, and other information. This Web page can authenticate them as they arrive (using the single sign-on capabilities of WS03 and Internet Information Server), validate that the information they enter is in the appropriate format, and automatically update the directory when completed. Such a Web page can easily be designed using the Active Directory Services Interface (ADSI) and simple content validation rules to ensure that all values are entered in a standard format. Figure 6-2 displays an example of such a Web page. Note that the entire Address portion can be further controlled through the use of drop-down lists since the choices for each address can be preset. Other fields such as State/Province, Zip/Postal Code, and so on can be automatically filled when the street address is selected. This removes the possibility of errors when users update their own information.

Creating User Objects

There are two ways to activate the User Creation Wizard: either through the use of the New command in the context menu or through the use of the New User icon in the AD Users and Computers console toolbar. Once the wizard is activated, two main panels are displayed. The first deals with the account names. Here you set the user's full name, the user's display name, their logon name or their user principal name (UPN), and their down-level (or pre-Windows 2000) logon name.

The next screen deals with the password and account restrictions. Type in the Default User password and make sure the checkbox for "User must change password at next logon" is selected. If the user is not ready to take immediate possession of the account, you should check the "Account is disabled" option as well. You can also set a password never to expire in addition to stating that the user cannot change the password. Both are usually set for non-user accounts—service accounts that are designed to operate services or generic purpose accounts.

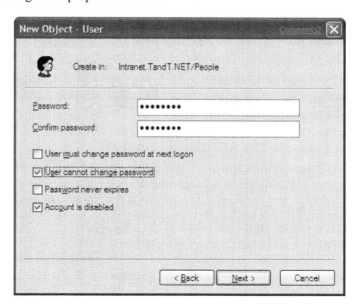

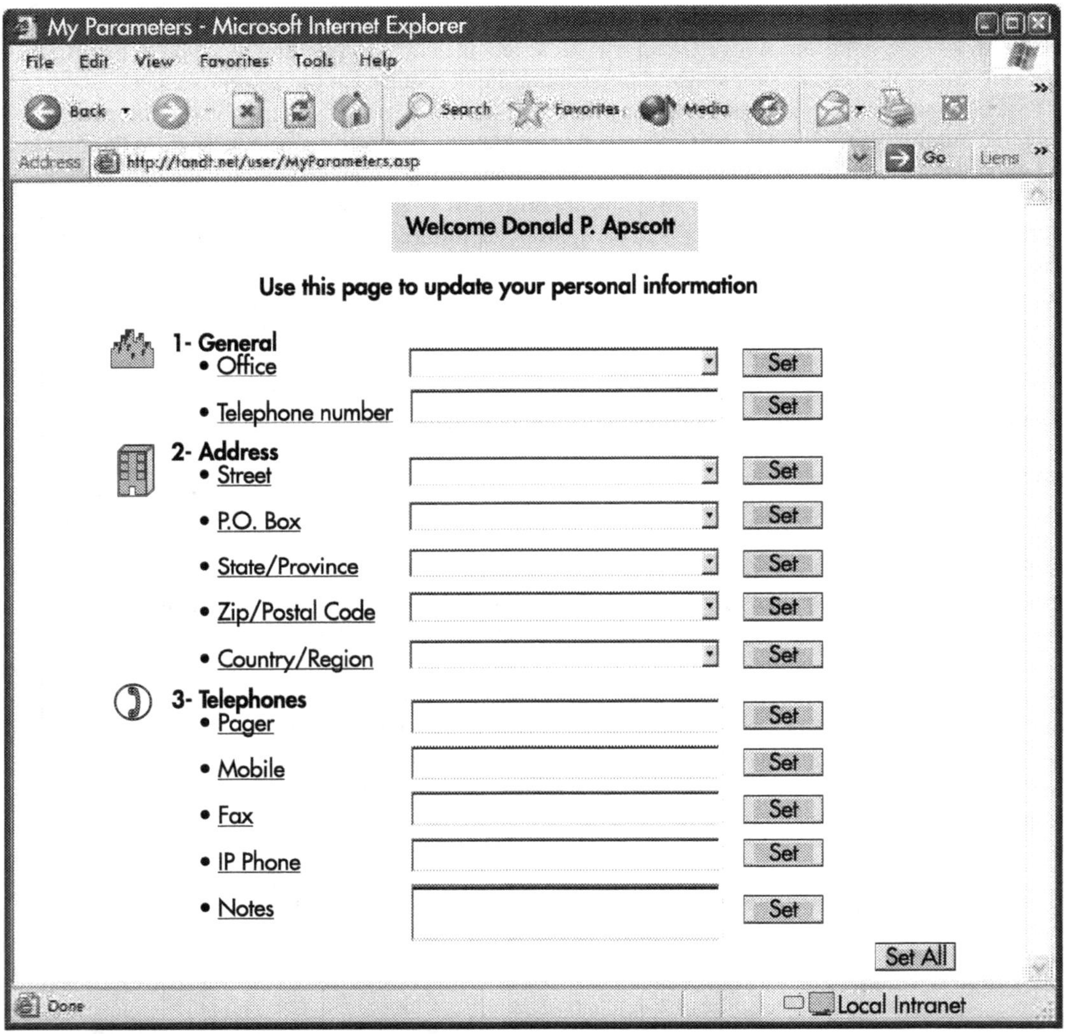

Figure 6-2 A user data management intranet page

Windows Server 2003 supports two types of logon names: the UPN and the down-level logon name. The latter is related to the Windows NT logon name you gave your users. If you are migrating from a Windows NT environment, make sure you use the same down-level name strategy (unless there are compelling reasons to change this strategy). Users will be familiar with this strategy and will be able to continue using the logon name they are most familiar with. Down-level logon names are most often used within the same WS03 domain.

User Principal Names

If your users must navigate from domain to domain or from forest to forest, you should get them used to working with their user principal name. The UPN is usually composed of the user's name and a suffix including the name of the domain or forest they log onto. Many organizations tend to use the user's email address as the UPN. Of course, since in the examples in this book your internal forest name is based on a .net extension and your external name is based on a .com or other public extension, you need to modify the default UPN suffix that is displayed when creating accounts.

This is done through the Active Directory Domains and Trusts console in the forest root domain with Enterprise Administrator credentials.

1. Launch the Active Directory Domains and Trusts console. This can be done through the Start Menu or through the Manage Your Server console.

2. Right-click on Active Directory Domains and Trusts and select Properties.

3. Move to the UPN Suffix tab, type in the new suffix, and click Add.

4. Type in as many suffixes as required. One is usually all you need if your forest has only one tree. If you host more than one tree in your forest, you will require more suffixes. Click OK when done.

5. Close the AD Domains and Trusts console.

The new suffix will now be displayed in the User Logon Name dialog box and can be assigned to users. Be careful how you use UPN suffixes. Removing a UPN suffix that is in use will cause users to be unable to log in. WS03 will give you a warning when you perform this operation.

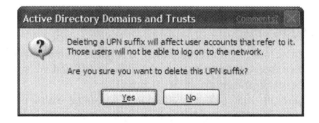

Default WS03 Accounts

WS03 installs several default accounts when you create your first domain controller. These are similar to the default accounts created on either workstations or Member Servers. They include:

- **Administrator** This is the global administration account for the domain. It should be renamed through a GPO and locked. A strong password should be set on this account. All domain management activities should be performed through accounts that are copies of this main account. Other administration tasks should be performed through accounts that have specific permissions for the services they must manage.

- **Guest**   This account is disabled by default and is not a part of the Authenticated Users group. It is designed to allow guests access to your network. Guest access is no longer very popular. It is always best to create limited access accounts and enable them on an as-needed basis.

- **HelpAssistant_*nnnnnn***   This account is designed to provide Remote Assistance within the domain. It is activated by default. At a minimum, its password should be reset so that you maintain control over the account. A strong password should be set for this account. If Remote Assistance is not planned for the site, change the password and disable the account. (Note: *nnnnnn* refers to a randomly generated number based on the domain name.)

- **krbtgt**   This account is the Key Distribution Center Service Account. It is disabled by default and is only used when you put a public key infrastructure (PKI) in place within your domain.

- **SUPPORT_388945a0**   This is an example of a vendor account, in this case Microsoft. It is provided to allow Microsoft to provide you with direct online support through Remote Assistance. It is disabled by default.

All of these accounts are also found on local systems except for the krbtgt account since a public key infrastructure requires a domain to function. In addition, the local HelpAssistant account name on Windows XP machines does not include any numbers. All default accounts are located within the Users container in the Active Directory.

Administrator   Guest   HelpAssista...   krbtgt   SUPPORT_3...

Using Template Accounts

The ideal way to create an account is to use a template. Template accounts have been supported in Microsoft networks since the very first versions of Windows NT and are supported in Windows Server 2003. There are some significant differences, though.

To create a template account, you use the standard user account creation process, but you assign different properties to the account. For one thing, the template account must always be disabled. It is not designed for regular use; it is designed to be the basis for the creation of other accounts. To do so, you simply need to copy the template account. WS03 launches the New Account Wizard and lets you assign a new name and password while retaining several of the template account's properties. Retained properties are outlined in Table 6-1.

> ► **QUICK TIP**
>
> *For profile path and home folder names to be modified, the setting used to create the template account's profile path and home folder must be performed with the %username% variable (that is, using a UNC plus the variable, for example: \\server\sharename\%username%).*

User Property Dialog Box Tab	Retained Values
General	None
Address	Everything except the street address
Account	Logon hours Log onto… User must change password at next logon Account is disabled Password never expires User cannot modify password
Profile (Note: This tab is becoming obsolete in WS03)	Everything, but profile path and home folder are both changed to reflect the new user's name
Telephones	None
Organization	Everything except the title
Terminal Services Profile	None; the account is reset to default settings
Environment	None; the account is reset to default settings
Sessions	None; the account is reset to default settings
Remote control	None; the account is reset to default settings
COM+	None
Published Certificates	None
Member of	Everything
Dial-in	None; the account is reset to default settings
Security	Everything

Table 6-1   Template Account Attribute Retention

Template accounts are ideally suited to the delegation of account creation. Designing a template account for a user representative and delegating the account creation process based on copies of this account instead of the creation of a new account from scratch ensures that your corporate standards are maintained even if you delegate this activity. In addition, user representatives cannot create accounts with more security rights than the template account you delegate to them.

You can also see that even with a template account, several values need to be reset each time you copy the account. This is an excellent argument for the use of Group Policy objects to set these values instead of limiting their use within each account. GPOs set values globally simply by being outlined at a central location. This is the recommended method to use.

Massive User Management

Windows Server 2003 offers several enhancements in regards to the ability to manage several objects at once. For example, you can now select multiple objects and drag and drop them from one location to the other within the directory because this functionality is supported in the AD consoles.

You can also select several objects and modify some of their properties at the same time. For example, you can select several User objects and modify their description in a single step. You can also move several accounts at once, enable or disable them, add them to a group, send mail to them, and use standard cut and paste functions.

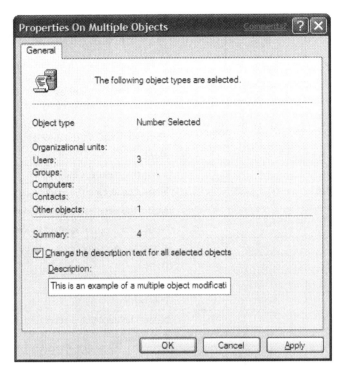

But when you need to perform massive user management tasks—for example, modify the settings on large numbers of users—you are better off using scripts. WS03, like Windows 2000, supports the Windows Scripting Host (WSH) toolset. WSH includes the ability to create and run scripts in either Visual Basic Script (VBS) or JavaScript. In addition, with the use of ADSI and WMI, you can truly create powerful jobs that will perform massive modifications for you.

When it comes to creating a vast number of users, you'll find that the Windows Server Support Tools and Resource Kit include a number of different tools that can be used to help out in these situations. Some of the most important are:

- **ClonePrincipal** A series of VBS scripts that copy accounts from NT to WS03.

- **AddUser** A VBS script that adds users found in an Excel spreadsheet to the directory.

- **Active Directory Migration Tool (ADMT)** Migrates users from Windows NT or Windows 2000 to WS03. Includes password migration. More information is available in Chapter 10.

There are also third-party tools that provide this functionality. Their advantage is that they provide full reporting capabilities while migrating or creating vast numbers of users.

> **QUICK TIP**
>
> *More information on user scripting is available at the Microsoft Script Center (http://www.microsoft.com/technet/treeview/default.asp?url=/technet/scriptcenter/sampscr.asp).*

Managing and Administering Groups

User objects are created within the directory for a variety of reasons. One of the most important is the assignation of permissions, both within the directory as well as permissions to access objects outside the directory such as printer queues and file folders. Permissions are assigned through the use of groups. In fact, one of the first best practices you learn in any network environment is that you never assign permissions to individual users; you always assign them to groups.

Assigning permissions is a complex task. If you assign permissions to a user and the next day another user comes along who requires the same permissions, you have to start over from scratch. But if you assign permissions to a group, even if there is only one person within the group, and another user comes along requiring the same permissions, all you need to do is place the user within the group.

On the other hand, this strategy works only if you have complete documentation about each of the groups you create in your directory. It's easy to include users into an existing group if you created the group yesterday and today someone requires the same rights. But if you created the group last year and someone requires the same rights today, chances are that you might not remember that the original group exists. This problem is compounded when group management is distributed. You might remember why you created a group, but other group administrators within your organization won't have a clue the group exists unless you find a way to tell them.

This usually leads to a proliferation of groups within the organization. Here's why. Admin 1 creates a group for a specific purpose. Admin 1 places users within the group. Admin 2 comes along a while later with another request for the same rights. Admin 2 does not know that the group Admin 1 created exists. So, just to be safe, Admin 2 creates a new group for the same purpose and so on. Most organizations that do not have a structured approach for group management will find that when they migrate from Windows NT to Windows Server 2003, they need to perform an extensive group rationalization— they need to inventory all groups, find out who is responsible for the group, find out the group purpose, find out if it is still necessary. If answers cannot be found for these questions, then the group is a good candidate for rationalization and elimination.

The best way to avoid this type of situation is to document all groups at all times and to make sure that this documentation is communicated to all affected personnel. Active Directory provides the ideal solution. Group management in AD is simplified since the Group object supports several new properties that assist in the group management process:

- **Description** This field was present in Windows NT, but it was seldom used. Use it fully in Windows Server 2003.

- **Notes** This field is used to identify the full purpose of a group. This information will provide great help in long-term group management. Both Description and Notes are on the General tab of the Group Properties dialog box.

- **Managed by** This field is used to identify the group's manager. A group manager is not necessarily the group's administrator as can be evidenced in the Manager can update membership list checkbox. Check this box if you have delegation rules in place and your group manager is also your group administrator. This entire property page is devoted to ensuring that you know who is responsible for the group at all times.

Filling out these fields is essential in an enterprise network group management strategy.

> ▶ **QUICK TIP**
>
> *Microsoft provides excellent reference information on this topic at http://www.microsoft.com/ technet/treeview/default.asp?url=/technet/prodtechnol/ad/windows2000/maintain/adusers.asp.*

WS03 Groups Types and Group Scopes

Windows Server 2003 boasts two main group types:

- **Security** Groups that are considered security objects and that can be used to assign access rights and permissions. These groups can also be used as an email address. Emails sent to the group are received by each individual user who is a member of the group.

- **Distribution** Groups that are not security-enabled. They are mostly used in conjunction with email applications such as Microsoft Exchange or software distribution applications such as Microsoft Systems Management Server 2003.

Groups within native WS03 forests can be converted from one type to another at any time.

In addition to group type, WS03 supports several different group scopes. Group scopes are determined by group location. If the group is located on a local computer, its scope will be local. This means that its members and the permissions you assign to it will affect only the computer on which the group is located. If the group is contained within a domain in a forest, it will have either a domain or a forest scope. Once again, the domain and forest modes have an impact on group functionality. In a native WS03 forest, you will be able to work with the following group scopes:

- **Domain Local** Members can include accounts (user and computer), other Domain Local groups, Global groups, and Universal groups.

- **Global** Members can include accounts and other Global groups from within the same domain.

- **Universal** Members can include accounts, Global groups, and Universal groups from anywhere in the forest or even across forests if a trust exists.

Group scope is illustrated in Figure 6-3. In a WS03 native forest, you can change the scope of a group. Global groups can be changed to Universal, Universal to Domain Local, and so on. There are some restrictions on scope changes, though:

- Global groups cannot become Universal groups if they already belong to another Global group.

- Universal groups cannot become Global groups if they include another Universal group.

- Universal groups can become Domain Local groups at any time because Domain Local groups can contain any type of group.

- Domain Local groups cannot become Universal groups if they contain another Domain Local group.

- All other group scope changes are allowed.

Groups can be *nested* in WS03. This means that a group can include other groups of the same scope. Thus, you can create "super" groups that are designed to contain other subgroups of the same type. As you can see, without some basic guidelines, using groups in WS03 can become quite confusing. First, you need to understand how default groups have been defined within the directory.

▶ | **QUICK TIP**

One of the best ways to become familiar with default groups in WS03 is to use the default group information table located on the companion Web site at http://www.Reso-Net.com/WindowsServer/.

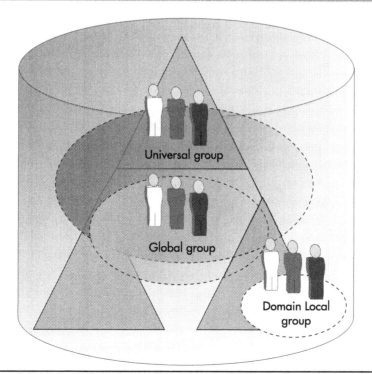

Figure 6-3   Group scopes within a forest

Best Practices for Group Management/Creation

Group management practices can become quite complex. This is why a group management strategy is essential to the operation of an enterprise network. This strategy begins with best practice rules and guidelines. It is complemented by a strategic use of Global groups or groups that are designed to contain users. The varying scopes of all of the groups within Active Directory will not help your group management activities if you do not implement basic guidelines for group usage. Thus there is a best practice rule for using groups. It is the User-Global Group-Domain Local Group-Permissions rule or UGLP rule. This rule outlines how groups are used.

It begins with the placement of users. All users are placed within Global groups and only within Global groups. Next, Global groups are placed within Domain Local groups and mostly in Domain Local groups. Permissions are assigned to Domain Local groups and only Domain Local groups. When users need to access objects in other domains, their Global group is included within the Domain Local group of the target domain. When users need to access objects located within the entire forest, their Global group is inserted into a Universal group. This rule is illustrated in Figure 6-4.

In short, this rule is summarized as follows:

- Global groups only contain users.
- Domain Local or Local groups only contain other groups (Global or Universal).
- Permissions are only assigned to either Domain Local groups or Local groups.
- Universal groups only contain Global groups.

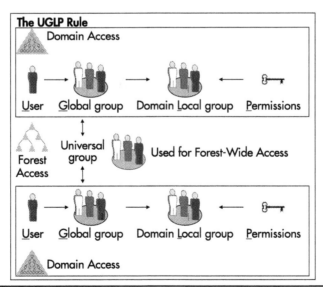

Figure 6-4 The UGLP rule

This rule is supported by the following additional guidelines:

- All group names are standardized.
- All groups include detailed descriptions.
- All groups include additional notes.
- All group managers are clearly identified.
- Group management staff is trained to understand and use these rules.
- Group purpose verification activities are performed on a regular basis.
- A group usage report tool is in place to provide regular group content updates.

Standard names and group manager administration are two areas that require further discussion before finalizing the Group Management Strategy.

> ## QUICK TIP
>
> *The companion Web site includes tools you can use to document your group strategy at http://www.Reso-Net.com/WindowsServer/.*

Standard Group Naming and Delegation

In Windows NT, many organizations implemented a standard naming strategy for both Global and Local groups. It was simple; place a "G_" or an "L_" at the beginning of the name of each group type. But in Windows 2000 and WS03, groups can have more complex names. In fact, groups have three names:

- The WS03 group name, which is the name you will use to manage the group.
- The down-level group name, which is similar to the name you used in Windows NT.
- The group email address, which is how you communicate with members of a group.

Thus, you should reconsider how you name groups to make a better use of the directory. You should take into consideration the possible delegation of group membership management. For example, if your public relations department wants you to create a special group for them that they will use to both assign file and folder permissions and communicate with all PR managers within the enterprise, you might very well decide that once the group is created, you don't want to be burdened with the day-to-day administration of the contents of this group. As such, you could delegate group content management to someone in the PR department. This could be done for a vast number of groups.

Since only Global groups can contain users, you only need to consider the delegation of Global groups. Also, by retaining the management of Domain Local groups, you retain control over the permissions and rights you assign to any user in the organization.

In addition, remember that users can search the directory. In an enterprise network, you'll want to keep a tight rein on the creation and multiplication of groups. Therefore, your core strategy should focus on combining group functions as much as possible. For example, if you integrate Microsoft Exchange to your directory, you will need to manage many more distribution groups. But if your security group strategy is well defined, then several of your existing security groups will double as distribution groups. Therefore, you should have considerably less distribution groups than security groups. You may not even have to create any new distribution groups at all if you've done your homework.

So, if you think you will be delegating Global group membership management at least for some Global groups or you think that you may one day need to have security groups, usually Global Security groups, double as distribution groups, you should reconsider your group naming strategy. Everyday users will not be comfortable with groups named G_PRMGR or L_DMNADM.

Thus an Enterprise Group Naming Strategy should take into account the following guidelines:

- Global and Universal groups should be named without identifying their scope. Scope identification is displayed automatically within the directory so this is not an issue for administrators.

HelpServicesGroup	Security Group - Domain Local
PC Technicians (Local)	Security Group - Domain Local
RAS and IAS Servers	Security Group - Domain Local
Central Technicians	Security Group - Global
Common Users	Security Group - Global

- Since they may be accessed by users for communication purposes or by user representatives for membership management purposes, Global and Universal groups should be named using common language.

- Universal groups should include the organization's name to identify that they are forest-wide groups.

- Down-level names should not include scope for Global and Universal groups because users can also access the down-level name.

- Domain Local groups should be named including the "(Local)" identifier at the end of the name. This allows administrators to search for all local groups more easily.

- Down-level names for Domain Local groups should be preceded by an "L_" to make it simpler to identify them in the directory (once again by administrators).

- All Domain Local groups should be contained within OUs that deny read rights to common users. This will ensure that user directory query results never include Domain Local groups and always only include groups to which users should have access. Special groups such as Domain Admins, Enterprise Admins, Schema Admins, and Administrators should be moved to containers that deny user read rights so that users cannot identify these special security roles in your organization.

Table 6-2 lists some sample names for different groups.

Group Scope	Name Example
Universal Group	T&T Public Relations Managers; T&T Technicians; T&T Administrative Assistants
Universal Group Down-level Name	T&T PR Managers; T&T Technicians; T&T Admin Assistants
Global Group	Public Relations Managers; Region 1 Technicians; Region 1 Administrative Assistants
Global Group Down-level Name	PR Managers; R1 Technicians; R1 Admin Assistants
Domain Local Group	Public Relations Managers (Local); Region 1 Technicians (Local); Region 1 Admin Assistants (Local
Domain Local Group Down-level Name	L_PR_MGR; L_R1_Techs; L_R1_AdmAss

Table 6-2   Group Name Examples

Using such a naming strategy will greatly reduce group management headaches. This naming strategy along with the guidelines outlined above should produce the following results:

- Universal groups are the fewest in number. They are used only for very special purposes.

- Domain Local groups are fewer than Global groups. Since permissions are assigned to Domain Local groups, you should be able to create fewer of these groups. It should be possible to identify that certain groups that may need to be segregated on user membership should nevertheless be assigned the same permissions.

- Global Security groups should be the most numerous group type in your forest. These groups perform double duty as both security and distribution groups.

- Global Distribution groups should be less numerous than Global Security groups. Distribution groups should be used only if there is no security group that can fulfill the same purpose.

Keep to these results. Group management requires tight controls, especially if it is a delegated task. Figure 6-5 outlines the Group Creation Process Flowchart to simplify your group management activities.

Group Ownership Management

One of the aspects of group management that is crucial to your strategy is the assignation of group managers. When you identify a group manager, you locate a user account in your directory and assign the manager's role to this user. When the manager changes, you must modify the ownership of each group. Active Directory provides an automated way to do this.

While people work with the user on the basis of the account name, Active Directory does not. It identifies all objects through special numbers: the Security Identifier (SID) or the Globally Unique Identifier (GUID). Security principals (user accounts) are identified through their SID. When a manager changes, if you deactivate the former manager's account and create a new account, you will have to reassign all of the former account's permissions and user rights.

If, on the other hand, you treat user accounts as user roles within your organization instead of individuals, you can take advantage of Active Directory features to facilitate your work. To do so,

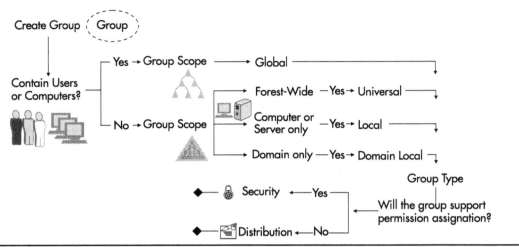

Figure 6-5 The Group Creation Process Flowchart

you need to deactivate and rename accounts instead of recreating them. For example, Ruth Becker, group manager for the PR Global Security group, leaves the company. Since you know that your organization will not operate without someone in Ruth's role, you do not delete her account, you only deactivate it. A few days later, John Purdy is hired to replace Ruth. Now you can reactivate Ruth's old account, rename it to John Purdy, reset the password, and force a password change at next logon. John automatically has all of Ruth's rights and permissions or rather, all the rights and permissions that come with his new role within the organization.

This even applies if a person only changes positions within the organization. Once again, since people work with names and AD works with SIDs, using a new account or a renamed account is completely transparent to them. On the other hand, the advantages of renaming the account are great for the system administrator because you only have to perform a few tasks and you're done.

In some cases, security officers will be against this practice because they fear they will not be able to track user activity within the network. They are right in a way. Since AD tracks users through their SIDs, the SID is the only value that is guaranteed when you view audit reports. When you change a user's name, you are continually reusing the same SID. If you do not maintain strict records that help you track when the user name for a SID was modified, you will not be able to know who owned that SID before the current user. Worse, you won't know when the current user became owner of the SID. This could cause problems for the user, especially if the former owner performed some less than honest actions before leaving.

Once again, strict record-keeping is an important part of a User and Group Management Strategy. In addition, you will need to perform a group manager identification process before you can proceed with the creation of any groups within your parallel network.

Best Practice: Managing Global Groups

Global groups are the groups that are used to contain users. In most enterprise networks, the Global groups you create will fall into four categories:

- **IT user roles**   This type of role identifies a person's IT user role within the organization. IT user roles include a variety of different activities. Examples of these group types include the following:

  - Generic user

  - Information worker

  - Management and management support

  - Professionals

  - End-user developer

  - Web/intranet editor

  - System developer

  - Systems or security administrator

  - Systems and user support

  These IT user roles allow you to create horizontal user groupings that span your organization and allow you to manage people who perform similar tasks no matter where they are located both within the organization and within your AD structure. These roles are related to the computer vocation roles identified in Chapter 5. Try to limit these roles to less than 20.

- **Line-of-business groups**   In most cases, you will also need to be able to manage users vertically. For example, if the Finance department wants to contact all of its members, a Finance Global group will be required. Many of these groupings will have been created with the organization unit structure in your domain, but you cannot use an OU to send email messages, thus a group will still be required. In addition, many departments will have personnel distributed in a vast number of OUs, especially if your organization includes regional offices and you need to delegate regional management activities. Try to keep these groupings to a minimum as well. In many organizations, the "Department minus 1" rule is all that is required. This means you follow the hierarchical structure of the company to one level below departments. Thus in the Finance department you would find the Finance group, then Payables, Payroll, Purchasing, and so on. You may require a more detailed division for your groups within the IT department itself.

- **Project-based groups**   Organizations are constantly running projects. Each project is made of different people from different sections of the organization. Projects are volatile and last only for definite periods of time. Thus, unlike the two previous group types, project-based groups are not permanent. Because of this, this group type is the one that gives you the most work. It is also because of this that this group type may involve the creation of other group scopes, not for the inclusion of users, but rather for the assignation of permissions to project resources. Once again, try to keep a tight rein on the number of groups you create.

- **Special administrative groups**   The last Global group type is the special administrative group type. Like the first two group types, this group type is more stable than project groups. It is required to support the application of special administrative rights to groups of users. For example, if you need to either filter Group Policy or assign specific Group Policy features through the use of security groups, you would do so through a special administrative group.

Whichever group type you create or manage, remember that the key to a successful group management strategy is documentation, both within and without the directory. Document your groups within the directory using the strategies outlined previously. Document your groups outside of the directory through external databases and other documentation methods. Once again, the tools on the companion Web site will be useful to support this task.

Creating an OU Design for User Management Purposes

Now that you have a good understanding of groups and what you intend to do with them, you can proceed to the finalization of your OU design for user management. First, you need to review the People OU structure that was proposed in Chapter 3. A People OU is used here because the User container in Active Directory is not an OU. Therefore you cannot use it to create an OU substructure or to apply Group Policy to your people objects.

The People OU Structure

The People OU structure must support both user-based Group Policy application as well as some user administrative task delegation. Since Active Directory is a database that should be as static as possible, you want to ensure that your People OU structure will be as stable as possible. Each time you perform massive changes to the OU structure, it is replicated to every domain controller within the production domain.

This is the reason why you do not want to include your organizational structure (as displayed in your enterprise organization chart) within the People OU structure. Many organizations tend to modify their hierarchical authority structure several times per year. Replicating this structure within your People OU design will only cause more work for you since you will be constantly modifying your OU structure to reflect the changes your organization chart has undergone.

Your OU structure still needs to represent the structure of your organization to some degree. This is why the People OU structure is based primarily on four concepts:

- **Business units**   By basing your OU structure on business units, you can ensure that you address the requirements of your user base through your organization's logical business structure. Business units are less volatile than organization charts. Organizations create new business units less often than they assign new responsibility centers.

- **Geographical distribution**   If your enterprise is distributed and includes regional offices, chances are that you will need to delegate some administrative tasks to regional officers. The best way to support delegation is to create organizational units that regroup the objects you want to delegate.

- **Special workgroups**   Your enterprise will most likely include groups of users that have special requirements that are not met by any other groups. Thus, you need to create OUs that will contain these special user groupings. For example, many organizations use special "SWAT" teams that can offer replacement services to anyone anywhere in the organization for sick leave and/or holidays. These SWAT teams must be treated specially within the directory.

- **Special interest groups**   These special interest groups require further segregation. An example of a special interest group is the IT department whose needs are different from anyone else.

You'll also remember that the best OU structure does not extend beyond five sublevels. The People OU illustrated in Figure 6-6 displays only three levels of OUs. The first is the OU type: People. It regroups all common users in the organization. The second covers business units, special workgroups, and projects. The third regroups either geographic distribution or administrative services. This last layer offers the possibility to delegate further sublevel creation to special interest groups. The final result of your People OU design aims to meet all user requirements. As such, chances are that you will need to perform some trial and error at first and refine the resulting OU structure within the first six months of its operation. The People OU structure proposed in Chapter 3 has now been supplemented with a refined vision of your needs.

A Group-Related OU Structure

Many organizations create a special OU structure to include groups in addition to the People OU structure. While the addition of such a structure has its merits, it will only lead to more work on your part if you do so. Remember that you will most likely want to delegate some of the group management or administration activities, perhaps not group creation, but certainly group membership management. To do so, you would need to implement delegation in two places: the People OU structure and the Group OU structure. In the end, it is best to have the People OU structure perform double-duty and include both Group and User objects.

Besides, the only group scope that needs to be included here is the group scope that actually includes User objects. This is the Global Group scope. This means that your People OU structure will house Global groups, but that all other groups—Domain Local, Local, and Universal—will be housed elsewhere. In fact, since these latter group scopes are of an *operational* nature, they should be stored within the Services OU structure (except for Local groups, of course). These groups are

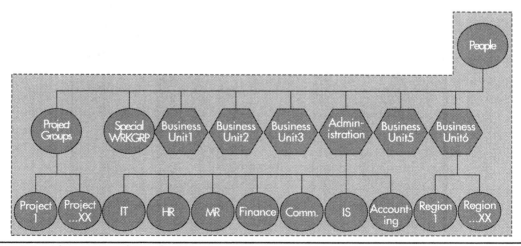

Figure 6-6   The proposed People OU structure

named "operational" for two reasons. The first is that they are designed to contain only other groups. The second is that they are designed to provide access to resources (either object access or forest access). They should, in fact, be hidden from common users—that is, users should not be able to find these groups when they search the directory. This means that you can use a more complex naming strategy for these groups and it also means that you must store these groups within an OU structure that is normally hidden from users. This is the Services OU structure which will be detailed in Chapter 7.

Delegation in the People OU

There are two main categories of delegation required in a People OU. The first relates to *user representatives*. User representatives are responsible for basic user administration activities. These should include at the very least password resets and user group membership management and at the very most user account creation based on template accounts. User representatives should not be allowed to create groups. You should have Global account operators to provide this service.

Unlike the delegation used in Chapter 5 for PC vocation management, the user representative delegation tasks are all standard delegation tasks that are included by default within Active Directory. Thus, when you delegate control of a People sub-OU to a user representative (of course this would be to the user representative *group* and not the individual), you can select the following standard delegation tasks:

- Create, delete, and manage user accounts
- Reset user passwords and force password change at next logon
- Read all user information
- Modify the membership of a group

Since these are standard delegation tasks, assigning delegation rights to user representative groups is a fairly simple activity.

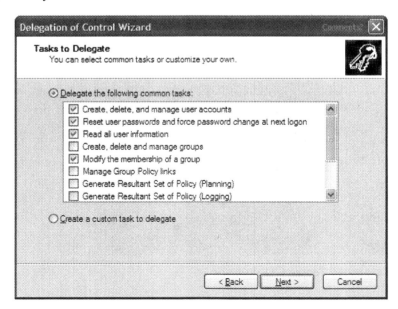

The second type of delegation is to *special interest groups*. As mentioned before, these focus on special departments such as IT itself. The task you want to delegate here is the creation of a sub-OU structure. It is within the third OU layer that you will probably find special interest groups that will require further OU segregation. Using a three-tiered main OU structure gives these groups two more levels they can use to perform this additional segregation.

Delegation here refers to process delegation rather than actual task delegation within Active Directory. You need to delegate the process so that these particular groups can identify their own needs in regards to sub-OU creation. For this, you will need to provide coaching to these groups so that they can determine why they need further segregation and decide what type of regroupings they want to use. Providing them with a preliminary coaching session can free you to continue with other design tasks while they debate among themselves on the model they require. Then, once they have decided, you can ask them to present you with their OU substructure proposal and determine with them if their needs are met. Once you both agree on the design, you can implement it and provide them with the same type of delegated tasks you gave to user representatives.

Delegation in both of these situations will only work if you have previously identified who you will delegate to. Like the group manager identification process, OU delegation requires a comprehensive user representative identification process before you can begin the implementation of your People OU design within the parallel network.

User-Related GPO Concepts

Chapter 5 identified the general operation of Group Policy objects as well as their breadth of coverage. In the application part of Chapter 5, only the computer GPO settings were covered. Since the People OU structure will house User objects, it is now necessary to detail user GPO settings.

In the PCs OU structure, the user portions of the GPOs were deactivated. This time, the computer portions of GPOs must be deactivated since only users are targeted in the People OU. Table 6-3 details the user portion of a GPO and applicable settings for the enterprise network.

GPO Section	Comment	Applicable
Software Settings	This section deals with software installations. If you want to assign a software product to a user instead of a computer using Windows Server 2003 software delivery, you set the parameters here.	No, see Chapter 5
Windows Settings	This section deals with general Windows settings and includes elements such as scripts and Security Settings.	Some
Remote Installation Services	This policy is related to the RIS installation options you offer to users.	Discussed in Chapter 7
Scripts	Controls access to logon and logoff scripts.	Required
Security Settings	Includes Public Key Policies and Software Restrictions.	Some
Public Key Policies	Controls renewal policies for certificates (more in Chapter 8). Also controls Enterprise Trust for the inclusion of certificate trust lists.	Required for all users
Software Restriction Policies	Allows you to determine which applications are allowed to run in your network (more in Chapter 8).	Required for all common users

Table 6-3   User Policy Categories and Contents

GPO Section	Comment	Applicable
Folder Redirection	Allows you to redirect local folders to network locations. Replaces both the Home Directory and the Roaming User Profile. Supports data protection by locating user folders on central servers.	Required for most users
Application Data	Includes two settings: basic and advanced. Basic redirects all folders to the same location. Advanced supports different redirection locations based on user groups.	Redirect for data protection
Desktop	Same as Application Data.	Redirect for data protection
My Documents	Same as Application Data. Can include My Pictures folder.	Redirect for data protection
Start Menu	Same as Application Data.	Redirect for data protection
Internet Explorer Maintenance	Controls Browser User Interface, Connection, URLs, Security, and Programs. Controls IE settings for your organization (logos, home page, support URLs, and so on). Programs are derived from the settings on the desktop or server used to create the GPO. Many of these settings can replace the configuration in the Connection Manager Administration Kit.	Required for all users Can be personalized further at sublevels
Administrative Templates	Administrative Templates are scriptable GPO components that can be used to control a wide variety of settings such as Windows Components, Start Menu and Taskbar, Desktop, Control Panel, Shared Folders, Network, and System.	Yes
Windows Components	Controls settings such as NetMeeting (for remote assistance), Internet Explorer behavior, Help and Support Center, Windows Explorer, Microsoft Management Console, Task Scheduler, Terminal Services, Windows Installer behavior, Windows Messenger, Windows Update, and Windows Media Player. Several settings are of use here. Help and Support Center settings help limit the Internet information that is provided to your users. MMC helps support the custom MMCs you deliver to delegation officers. Terminal Services determines how the TS session is established between the local and the remote systems. This section should be used to avoid having to set these parameters for each user's account (see Chapter 7). Windows Update in particular allows you to control user access to this feature.	Yes
Start Menu and Taskbar	Controls the appearance and content of users' Start menus.	Yes
Desktop	Controls Desktop content and appearance as well as Active Desktop usage and Active Directory search behavior.	Yes
Control Panel	Controls access to the Control Panel as well as Add or Remove Program, Display, Printers, and Regional and Language Option behaviors.	Yes
Shared Folders	Controls user access to shared folders and DFS roots within the directory.	Yes

Table 6-3   User Policy Categories and Contents *(continued)*

GPO Section	Comment	Applicable
Network	Controls network related settings such as Offline Files and Network Connections. Offline Files settings should be set so that users cannot configure them for themselves. Network connections should be set so that common users do not modify their configuration.	Yes
System	Controls system-wide settings such as User Profiles, Scripts, CTRL-ALT-DEL Options, Logon, Group Policy, and Power Management. These settings should be set to automate most system functions for users.	Yes

Table 6-3   User Policy Categories and Contents *(continued)*

As you can see, there is a wide variety of configuration parameters available to you through user GPOs. Detailing each and every one is beyond the scope of this book, but the most important are outlined in the following sections. The settings you apply and the settings you activate will mostly depend on the type of environment you want to create. Take the time to review and understand each setting, then decide which you need to apply. Once again, comprehensive documentation is the only way you will be able to make sure you maintain a coherent user GPO strategy.

Managing User Data

If you're used to a Windows NT network, you'll have become quite adept at generating new user accounts that automatically manage all of a user's data deposits. Few administrators today don't use template accounts that automatically create a user's home directory or a user's roaming profile directory if roaming profiles are in use. In NT, it is fairly simple to apply these settings to a template user account. Both are based on a universal naming convention (UNC) share structure coupled with the username variable (%username%). Since NT is based on the NetBIOS naming standard, everything needed to be in capital letters for the operation to work.

User data management is fairly straightforward in NT: create a home directory, create a profile directory if required, implement a quota management technology, and start backing up the data. If this is what you're used to, you'll find that while all of these operations work in Windows Server 2003, many of these concepts are no longer used.

With the introduction of IntelliMirror in Windows 2000, Microsoft has redefined user data management in the Windows platform. In WS03, home directories are no longer required. Much the same applies to the roaming profile. In a parallel network, one where you endeavor to avoid the transfer of legacy procedures, you'll want to seriously rethink your user data management strategies if you want to make the most of your migration.

Originally, the home directory was designed to provide a simple way to map user shares on a network. In Windows NT, using the %username% variable automatically generated the folder and automatically applied the appropriate Security Settings giving the user complete ownership over the folder. In addition, Windows NT Workstation automatically mapped the appropriate network drive at logon. Since the folder was on a network drive, you could easily back it up and thus protect every user's data. In Windows Server 2003 and Windows XP, it is no longer necessary to use mapped drives. Windows Server 2003 offers much more interesting technology, technology based on the UNC concept, to manage all network shares. This is the Distributed File System (DFS), which is covered in Chapter 7. It is designed to provide a unified file share system that is transparent to users *without* the need for mapped drives. Of course, it may happen that you require some mapped drives since you will most likely still be hosting some legacy applications, especially those that have been developed in-house. But for user folders, mapped drives are no longer necessary.

Since Windows 2000, Microsoft has focused on the use of the My Documents folder as the home of all user documents. This folder is part of the security strategy for all Windows editions beyond Windows 2000. It is stored within a user's profile and is automatically protected from all other users (except, of course, administrators). The same goes for all of a user's application settings. These are no longer stored within either the application or the system directory. Applications that are designed to support the Windows 2000 and beyond Logo program will all store their user-modifiable settings within the user's profile.

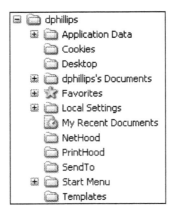

The Folder Redirection portion of a user's Group Policy can manage four critical folders and assign network shares for each. These include:

- **Application Data**   This folder stores all application-specific settings.
- **Desktop**   This folder includes everything users store on the desktop.
- **My Documents**   This folder is the user's data storage folder. Storing the My Pictures subfolder on the network is optional.
- **Start Menu**   This folder includes all of a user's personal shortcuts.

When redirection is activated through Group Policy, the system creates a special folder based on the user's name (just like in the older home directory process) and applies the appropriate Security Settings. Each of the above folders is created within the user's parent folder. Data in these folders is redirected from the desktop PC to the network folders. Because of the Fast Logon Optimization process, it takes a user three logons before all of the data is redirected (see Chapter 5).

Replacing the Home Directory

Folder redirection is completely transparent to the user. While they think they are using the My Documents folder located on their desktop, they are actually using a folder that is located on the network. This way you can ensure that all user data is protected.

Using this folder redirection strategy rather than using a home directory simplifies the user data management process and lets you take advantage of the advanced features of the WS03 network. For example, even though data is stored on the network, it will be cached locally through offline files. Redirected folders are automatically cached through client-side caching when they are activated through a GPO so long as the client computer is Windows XP (as would be the case in the ideal parallel network). This means that the files in these folders will be cached locally and will be available to users whether they are connected to the network or working offline. There are issues with client-side caching of files. These are covered in Chapter 7 since offline files are a feature of network shares rather than Group Policy.

Data in these folders can also be encrypted through the Encrypting File System (EFS). If the client is Windows XP, all offline files can be encrypted. But if you choose to continue to use a home directory structure and redirect My Documents to the home directory, you will not be able to activate data encryption on a user's files since the user will not be able to decrypt data stored in the redirected folder—one more reason for avoiding the use of home directories. EFS is covered in Chapter 8.

Replacing the Roaming Profile

Three of these folders—Application Data, Desktop, and Start Menu—are special folders. They are used to store a considerable portion of the user's profile—that is, all of a user's application-specific settings, the user's desktop contents, and the user's custom Start Menu. Redirecting these folders through Group Policy is very much the same as using a Roaming User Profile. The major difference is the time it takes for activating a profile.

When you use a roaming profile and you log onto a workstation, WS03 copies the entire contents of the roaming profile to the workstation. This can take a considerable amount of time. It is practical, though, since the user can find his or her own environment no matter which computer they logon to. In addition, when the user logs off, the entire profile is copied back to the server. Using roaming profiles has a considerable impact on network performance since the entire contents of a user's profile is copied at logon and logoff.

Quotas are also difficult to enforce when User Profiles are set to roam since users will encounter errors when logging off because they are using more space in their profile than they are allowed on the network. In some cases, organizations using Windows NT and roaming profiles were forced to remove quotas to ensure the roaming profiles worked all of the time. This led to users having profiles whose size was simply excessive. Imagine how long it would take to log onto a system with a profile in excess of 1 GB. Even in the best of networks, it is a great justification for an early morning coffee break while you wait for the logon process to complete.

Roaming profiles are no longer required in the WS03 network for three major reasons:

- The core of a user's profile can be redirected through Group Policy, making it available to the user at all times.

- If profile backup is the justification for implementing roaming profiles, then local profiles can be backed up regularly through the User State Migration Tool (USMT). This tool can be used to create a recurring task that regularly copies all local content of User Profiles to a central location that can then be backed up.

- Windows XP and Windows Server 2003 both support the Remote Desktop. When properly managed, the Remote Desktop allows users to have access to their own local desktop from any location in the enterprise network. This virtually eliminates the need for Roaming User Profiles.

> ▶ **QUICK TIP**
>
> *Remote Desktop uses the Terminal Services port 3389 for communication. In some networks, this is blocked at the router and switch level. It must be opened for this strategy to work.*

If you find you still need Roaming User Profiles, make sure you take the following restrictions into account:

- Do not use client-side caching on roaming profile shares. The roaming profile mechanism has its own caching system that will conflict with the offline files system.

- Do not encrypt files in a roaming profile. EFS is not compatible with roaming profiles. Any portion of the profile that is encrypted will not roam, proving once again that roaming profiles are becoming outdated.

- Be wary of the quota size you set on users with roaming profiles. If the disk quota is set too low, profile synchronization will fail at logoff.

The best thing to do is to begin to use the new network strategy and focus on folder redirection rather than either home directories or roaming profiles.

Other Profile Types

A special profile type, the mandatory profile, was also in use within the Windows NT environment. The mandatory profile is a locked profile that forces desktop settings on the system when a user logs on. Once again, while this profile type is supported in Windows Server 2003, it is no longer really required. Like the home directory and the roaming profile, the mandatory profile must be inscribed into the user's account properties. Having to inscribe specific settings on a user per user basis is less than practical. This is why Group Policy should be your favored approach. GPOs provide a central location for applying changes.

Chapter 5 outlined how the Group Policy Loopback feature could be used to ensure that computers that were exposed to security risks such as computers in a kiosk could be protected. Loopback is a device that will protect computers that have generic roles. Temporary personnel that must be given a very secure and very controlled desktop environment should fall into this category. If you find that you need to create and maintain mandatory profiles, ask yourself first if you can secure the desktop through a kiosk-type computer configuration.

Folder Redirection and Offline File Settings

Two different client-side caching settings apply to the different types of folders that will be redirected. The My Documents and My Picture folders are document folders that contain documents and document-related information. In contrast, the three special folders you can redirect contain mostly application data. In Windows 2000 and XP, you had to choose two different offline settings for the different types of data, but in WS03, one single setting is required: the automatic setting. If applications are also included in the shared folder, you should include the Optimized for performance setting. This will ensure that applications are automatically cached on the user's PC and thus improve overall application performance.

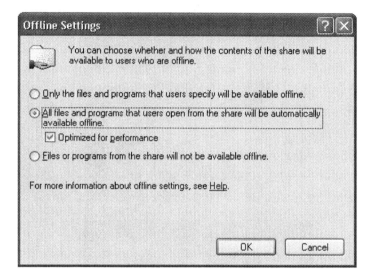

In addition, when you assign folder redirection, you should also ensure that caching settings are globally defined in your user GPO. Since folder redirection and caching are closely related, you need to make sure your users are always working with the latest data. To do so, you need to set the Offline Files settings under Network in Administrative Templates. Three settings should be modified:

- Synchronize all offline files when logging on
- Synchronize all offline files before logging off
- Synchronize all offline files before suspend

The latter setting offers two choices for synchronization: Quick or Full. Quick ensures that all files in the local cache are synchronized. Full performs a complete synchronization. Since users are often in a hurry when putting a system in suspend mode, it is recommended to use the Quick setting. Full synchronizations are performed when they log on or log off the network.

Enabling Folder Redirection

There are special considerations when enabling folder redirection. First, you need to ensure that each user is redirected to the appropriate server. It wouldn't do to have a user in New York redirected to a server in Los Angeles. Thus you must create special administrative groups that can be used to regroup users and ensure that each user is assigned to the appropriate server. You must also ensure that offline settings are appropriately configured to guarantee that users are working with the latest version of their offline files.

Redirecting folders through user groupings is very similar to creating regional or rather geographically-based user groups. Since each server is a physical location, you will need to create a user group for each server. Remember to create both Global groups to contain the users and Domain Local groups to assign the permissions. Begin by enumerating the location of each file server that will host user folders, then name each Global and Domain Local group accordingly. Once the groups are created, you can begin the redirection process. Using groups allows you to limit the number of GPOs required for the People OU structure.

1. In your Global People GPO, move to User Configuration | Windows Settings | Folder Redirection | Application Data, since it is the first folder listed.

2. Right-click on Application Data and select Properties.

3. Under the Target tab, select Advanced – Specify different locations for various user groups and then click Add.

4. In the Specify Group and Location dialog box, type in the group (using the down-level group name, domain\groupname) or click Browse to find the appropriate group.

5. Under Target Folder Location, select Create a folder for each user under the root path.

6. Under Root Path, type in the UNC path to the share name or click Browse to locate it.

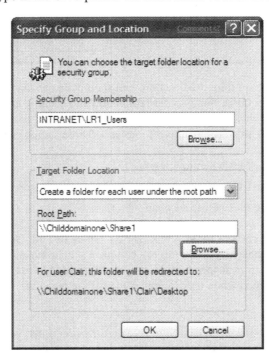

7. Click OK to return to the Application Data dialog box. Repeat for each group and server location you need to enter. Move to the Settings tab.

8. Under Policy Removal, select Return the folder back to the local User Profile location when policy is removed. This will ensure that redirected folders return to original locations if for some reason the policy is removed. Leave all other settings on in this tab.

9. Click OK when done.

10. Perform the same operation for the Desktop, My Documents, and Start Menu. Ensure that you have My Pictures follow My Documents by selecting the appropriate option under the Settings tab (according, of course, to your redirection policy).

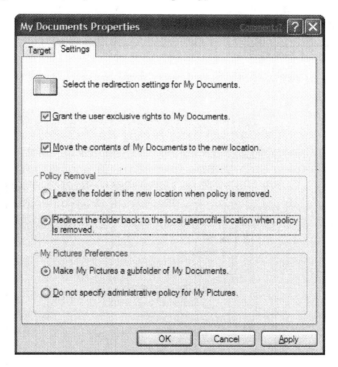

Now that your folder redirection is set, make sure you modify the Offline Files settings in this GPO as outlined in the previous section.

Logon and Logoff Scripts

Scripts are managed through Group Policy and are no longer managed through user account properties. Windows NT compatibility is the only reason why it is still possible to type in a logon script as a property of a user account. Since Windows 2000, all Windows editions support start up, shut down, log on, and log off scripts. This means that while the script has become a much more popular and powerful tool within Windows, it is no longer applied on an individual user basis.

In addition, the logon script has also changed in nature. Many organizations used the logon script to map both network drives and network printers. Printers can now be assigned through Group Policy.

Printer names are also now stored within Active Directory and are directly searchable, making it much easier for users to find and use network printers. The same applies to network shares through the features of DFS. Thus, enforcing mappings through a logon script is becoming a thing of the past.

It may be necessary to enable certain network drive mappings in order to provide support for legacy applications that have not yet been updated to take full advantage of features like DFS, but in most cases, this will be a temporary measure. If this is the case, you can assign logon scripts through the user settings portion of Group Policy.

What is certain is that you will need to rethink your logon script strategy in order to ensure that you do not duplicate efforts that can be provided through Group Policy configuration. What is also certain is that when you configure and create user accounts, you will no longer require the use of the user account's Profile tab. Scripts are now located in the Sysvol share under the Group Policy object identifier in which they are activated.

Managing the Active Desktop

Chapter 1 presented the PASS model for the server construction and design. This same model can be used to represent PCs as well. One of the innovative aspects of this model is the introduction of a specific layer for presentation. In the enterprise network, this layer is managed through the Active Desktop. In turn, the Active Desktop is managed through Group Policy objects.

The Active Desktop is very practical because it supports the storage of Web content on the desktop. This means that it will support a greater variety of image formats for desktop backgrounds including JPEG and GIF, both considerably smaller than standard bitmap images. Once the Active Desktop is activated, the desktop image can be set centrally through Group Policy.

You can also set personal Web pages to display within the desktop through GPO settings. This can allow you to create custom intranet pages containing a series of links or even portals for each IT user role within your organization. Since Web content is considerably smaller in size than traditional desktop content, you can use this GPO setting to manage corporate tool access and create a virtual desktop.

Completing the People OU Structure

Now that you have a better understanding of the major changes within WS03 for user management and administration, you are ready to begin the completion of your People OU infrastructure. The easiest way to do so is to detail the requirements for each OU within a table much like the one you used for the PCs OU design in Chapter 5 (Table 5-1).

Table 6-4 outlines a possible People OU structure for T&T Corporation. As mentioned before, T&T has several main offices where user creation is delegated to each business unit. In addition, T&T has several regional offices that have local security officers who perform many of the user administration

OU	Level	Objective	GPO	Notes
People	One	Grouping of all users in the organization	Global People GPO	Applies to all users Mostly a placeholder OU Includes all IT user role Global groups
Business Unit 1 to *x*	Two	Grouping of all users according to organizational business units	Possible but not absolutely required Avoid if possible	Segregates users by business unit Includes only users for central offices Includes Global groups for the business unit User creation (from template accounts) and group membership management is delegated to user representatives
Region 1 to *x*	Three	Grouping of all users within a region; created under the Regional Operations Business Unit	Possible but not absolutely required Avoid if possible	User creation (from template accounts) and group membership management is delegated to user representatives Includes regional special administrative groups
Special Workgroups	Two	Grouping of all users such as SWAT teams	SWG GPO	GPO focuses on Terminal Services settings All users have access to their own remote desktop as well as regional operations
Projects	Two	Grouping of all Project OUs		Categorization only Contains mostly other OUs Can contain an administration group if project-based OU administration and creation is delegated
Project 1 to *x*	Three	Grouping of all user groups that are related to any given project		Group membership management is delegated to project user representative
Administration	Two	Grouping of Global groups and sub-OUs for the Administration Business Unit		Group membership management is delegated to user representative

Table 6-4 A People Administration OU Structure

OU	Level	Objective	GPO	Notes
Human Resources, Material Resources, Finance, Communications, Accounting	Three	Grouping of all users according to organizational administrative service		Segregates users by service Includes only users for central offices Includes Global groups for the service User creation (from template accounts) and group membership management is delegated to user representatives
IT and IS	Three	Grouping of all users according to organizational administrative service	Possible, but not required Avoid if possible	Segregates users by service Includes only users for central offices Includes Global groups for the service User creation (from template accounts) and group membership management is delegated to user representatives Sub-OU creation is also possible here and may be delegated

Table 6-4   A People Administration OU Structure *(continued)*

tasks. Since objects can only be contained within one OU, several users from different business units are located within the regional OUs. Thus, the actual business unit OU must contain both the users from central offices as well as the Global groups that are used to regroup all users from the business unit no matter where their user account is located within the directory. T&T also has special workgroups, notably a special SWAT-like team that is used to provide emergency replacement for personnel who are absent for one reason or another. Since the members of this group must be able to play any operational user role within the organization, they are regrouped in a special OU. Finally, T&T manages all operations through projects. Thus, its People OU structure must include project-based group management. All of these needs are taken into account in the T&T Corporation's OU structure. The resulting structure is graphically represented in Figure 6-7.

> **QUICK TIP**
>
> *Maintain a tight control over the sub-OU creation process since you want to make sure that directory performance is not impacted by an OU structure tant is too complex (more than five levels).*

Putting the People OU Infrastructure in Place

You can proceed to the creation of this OU infrastructure since you have designed your People OU infrastructure matrix (Table 6-4). This assumes that you have performed all of the identification activities listed earlier such as preparing a group purpose matrix, identifying all group managers, OU owners, and user representatives.

Once this is done, you can proceed to the creation of the infrastructure. The activities you need to perform to create this structure are:

- Create each OU.
- Create the Global People GPO and modify its settings (see Table 6-3).

- Create the group structure required to both assign rights and to delegate management; these should include:
  - Global groups for each business unit (Department minus 1).
  - Project groups for each project OU.
  - Special administrative groups for both folder redirection and user representatives (for delegation purposes).
  - IT user role Global groups (should be stored in the People top-level OU).
  - Operational groups for rights assignation. These are not stored in the People OU infrastructure, but rather in the Services OU structure—see Chapter 7. For the time being, these groups can be stored in a temporary OU. They can then be moved to the Services OU when you are ready.

All groups should be fully documented and each should have an assigned manager.

- Assign delegation rights to each OU.
- Create personalized Microsoft Management Consoles for each OU that includes delegation rights.

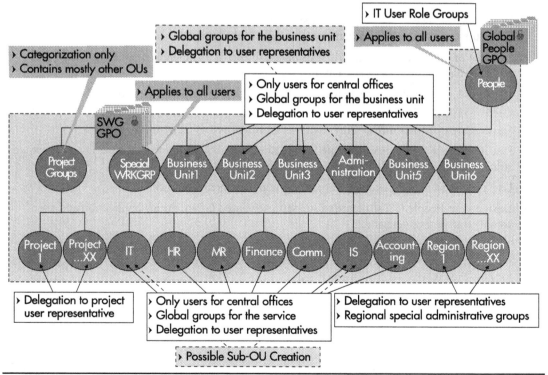

Figure 6-7   GPO application and delegation in the People OU structure

Use Active Directory Users and Computers as well as the Global Policy Management Console and when in doubt, return to Chapter 5 to see how each activity is performed. As you will see, creating this OU infrastructure is one of the most intensive operations you have to perform while preparing the Parallel Enterprise Network. Take your time and make sure you do it right. Now is not the time to cut corners since you will be living with this structure for quite some time.

You're almost ready to migrate users to the parallel network, but you can't do so quite yet. User migration should not occur until everything has been prepared in your parallel network. You still need to implement your Services structure, define enterprise security measures, and prepare your risk management strategies. Until you do so (in the next three chapters), you won't be able to start hosting massive numbers of users within your network. Massive user migration will not occur until Chapter 10 since this activity is highly related to recurring user and group administrative activities.

⬐ Best Practice Summary

This chapter recommends the following best practices:

- When implementing Active Directory, determine which data fields you want to manage and who is responsible for their update, especially for the User object.
- When creating users, use the User object type in the intranet and determine whether to use either the User or the InetOrgPerson object type in the extranet.
- Because of the hierarchical nature of its database and of its inherent replication latency, do not store data that is of a timely nature within the directory.
- Use template accounts to create users within the directory, especially if you delegate the account creation task.
- Never assign permissions to individual users, always assign them to groups.
- Document each of the groups created in the directory and ensure that a proper communications strategy is in place for all interested parties.
- Use a standard naming strategy to reduce group management issues.
- Design your People OU structure to support user-based Group Policy application and user administrative task delegation.
- Take the time to review and understand each GPO setting in order to determine which one you will need to apply in your environment. Test them in your technological lab to get a better feel for how they work.

- Create as few user-based GPOs as possible.
- The profile tab for the User object is no longer required because it is replaced by GPO settings.
- Do not configure Terminal Services on a per user basis, use GPO settings instead.
- If you choose to use Roaming User Profiles:
    - Do not use client-side caching on roaming profile shares.
    - Do not encrypt files in a roaming profile.
    - Be wary of the quota size you set on users with roaming profiles.
- Before putting the People OU infrastructure in place, perform all of the following identification and documentation activities:
    - Create the group purpose matrix.
    - Identify all group managers.
    - Identify all OU owners and user representatives.
- Use GPO settings to configure Internet Explorer to supplement the Connection Manager Administration Kit.
- Perform all folder redirection based on security groups (advanced redirection) in order to limit the number of GPOs required.
- When redirecting My Documents, keep My Pictures with it unless there are compelling reasons not to do so. Separating these two folders is not good practice because you will need to provide two different service levels for each folder.
- Review the best practice list for the UGLP rule.
- Review the best practice list for managing Global groups.
- Create custom Microsoft Management Consoles when delegating tasks to user representatives.

Chapter Roadmap

Use the illustration in Figure 6-8 to review the contents of this chapter.

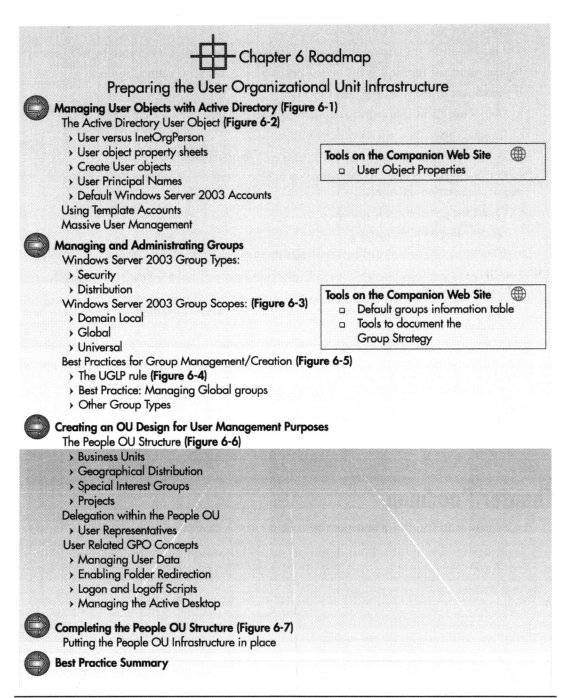

Chapter 6 Roadmap

Preparing the User Organizational Unit Infrastructure

Managing User Objects with Active Directory (Figure 6-1)
The Active Directory User Object **(Figure 6-2)**
  › User versus InetOrgPerson
  › User object property sheets
  › Create User objects
  › User Principal Names
  › Default Windows Server 2003 Accounts
Using Template Accounts
Massive User Management

Tools on the Companion Web Site
□   User Object Properties

Managing and Administrating Groups
Windows Server 2003 Group Types:
  › Security
  › Distribution
Windows Server 2003 Group Scopes: **(Figure 6-3)**
  › Domain Local
  › Global
  › Universal

Tools on the Companion Web Site
□   Default groups information table
□   Tools to document the Group Strategy

Best Practices for Group Management/Creation **(Figure 6-5)**
  › The UGLP rule **(Figure 6-4)**
  › Best Practice: Managing Global groups
  › Other Group Types

Creating an OU Design for User Management Purposes
The People OU Structure **(Figure 6-6)**
  › Business Units
  › Geographical Distribution
  › Special Interest Groups
  › Projects
Delegation within the People OU
  › User Representatives
User Related GPO Concepts
  › Managing User Data
  › Enabling Folder Redirection
  › Logon and Logoff Scripts
  › Managing the Active Desktop

Completing the People OU Structure (Figure 6-7)
Putting the People OU Infrastructure in place

Best Practice Summary

Figure 6-8   Chapter Roadmap

CHAPTER 7

Designing the Network Services Infrastructure

IN THIS CHAPTER

The very purpose of an enterprise network is the delivery of services to a community of users. Thus, one of the most critical tasks you will undertake when designing the parallel network will be the implementation of the services infrastructure. Implementing this infrastructure will involve two major steps: creating the servers that will host each service type and creating the organizational unit infrastructure that will support service administration within the directory.

Chapter 1 identified eight server roles within the enterprise. Two of these have already been covered to some extent: Identity Management Servers (domain controllers) and Network Infrastructure Servers. Another, the Failsafe Server is really a duplicate of existing servers. This leaves five key roles to cover when designing your service infrastructure:

- **File and Print Servers** Servers that provide storage and structured document services to the network.

- **Application Servers** Servers that provide application services based on either commercial software such as Exchange Server, SQL Server, Commerce Server, and so on, or on custom corporate applications. This also includes applications based on the .NET Framework.

- **Terminal Servers** Servers that provide a central application execution environment; the entire execution environment resides on the server itself.

- **Dedicated Web Servers** Servers that provide Web services. The Dedicated Web Server role will be covered in Chapter 8 since the Web service is highly related to security issues.

- **Collaboration Servers** Servers that provide the infrastructure for collaboration within the enterprise. Their services include, among others, SharePoint Team Services, Streaming Media Services, and Real Time Communications (RTC).

▶ NOTE

Streaming Media Services are also known as the Windows Media Center or Windows Media 9 Studio. More information is available at http://www.microsoft.com/windows/windowsmedia/9series/server.asp.

In addition, it will be important to complete the coverage of the Network Infrastructure Servers because only two functions have been covered for this server role to date: DHCP and WINS.

The structure for the coverage of each of these server roles includes:

- **Functional requirements** Discussions on how the service must be designed for the enterprise network and the rationale for the service.

- **Features** Features supporting the role or service within WS03 (includes new features).

- **Implementation instructions** How to proceed with the preparation of the server role within the parallel network environment.

Each server role will be based on the Server Construction Model outlined in Chapter 1, the PASS model, and the basic Server Construction Process detailed in Chapter 2, the design of the Server Kernel. In fact, here you only add functional roles to the core server design.

All of the roles mentioned here are normally assigned to Member Servers. Domain controllers are reserved for one of two roles: Identity Management Servers and multipurpose servers—servers that combine more than one role because of the size of the user base they support. Multipurpose servers are often found in smaller regional offices. These servers must be constructed with care because of the security risk involved in offering multiple user services on a domain controller.

It will also be important to cover specific considerations for all server types such as the Network Load Balancing and Server Cluster services. Both offer powerful redundancy features that minimize risk within the enterprise. These topics will be further discussed in Chapter 9. Table 7-4 at the end of this chapter outlines the hardware requirements to build each server role. It will serve as a guide for server construction.

Finally, once the basis for enterprise services has been covered, it will be time to design the Services OU structure within the directory. As for the People and PCs OU structures, this design will include both GPO and delegation principles, but uniquely, it will also involve the design of a Services Administration Plan. As with Windows 2000, WS03 offers the capability to assign specific administrative rights based on the task the administrator is responsible for. Unlike Windows NT, you will no longer need to grant Domain Administration rights to one and all just to let them perform their work. This Services Administration Plan will be a key element of your security infrastructure for the enterprise network.

The Services OU structure will be built as each service is added to the network. It is at this point that OU contents will be identified. Once each service has been covered, the administrative, delegation, and Group Policy requirements for each will be covered in detail.

► **NOTE**

Covering the detail for each of the server roles is beyond the scope of this book. This book focuses on new features inherent to Windows Server 2003. Thus, only specific new features are covered in the server role section of this chapter.

Preparing File and Print Servers

The most basic network server is the File And Print Server. Both services are one of the main reasons why groups of people tend to put networks in place. Central file storage provides the ability to share information as well as protect it and provide a single location for backup and recovery operations. Print servers allow the reduction in hardware printer costs by sharing fewer printers among more users. In addition, central file storage servers can index content for all users, making it easier for everyone to reuse information.

Windows Server 2003 offers several features for the support of both operations. In fact, file and print sharing on WS03 has become quite sophisticated.

Sharing Files and Folders

One of the key aspects of the enterprise network is server standardization. When staging and preparing servers for file and folder sharing, you must begin by identifying the purpose, or rather, the type of file sharing you intend to perform. After years of existence, file sharing has become concentrated on a few core file sharing functions. The types of files most organizations need to share today are the following:

- **User data** The files that make up both personal user information and the user's profile. This is a private share.

- **Public data** Information that is made widely available to all corporate personnel on both a permanent and volatile basis, though with the advent of internal Web technologies, this file share is becoming less and less useful.

- **Departmental data** Information that is widely available to a department and to the services that are located within that department. Once again, this file share is becoming less used in favor of Web-based technologies.

- **Project data** Information that is shared between the members of a project.

- **Software applications** Applications that operate from a central location.

- **Installation sources** Source files for software installed on either servers or PCs.

- **System administration** Special system administration files used by technical and operational personnel.

As you can see, several of these shares are being replaced with Web technologies, though not at an alarming rate. Most people are comfortable with the traditional file share and continue to use it even though more innovative technologies are now available to replace this function.

File and folder sharing are supported by two core features: the file system itself and its capability for disk management and the Windows sharing subsystem. The first is the most important in terms of information storage.

Expanding Disks for File Storage

The one undeniable fact of file storage is that it always increases. Fortunately, disks are a low-cost commodity today. But since you know that you will probably be expanding the disk storage system at some point in time, it makes sense to use a disk subsystem that can easily accept physical expansions with little or no impact on logical partitions. This is why hardware-based RAID systems are so important.

Take, for example, the following situation. Your users are all storing their information on a central file share. Each user is allowed no more than 200 MB of storage space, and you have at least 2 GB of free space. But your organization is expanding and 50 more users will be hired. You now have a choice: install another file server for these 50 new users or simply expand the storage capabilities of your existing file server. When using a hardware-based RAID system, you can acquire the appropriate number of disks, insert them into your server, expand the existing disk with your hardware RAID controls, and use the DISKPART.EXE command to extend the existing disk in Windows.

The DISKPART.EXE command launches an execution environment. If you use it interactively, type in the following commands:

```
diskpart
extend
exit
```

The extend command will automatically extend the disk to take up all of the available space you just added. Remember that disk expansion can only be done on non-system disks.

You can also use scripts with DISKPART.EXE. Simply insert your commands in a text file. Scripts are especially useful when you are staging servers with either the unattended or disk imaging installation techniques. In this case, you'll also want to log all errors. To do so, use the following command:

```
diskpart /s scriptfile.txt >logfile.txt
```

▶ | **QUICK TIP**

Microsoft has written a knowledge base article on disk and volume management. Search for article number Q329707 at http://support.microsoft.com/.

Disk Structure Preparation

Expanded disks ensure that your main disk partitions always remain the same. This means that you can create a standard disk structure for all servers. This structure should include the following:

- **C: drive**   This is the system disk.
- **D: drive**   The data storage disk.
- **E: drive**   An optional disk for servers hosting database applications. In the Microsoft world, this includes servers hosting Active Directory (domain controllers), SQL Server, Exchange, and SharePoint Portal Server. This disk is used to store transaction journals for these database applications. It can also be used to store shadow copies for file servers.
- **F: drive**   The DVD/CDRW server drive.

No matter how your server is constructed, it should use this structure for its logical appearance. Since all disks can be extended, no other drive letters should be required.

The disk that requires the most structure is the D: drive since it is the disk that will store user and group shared data and documents. This disk should include a master folder for each of the different data types identified earlier. In addition, it is a good idea to structure the disk folders according to content. Thus, the D: drive would appear as illustrated in Figure 7-1.

There are a few principles to use when creating the folders in the D: drive.

- First, group information according to content. This means that three top-level folders are required: Data, Applications, and Administration. Each will be used to regroup subfolders that will store similar content.
- Second, use representative folder names. If a folder will be used to store user data, call it UserData.
- Third, use combined words. That is, do not include spaces or special characters between words. Thus, if your folder name is User Data, type it as UserData. Unfortunately, there are still some vestiges of NetBIOS in WS03. NetBIOS prefers word strings that do not use spaces or other special characters.
- Fourth, name your folders the way you will want to have your shares appear. A good example here is the use of the dollar sign ($) at the end of a folder name. Remember that when you share

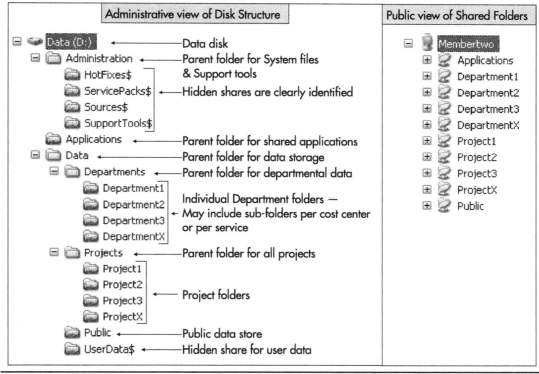

| Administrative view of Disk Structure | Public view of Shared Folders |

Data (D:) ———————————Data disk
  Administration ———————Parent folder for System files
    HotFixes$ & Support tools
    ServicePacks$ ————————Hidden shares are clearly identified
    Sources$
    SupportTools$
  Applications ——————————Parent folder for shared applications
  Data ——————————————————Parent folder for data storage
    Departments ————————Parent folder for departmental data
      Department1
      Department2   Individual Department folders —
      Department3   ← May include sub-folders per cost center
      DepartmentX   or per service
    Projects ——————————Parent folder for all projects
      Project1
      Project2
      Project3   ← Project folders
      ProjectX
  Public ————————————————Public data store
  UserData$ —————————————Hidden share for user data

Membertwo
  Applications
  Department1
  Department2
  Department3
  DepartmentX
  Project1
  Project2
  Project3
  ProjectX
  Public

Figure 7-1   D: drive folder and share structure

a folder with the dollar sign at the end, it becomes a "hidden" share—that is, it cannot be seen through the network browsing mechanism.

- Fifth, create the same folder structure on all servers that have a file and print vocation even though you will not share each of the folders on each server. This strategy allows you to quickly activate a folder share when a file server is down. Since each server has the same folder structure, activating a shared folder in an emergency is quick and easy. This also facilitates file server replication modifications in case of a server crash.

Using these guidelines, folders should be created according to the details outlined in Table 7-1.

NTFS Permissions

Windows Server 2003 is similar to Windows NT and Windows 2000 in that permissions on shared folders are based on a combination of NTFS and shared folder permissions. As such, the same rules apply. This means that since it is complex to manage both file and share permissions, it becomes much easier to focus on NTFS permissions since these are the last permissions applied when users access files through network shares. This process is illustrated in Figure 7-2.

Folder Name	Share Name	Offline Settings	NTFS Permissions	Share Permissions	Comment
Applications	Applications	Automatically available offline and Optimized for performance	Users: Read Administrators: Full Control	Everyone: Read	This folder shares centrally-located applications.
Department*n*	Department*n*	User-determined	Department: Read User Representative: Change Administrators: Full Control	Everyone: Change	Data can be encrypted, but should not be compressed. This folder is the main folder for the department; only user representatives can write to this folder and create subfolders.
Project*n*	Project*n*	User-determined	Project Members: Change Administrators: Full Control	Everyone: Change	Data can be encrypted, but should not be compressed.
Public	Public	Not available offline	Everyone: Change Administrators: Full Control	Everyone: Change	Data should not be either encrypted or compressed.
UserData$	UserData$	Automatically available offline and Optimized for performance	Everyone: Change Administrators: Full Control	Everyone: Change	Data can be encrypted, but should not be compressed. This folder will be used to redirect the My Documents, Application Data, Desktop, and Start Menu folders for all users.
HotFixes$	HotFixes$	Not available offline	Everyone: Read Administrators: Full Control	Everyone: Read	Data should not be either encrypted or compressed.
ServicePacks$	ServicePacks$	Not available offline	Everyone: Read Administrators: Full Control	Everyone: Read	Data should not be either encrypted or compressed.
Sources$	Sources$	Not available offline	Everyone: Read Administrators: Full Control	Everyone: Read	Data should not be either encrypted or compressed.
Tools$	Tools$	Not available offline	Everyone: Read Administrators: Full Control	Everyone: Read	Data should not be either encrypted or compressed.

Table 7-1 Folder and Share Structure

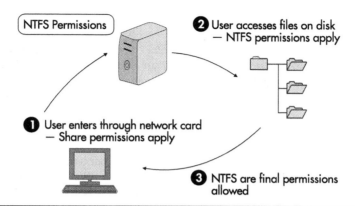

NTFS Permissions

❷ User accesses files on disk
— NTFS permissions apply

❶ User enters through network card
— Share permissions apply

❸ NTFS are final permissions
allowed

Figure 7-2   The File Permission Process

Combining shared folder permissions with NTFS permissions can become very confusing and difficult to troubleshoot if you mix and match them. In order to simplify the process, you should only use NTFS permissions because the most restrictive permissions are always applied.

In Windows Server 2003, every new shared folder receives the same basic permissions: Everyone Read. This is different from all previous versions of Windows! If users need to write into a shared folder, these permissions must be modified to Everyone Change. If not, the most restrictive permissions apply and no one is allowed to write into a shared folder.

▶ *CAUTION*

It will be important for you to ensure that you take the time to verify shared folder permissions before finalizing the share. Otherwise, you will receive several support calls on nonfunctioning shares.

It is quite all right to set share permissions on just about anything to Everyone Change because NTFS permissions will apply even though your share permissions are not restrictive. Microsoft modified the default behavior of the shared folder process in order to provide better security for enterprises that did not prepare their NTFS settings beforehand. Thus, if you use the share preparation process outlined here, you will be quite safe from prying users when you share your folders because NTFS permissions are always applied *before* the share is enabled.

Nevertheless, the best practice in terms of shared folder permissions is to set permissions according to the following:

- Set Everyone Read for all shared application folders, installation folders, support tool folders, and so on.

- Set Everyone Change for all shared data folders and set appropriate NTFS permissions on a folder per folder basis.

There is rarely any need for the Everyone Full Control shared folder permission setting.

▶ *CAUTION*

It is important to set Everyone Change as the shared folder permissions for the shared folder hosting the redirection of user data. Otherwise, the automatic folder creation process that is enabled whenever the policy applies to a new user will not be able to create the user's data folders.

Disk Quotas

Another important factor in file sharing is disk quotas. Windows Server 2003 offers a disk quota management process that supports the assignation of quotas on a per user, per disk basis. In addition, WS03 quota usage is identified by file ownership. This means that if you create all of your shared folders on the same disk, a user's total quota usage will apply to every file on the disk that was created or is owned by the user no matter which shared folder it is located in.

You begin by setting general quotas on a disk, and then you can set different quotas for users who require more than the average amount of space. You cannot manage quotas on a per group basis. This is not very practical in an enterprise network. WS03 quotas do not apply to administrators.

Some rules apply if you intend to use WS03 quotas:

- Use the quota tracking option to analyze disk usage before enforcing quotas. This will tell you the size of the quotas you need to apply.

- Group users according to file types; if some users have a tendency to work with files that have large formats, such as graphic files, then place them on a separate disk and assign a higher quota to this disk. This is the same as assigning quotas to groups, but instead of using groups, you use different disks.

- Create separate disks for private user data and group shared folders and assign different quotas to each disk.

If you find that these rules are too constricting, then use a commercial quota management tool. These tools will allow you to perform policy-based management of quotas on a user or group basis no matter how many disks you have for shared folder storage.

Shadow Copies

Windows Server 2003 includes a new feature for shared folder support: volume shadow copies (VSC). This feature automatically takes a snapshot of the files located in a shared folder at regular intervals (in fact, it takes a copy of the entire disk on which the shared folder resides). The shadow copy feature is designed to assist in the process of recovering previous versions of files without having to resort to backups. The shadow copy feature is very much like a server "undelete" feature. It is useful for users who often require a return to either a previous version of a file or who accidentally destroy files they still require.

WS03 uses a default schedule for creating shadow copies: 7:00 A.M. and 12:00 noon. If you find that this schedule does not meet your requirements, you can change it. For example, you might prefer to create shadow copies at 12:00 noon and 5:30 P.M. if your staff tends to start early in the morning. Also, use a separate disk for shadow copies and set the maximum size of the shadow copies on this disk. The number of copies kept on the shadow copy disk will depend on the amount of space allocated to shadow copies. Once full, shadow copies are overwritten by newer versions. There is also a hard limit of 64 versions. Once you reach this limit, older versions are automatically overwritten. If you expect a large number of file changes, you should assign a larger amount of space for shadow copies.

Shadow copies do not replace backups. Even though the WS03 Backup tool uses the shadow copy process to perform backups, the automatic shadow copies the system creates are not backed up so you cannot count on previous versions of a shadow copy. Finally, the shadow copy process is in fact a scheduled task. If you intend to delete the disk on which a shadow copy is performed, begin by deleting the shadow copy scheduled task. Otherwise, this task will generate errors in the event log.

> ### QUICK TIP
>
> *One of the great advantages of disk shadow copies is the ability for users to recover their own files. The VSC service adds a tab to file and folder properties that allows users to retrieve older versions of a file from the shadow copy so long as the image of the shadow copy has not been overwritten. This feature is a boon to disk administrators because it greatly reduces the number of restores they need to perform. To enable this feature, you will have to deploy the Previous Versions client on Windows XP systems. The client software is located in \\%systemroot%\system32\clients\twclient.*

Indexing Service

The Indexing Service is one of Windows' best features for the support of knowledge management. WS03 can index all sorts of information and documents inside shared folders and on internal and external Web sites. The Indexing Service is installed by default, but it is not activated. Therefore, one of the most important steps in preparing a file share server is to set the Indexing Service startup to automatic.

The Indexing Service will index documents in the following formats:

- Text
- HTML
- Office 95 and later
- Internet mail and news
- Any other document for which a filter is available

For example, Adobe Corporation provides an indexing filter for documents in the PDF format. The Adobe PDF IFilter can be found at http://download.adobe.com/pub/adobe/acrobat/win/all/ifilter50.exe. Installing this filter will ensure that all PDF documents will be indexed and searchable. In addition, the Indexing Service can index files for which it doesn't have specific filters. In this case, it will do the best it can.

In general, the default settings of the Indexing Service are sufficient for shared folders storing data and documents. This is because even though all documents on a file server are indexed, users will only see the query results for which they have access rights. So even if you have five documents about system administration on a file share, but the user performing the query has access to only one of those, the Indexing Service will respond with only one query result.

If you find you require more refined filtering, you can use the Indexing Service to create special indexing catalogs for groups of users. These catalogs increase the speed of a search since they limit the number of possible hits for user queries. Indexing is a memory intensive task. This means that your file server will require sufficient RAM to support the indexing of documents. For large file shares including more than 100,000 documents to index, you should dedicate at least 128 MB of RAM to the Indexing Service.

Offline File Caching

By default each share that is created with Windows Server 2003 is set to allow the user to determine if they want to make the files available offline. Offline file caching allows users to transport files with them if they are using a portable computer or to continue working in the event of a network failure. Through offline files, users actually work on local copies of the files and the Windows Synchronization Manager automatically synchronizes files between the server and the client. Synchronization Manager includes a conflict resolution process allowing even multiple users to work with offline files without fear of damaging information created by one or the other.

There are some issues with offline files. The most important of these is that not all files are supported through the offline files process. Database files, in particular, are not supported. Thus if you intend to use offline folders, you must educate your users to store their database files elsewhere, either locally or in file shares that do not offer offline file possibilities. Non-supported file types cause error messages during the synchronization process which occurs at either logon or logoff. This can cause a security breach because the logoff process is not completed when non-supported file types are included in an offline folder until the error message dialog box is closed manually. And, if the user leaves before the logoff is complete, their system remains in this state until they return. Of course, it would be difficult for a hacker to reopen the session, but leaving a session in a semi-open state is not good practice.

Caching options include:

- **No caching**   Files or programs from the share are not available offline.
- **Manual caching**   Only the files and programs that users specify will be available offline (this is the default setting).
- **Automatic caching**   All files and programs that users open from the share will be automatically available offline. This setting can be optimized for performance.

Offline files are a boon, especially for mobile users, because they offer local access to files while at the same time allowing central backup and protection of data.

Creating the File Server

There are several process involved in the creation of a File Server. The overall File Server Creation Process is outlined in Figure 7-3.

The place to start is with the creation of the server itself. Use the process outlined in Chapter 2 to create a basic Member Server. This server is based on the Server Kernel, but its primary role will be

Figure 7-3   The File Server Creation Process

file sharing. Thus, you now need to add a server role on top of the kernel. This server should include a disk structure as outlined previously in the "Disk Structure Preparation" section. Once the server has been prepared, move to the first activity: Creating the Folder Structure.

Creating the Folder Structure

The folder structure is not the same as the shared folder structure because shares are regrouped by content type (refer to Figure 7-1). Though WS03 provides a Share a Folder Wizard that supports the creation of a folder structure on a NTFS disk, it is easier to use Windows Explorer to create the folders that will host file sharing.

1. Move to Windows Explorer (Quick Launch Area | Windows Explorer).

2. Select the D: drive.

3. Create the three top level folders: Administration, Applications, and Data. To do so, right-click in the right pane of Explorer, select New | Folder and type in the name of the folder. Press ENTER when done. Repeat for each folder you require.

4. Apply appropriate NTFS security settings for each folder. Security settings are applied according to the details of Table 7-1. To do so, right-click on each folder name and select Properties. Move to the Security tab. Add the appropriate groups and assign appropriate security settings to each group. Also, modify the default security settings per the requirements in Table 7-1. You modify security settings now because they are inherited whenever you create subfolders. Thus, you will only need to fine-tune subfolder security settings from now on instead of recreating them all.

5. Create all of the subfolders for each section:

- In Administration, create HotFixes$, ServicePacks$, Sources$, and SupportTools$.

- In Data, create Departments and Projects. These subfolders are parent folders for each of the department-specific and project-specific shared folders. Also create Public and UserData$ at this level.

- Within Departments and Projects, create the required subfolders for each department and each project.

6. Modify the NTFS security settings for each folder. Remember to modify the parent folders first before creating their subfolders in order to simplify your creation process.

Once the folder creation process is complete, make a copy of the entire structure in another secure place on the network. This way, you will not have to recreate the entire folder structure each time you create a file server. You will simply have to copy it from your file structure template. Ensure that this master folder structure is always up to date in order to simplify the file server creation process.

Enabling File Server Services

Three special services must be put in place to support file sharing: quotas, shadow copies, and indexing. These are activated next.

1. Once again, move to Windows Explorer.

2. Right-click on the D: drive and select Properties.

3. Move to the Quota tab and activate quotas for this disk:

- Select Enable quota management.

- Select Deny disk space to users exceeding quota limit.

- Select Limit disk space to and assign at least 200 MB per user.

- Set warning level to 15 to 20 percent lower than the assigned quota limit.

▶ | **QUICK TIP**

It is very important to assign appropriate quota levels to users. It is highly recommended to validate the space required on a per user basis before assigning quota levels. Do not deny disk space to users exceeding quota limits to test required quota levels. To test these limits, you will need to monitor quota usage through the use of the Quota Entries button at the bottom of the dialog box.

- Select both Log event when a user exceeds their quota limit and Log event when a user exceeds their warning level. Both of these tools are used to identify long-term quota requirements.

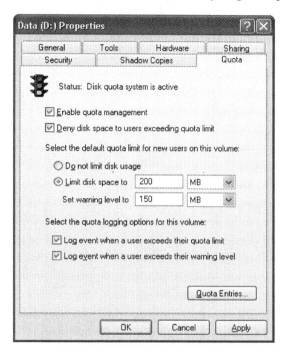

QUICK TIP

Event logs don't actually provide the name of the person who exceeds the limit. You have to use WMI scripts to extract this information. But event logs will tell you that someone has exceeded the limit. Don't worry, you'll know who it is soon enough because users who exceed their limits are quick to call the help desk to complain.

4. You can select Apply if you want to, but you don't have to because you aren't done with this dialog box yet. Move to the Shadow Copies tab.

5. Before enabling this feature, you must modify the drive that will store shadow copies. To do so, click the Settings button. In the new dialog box, use the drop-down list to select the E: drive. Set the limit for the copy as appropriate and change the schedule if required. Click OK when done.

6. The default schedule is at 7:00 A.M. and at 12:00 noon. If this schedule is not appropriate, click the Schedule button to modify it. This is a scheduled task. Its scheduling features are the same as all scheduled tasks.

7. Click Enable to activate shadow copies.

8. WS03 will give you a warning about enabling this feature. Click OK to close it. WS03 will perform an immediate shadow copy.

9. Move to the General tab to ensure that the Allow Indexing Service to index this disk for fast file searching checkbox is checked, and then click OK to close the dialog box and assign the settings.

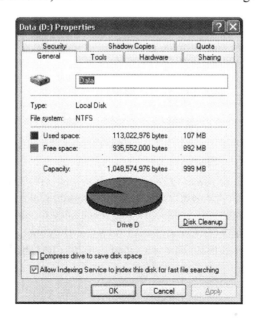

10. You need to enable the Indexing Service. The easiest way to do this is to use the Manage Your Server console to add a new server role. Of course, you can change the service settings in the Computer Management console, but the Manage Your Server console will also install a special File Server Management console as well as enabling the Indexing Service. Start the Manage Your Server console if it is closed (use the Quick Launch Area icon).

11. Click Add or remove a role. Select File Server in the Configure Your Server Wizard, and then click Next.

12. Select Yes, turn the Indexing Service on, and then click Next. Click Finish when done.

Now your server is ready to share folders, and the File Server Management console is open.

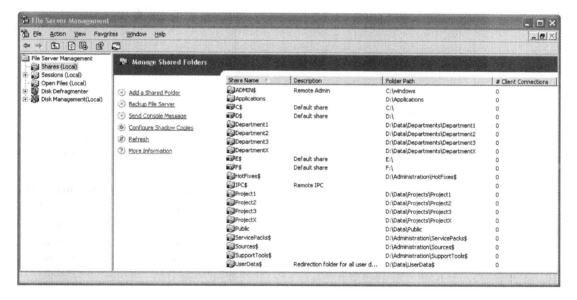

Sharing Folders

The next stage involves creating the shares themselves, setting share permissions, and setting caching options for each share. Everything is performed through the File Server Management console and the Share a Folder Wizard (you can also use the Computer Management console to do this).

1. Click Add a Shared Folder at the left of the File Server Management console's right pane. This launches the Share a Folder Wizard. Click Next.

2. Either type in the pathname or click Browse to identify the folder you want to share, and then click Next.

3. Identify the name for the share—in this case the name of the folder—and type in a description.

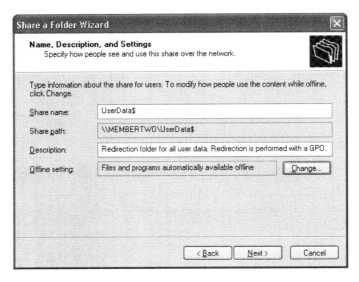

4. This is also where you can set caching options for the share. By default all shares are set to allow users to determine if they need to cache information. Caching should be set according to the information in Table 7-1. To change caching options from the default, click Change.

5. Select the appropriate setting, and then click OK to return to the Share a Folder Wizard. Click Next.

6. Now set share permissions. Remember that by default, all shares are Everyone Read. The wizard provides you with a default set of permissions. Assign share permissions according to the information in Table 7-1. If custom permissions are required, click Use custom share and folder permissions, and then click Customize. Use the Customize dialog box to change share permissions. You can also use this dialog box to review and change NTFS permissions if required. Click OK when done.

7. Once you return to the wizard, click Finish. The share is now created. If you need to create a new share, select the When I click on Close, run the wizard again to share another folder check box. Repeat until all shares have been created.

You're almost done. Now, the only thing left is to make the shares available to users. This is done through Active Directory.

Publishing Shares in Active Directory

Shares are published in Active Directory to simplify their access by users. Users can search the directory to locate the shares they require access to, reducing the requirement for mapped shares in logon scripts.

1. Move to a domain controller and open the Active Directory Users and Computers console.

2. If it isn't already done, create a new organizational unit structure and name it Services. Under Services, create a new OU named File and Print.

3. Within the File and Print OU, create new shares. To do so, move to the right pane and right-click. Select New | Shared Folder from the context menu.

4. Type in the name of the share and the path to the shared folder (using UNC format). Click OK when done. Repeat for all the shares you need to publish.

▶ *CAUTION*

Do not publish hidden shares because they will no longer be hidden. Any share that is published in AD will be visible to users.

5. Once the shares are created, you will need to add a description and keywords to each. Folder descriptions are important since they will serve to tell users the purpose of the shared folder. Keywords are also useful because users can search for a shared folder by keyword instead of share name. To enter both, view the Properties of each shared folder in AD.

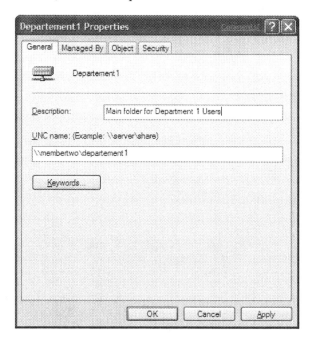

6. Use this dialog box to add complete descriptions to each share and to identify its manager. To add keywords, click the Keywords button. Type the keyword and click Add. Click OK when done.

7. Close the dialog box when done. Repeat for each share you publish in AD.

Your shares are now ready for access by users.

Finding a Share in AD

Finding shares is performed through Windows Explorer's Search function.

1. Open My Network Places on either Windows XP or WS03.
2. Use the task pane (on the left) to click on Search Active Directory.
3. In the Find dialog box, select Shared Folders from the Find drop-down menu. The title of the dialog box will change to reflect the fact that you are searching for shared folders.
4. Type in either the folder name or its keywords and click Find Now.
5. The Find dialog box will display the shared folders matching the search criteria. To access a shared folder, double-click on its name.

Your users will require this operation only once because each time a new shared folder is accessed from a client computer, it is added to the Network Favorites portion of the Explorer. Users can access their shared folders from there the next time they need it.

> ► **QUICK TIP**
>
> *Don't forget to deploy the Previous Versions client to both PCs and servers. In fact, this client should be part of the PASS System Kernel for both (storage layer).*

Managing Folder Availability

Though they are fully supported, mapped drives are no longer an orientation in Windows Server 2003. It is the Universal Naming Convention (UNC) that is the favored method of rendering shared folder access. This method is based on a \\Servername\sharename naming structure. But there are features of mapped drives that cannot be rendered by a simple UNC name. For example, since a mapped drive is usually created through a logon script, it is easy for administrators to change the address of the mapped drive overnight, an operation that is completely transparent to users. As far as they are concerned, the K: drive remains the K: drive no matter where it connects.

Thus, mapped drives supported administrative tasks such as replacing servers and moving shared folders. They were not without problems, though. For example, ever since version 97, Microsoft Office tracks the UNC behind the mapped drive, making it difficult to use conventional drive mappings. With the advent of Windows Installer compatible software, the UNC is becoming more and more important. For self-healing purposes, Windows Installer must remember the original installation source of a program. It prefers a UNC format to a mapped drive for this function. This is why Microsoft has developed two technologies that support fault tolerance for UNC shares. These two technologies are Distributed Link Tracking and the Distributed File System. Both can be used individually or together to provide many of the same administrative advantages of mapped drives.

Distributed Link Tracking

Windows 2000 first introduced the Distributed Link Tracking (DLT) service. This service is composed of a client and a server component. Both components are available on WS03, but only the client component is available on Windows XP. This service is designed to track distributed links, or rather shortcuts that have been created on a client computer. The basic purpose of the service is to ensure that shortcuts are always functional. For example, when a workgroup is working with a given set of files that are located on a specific file server, each either creates their own shortcut to these files or a global shortcut is distributed by the project administrator to all team members. This shortcut is functional because it points to the shared folder containing the files. If both the client and the server services for DLT are enabled, then the shortcut will always work even if an administrator must move the shared folder to a different server.

The client service is set to automatic startup. It tracks local shortcuts or shortcuts whose targets are modified by the user of the local system. The server portion tracks shortcuts linked to central file shares. It stores all link information into Active Directory (in the System | FileLinks container). If a shortcut no longer works, the client application will search the directory to locate the new path to the link and automatically repair it.

While the server portion was set to automatic startup in Windows 2000, it is now disabled in Windows Server 2003. The reason for this deactivation is the inordinate amount of information DLT stores within the directory. It can have a serious impact on intersite replication and can lead to other problems if organizations do not take its contents into account when calculating the size of the AD database. In fact, Microsoft has a support article on this subject (Q312403). This article outlines a "fictitious" case where a client did not know that DLT stored information into the directory and found that when it was time to upgrade from Windows 2000 to Windows Server 2003 (1.5 GB free space is required), they could not do so because their domain controllers were topped out in terms of physical disk additions.

Therefore, be warned: DLT uses a lot of space in the directory if you enable the server portion. Make sure your storage system for directory files has sufficient space and can grow with your Directory Database requirements. To enable the DLT Server service, set it to Manual startup.

Working with the Distributed File System

The preferred technology for fault tolerance of file shares is the Distributed File System (DFS). DFS offers several enterprise features for the support and administration of file shares:

- DFS creates a file share alias that is unique through which users can access files on a server. This means that you can change the target file share without impacting users because they access the alias and not the physical file server.

- The DFS alias does not only apply to file shares, it can also be applied to Web server addresses, allowing you to modify background Web servers without impacting the use of your internal or external Web applications.

- The DFS namespaces can be linked to any number of actual physical file shares. This is because the DFS namespace can be replicated. If a server must be shut down for any reason, users continue to work by being redirected by DFS to another physical server.

- DFS can provide load balancing by distributing file access to a number of physical locations or targets.

- DFS provides transparent consolidation of distributed file shares. If files for a given department are distributed on several physical servers, then DFS can make it appear as if they are all located within a single virtual DFS structure.

- DFS is site aware—that is, it can identify AD sites and use them to redirect users to a file server located within their site. Thus DFS is ideal for distributing file shares that span regions.

- DFS clients can cache referrals for DFS roots or links for a definable period of time, improving performance by accessing resources without having to perform an AD lookup.

The Distributed File System works in conjunction with the File Replication System (FRS) in Windows Server 2003 to provide fault tolerance and link tracking features. DFS roots that are integrated to AD are named domain DFS roots. WS03 domain DFS roots cannot include more than 5,000 targets or links.

DFS also supports stand-alone DFS roots. Stand-alone roots are not fault tolerant in the same way as domain DFS roots because they are located on a single machine. On the other hand, a stand-alone DFS root can be on a cluster server and provide fault tolerance through cluster services. It can contain up to 50,000 targets.

DFS is extremely powerful. For example, if your developers need to work in different environments when preparing corporate applications, they can take advantage of DFS by creating a standard DFS root for development purposes in each staging environment and using the same DFS name that will be used in the production network. Thus they do not have to modify paths within the code whenever they change environments, even into production.

Another example is the source file for all installations and for the support of Windows Installer features such as self-healing. By using DFS, you can have one single installation source path that is available in all sites and that automatically replicates all of the source files from site to site.

There are many other useful implementations of DFS/FRS: public folders that are replicated in each regional site, project folders that span a specific number of regions, or file shares that are transparent to mobile users, just to name a few.

Installing a Domain DFS Root

Domain DFS roots are more useful when shared folders must span regions. Begin by installing the domain DFS root. It is recommended to perform this action on a Member Server. You normally need domain administrator credentials to create a domain DFS root, but it is possible to delegate this right in AD. Delegate this right only if you need to create DFS roots on a recurring basis. If you only need to set them up once during the creation of the parallel network, don't bother. Use the process outlined in Figure 7-4 to identify the steps required to create your DFS configuration.

1. Launch the Distributed File System console (Start | Administrative Tools or in the Quick Launch area).

2. Right-click on Distributed File System in the console's left pane. Select New Root. This launches the New Root Wizard. Click Next.

3. Select Domain Root, and then click Next.

4. Select the host domain—this should be the production domain—in this case, Intranet.TandT.net, and then click Next.

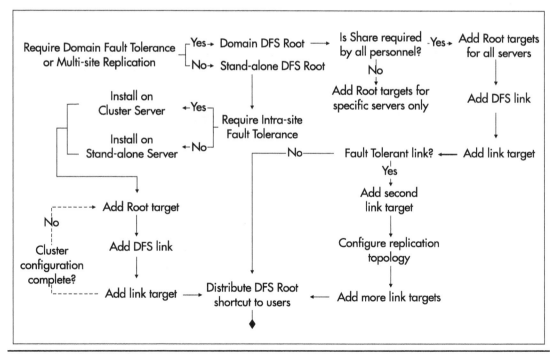

Figure 7-4   The DFS decision tree

5. Select the host server. Click Browse to find the name of the server. This should be one of your file servers. Click Next when done.

6. Name the DFS root. Use a common name that will not be duplicated within the enterprise and that will be resilient (last a long time). Think of the resilience of network drives when choosing DFS root names. For example, for the public share, use Public as the root name. Type in a short description for the root. Click Next when done.

▶ **CAUTION**

Keep your descriptions to a minimum. Large DFS descriptions will impact performance and slow down the DFS search process.

7. DFS will locate the shared folder automatically if it has already been shared. If not, it will display an additional screen that allows you to create and share a folder.

▶ **CAUTION**

If your domain DFS roots will be hosted on both Member Servers and domain controllers (for example, domain controllers that are used as multipurpose servers in regional sites), you should ensure that the shared folder name you use on the Member Server to host the domain DFS root is not the same as the share name used on the domain controllers because by default, clients will be directed to the domain controller if the names are the same. Not only will they not be able to access the Member Server share, but it may impact performance.

8. Click Finish. The DFS root will be created. Now you must add additional information to the root. To do so, right-click on the DFS root name and select Properties. Move to the Publish tab, select Publish this root in Active Directory, type in a comment for the root, and identify its owner. Click OK when done.

► *NOTE*

The information stored in the Publish tab of the DFS root properties dialog box can only be viewed through the Distributed File System console.

9. Now add an additional root target (the first root target was added when you created the DFS root). Root targets are the elements that provide fault tolerance and redundancy within same sites and provide local site access when they are in different sites. If this share will be required by all personnel, such as the public share, you need to add as many root targets as you have Active Directory Sites. To add a root target, right-click on the name of the new domain DFS root in the left pane and select New Root Target.

10. Follow the instructions in the Add a Root Target Wizard. Repeat as many times as required.

Your DFS root is ready. It now requires links to provide user access to information. The root creation process allows you to change the default setting for client caching of root targets. By default this setting is 300 seconds or five minutes. This setting is usually appropriate for domain DFS roots.

Adding DFS Links

Now that your DFS root has been prepared and is fault tolerant, you can begin to add DFS links. Links are the elements that users see when accessing DFS shares.

1. To add a link, right-click on the DFS root and select New Link.

2. In the New Link dialog box, type in the name of the link and either type in the UNC path to the shared folder or use the Browse button to locate the appropriate share. Type in a description for the link. Click OK when done.

3. If this is a fault-tolerant link, you will need to add new link targets to the initial link. Additional link targets make the shared folder redundant. To add a new target, right-click on the link name in the left pane and select New Target from the context menu.

4. Either type in the UNC path to the shared folder or use the Browse button to locate the appropriate share. Click OK when done.

5. As soon as you add a second target, DFS will request that you configure replication for the shares within the link. In the Distributed File System dialog box, click Yes to launch the Configure Replication Wizard. Click Next.

6. Identify the Initial Replication Master by clicking on the share name. This server should be the server acting as the initial source for all files. You can also configure the staging directory. On a file server, this should be the same as the Shadow Copy drive, or the E: drive. DFS will create its own staging directory on this drive. Modify this option only if required.

7. Click Next. You now need to select the replication topology. See Figure 7-5 for FRS replication topology types. Four choices are available:

   • Select Ring if all the servers are in a ring topology. This is best when only one server contains the data in each site.

- Select Hub and Spoke if your servers are located in different sites and your wide area network includes links at differing speeds. The T&T WAN example used in Chapter 3 is an example of a hub and spoke replication topology. You will need to identify the hub server if you select this replication topology. This should be the central server.
- Select Full Mesh if the servers staging the share are all in the same site and are connected with high speed links or if your WAN links are all at the same speed.
- Select Custom if you want to configure your own replication topology later.

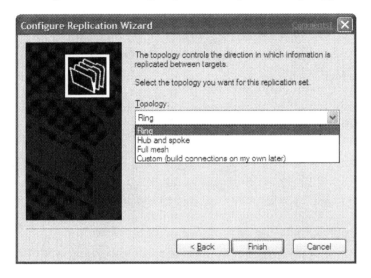

8. Click Finish when done. This will launch an initial replication.

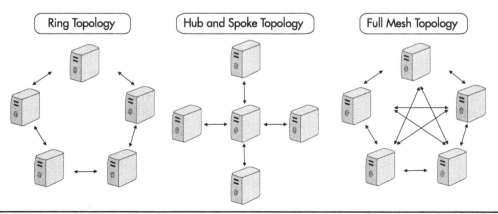

Figure 7-5 FRS replication topologies

> ▶ **QUICK TIP**
>
> *You should consider turning off the antivirus software on file servers during initial replication, so long, of course, as you know that all files to be replicated are free of viruses. If massive volumes of files must be replicated, the antivirus engine will impact the replication process.*

The link creation process allows you to change the default setting for client caching of link targets. By default this setting is 1800 seconds or 30 minutes. This setting is usually appropriate for DFS links.

> ▶ **QUICK TIP**
>
> *The DFS process is fully detailed in the book* Windows Server 2003 Deployment Kit: Designing and Deploying File Servers in the Planning Server Deployments *(Microsoft Press, 2003). It is highly recommended reading if you want to make full use of DFS in your enterprise.*

DFS Clients

Clients can view DFS shares in the same way they view standard shared folders, through My Network Places. But the best way to give access to domain DFS roots to clients is to send them a shortcut to the root. The advantage of the DFS alias is that it is not tied to a single server, but rather to the domain as a whole. Thus, the shortcut must point not to a server UNC, but to a domain UNC. In this case, the domain UNC would be: \\Intranet.TandT.net\BulletinBoard.

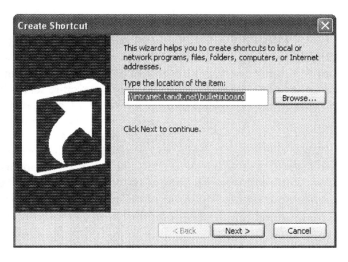

The domain DFS root is listed as a component of the Entire Network.

The shortcut can be made available to users through the logon script. By double-clicking on the shortcut, users have access to all of the published folders in the root; this access is independent of the location of the user. In fact, the server they are connected to is completely transparent to them.

If you want your users to use the DFS links instead of standard shared folders, you should name all of your actual shared folders with a dollar sign (example: Server$). This will hide your actual shares from being displayed on the network. Users will thus only see DFS shares and not actual shares.

As stated throughout this book, when implementing a Windows Server 2003 network, you should strive to make use of the latest standards it offers so long as they are applicable to your situation.

> **QUICK TIP**
>
> *The migration of files from the legacy network to the parallel network and your new DFS structure is detailed in Chapter 10.*

Working with DFS instead of mapped drives is an excellent example of this principle. DFS and FRS will automatically synchronize content between sites while making user access to shares completely transparent—something network drives will never do. And by using DFS today, your network will be ready to support tomorrow's requirements.

Sharing Printing Services

The print server has greatly evolved with Windows 2000 and Windows Server 2003. WS03 now supports Version 3 print drivers. Version 3 drivers are designed to integrate more properly with the operating system to provide better fault tolerance. One of the great advantages of Version 3 print drivers is that when the printer driver fails, it does not require a server restart but only a print spooler restart. In fact, WS03 can automatically restart the print spooler on a failure, making the failure transparent to the majority of the users connected to the printer. The only user who will notice the failure is the one whose job caused the print spooler to fail.

This is because Windows 2000 and Windows Server 2003 drivers are user-mode drivers. Drivers can be either user-mode or kernel-mode. In Windows NT, drivers were moved to kernel-mode because kernel-mode drivers provided better performance. Kernel-mode drivers are Version 2 drivers. But a faulty kernel-mode driver can crash the entire kernel, or rather, the entire server. Thus, to provide better performance and better reliability, Windows 2000 and WS03 drivers were moved to user-mode. In Windows Server 2003, a default Group Policy blocks the installation of Version 2 drivers.

In addition, user-mode drivers allow users to set their own printing preferences, something that was an issue in Windows NT. Since the drivers operated in kernel-mode, they did not provide the ability to separate user printing preferences from default driver configurations, causing a lot of frustration in the Windows NT user market. WS03, like Windows 2000, offers the ability to set printing defaults for the shared printer as well as printing preferences for each user of the shared resource.

Printing preferences are separate from the printer properties, but are derived from the defaults you set. For example, if you use a double-sided printer and you set its default properties to double-sided output, the user's default preferences will be double-sided printing, but the user now has the choice to modify the setting for their own personal environment to single-sided, without affecting general settings for other users. It is surprising how many organizations use double-sided printers but set the default print spooler setting to single-sided, forcing conscientious users to manually reset their preferences. One of the most important aspects of a shared printer implementation in any organization is the establishment of an enterprise-level shared printer policy. This policy should include elements such as default settings for all printers. A sample shared printer policy is outlined later in this section.

WS03 Printer Drivers

WS03, like Windows 2000, uses three core printer drivers: the Unidriver, Postscript, and a Plotter driver. Each of these drivers provides the core printer protocol. Along with the core drivers, Windows Server 2003 calls upon a printer definition file for each type of printer in your network. This vastly simplifies the driver development process because all driver structures are standardized. These core drivers have been defined in conjunction with independent hardware vendors to ensure stability and robustness.

Another advantage of this shared development process is that drivers can now be certified. A certified driver is a driver that conforms to the Microsoft "Designed for Windows" Logo guidelines. Certified drivers are all Version 3 drivers and all include a digital certificate that is used for code signing purposes. Digitally signed drivers ensure their reliability. Your enterprise shared printer policy should be based on digitally signed and thus certified drivers.

The Microsoft Hardware Compatibility List (HCL) Web site (http://www.microsoft.com/hcl/) lists all products that have been designed for Windows. You should use this site when selecting new printers for your organization. If you want little trouble with your shared printer pool, only use printers that include Designed for Windows drivers. When you install printer drivers, Windows will indicate if the driver is digitally signed or not. The Add Printer Wizard dialog box even includes a Web link to the HCL Web site.

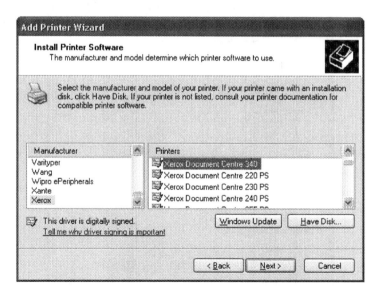

But if your current printer pool includes a number of older printers, it is obvious that you will not be able to include only certified drivers in your shared printer policy. Try your best to use only certified drivers (updated versions are included in WS03), but if you can't, then consider a printer obsolescence strategy that will gradually replace older printers with new engines that include better support for the Windows operating system.

► **QUICK TIP**

The best way to do this is to create a small database that includes information about all printers and the associated printer drivers. This way, each technician that must work with printers will have access to centralized information about all printers, making sure that only one version of a driver is in use in the enterprise network.

Integration with Active Directory

Full support for the Windows operating system today also means integration to the Active Directory. Each shared printer is now published within the directory, much in the same way file shares are. Printers are published in the directory by default. Their object names are stored in their parent domain. Users can use the directory to search for printers and automatically connect to the appropriate printing service.

AD stores information about printer features and locations. Locations especially are very important since it is one of the best ways for users to locate printers within your network. Descriptions are also very important since these are included in the elements users have access to when searching for printers in the directory.

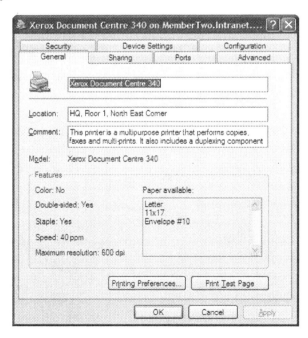

Users now search for printers in much the same way as they search for file shares, through the Active Directory Search tool. They can search based on printer name, printer location, or model. They can also search based on features such as double-sided printing, stapling, color output, and resolution.

Windows Server 2003 supports Printer Location Tracking. This component is based on the Active Directory Site Topology you designed in Chapter 3. One of the key elements of the Site Topology is the subnet. Each subnet includes a name and a description. It can also include location information. Location information is stored in hierarchical form in the subnet properties under the Location tab. Each level is separated by a slash. You can use up to 256 levels in a location name, though the entire location name cannot be more than 260 characters long. Each part of the name can include up to 32 characters. For example, a printer located in the northeast corner of the first floor of the headquarters building could be identified as HQ/First Floor/Northeast Corner.

To enable Printer Location Tracking in your domain, you need the following elements:

- Subnets and subnet locations entered into Active Directory Sites and Services
- A printer location naming convention
- Location Tracking GPO enabled
- Location settings for all printers
- Location settings for all PCs and servers

The Location Tracking GPO should be set at the domain level in order to have it apply to every object within the domain. In Chapter 5, you learned that you didn't want to modify Default Domain Policies since there is no rollback feature (unless you use a commercial policy management tool). Thus, you need to create an Intranet Domain GPO. This should be the GPO that includes the Printer Location Tracking setting. This setting is part of the Computer settings, under Administrative Templates | Printers. To turn Printer Location Tracking on, you must enable the "Pre-populate printer search location text" setting. This setting enables the Browse button in the Location tab for printer and computer properties within the directory. It also enables this button in the Search Printers tool on servers and PCs.

To enter location settings for printers, first locate all of the printers in your directory, and then open their Property page. In the General tab, enter their location or click Browse to select a location for the printer. You will usually want to be more specific when identifying printer locations. You can thus include more detail such as room number within the printer's location information. Perform this operation for each printer.

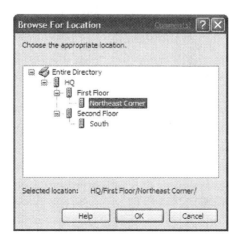

Perform the same operation on all computer objects in the directory. Open their Property page and use the Location tab to either enter the location or use the Browse button to select it. By entering locations for each object, you will facilitate the user printer search process. Then, whenever users use the Search tool to locate a printer, printer location will automatically be entered in the location field enabling your user community to find printers near them without having to know your location naming strategy. Because of this, you may not need to include user printers in their logon script. You only need to show them how to locate printers close to them and how to connect to them during migration training.

As in Windows NT, printer drivers are automatically downloaded to user systems when a user connects to the printer. If you are using the parallel network, you will not require the installation of multiple client drivers on your print spoolers. If not, you will need to add other versions of printer drivers—one to support each client type in your network. Keep in mind that you do not need Version 2 drivers for Windows NT clients. Windows NT clients can usually operate with Version 3 drivers.

Managing Printer Permissions

Printer permissions are much the same in Windows Server 2003 as they are in Windows NT. Print management is divided into printer queue and printer management. Print operators are allowed to manage both the physical device and the logical queue. In addition, each user that prints a job has control over their own job. That is, they can delete the job, but cannot change its priority.

WS03 supports the segregation of printer and document management. Printer management allows operators to stop, pause, and restart the printer itself. But it does not give the operator control over the documents in a queue. Document management allows the operator to start, stop, pause, and reorder documents that are in a print queue. By default, print operators in WS03 have both these rights. If you need to segregate these rights within your organization, you will need to create the appropriate administrative groups and delegate the appropriate rights to each. For example, if you want to delegate document management to administrative assistants, you will need to create the appropriate Security group.

Internet Printing Protocol

Windows Server 2003 also supports the Internet Printing Protocol (IPP). This means that users can print directly to a Uniform Resource Locator (URL) address. This operation requires the print server to host Internet Information Services (IIS) and IIS printer support. IPP also allows you to manage printers through a Web-based interface. This can have great advantages in a corporate intranet. On the other hand, installing IIS on servers that do not absolutely require it may also be an issue.

If you determine that IPP is not for you, you can disable it through a GPO. Once again, this should be done at the domain level with the Intranet Domain GPO discussed earlier. The GPO setting for disabling IPP is under Computer Configuration | Administrative Templates | Printers. To deactivate IPP on all your print servers, disable the Web-based Printing setting in this GPO.

▶ **QUICK TIP**

IPP should be disabled by default on all IIS servers facing the Internet.

Establishing a Shared Printer Policy

Now that you have a basic understanding of the printing support features of Windows Server 2003, you can begin to establish your enterprise shared printer policy. This policy should be fully documented and distributed to all technicians. It should include:

- Printer selection criteria (based on "Designed for Windows" certified printers)
- Minimum criteria for the addition of a shared printer
- Default printer setting standards
- Version 3 digitally signed drivers for all printers
- A standard printer naming convention
- A standard printer location naming convention in Printer Location Tracking format
- Standard description formats
- Printer Location Tracking activation
- Documented printer sharing procedures and processes
- Printer server construction principles

This list is not exclusive. Include in your printer policy anything you deem necessary. Keep in mind the following elements:

- Printing has a lower priority than file sharing especially with the use of Version 3 (user-mode) drivers. So if you have a region that requires high printing throughput, do not create File and Print Servers. Instead create dedicated Print and dedicated File Servers.

- When you have more than one Print Server, create redundancy in your shared printer setups. Create all of the printers on each server, then share only a portion (for example, half) of the printers on one server and the other portion on the other server. Thus if one of your print servers goes down, you can quickly share and thus reactivate the lost printers on the other server. Each server acts as a standby server for the other.

- Almost everything can be done with the Unidriver today. Acquire Postscript in your printers only if you absolutely require it (for example, if you have non-Windows clients). Instead, select additional features such as duplex or stapling to create multifunctional devices for the same printer cost.

- When determining your default print setting standards, keep in mind that long jobs take a long time to spool. By default, WS03 printers begin printing as soon as the job begins spooling. But if you are spooling a 200-page document, other users would most likely have the time to print numerous 10-page documents before the job is done. If you set printing properties to spool, then print, small jobs will often clear much faster than long jobs.

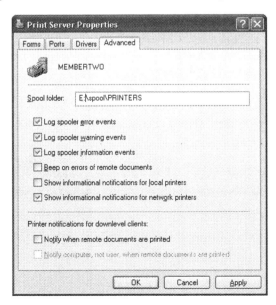

- To speed printing on a shared printer and file server, move the spooling directory to a dedicated disk. This is done through Print Server Properties in Printers and Faxes. Use the Advanced tab to redirect spooling to another disk. This should be a folder you create on disk E:.

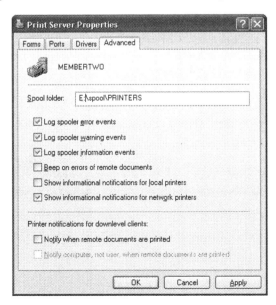

- Finally, use the Standard Port Monitor (SPM) instead of the LPR port when printing directly to network-enabled printers. The SPM is Windows Server 2003's new support mode for TCP/IP printer ports. It generally provides much more detailed status information than LPR can. For example, it can indicate status errors such as paper jams, low toner, non-responding documents, and much more. It also performs much better.

These are not the only considerations you will need to take into account for your enterprise shared printer policy, but they are often elements that are forgotten. Remember, printers are really there for users and should be designed in a way that facilitates the printing process for them.

Creating the Print Server

Print servers are normally linked with file servers. Thus, since your file servers have already been staged, you only need to add a print server function to existing servers. Before you proceed, though, remember to use the Print Server Preparation Process illustrated in Figure 7-6. This process includes several activities and it is heavily based on your enterprise shared printer policy.

Printers should have been identified in the inventory process outlined in Chapter 1. Use this inventory to create your print servers now. Then activate the print server role on your Member Server. Ensure that all printers are physically installed on the network and powered on.

1. Start the Manage Your Server console if it is closed (use the Quick Launch Area icon).
2. Click Add or remove a role. Select Print Server in the Configure Your Server Wizard, and then click Next.
3. Identify if you will be supporting only Windows 2000 and Windows XP clients or if you need to support other Windows clients as well, then click Next. (In the parallel network, you should only have Windows XP clients.)
4. The Configure Your Server Wizard will now be ready to start the Add Printer Wizard. Click Next.

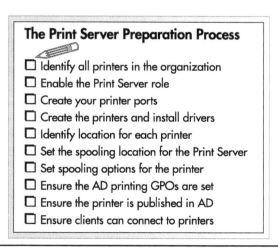

The Print Server Preparation Process

☐ Identify all printers in the organization
☐ Enable the Print Server role
☐ Create your printer ports
☐ Create the printers and install drivers
☐ Identify location for each printer
☐ Set the spooling location for the Print Server
☐ Set spooling options for the printer
☐ Ensure the AD printing GPOs are set
☐ Ensure the printer is published in AD
☐ Ensure clients can connect to printers

Figure 7-6   The Print Server Preparation Process

5. Create your printer ports. Click Next. In the Add Printer Wizard, select Local Printer attached to this computer and deselect Automatically detect and install my Plug and Play printer, and then click Next.

6. Select Create a new port and in the Port Type drop-down list, select Standard TCP/IP Port. Click Next.

7. This launches the Add Standard TCP/IP Printer Port Wizard. Click Next. Under Port Name or IP Address, type the printer FQDN. The FQDN is preferred since it will not change, whereas the IP address may, especially if you assign printer addresses through DHCP. Windows will automatically enter the port name as you type the printer name. Change this name only if you must. Click Next.

8. Windows will contact the printer and identify it. If the printer is turned off, Windows will allow you to select the printer type. Ensure the appropriate printer is selected and then click Next.

9. Click Finish to create the new port. Windows returns you to the Add Printer Wizard. You can click Back to repeat the Standard Printer Monitor creation process or you can proceed to finish printer installation. If you choose to return to create more ports, repeat steps 6 through 8. When you return to create other printers, you can then select Use the following port to connect to the printer since all of your SPM ports will have been created. When done, create the new printer by selecting the appropriate printer manufacturer and the appropriate model. Click Next.

10. Name your printer according to your naming strategy, and then click Next.

11. Share the printer, and then click Next.

12. Type in or select the printer location and type in a complete description. Click Next.

13. Determine if you need to print a test page, then click Next. It is always a good idea to print the test page at this time, just to make sure the printer actually works.

14. Check the Restart the wizard to add another printer box if you need to repeat the procedure.

15. The Configure Your Server dialog box returns. Click Finish.

When your operation is complete, your server will have an additional role. You will now be able to complete the print server setup operation. Now you should review each shared printer to ensure that it has the proper spooling settings and move the print spooler to the dedicated disk.

1. In Manage Your Server, click Open Printers and Faxes. Select Server Properties from the File menu (or use the right mouse button anywhere in the right pane to select Server Properties from the context menu).

2. Move to the Advanced tab and type in the location for printer spooling. This should be E:\Spool\Printers. Click OK when done.

3. Select each printer, view its Properties, then move to the Advanced tab and set its spooling properties. Select Start printing after last page is spooled and Print spooled documents first. Other settings can remain at the default setting.

4. Move to the Configuration tab and ensure the device is properly configured. Then move to Device Settings and apply default printer settings such as duplex printing, stapling, and paper type in each paper tray.

5. Click OK when done. Perform this task for each printer.

You should now ensure that printing GPOs have been set. These are set according to Table 7-2. They should be set at the domain level since they affect all computers and users.

Location	Setting	Comment
Computer Configuration/ Administrative Templates/Printers	Allow printers to be published	The default behavior is for printers to be published. Use this setting only if you want to disable the function on specific print servers.
Computer Configuration/ Administrative Templates/Printers	Allow pruning of published printers	Disable this setting for permanent print servers, otherwise AD will prune the server's printer from the directory if the server is temporarily down.
Computer Configuration/ Administrative Templates/Printers	Automatically publish new printers in Active Directory	The default behavior is to publish printers. Use this setting only if you want to disable the function on specific print servers.
Computer Configuration/ Administrative Templates/Printers	Check published state	Should not be necessary. Activate only if you see that printers are removed from AD when they should still be there.
Computer Configuration/ Administrative Templates/Printers	Computer location	Used for Printer Location Tracking; enable only if you want to force a given printer for a specific set of computers.
Computer Configuration/ Administrative Templates/Printers	Custom support URL in the Printers folder's left pane	Enable and set to an internal printing support Web page.
Computer Configuration/ Administrative Templates/Printers	Directory pruning interval	Applies only to domain controllers; not required if you disabled pruning of published printers.
Computer Configuration/ Administrative Templates/Printers	Directory pruning priority	Not required if you disabled pruning of published printers.
Computer Configuration/ Administrative Templates/Printers	Directory pruning retry	Not required if you disabled pruning of published printers.
Computer Configuration/ Administrative Templates/Printers	Disallow installation of printers using kernel mode drivers	Enable this setting if you can. By default, kernel mode printers are allowed on Windows XP Professional and not on Windows Server 2003.
Computer Configuration/ Administrative Templates/Printers	Log directory pruning retry events	Not required if you disabled pruning of published printers.

Table 7-2   Printing GPO Settings

Location	Setting	Comment
Computer Configuration/ Administrative Templates/Printers	Pre-populate printer search location text	Enable in order to use Printer Location Tracking.
Computer Configuration/ Administrative Templates/Printers	Printer browsing	Not required wherever there is a domain controller because printers are published in AD.
Computer Configuration/ Administrative Templates/Printers	Prune printers that are not automatically republished	Required only if you have non-Windows 2000 or Windows Server print servers or if you publish printers across forests.
Computer Configuration/ Administrative Templates/Printers	Web-based printing	Required for Internet Printing Protocol. Only necessary if IIS is installed on the print server or if you want users to use a central Web page to locate printers.
User Configuration/Administrative Templates/Control Panel/Printers	Browse a common web site to find printers	Used in conjunction with Web-based printing. Can be used to redirect users to a common centralized Web page to locate shared printers.
User Configuration/Administrative Templates/Control Panel/Printers	Browse the network to find printers	Used to automatically list shared printers in the network printers dialog box of the Add Printers Wizard. Not required when using AD to add printers.
User Configuration/Administrative Templates/Control Panel/Printers	Default Active Directory path when searching for printers	Only required on very large networks to speed directory searches or for distributed environments with slow links between sites.
User Configuration/Administrative Templates/Control Panel/Printers	Prevent addition of printers	Used only for highly restrictive accounts.
User Configuration/Administrative Templates/Control Panel/Printers	Prevent deletion of printers	Used only for highly restrictive accounts.

Table 7-2 Printing GPO Settings *(continued)*

Finally, ensure that your printers are published within the directory. This is the default behavior, but it should be verified anyway. This can be done at the same time as the last activity, ensuring users have access to the printers. Return to your workstation and log on with your normal user account.

1. Use the Start Menu to select the Search command.

2. Under Search, select Printers, Computers or People, then A printer on the network.

3. The Find Printers dialog box will be launched and the location field will automatically be filled in if your Printer Location Tracking is activated. Click Find Now.

4. Windows will display all of the printers near you. Double-clicking on any printer will connect you and install the driver.

5. Move to Printers and Faxes. Right-click on the printer and select Printing Preferences. Your default printing preferences should be those set on the shared printer object. Modify them as you require. Click OK when done.

Printing configuration is now done. You will need to perform this activity for each print server in your organization.

> **QUICK TIP**
>
> *You may find that you have too many printers to create manually. If this is the case, you can use the Microsoft Print Migrator to move printers from the legacy network to the parallel network. Print Migrator (including its documentation) is available at http://www.microsoft.com/windows2000/ technologies/fileandprint/print/download.asp. This tool will automatically convert printers from Version 2 to Version 3 during the migration.*

Sharing Files and Printers for Non-Windows Clients

Windows Server 2003 also supports printing and file sharing for non-Windows computers. These include the Macintosh as well as UNIX computers. Chances are that most enterprise networks will contain either one or the other or even both.

Macintosh Computers

Windows NT has supported Macintosh connectivity since its very earliest versions. Windows Server 2003 is no different. Macintosh connectivity is provided through Services for Macintosh, a service that includes both File Services for Macintosh and Print Services for Macintosh and must be added to the File and Print Server. The service automatically adds support for the AppleTalk protocol, but file and printer sharing over AppleTalk networks can be added either together or separately.

In addition to the service, you must install the Microsoft User Authentication Module (MSUAM) on client computers in order to ensure user passwords are encrypted over the network. Once this is done, Macintosh file shares can be managed in the same manner as normal file shares through the Computer Management console. Remember that all Macintosh shares must be on NTFS disks.

For printing, once the service is started, Macintosh users will see Windows Server 2003 printers as AppleTalk printers. Thus they will be able to operate as if they were within a Macintosh network. The printing service requires an account to operate. This should be configured as a service account and highly secured. Once it is up and running, Macintosh users will gain several benefits from the WS03 print service, but the greatest is that Postscript printers are not required. Print Service for Macintosh will automatically convert the Postscript header to non-Postscript when users print jobs. In addition, Windows users can print to AppleTalk printers as if they were on a WS03 network.

UNIX Integration

Windows Server 2003 also supports UNIX integration at several levels. With Print Services for UNIX, WS03 installs the Line Print Monitor allowing UNIX clients to print to WS03 print servers. In addition, WS03 uses the Server Message Block (SMB) or the Common Internet File System (CIFS), as it is now known, to share file services. Technologies like SAMBA (http://www.samba.org/) enable UNIX servers to share files in a way that Windows clients can view them (Windows 2000 and up) because they are compatible to the CIFS standard.

In terms of security, you can integrate Kerberos realms including WS03 domains and UNIX networks since Kerberos Version 5 is a standard and is able to interoperate between the two environments. A Kerberos realm ensures that users can access files from both environments without having to use or remember two accounts and passwords. More on Kerberos is covered in Chapter 8.

Finally, if you need a higher level of interaction between UNIX and Windows Server 2003 networks, you can acquire Services for UNIX, a comprehensive set of tools that is designed to integrate UNIX and WS03 networks and even allow UNIX applications to run on WS03 servers.

▶ **NOTE**

More information on WS03 File and Print Services can be found at http://www.microsoft.com/ windowsserver2003/evaluation/overview/technologies/fileandprint.mspx and http://www.microsoft.com/ windowsserver2003/techinfo/overview/print.mspx.

Preparing Application Servers

The Application Server is a multifunctional server role because it is required to support commercial server software as well as corporate applications. Whether it is for software or applications, this server role, like all others, is based on the core Server Kernel installation. Thus, you need to stage this server in the same way you stage all the other servers in WS03 enterprise network. There are some particularities depending on the type of software or application the server will host. In addition, each software or application will most likely require a detailed architecture of its own before implementation. For example, you could not install Microsoft Exchange Server without first determining its impact on your Active Directory, domain controllers, replication topology, and other elements of the infrastructure you already have in place.

Sharing Applications: Commercial and Corporate

Most organizations will have a vast number of software and applications already in place. This is, after all, the basis of the client/server model. Organizations who are using Windows NT or Windows 2000 today will also know that both software and applications hosted on these operating systems must conform to a specific set of guidelines in order to operate. This is outlined as the "Designed for Windows" specification. Ideally, all applications and software can be upgraded to versions that are completely compatible to Windows Server 2003, but this is an improbable scenario.

Few organizations will be able to afford the upgrade of all of their software or the redesign of all of their applications during the migration to WS03. The best you can hope for is to upgrade a few core or critical software products and redesign a few core applications. For example, on the software side, if you're using Microsoft Exchange 5.5, it makes a lot of sense to upgrade to the current version of Exchange because it integrates directly with Active Directory. You should also upgrade other core software such as the products found in the Microsoft .NET Enterprise Servers if you can. It also makes sense to upgrade your mission-critical corporate applications because they will gain from the new capabilities of WS03 and integration to the .NET Framework.

If you can't upgrade everything or redesign your applications, don't despair. Like Windows XP, Windows Server 2003 now boasts a Compatibility Mode that can emulate Windows 95, Windows 98, Windows NT, or Windows 2000 operating systems. In addition, WS03 includes a Program Compatibility Wizard that steps you through the assignment of compatibility parameters for legacy software or older applications. The wizard can be launched in two ways:

- Start Help and Support from the Start Menu (or from the Quick Launch Area) and search for Program Compatibility Wizard. Select Troubleshooting Compatibility Issues from the Suggested Topics listed in the left pane. In the right pane, click Program Compatibility Wizard and follow the wizard's instructions.

- Click Run from the Start Menu and type in hcp://system/compatctr/compatmode.htm and follow the wizard's instructions.

▶ **QUICK TIP**

In addition, Microsoft offers the Application Compatibility Tool which helps you verify the compatibility of your applications with Windows Server 2003. It is available at http:// www.microsoft.com/downloads/release.asp?ReleaseID=42071&area=search&ordinal=2.

One of the important aspects of application compatibility is security. Microsoft changed the security model for applications between Windows NT and Windows 2000. Now neither users nor applications have the right to change or modify information in critical folders. Therefore, if you have a legacy application that must run on a Windows Server 2003, you must either modify security settings to allow users to modify specific files in critical folders or run the Program Compatibility Wizard to redirect program data to the user's profile area.

▶ **CAUTION**

If you need to run multiple legacy applications on a server, you may decide to apply a special Security Template on the server by using the following command:
`Secedit /configure /cfg compatws.inf /db compatws.sdb`
This, however, will reset your server's security level to Windows NT. This is not recommended. Rather, it is best to use the Program Compatibility Wizard to apply special settings to each program that requires it.

Application Development Support

If you choose to redesign your corporate applications, you'll find that Windows Server 2003 offers a wealth of new features focused on application support. These fall into several categories such as scalability, availability, manageability, and enhancements to the program model. They are regrouped under WS03 Enterprise Services and include:

- **Application pooling**   With WS03, it is possible to create thread pools and apply them to legacy applications that would normally operate in a single process. This gives the application more robustness since it is no longer tied to a single process.

- **Application recycling**   Some applications have a tendency to have degraded performance over time due to memory leaks and other programmatic issues. WS03 can recycle a process by gracefully shutting it down and restarting it on a regular basis. This can be done either administratively or through the COM+ software development kit. Administratively, it is applied through the Component Services console, by right-clicking on a COM+ component, selecting Properties, and modifying the elements on the Pooling & Recycling tab.

- **Applications as NT services**   Now all COM+ applications can be configured as NT services, making applications load at boot time or on demand as required.

- **Low-memory activation gates**   WS03 can check memory allocations before it starts a process, allowing it to shut an application down if it will exhaust memory resources. This allows other applications running on the server to continue operation while only the faulty application fails.

- **Web services**   Any COM+ object can be treated as a Web service and any Web service can be treated as a COM+ object greatly extending the remoting capabilities of your applications.

- **Application partitions**   These were discussed in Chapters 3 and 4 when using Active Directory. In terms of application support, these partitions allow you to host several instances of the same or different versions of COM+ objects on the same server. If, for example, you have 500 customers running a hosted application, you can create 500 partitions, one for each customer, segregating their operational environment from all of the others. Application partitions are created in Active Directory Users and Computers under System | ComPartitions and ComPartitionSets (Advanced View must be enabled). In addition, Member Servers must have partitions enabled. This is done through Component Services | Computer | Properties.

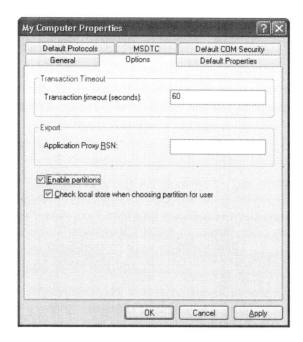

- **.NET Framework** WS03 includes an integrated version of the .NET Framework. Therefore you can program applications to make use of the Common Language Runtime and integrate them with XML Web services to take advantage of this powerful new programming model.

▶ **QUICK TIP**

More information on .NET Framework administration can be found in Admin.CHM from %systemroot%/Microsoft.NET/Framework.

- **UDDI services** WS03 also includes Universal Description, Discovery, and Integration services, allowing you to publish your Web services either internally or externally. UDDI services can be found under Windows Components in the Add or Remove Programs component of the Control Panel.

- **Simple Object Access Protocol (SOAP)** WS03 includes this XML-based protocol to allow full integration into the Web services programming model.

- **Message Queuing** WS03 also includes Microsoft Message Queuing (MSMQ) services. MSMQ provides an asynchronous messaging infrastructure for applications. This allows applications to operate under non-constant networking conditions. MSMQ is integrated with Active Directory where it stores all configuration, security, and status information. MSMQ provides guaranteed network communications even in non-optimal networking conditions. The WS03 version of MSMQ fully supports the SOAP Reliable Messaging Protocol (SRMP) allowing message queuing over the HTTP and HTTPS protocols.

Redesigning corporate applications is not a speedy process. It must be planned well before you begin your Windows Server 2003 migration so that applications will be ready to deliver when you perform your infrastructure deployment.

Application Compatibility Servers

If it turns out that you have legacy applications that simply won't run under WS03 or that require different versions of other software products to work (for example, an application requiring SQL Server 7 and another requiring SQL Server 2000), you can always create virtual servers on the Application Server through the use of virtual machine software such as VMware (http://www.VMware .com/). VMware GSX Server supports multiple CPUs, enterprise-level RAM partitions, and even server clusters. With GSX Server, you can create virtual machines on your Application Servers and have them host legacy applications through older operating systems (for example, Windows NT or Windows 2000). This gives you more time to convert applications while ensuring that your service levels stay the same for all users. In addition, it allows you to upgrade all servers to WS03 because they are no longer held back by legacy applications or software.

Finally, GSX Server can also be used for other purposes such as server consolidation. In many instances, server resources are barely used because each project tends to bring in their own server. Using GSX Server, you can consolidate multiple server roles onto fewer physical machines while at the same time making more effective use of your hardware capabilities. Keep in mind that you must ensure that you have full support from the application software manufacturer before using this strategy.

Legacy Application and Software Testing

Whether or not you convert your applications and upgrade your software, one of the key elements of your WS03 migration will rest with your application testing strategy. Every application and software product that will be migrated from your legacy network must be tested in your new network in order to ensure that it behaves in the proper manner while running under Windows Server 2003. It is also a good idea to repackage legacy application installations to integrate them with the Windows Installer service (see Chapter 5).

> **QUICK TIP**
>
> *A white paper on "Enterprise Software Packaging Practices, Benefits and Strategic Advantages" is available at http://www.wise.com/dyn-form.asp. You will need to fill in a short survey before downloading the white paper.*

This will give all of your applications additional robustness and stability at little cost since every software component or application must be configured to install automatically anyway. In addition, it will provide you with a single unified installation and deployment method for all software products.

Use rigorous testing methods and ensure that expert users are part of your acceptance test group for each application or software product. This will help you guarantee that the software or application provides all the features they expect since you can't be an expert on every aspect of every program in your network.

► *CAUTION*

Remember to test all of your software and application installations in user mode to ensure that they behave properly on WS03 with limited access rights.

Preparing Terminal Servers

One of the greatest features of Windows servers is the Terminal Service (TS). This service enables you to publish applications to remote computers giving them full access to programs running on Windows Server 2003 environment. The greatest advantage is in deployment. Since the application operates on the Terminal Server, that is the only place it needs to be installed, updated, and maintained. Also, since the application runs from the server, you only need to deploy shortcuts to users, nothing else, saving vast amounts of time. And this shortcut doesn't change even though you may upgrade or otherwise modify the application.

The WS03 version of Terminal Services also provides a richer experience for users than the Windows 2000 version. TS now supports sound redirection to client PCs, thus if you operate a multimedia application on the server, users will hear the information just as if the application was running on their own workstation. In addition, the WS03 version of Terminal Services supports higher quality graphics including True Color and the highest level of resolution supported by client hardware. Resolution and color must be set on both the client and the server to operate. Finally, TS is now integrated with Group Policy, allowing you to control Terminal Service features centrally.

Thin client models are becoming more and more popular, especially with the proliferation of wireless Pocket PCs and the new Tablet PC device. Both have more limited resources, making server application hosting more and more attractive to these user bases. Thus the Terminal Server is a server role that has a bright future in the enterprise.

Sharing Applications: Terminal Services

The Terminal Service is a core WS03 feature. In fact, with WS03, Terminal Services can now automatically provide load balancing of terminal applications. For this feature to work, Terminal Servers must be clustered at the network level to work together to run a common set of applications and appear as a single system to clients and applications. To do this, they must be clustered through the Network Load Balancing service. Once this is done, Session Directories can be used to transparently balance workloads between groups of Terminal Servers.

In addition, the WS03 version of Terminal Services supports roaming users. This means that users can open a session on a Terminal Server or a Terminal Server cluster, disconnect from the server without closing the session, move to another computer, and reconnect to their existing TS session. This is a great advantage over previous TS capabilities. Use the process outlined in Figure 7-7 to prepare to use Terminal Services.

Installing and Configuring Terminal Services

The Terminal Server role is defined in the same way all other server roles are defined in the enterprise. It begins with the Server Sizing Exercise outlined in Chapter 2. Then it involves the basic server

> **The Terminal Services Preparation Process**
>
> ☐ Install and configure Terminal Services
> ☐ Define the Terminal Server licensing model
> ☐ Determine the Application model for hosted applications
> ☐ Install hosted applications
> ☐ Define Terminal Services Group Policy objects
> ☐ Determine how to deploy Shared applications

Figure 7-7   The Terminal Services Preparation Process

staging process applying your customized kernel to the server, again as outlined in Chapter 2. Next, proceed as follows:

1. Using the Manage Your Server console, click Add or remove a role.
2. Once WS03 has identified existing roles on this server and displays available roles, select the terminal server role and then click Next. No CD is required for this operation.
3. Click Next again. This will launch the Configure Your Server Wizard. The first task this wizard performs is warn you to close applications because this process will cause the server to restart. Close running applications and click OK in the warning dialog box.
4. If existing applications and services have been installed on your server beforehand, Configure Your Server will reconfigure them to enable them to operate in multiuser mode. Then it will finalize the installation of Terminal Services in application mode. Once this is done, your server will restart. Log in again once it has restarted.
5. Once your session is open, the Configure Your Server Wizard indicates that the operation is complete. Click Finish. The Manage Your Server console will list a new server role and Terminal Services Help is started to help you complete Terminal Services configuration tasks.

Now you're ready to proceed to the license configuration.

Terminal Server Licensing

Terminal Services require special client access licenses (CALs) for each client that connects to the server. This is because each client connecting to Terminal Services in application mode (as opposed to administrative mode) is actually opening a Windows Server 2003 remote session. Thus even if you have hardware that does not support Windows XP, you can give users access to all of its features through remote terminal sessions on WS03 servers. If on the other hand, you do have client hardware that supports Windows XP, you gain a lot of advantages through Terminal Services. For example, there is no client component to deploy to have Terminal Sessions operate on a Windows XP client because Windows XP includes its own Remote Desktop capability. This means that you can then focus on centralizing applications and use a simpler application deployment model.

▶ **CAUTION**

It is important to activate the Themes service on a WS03 Terminal Server and enable the Windows XP theme because otherwise Windows XP users will be faced with a Windows 2000-like interface when accessing remote applications in Terminal Services mode. This will most certainly lead to confusion (Windows XP on the desktop and Windows 2000-like on remote sessions) and increase support calls.

Unlicensed servers will only allow clients to operate for 120 days after the first client logon. Once this delay has passed, all sessions will end and the Terminal Server will no longer respond to client requests. In order to license servers, you must install a Terminal Services Licensing server. This server must be activated by Microsoft before it can begin to issue licenses to your enterprise. Activation is automatic if your server is connected to the internet.

To install a Terminal Services Licensing server and activate it, use the following procedure. The Windows Enterprise Server CD is required for this installation.

1. Ensure that you log on with Domain Administrator or Enterprise Administrator credentials.

2. Open Add or Remove Programs from the Control Panel.

3. Select Add/Remove Windows Components.

4. Under Windows Components, select Terminal Services Licensing and click Next.

5. Since the Licensing Server will be for the enterprise, select Your entire enterprise and click Next. You can also modify the location of the license server database. This should be on the D: drive.

6. Click OK once the installation is complete. Close Add or Remove Programs.

7. Open Terminal Services Licensing from Start | Administrative Tools.

8. The Terminal Services Licensing console will automatically locate the Licensing Server.

9. Right-click on the server name and select Activate. This will launch a wizard that will automatically connect to the Microsoft Clearing House and proceed with the activation. Follow the steps it presents to complete the activation.

10. Once the server is activated, you need to install client license key packs. This can be done through the Internet as well. Right-click on the server name and select Install Licenses. This starts the Terminal Server CAL Installation Wizard.

11. Enter the appropriate licensing information in Program and Client License Information and then click Next.

12. The wizard then connects to the Microsoft Clearing House and installs the license key packs. Click Finish when done.

Now you're ready to start issuing licenses to TS sessions. This is an area where you will want to apply Group Policy settings. By default, Terminal Servers issue licenses to any computer that requests one. By using the License Server Security Group GPO setting (under Computer Configuration | Administrative Templates | Windows Components | Terminal Services | Licensing), you can restrict TS sessions to authorized groups of computers or users only. To do so, you will need to create Global groups for users (or computers) that are allowed to use Terminal Services and place these groups within the Local Terminal Services Computers group that is created by the policy. At the very least, you should place the Domain Users group within this Local group.

Determining the Application Model and Installing Applications

Terminal Services applications should be installed through Add or Remove Programs because this component ensures that applications are installed in multiuser mode. If you prefer to install remotely or through the command line, you must use the change user command. Use `change user /install` to set the Terminal Server to installation mode, perform the installation, and then use the `change user /execute` command to reset the server into execution mode.

Applications and software should be installed before allowing users to connect to the server so that you can test their operation properly before users start activating them. In addition, you should take the following guidelines into consideration when deciding which applications should be installed on a Terminal Server:

- Do not run 16-bit applications since they can reduce the number of concurrent users by up to 40 percent and require 50 percent more RAM per user.

- Do not run MS-DOS applications since they can consume all of the CPU resources of a server.

- Applications that run constant processes in the background (spell-checking in MS Word, for example) consume more resources.

- Applications that use high-quality graphics consume more bandwidth.

Your Terminal Services should be used to run applications that fall into the following categories:

- Applications that require complex installations. Placing these applications on Terminal Servers reduces the number of installation points and thus the risks of having problems with the installation.

- Applications that require frequent changes. Placing these applications on Terminal Servers reduces the number of installation points and thus the installation and deployment workload.

- Applications that are prohibitively expensive on a per user basis so long as their licensing model allows TS sharing. Placing them on Terminal Servers allows you to control how many licenses are used.

- Applications for users having low bandwidth access. This is ideal for wireless devices.

- Applications for users in sites where there are no local servers. If the number of users in a site (10 and below) does not warrant a local server, you can give these users access to the same service level by allowing them to use applications remotely.

The Terminal Services application operation model is slightly different from the standard WS03 model because of the multiuser environment. You should also check for compatibility scripts for the applications you install. These scripts modify standard installations to make them TS compatible. They should be run after the application installation. Scripts are found in the %systemroot%\Application Compatibility Scripts\Install folder.

GPOs for Terminal Services

There are over 40 Group Policy object settings for Terminal Services. This means that most every TS setting can be managed through GPOs. Like the user folder information outlined earlier in "Sharing Files and Folders," user terminal service information is no longer entered in the user account properties (see Chapter 6) because it must be done on a per user basis. User parameters are now set through the User Configuration of a GPO. Server and PC settings are set through the Computer Configuration of a GPO. Table 7-3 outlines the settings you should apply to each section. Settings that have no comment are optional.

Location	Settings	Applied to...	Comments
Computer Configuration/ Administrative Templates/ Windows Components/ Terminal Services	Keep-Alive Connections	Server	Enable to synchronize the client and the server connection state
	Automatic reconnection	PC	Enable
	Restrict Terminal Services users to a single remote session	PC	Enable to control resource use on servers
	Enforce Removal of Remote Desktop Wallpaper	Server	Enable to reduce bandwidth use
	Limit number of connections	Server	*Perhaps*—monitor server loads
	Limit maximum color dept	Server	Enable to limit bandwidth use
	Allow users to connect remotely using Terminal Services	PC	Enable to allow Remote Desktop
	Do not allow local administrators to customize permissions		
	Remove Windows Security item from Start Menu		
	Remove Disconnect option from Shut down dialog box		
	Set path for TS Roaming Profiles		
	TS User Home Directory		
	Sets rules for remote control of Terminal Services user sessions	Server	Enable—Full Remote Control with user's permissions
	Start a program on connection		

Table 7-3   Terminal Services GPO Settings

Location	Settings	Applied to...	Comments
Terminal Services/Client/ Server Data Redirection	Allow time zone redirection	Server	If required in multiple time zones
	Do not allow clipboard redirection		
	Do not allow smart card device redirection		
	Allow audio redirection	Server	*Perhaps* to limit bandwidth use
	Do not allow COM port redirection		
	Do not allow client printer redirection		
	Do not allow LPT port redirection		
	Do not allow drive redirection		
	Do not set default client printer to be default printer in a session		
Terminal Services/ Encryption and Security	Always prompt client for password upon connection	Server	Enable
	Set client connection encryption level	Server	Enable—Set to Client Computer capabilities
Terminal Services/ Encryption and Security/RPC Security Policy	Secure Server (Require Security)	Server	Enable when all clients are Windows XP
Terminal Services/Licensing	License Server security group	Server	Enable to include at least domain users
	Prevent License Upgrade		
Terminal Services/ Temporary Folders	Do not use temp folders per session		
	Do not delete temp folder upon exit		
Terminal Services/Session Directory	Terminal Server IP address redirection	Server	Enable to support NLB cluster
	Join Session Directory	Server	Enable
	Session Directory Server	Server	Enable to identify Session Directory Server
	Session Directory Cluster Name	Server	Enable to identify cluster name

Table 7-3 Terminal Services GPO Settings *(continued)*

Location	Settings	Applied to...	Comments
Terminal Services/Sessions	Set time limit for disconnected sessions	Server	*Perhaps* if long disconnections turn out to be common behavior
	Set a time limit for active Terminal Services sessions		
	Set a time limit for active but idle Terminal Services sessions	Server	*Perhaps* if long idle times turn out to be common behavior
	Allow reconnection from original client only	Server	*Perhaps* if you determine that it is a security issue
	Terminate session when time limits are reached	Server	*Perhaps* if time limits are set
User Configuration/ Windows Components/ Terminal Services	Start a program on connection	User	Enable for single application users
	Sets rules for remote control of Terminal Services user sessions		Set at computer level
Terminal Services/Sessions	Set time limit for disconnected sessions		Set at computer level
	Set time limit for active Terminal Services sessions		Set at computer level
	Set time limit for active but idle Terminal Services sessions		Set at computer level
	Allow reconnection from original client only		Set at computer level
	Terminate session when limits are reached		Set at computer level

Table 7-3 Terminal Services GPO Settings *(continued)*

Deploying Terminal Services Applications

As outlined in Table 7-3, Terminal Services can be set to operate in either single application mode or in full desktop mode. Single applications are deployed to users already having access to full desktops. Full desktop mode should be reserved for users lacking the capability on their own system or users requiring access to multiple applications on the Terminal Server. In either case, deploying the Terminal Server application is the same process. It simply requires the delivery of a Terminal Services connection file.

These files are simply Remote Desktop Connections (RDC) that include the proper parameters for accessing Terminal Services. To create an RDC file, use the following procedure:

1. Open Remote Desktop Connection (Start | All Programs | Accessories | Communications).

2. Type in the computer name or IP address (use the Terminal Server cluster name if you are using load balancing through Session Directory).

3. Click Options to set the parameters for this connection.

4. Save the RDC file (.rdp extension) when complete.

5. Test the connection through the RDC file.

6. Deploy the RDC file to users through a logon script or other deployment mechanism.

Users will now have access to your Terminal Server applications.

▶ **NOTE**

RDC files are also often called RDP files for Remote Data Protocol. The shortcut files are called Remote Desktop Connections or RDC in Windows XP and WS03.

In addition, Windows Server 2003 supports *Remote Desktop Web Connections (RDWC)*. The advantage of this model is that no deployment is required since client access is located on an internal Web page (never on an IIS server facing the Internet). WS03 includes a sample Web page that can serve as a starting point for your Terminal Services Web access. The RDWC client is not installed by default. Use the following procedure to install it. The WSE CD is required for this operation.

1. Open Add or Remove Programs in Control Panel and select Add/Remove Windows Components.

2. Click Application Server (don't check the box) and click Details.

3. Click Internet Information Server and click Details.

4. Click World Wide Web Service and click Details.

5. Select Remote Desktop Web Connection and click OK. Click OK three times to return to the Web Components dialog box. Click Next.

6. Once the client is installed, you can move to the %systemroot%\Web\TSWeb folder and open Default.htm to view the default RDWC page.

7. This page can be edited to meet your corporate standards and placed on your intranet to give users access to specific applications through a Web interface.

Your Terminal Services environment is now ready for production. Ensure that you use a thorough testing policy before giving users access to the applications you host on Terminal Servers.

Collaboration Servers

In its first iterations, Windows Server 2003 was touted as the platform for collaboration in the Windows world. But as the release product progressed toward final code, Microsoft saw fit to remove several collaboration features and release them separately as free add-ons. These include mainly the Real Time Collaboration service. In addition, SharePoint Team Services which were also to be part of the collaboration features of WS03 were moved to SharePoint Portal Server. Thus, Collaboration Servers are really only hosts that are prepared to support applications such as Microsoft Exchange, SharePoint Portal Server, the Real Time Collaboration add-on, and other services that promote user interaction in a networked environment.

Once again, these servers are based on the PASS model and are configured with the Server Kernel. Refer to each product's documentation to finalize the server role.

Additional Network Infrastructure Server Functions

Chapter 4 outlined how to construct Network Infrastructure Servers for two specific roles: Dynamic Host Configuration Protocol (DHCP) and Windows Internet Naming Service (WINS). One more Network Infrastructure Server role is required to complete the Parallel Network Design. It is the Remote Installation Services (RIS) server role. This server is closely related to the DHCP server role since its very operation is based on the DHCP protocol. Also, Chapter 2 outlined how the RIS server role helped support the preparation and staging of both servers and computers in the Windows Server 2003 enterprise network.

Preparing Remote Installation Services Servers

Once again the preparation of a RIS server is performed through the Add or Remove Programs component of the Control Panel. To prepare a RIS server, use the following steps. The WSE installation CD is required for this process.

1. Log on as an Enterprise Administrator. The RIS installation process includes RIS server authorization in Active Directory (because it is based on the DHCP service), thus you need proper credentials.

2. Move to Add or Remove Programs in Control Panel and select Add/Remove Windows Components.

3. Select Remote Installation Server and click Next.

4. Type in the Remote Installation Folder Location (this cannot be the system or boot drive and should be a dedicated drive). Then click Next.

5. In the Initial Settings dialog box, check both Respond to client computers requesting service and Do not respond to unknown client computers and then click Next. Checking the latter

setting means that RIS will only respond to computer names that exist in Active Directory. This means all computer names must be prestaged.

6. Identify the location of your Windows System CD and click Next.

7. Name your Windows Installation Image Folder and click Next.

8. Type in a friendly description for the image and add descriptive text. Remember that this is the name and description users will see when selecting installations. Click Next when done.

9. Review your settings and click Finish when ready.

10. The RIS installation process will begin outlining each step and identifying installation progress. Click Done when all tasks are complete.

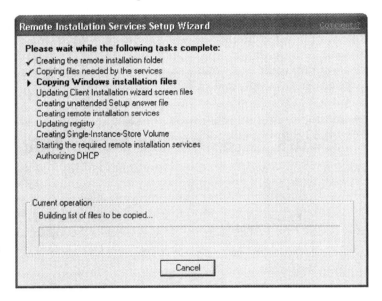

Once installation is complete, RIS will have created an entire folder structure designed to support remote system installation. You can now use the RIPrep utility to create custom images for both servers and PCs.

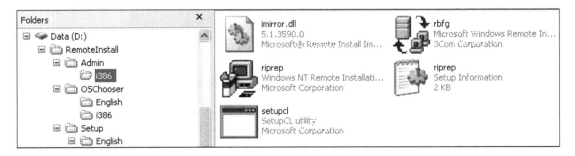

Prestaging Client PCs and Servers

During the RIS service installation, you identified that you wanted to respond only to known computers. This means that in order to apply RIS to stage systems, you will need to prestage each system in Active Directory before it can be prepared through RIS. Prestaging is a straightforward task. It implies creating the computer or server object in Active Directory, indicating that it is a managed computer, identifying its globally unique identifier (GUID) and identifying which RIS server can stage this system.

Prestaging allows you to coordinate your organizational unit strategy with Remote Installation Services to install both PCs and servers and have them immediately located in the right portion of your directory structure. Now the only thing you need to do is ensure that machines are placed within the appropriate OU and the appropriate software category group when you integrate them into the parallel network.

▶ *CAUTION*

Make sure the system manufacturer supplies you with the GUIDs for the systems you purchase. An Excel spreadsheet is ideal when buying computers in lots. You can change it to a script and prestage computers automatically. If not, the GUID can also be found in the system's BIOS settings.

Preparing the OU structure before integrating new machines into the network also ensures that they will be managed as soon as they join the network. No mistakes can be made when you use this procedure (see Chapter 5 for more information on software category groups).

▶ *CAUTION*

Deploying servers through RIS still requires discipline. Even though you facilitate deployment and server rebuilds through RIS, it is important to ensure that technicians still follow proper operational procedures.

Server System Requirements by Role

Now that you have reviewed the creation process for each server role identified in Chapter 1, you have an idea of the hardware requirements to construct each server role. Table 7-4 outlines the CPU, RAM, disk sizes, and network capabilities required for each server role discussed in this chapter. Use it as a guideline to prepare your servers when you stage the parallel network.

Server Role	CPU	RAM	Drive D	Drive E	Network
File Server	Low load	Required for Indexing Service	Hosts shares	Hosts shadow copies	Higher speeds required for file sharing throughput

Table 7-4   Hardware Requirements per Server Role

Server Role	CPU	RAM	Drive D	Drive E	Network
Print Server	Medium load	Required for large documents	Not required	Hosts spool files	Required for networked printers
Application Servers & Dedicated Web Servers	Medium to high load	Required to increase processing speeds	Hosts data files	Hosts transaction logs	Required for large user bases
Terminal Servers	High load (depends on the number of users)	Required for server processes as well as for each user (20 MB per user)	High-speed SCSI RAID adapters are recommended	Required only if the server hosts database applications	Required for better Remote Desktop Protocol throughput
Collaboration Servers	High load	Required for collaboration services	Hosts data files	Hosts transaction logs	Required for better collaboration throughput
Network Infrastructure Server (RIS role)	High load	Required to support multiple system construction processes	Hosts RIS service and image files; use large, dedicated drives	Not required	High speed network card is required for better performance

Table 7-4   Hardware Requirements per Server Role *(continued)*

▶ **QUICK TIP**

An updated version of this table is available at http://www.Reso-Net.com/WindowsServer/.

Designing the Services OU Structure

The final step of service preparation is the design of the Services OU structure and the application of proper delegation and Group Policy settings to each service. This should be done according to the elements outlined in Table 7-5. As can be seen, this OU structure is fairly flat, but it supports the ability to create substructures. When the Services OU structure was first introduced in Chapter 3, its purpose was to identify the type of content you could expect it to host. Now you have had the opportunity to refine your understanding of the content for this OU structure, thus you will find that it is slightly different than the initial presentation in Chapter 3. For example, while in Chapter 3, this OU structure presented the type of Member Server contained within the OU, in this chapter, it now presents the server role at the *second level*. This categorization allows further refinement. For example, if you find you need to further segregate Collaboration Servers because your policies for Exchange Server are not the same as those for SharePoint Portal Server (SPS), you can create a third level of OUs under Collaboration Servers and place Exchange and SPS servers in separate OUs.

OU	Level	Objective	GPO	Notes
Services	One	Grouping of all services and utilitarian objects in the organization	Baseline GPO	This is a Security GPO. Detailed in Chapter 8.
File and Print	Two	Regroups all File and Print Servers	Global File and Print GPO	This GPO controls all aspects of file sharing, Distributed File System, and printing. Delegated to file and print operators.
Application Servers and Dedicated Web Servers	Two	Regroups all Application Servers Also regroups all Windows Web Servers	Global Application Server GPO	This GPO controls database servers, general purpose Web servers, .NET Framework, and corporate applications. Also controls all settings for IIS and Web services. Items can be subdivided if further segregation is required. Delegated to application server operators.
Terminal Servers	Two	Contains all Terminal Servers	Global Terminal Server GPO	Contains server-side Terminal Services settings. Delegated to terminal server operators.
Collaboration Servers	Two	Regroups all servers dedicated to collaboration services	Global Collaboration GPO	Contains settings for Real-time Communications Services, Exchange Server, SharePoint Portal Server, Content Management Server, and Streaming Media Services. Delegated to collaboration server operators.

Table 7-5   The Services OU Structure

OU	Level	Objective	GPO	Notes
Network Infrastructure	Two	Regroups all operational servers	Global Infrastructure GPO	Contains settings for DHCP, WINS, RIS as well as operational servers such as Microsoft Operations Management, Systems Management Server, Internet Security & Acceleration Server, and so on. Can be subdivided for further segregation. Delegated to infrastructure server operators.
Operational Accounts	Two	Regroups all special operational accounts such as support technicians and installers		No delegation, managed by domain administrators.
Service Accounts	Two	Regroups all special service accounts		No delegation, managed by domain administrators.
Hidden Objects	Two	Regroups all special groups including operational groups		Includes Domain Local and Universal groups. Includes special permissions (Deny List Contents) to stop regular users from locating these groups when searching Active Directory.

Table 7-5   The Services OU Structure *(continued)*

▶ *CAUTION*

The Hidden Object OU should deny List Contents to normal users to protect access to Universal and Domain Local groups. Make sure you do not assign this right to a group that contains Administrators because you will not be able to view its contents either.

The final result of this OU structure is presented in Figure 7-8.

One of the key aspects of this OU design is the preparation of appropriate security groups for server operators through the creation of the Services Administration Plan. Since it is mostly the preparation of special groups with limited administrative security rights, this operation will be performed in Chapter 8.

As for the preparation of this OU structure, use the same operations outlined in Chapters 5 and 6 to create the OU structure and delegate the management of the content of each OU to appropriate operational groups.

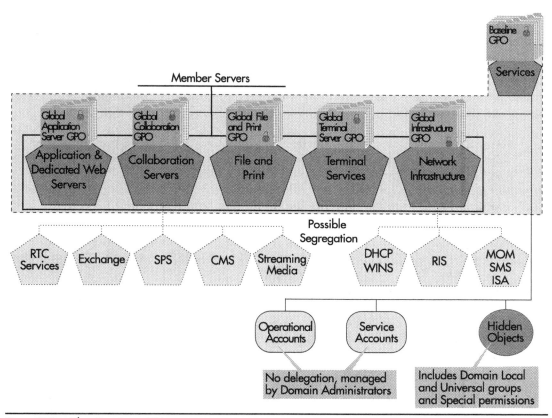

Figure 7-8   The Services OU structure

> ► **QUICK TIP**
>
> *An additional GPO was prepared in this chapter, the Intranet Domain GPO. It is applied at the domain level and includes global printer and other service settings.*

Considerations for the Migration of Services to the Parallel Network

Remember, when you migrate services from your existing network to the parallel network, you must perform a server rotation. Thus when you select a service to migrate, you should prepare the new servers first and ensure that you have a fallback solution in case of service failure. Ideally, you will be able to migrate a service, stabilize the servers, and then proceed to client migration. For client migration, you will need to migrate their PCs to Windows XP in order to fully profit from the new services infrastructure. As you migrate PCs, you will need to move users to the new service and monitor service performance. It will usually take one to two months of operation before services are fully stabilized. Afterwards, you will want to monitor services for growth potential.

The order you migrate services in will vary with your needs, but you might consider the following order for service migration:

- **Network Infrastructure** Begin with the migration of DHCP and WINS because no special client is required for computers to use these services. They work with all versions of Windows. Next, create the RIS Servers because they are required to build servers and PCs. Finally, create your systems management and operational servers so that your management infrastructure will be ready to manage new servers as they are added to the parallel network.

- **Dedicated Web Servers** Dedicated Web Servers can be next since IIS provides backward compatibility for Web applications. Be sure to thoroughly test all applications before putting them into production. There are serious security modifications in IIS 6 that may affect application operation. Once again, no special client is required to operate with IIS.

- **Application Servers** General purpose Application Servers can be next for the same reason as the Dedicated Web Servers. Database servers can also be migrated since once again, they will operate with existing clients. Corporate Application Servers can also be migrated since they will operate with existing clients. For these, you will require thorough testing.

- **Terminal Services** WS03 Terminal Services can operate through the Remote Desktop Web Connections, thus they will also support legacy clients as well as new clients.

- **File and Print Services** These services require new clients to operate properly or they require deployments to existing clients (for DFS and Shadow Copy Restore, for example). As such, they should be kept toward the end of your migration or at the very least, they should be coordinated with PC migrations (servers first, then PCs). Special attention should be paid to file ownership and access rights when files are migrated from the legacy network to the parallel network.

- **Collaboration Services** These services should be kept for last because they are at the basis of network service evolution. WS03 collaboration services extend the capabilities of your network. As such, they require the full capabilities of the new parallel network.

Remember to create your OU structure first and pre-stage servers in the directory, then use RIS to create the Server Kernel and follow through with the server role staging process.

Best Practice Summary

This chapter recommends the following best practices:

- Use the server lifecycle to prepare and plan for servers in your Enterprise Network Architecture.

- Prepare the Services OU structure before staging any of your server roles in order to ensure that servers are properly managed and delegated as soon as they are introduced into the enterprise network.

File Servers

- Focus on NTFS permissions rather than Share permissions.
- Use the same disk structure for all file servers. Use a template structure to recreate folders and shares on each file server.
- Try to avoid using Distributed Link Tracking unless absolutely necessary. Try to use the Distributed File System instead.
- Store your DFS roots on a domain controller. Document each portion of your DFS configuration.

Print Servers

- Use Version 3 printer drivers on Windows Server 2003.
- Use the Windows Unidriver (PCL) instead of Postscript drivers; invest savings into additional printer features such as duplexing and stapling.
- Design a shared printer policy when designing your network.
- Include detailed information about your printers when sharing them.
- Standardize your location naming strategy before sharing your printers and activate Printer Location Tracking.

Application Servers

- Upgrade your server software programs to "Designed for Windows" versions if possible.
- Redesign your corporate applications to take advantage of application support features in Windows Server 2003 and the .NET Framework if possible.
- Repackage all of your software and application installations to take advantage of the Windows Installer service.
- Thoroughly test all of your software and applications on your new network infrastructure before deploying them.
- Use the Program Compatibility Wizard to modify legacy applications to run on WS03.
- Use VMware to support legacy applications that are still required but are not compatible with Windows Server 2003.

Terminal Servers

- Combine Network Load Balancing services with Terminal Services and Session Directories to enable dynamic load balancing of Terminal Services.

- Enable the Themes service on Terminal Servers to ensure that users are faced with the same interface as that of their desktop.
- Use security groups to assign the right to use Terminal Services within your organization.
- Manage Terminal Services through Group Policy objects. This gives you one central location for TS management operations.
- Assign only single applications unless users require access to multiple applications on the same Terminal Server.

Infrastructure Servers

- Store Remote Installation Services on a dedicated disk separate from the operating system or boot drive.
- Prestage all systems to ensure that only authorized systems are staged through RIS in your organization.
- Place the prestaged machines in the appropriate OU and software categorization group to provide a complete machine construction process.

Chapter Roadmap

Use the illustration in Figure 7-9 to review the contents of this chapter.

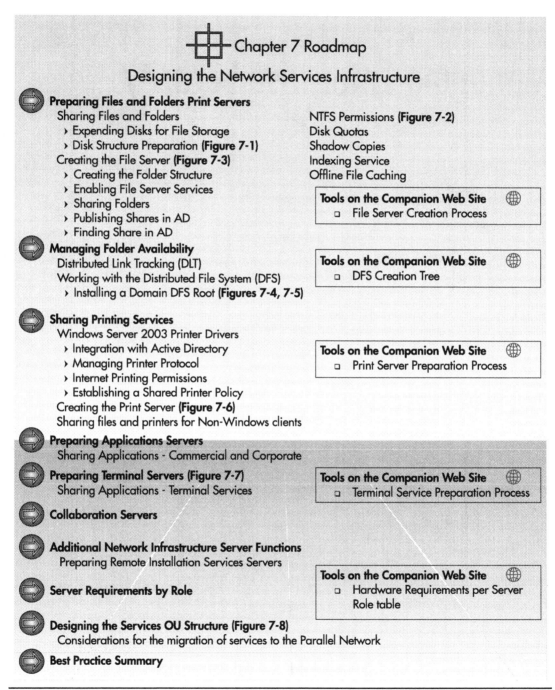

Figure 7-9 Chapter Roadmap

CHAPTER 8

Managing Enterprise Security

IN THIS CHAPTER

Security is a full-time occupation. On the technical side, it begins with the installation of a computer system and lasts throughout its lifecycle until its retirement. But security is not only a technical operation; it must involve everyone in the organization. Microsoft's goal with Windows Server 2003 is to help you master security in the enterprise network. Their new motto is "Secure by Design, Secure by Default, and Secure in Deployment." That means they've raised the bar with WS03. In fact, Microsoft is so confident that WS03 is secure that it has submitted it (as well as Windows XP) to Common Criteria evaluation and certification. Windows 2000 has already achieved this certification level. The Common Criteria are an internationally recognized method for certifying the security claims of information technology (IT) products and systems. They define security standards and procedures for evaluating technologies. The Common Criteria are designed to help consumers make informed security decisions and help vendors secure their products. More information is available on the Common Criteria at http://www.commoncriteria.org/.

The Common Criteria is not the only security standard on the marketplace. There are others. ISO 17799 (http://www.iso-17799.com/) is a generic standard on best practices for information security. The Operationally Critical Threat, Asset, and Vulnerability Evaluation (OCTAVE at http://www.cert.org/octave/) is an IT security risk assessment method that is based on industry accepted best practices. The Federal Information Technology Security Assessment Framework (FITSAF at http://www.cio.gov/documents/federal_it_security_assessment_framework_112800.html) is a methodology that allows federal agencies to assess their IT security programs. While Microsoft does not necessarily embrace all of these standards, it is their goal to do away with the common security threats people using their technology have faced in the recent past. As such, they have created a new operating system that is secure by default. This is a new direction for Microsoft who, in the past, has been known for pushing features above all else.

With commitments of this level, there is no doubt that Microsoft has designed this operating system to be chock full of security features. But like every other operating system, these security features will only protect your organization if they are implemented properly.

Security Basics

Security is a pervasive issue because it involves almost everything within the enterprise network. In fact, security has been discussed at every stage of the Enterprise Network Creation Process so far. The object of security is to protect information. To do so, you must put in place a layered protection system that will provide the ability to perform the following activities:

- Identify people as they enter your network and block all unauthorized access
- Identify appropriate clearance levels for people who work within your network and provide them with appropriate access rights once identified
- Identify that the person modifying the data is the person who is authorized to modify the data (irrevocability or non-repudiation)
- Guarantee the confidentiality of information stored within your network

- Guarantee the availability of information stored within your network
- Ensure the integrity of the data stored within your network
- Monitor the activities within your network
- Audit security events within the network and securely store historical auditing data
- Put in place the appropriate administrative activities to ensure that the network is secure at all times
- Put in place the appropriate continuing education programs to ensure that your users are completely aware of security issues
- Test your security processes regularly; for example, fire drills are the best way to ensure that your staff will be prepared when a security event occurs

For each of these activities, there are various scopes of interaction:

- **Local**   People interact with systems at the local level, thus these systems must be protected whether or not they are attached to a network.
- **Intranet**   People interact with remote systems. These systems must also be protected at all times whether they are located on the LAN or the WAN.
- **Internet**   Systems that are deemed public must also be protected from attacks of all types. These are in a worse situation because they are exposed outside the boundaries of the internal network.
- **Extranet**   These systems are often deemed internal, but are exposed to partners, suppliers, or clients. The major difference between extranet and Internet systems is authentication—while there may be identification on an Internet system, authentication is *always* required to access an extranet environment.

Whatever its scope, security is an activity (like all IT activities) that relies on three key elements: *People, PCs,* and *Processes*.

- **People** are the executors of the security process. They are also its main users.
- **PCs** represent technology. They include a series of tools and components that support the security process.
- **Processes** are made up of workflow patterns, procedures, and standards for the application of security.

The integration of these three elements will help you design a Security Policy that is applicable to the entire enterprise.

▶ | **QUICK TIP**

More information is available on the interaction of People, PCs, and Processes in Preparing for .NET Enterprise Technologies, *by Ruest and Ruest (Addison-Wesley, 2001).*

Designing a Security Policy

The design of an Enterprise Security Policy (ESP) is only one step in the security lifecycle, but it is not always the first step. People often think of the security policy only after they have been victims of a security threat. But since your implementation of WS03 is based on the design of a parallel network, it is an ideal opportunity to review your ESP if it is already in place or design one if it is not.

Like any other design process, you must begin by assessing your business model. Much of the information required at this level has already been collected through other design exercises you have already performed. In Chapter 1, you analyzed business and technical environments to begin the design of the enterprise network. You reviewed this information again in Chapter 3 when you created your enterprise Active Directory Design. This information will need to be reviewed a third time, but this time with a special focus on security aspects. This includes the identification and revision of current security policies if they exist.

Next, you will need to identify which common security standards you wish to implement within your organization. These will involve both technical and non-technical policies and procedures. An example of a technical policy would be the security parameters you will set at the staging of each computer in your organization. A non-technical policy would deal with the habits users should develop to select complex passwords and protect them. Finally, you will need to identify the parameters for each policy you define.

The Castle Defense System

The best way to define an ESP is to use a model. The model proposed here is the Castle Defense System (CDS). In medieval times, people needed to protect themselves and their belongings through the design of a defense system that was primarily based on cumulative barriers to entry. If you've ever visited a medieval castle or seen a movie with a medieval theme, you'll remember that the first line of defense is often the moat. The moat is a barrier that is designed to stop people from reaching the castle wall. Moats often include dangerous creatures that will add a second level of protection within the same barrier. Next, you have the castle walls. These are designed to repel enemies. At the top of the walls, you will find crenellated edges, allowing archers to fire on the enemy while still being able to hide when fired upon. There are doors of various sizes within the walls, a gate, and a drawbridge for the moat. All entry points have guards posted. Once again, multiple levels of protection are applied within the same layer.

The third defense layer is the courtyard within the castle walls. This is designed as a "killing field" so that if enemies do manage to breach the castle walls, they will find themselves within an internal zone that offers no cover from attackers located either on the external castle walls or within the castle itself. The fourth layer of defense is the castle itself. This is the main building within which are found the crown jewels. It is designed to be defensible on its own; stairways are narrow and rooms are arranged to confuse the enemy. The fifth and last layer of protection is the vault held within the heart of the castle. It is difficult to reach and highly guarded. This type of castle is illustrated in Figure 8-1.

This is, of course, a rudimentary description of the defenses included in a castle. Medieval engineers worked very hard to include multiple defense systems within each layer of protection. But it serves its purpose. An IT defense system should be designed in the same way as a Castle Defense System. Just

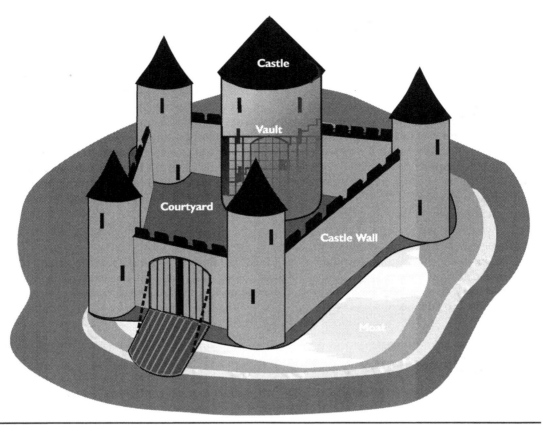

Figure 8-1   A typical medieval castle

like the CDS, the IT defense system requires layers of protection. In fact, five layers of protection seem appropriate. Starting from the inside, you'll find:

- **Layer 1: Critical Information**   This is the information *vault*. The heart of the system is the information you seek to protect.

- **Layer 2: Physical Protection**   Security measures should always begin with a level of physical protection for information systems. This compares to the *castle* itself.

- **Layer 3: Operating System Hardening**   Once the physical defenses have been put in place, you need to "harden" each computer's operating system in order to limit the potential attack surface as much as possible. This is the *courtyard*.

- **Layer 4: Information Access**   When you give access to your data, you'll need to ensure that everyone is authenticated, authorized, and audited. These are the *castle walls* and the doors you open within them.

- **Layer 5: External Access**   The final layer of protection deals with the outside world. It includes the perimeter network and all of its defenses. It is your castle *moat.*

The five-layer Castle Defense System is illustrated in Figure 8-2. In order to become a complete Enterprise Security Policy, it must be supplemented by two elements: People and Processes. These two elements surround the CDS and complete the ESP picture it represents.

Defining the various layers of defense is not the only requirement for an ESP, but it is a starting point. The activities required to define the ESP are outlined in Figure 8-3. This blueprint outlines a step-by-step approach to an ESP definition. It will need to be supported by additional activities which focus on the way the ESP is managed and administered once in place.

This chapter focuses on the solution design portion of the blueprint, specifically the application of the Castle Defense System itself.

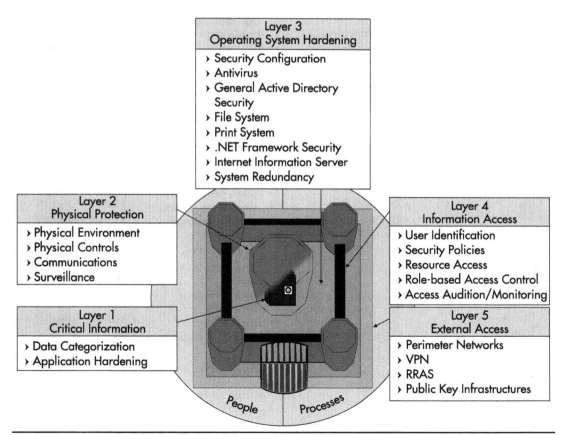

Figure 8-2   The Castle Defense System

Analysis

① Business Requirements

1- Business Model
- ▶ Organization Model
- ▶ Organization Goals
- ▶ Products & Services
- ▶ Geographic Scope
- ▶ Organization Processes

2- Organization Structure
- ▶ Management Model
- ▶ Organization Structure
- ▶ Vendors/Partner/ Customer Relationships
- ▶ Acquisition Plans (Business)

3- Organization Strategies
- ▶ Business Priorities
- ▶ Project Growth and Strategy
- ▶ Legal Implications
- ▶ Tolerance for Risk
- ▶ TCO Objectives

4- IT Management
- ▶ Centralized/ Decentralized Management
- ▶ Funding Model
- ▶ Outsourcing/ In-house?
- ▶ Decision-making Process
- ▶ Change Management Process

② Technical Requirements

1- Existing/Planned IT Environment
- ▶ Organization Size
- ▶ Number of Users
- ▶ Resources Location
- ▶ Network Geographic Distribution and Links
- ▶ Available Bandwidth
- ▶ H/S Performance Requirements
- ▶ Data Patterns
- ▶ Network Roles and Responsibilities

2- Security Issues
- ▶ Existing Systems and Applications
- ▶ Technology Support Structure
- ▶ IP Infrastructure
- ▶ Authentication Services
- ▶ Mobility Issues
- ▶ Remote Workers
- ▶ External Connections

Solution Design

③ Castle Defense System

1- Critical Information
- ▶ Data Categorization
- ▶ Application Hardening

2- Physical Protection
- ▶ Physical Environment
- ▶ Physical Control
- ▶ Communications
- ▶ Surveillance

3- Operation System Hardening
- ▶ Security Configuration
- ▶ Antivirus
- ▶ General Active Directory Security
- ▶ File System
- ▶ Print System
- ▶ .NET Framework Security
- ▶ Internet Information Server
- ▶ System Redundancy

4- Information Access
- ▶ User Identification
- ▶ Security Policies
- ▶ Resource Access
- ▶ Role-based Access Control
- ▶ Access Auditing/ Monitoring

5- External Access
- ▶ Perimeter Networks
- ▶ VPN
- ▶ RADIUS/IAS
- ▶ Public Key Infrastructure

④ Defense Planning

1- Threat Assessment
- ▶ Attack Type Identification
- ▶ Proactive Response Strategies
- ▶ Reactive Response Strategies

2- Risk Assessment
- ▶ Risk Identification
- ▶ Risk Calculation
- ▶ Risk Prioritization

3- User Awareness
- ▶ Mandatory Training
- ▶ Communication Plans
- ▶ Technical Training Program

4- Monitoring Procedures
- ▶ Events to Monitor
- ▶ Monitoring Infrastructure

5- Attack Reaction Plans
- ▶ Incident Response Team
- ▶ Response Procedures
- ▶ Escalation Procedures

6- Recovery Program
- ▶ Core System Protection
- ▶ Backup Systems
- ▶ Restoration Procedures

7- Industry Watch
- ▶ Security Event Watch
- ▶ Virus Watch
- ▶ New Product Watch
- ▶ Product Upgrade Watch

Figure 8-3   The Enterprise Security Policy Design Blueprint

The Security Plan

The ESP is only the first step to a complete security plan. Once the policy has been issued, you need to design and implement your defenses, monitor them on an active basis, and regularly test and update them. These four security management activities—policy design, defense planning, monitoring, and testing—make up the Security Plan. These interact with the Castle Defense System to complete the practice of security management. Their relationship is illustrated in Figure 8-4.

The key to the security plan is in knowing what to cover and knowing why it needs to be covered. As it is illustrated in Figure 8-3, the first part—knowing what to cover—is outlined in the Castle Defense System. It identifies all of the areas that require coverage by the security policy and helps you prepare for any eventuality. Next is defense planning. Here, the first step lies in knowing the type of attacks you may face. Some examples include:

- **Accidental security breach** These attacks are usually caused accidentally by users or system operators. They stem from a lack of awareness of security issues. For example, users who do not protect their passwords because they are not aware of the consequences can be the cause of accidental attacks. Another example is when operators place users in the wrong Security Groups and assign them the wrong privileges.

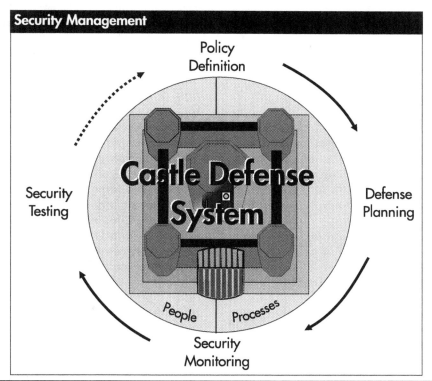

Figure 8-4   Security management activities

- **Internal attack**   These are one of the major sources of attacks. They are caused from within the internal network. Their source can be the organization's personnel or other personnel who are allowed access to the internal network. These attacks are sometimes the result of a lack of vigilance. Internal personnel often assume that since the internal network is protected from the outside, everyone who has access to it can be trusted.

- **Social engineering**   Once again, these attacks stem from a lack of awareness. They are caused by external sources that impersonate internal personnel and cause users to divulge compromising information—for example, someone calling a user while impersonating the help desk and asking the user for his or her password.

▶ *CAUTION*

It is common practice even today for help desk personnel to ask users for their password. This behavior is completely *unacceptable. There is no reason for help desk personnel to ever have access to a user's password.*

- **Organizational attack**   These attacks stem from competitive organizations who want to penetrate your systems to discover your trade secrets.

- **Automated attacks**   These are now one of the most common attack types. Basically an external computer scans Internet addresses until it finds a response. Once it has found a working address, it then scans this address to identify potential vulnerabilities. These attacks have become extremely sophisticated today and protecting yourself from them has now become a full-time occupation. Examples of these attacks are the Nimda and Code Red viruses.

- **Denial-of-Service (DoS) attacks**   These attacks are designed to stop the operation of a service on your network. Attacks that target generic Microsoft technologies instead of your organization specifically are excellent examples of DoS.

- **Viral attacks**   These attacks are in the form of viruses, worms, or Trojan horses and are designed to infiltrate your systems to perform some form of damage to either services or data.

▶ *QUICK TIP*

More information on attack types and defense strategies can be found at the Microsoft Security Center at http://www.microsoft.com/security/.

Each attack type requires a different defense strategy. Most are already in place with the CDS, but the processes that surround attacks and reactions to attacks must also be defined. This is the core of defense planning.

The Microsoft Security Operations Guide

Microsoft has produced an excellent overview for securing Windows 2000 technologies in the Security Operations Guide for Windows 2000 Server (search for Security Operations Guide at http://www.microsoft.com/security/). It uses an approach that is similar to the Castle Defense System. This approach is called Defense in Depth. The best part of this guide is that it includes a series of tools—specifically Group Policy Templates—that can be used to secure servers by role. To do so, it uses an Organizational Unit Structure similar to the one you designed in Chapter 7. Each server type is located within a specific OU, and Group Policy objects that include specific settings per server role are applied to the appropriate OU. This approach is also at the basis of the Castle Defense System since it is the core approach for the Active Directory Design illustrated throughout this book. This AD design is conceived with the purpose of managing objects according to object type. Thus, you use the same management approach whether you are managing object properties or you are applying security settings.

One of the best portions of the Security Operations Guide is its coverage of incident response (Chapter 7 in the guide). It offers extensive information about the different approaches you should take when responding to specific incidents. There is also a very interesting Job Aid (number 2) that outlines the most common security blunders; definitely recommended reading for anyone designing a security policy.

▶ | **QUICK TIP**

For a more complete overview of securing Windows Server platforms, see the Microsoft Solution for Securing Windows 2000 Server at http://www.microsoft.com/technet/treeview/ default.asp?url=/technet/security/prodtech/ Windows/SecWin2k/01intro.asp.

It is important for systems administrators to review the information available at both the Microsoft security Web site and other Web sites on an ongoing basis to remain secure once the Castle Defense System is in place. For example, an excellent source of information on security is the SANS Institute at http://www.sans.org/.

Windows Server 2003 Security

Windows Server 2003 is one of the key elements of Microsoft's Trusted Computing Initiative. As such, Microsoft has reviewed and improved the basic security features included in Windows 2000. The Windows 2000 foundation was already a major improvement over Windows NT; technologies such as Kerberos, Encrypted File System (EFS), Public Key Infrastructure (PKI), smart card and biometric support, and especially Active Directory, to name a few, were significant improvements over the basic security capabilities of NT.

With WS03, Microsoft has enhanced and improved these features as well as provided new security capabilities. The .NET Framework is a significant security improvement in and of itself, though it won't be at the core of organization's security strategies until existing code is migrated to this new development paradigm. Nevertheless, it does greatly enhance the capability to run secure code because it provides the execution environment for software, thus limiting the possibility of errors in code you run. It also identifies if code is digitally signed by someone you trust as well as its origin, ensuring a higher degree of trust within your execution environment.

Once again, this will not be a major opportunity until most code is migrated to the new platform. Meanwhile, WS03 offers several other new and improved features that help secure more traditional applications. These include:

- **Software Restriction Policies**   These policies can control which code is allowed to run within the enterprise network. This includes any type of code—corporate applications, commercial software, scripts, batch files—and can even be defined at the Dynamic Link Library (DLL) level. This is a great tool to prevent malicious scripts from running in your network.

- **Wireless LAN support**   WS03 includes special policy objects and other features designed to support secure wireless networking.

- **Remote access authentication**   WS03 includes a policy-based structure to manage remote access and virtual private network connections through the Active Directory. This feature is focused on an improved Internet Authentication Server (IAS) and Remote Authentication Dial-in User Server (RADIUS). IAS even includes a quarantine mode that restricts access to specific servers if user's machines are not configured to corporate standards. It serves to help users bring their machines up to standards before they gain full access to the network.

- **Multi-forest operations**   Chapter 3 outlined how WS03 Active Directory forests can use forest trusts to extend the authentication capabilities of Active Directory. In addition, the use of Active Directory in Application Mode allows you to create a central NOS directory and the required number of application directories to support your corporate application needs.

- **Public Key Infrastructure**   WS03 includes an improved PKI that supports user and computer auto-enrollment and automatic X.509 certificate renewal. It also supports the use of delta certificate revocation lists (CRL) simplifying the CRL management process.

- **Web server security**   Internet Information Server (IIS) version 6 is secure by default. It is not installed by default and once installed will only serve static content. The first management task for IIS 6 is to define its security parameters through the IIS Manager console.

- **Temporary and offline file protection**   WS03 supports the encryption of temporary and offline files.

- **Credential management**   The WS03 Credential Manager can securely store passwords and digital certificates (X.509). This supports seamless access to multiple security zones.

- **Kernel-mode encryption**   WS03 supports Federal Information Processing Standard (FIPS) approved cryptographic algorithms. This means that both governmental and non-governmental organizations can take advantage of this cryptography module to secure client/server communications.

- **Digest Authentication Protocol (DAP)**   WS03 includes a new digest security package that is supported by both IIS and Active Directory.

- **Digitally signed Windows Installer packages**   WS03 supports the inclusion of digital signatures within Windows Installer packages so that administrators can ensure that only trusted packages are installed within the network, especially on servers.

- **Passport usage**   WS03 supports the mapping of Microsoft Passports to Active Directory accounts enabling users and business partners to have a single sign-on experience when accessing external company services.

- **Role-based access control**   WS03 includes the Authorization Manager, which supports the use of role-based access controls (RBAC) for applications. RBAC stores can be in either XML format or within Active Directory.

- **Authentication delegation**   WS03 supports constrained delegation. This means that you can specify which servers can be trusted for user impersonation within the network. You can also identify for which services the server is trusted for delegation.

- **Permissions management**   It is now possible to view effective permissions with WS03 through the property dialog box for file and folder objects.

- **Limited Everyone membership**   The Everyone group continues to include Authenticated Users and Guests, but members of the Anonymous group are no longer part of the Everyone group.

- **Changed folder sharing process**   Folder shares are automatically set to read-only by default in WS03. This prevents errors and protects information.

- **Auditing**   Auditing in WS03 is not operations-based. This means that it is more descriptive and offers the choice of which operations to audit for which users or groups. WS03 also includes the Microsoft Audit Collection System (MACS) that helps you centralize and analyze server security logs.

- **Reset defaults**   It is now much simpler to use the Security Configuration and Analysis tool to reapply computer security settings from base templates, even customized base templates.

- **Optional subsystems**   Optional subsystems such as POSIX (support for UNIX applications) are no longer installed by default.

- **Security help**   Windows Server now includes comprehensive help on security issues and securing your computers. Access to security help is located directly on the home page of the WS03 Help and Support Center. Clicking on this Security item leads to a page that aggregates security information on a complete series of issues.

This is not a comprehensive list of all the new security features of Windows Server 2003, but it is a list of the most important features for enterprise networks. These features along with the basic features that stem from Windows 2000 will allow you to design your enterprise network Castle Defense System.

Applying the Castle Defense System

Since you are designing a new, parallel network based on WS03, you have the opportunity to review your entire security infrastructure. You should use the CDS to do this. This means reviewing each of its five layers and determining if changes or modifications are required to your existing security approach, if it is already in place.

QUICK TIP

A Castle Defense System job aid is available on the companion Web site at http://www.Reso-Net .com/WindowsServer/. It includes a point evaluation system that helps you rate your current security system and identify where it needs to improve.

Level 1: Critical Information

The place to start is with what you need to protect. Organizations have no choice. For collaboration and cooperation to work within a network, they must share data. They must also often allow users to store data locally on their hard drives. This is not so much an issue when the user has a workstation, because it is designed to remain within the internal network (although it is no reason to be lax in your policy design), but it becomes critical when the hard drive leaves the premises. The level of risk must be identified so that the solutions you design to protect data are appropriate.

To do so, you need to categorize data. This categorization must begin with an inventory of all the data within your network. Once this has been done, you can group it into four categories:

- **Public** Information that can be shared publicly inside and outside the network.

- **Internal** Information that is related to organizational operations. It is deemed as private, but not confidential. As such, it should be protected to some degree. This should include technical information about your network such as network diagrams, IP addressing schemes, internal user names, and so on.

- **Confidential** Information that should not be divulged to other than authorized personnel (for example, personnel data such as salaries).

- **Secret** Information that is critical to the operation of the organization. If this information is divulged to the wrong parties, the organization itself can be at risk.

For each data category, you will also need to identify which elements are at risk. For example, if data that is on your Web site—data that is deemed public—is modified without your knowledge, the reputation of your organization can be at risk. If payroll data is leaked within your organization, you will lose the trust of your employees and probably have a lot of employee discontent. The risk is different in each case and so is the required investment.

Information is made up of two elements: data and documents. Data is usually stored within structured tables and is usually within some type of database or list. Documents contain unstructured data and are within discrete objects such as text files, presentations, images, or other document types. Both types of information require protection. Documents are protected through the capabilities of file storage systems.

Data is protected at two levels. First, it is protected through the same mechanisms as documents because databases store information in files just like documents. Second, it is protected through the features of the database system used to store it. For example, while Microsoft SQL Server stores databases in .mdb files, it also offers several security features for the data contained within these files. Thus, for the protection of information, organizations must also look to the *hardening of applications*, especially when it comes to data. In this case, "hardening" means ensuring that security holes have been removed as much as possible within the applications the organization has developed. It also means that the security features of the database engine have been implemented to protect the data it contains. Thus, rows and columns that contain confidential and secure information will be secured at the database level, maybe even encrypted, and their access will be audited.

> **QUICK TIP**
>
> *Microsoft has also released a Security Operations Guide for SQL Server. Like all SOGs, it is available both online (http://www.microsoft.com/ technet/prodtechnol/sql/maintain/operate/ opsguide/default.asp) and from Microsoft Press.*

Information categorization and application hardening are both aspects of an information architecture—a structured approach to information management and organization within the enterprise. If you already have an information architecture in place, then you can rely on it to prepare this first level of defense.

Level 2: Physical Protection

The second level of security lies with physical protection of your computing systems. Physical protection deals with a variety of issues. A domain controller that is located under a stairway in some regional office cannot be considered secure by any means. The elements that you need to cover at the physical protection level include:

- **Geographical location**   Is the physical location of your buildings within environmentally endangered locations? Is there the possibility of floods, avalanches, or cave-ins that may affect the buildings you do business in? Are they near roads where accidents may affect the building?

- **Social environment**   Is your personnel aware that physical access to computing equipment should be protected at all times? Are they aware that they should never divulge passwords under any circumstance?

- **Building security**   Are your buildings secure? Are entries guarded and are visitors identified at all locations? Are guests escorted at all times? Are rogue computing devices allowed within your buildings? Is the electrical input to the building protected? Does it have a backup, especially for computer rooms? Is the building's air control protected and does it include a backup system? Is there a good fire protection plan in all buildings? Is the wiring inside and outside the building secure?

- **Building construction**   Is the building construction safe? Are the walls in your computer rooms fireproof? Is the computer room door a firebreak? Are floors covered in antistatic material? If there is a generator on the premises, is it in a safe and protected location? Does the computer room protect communication equipment as well as computer equipment? Does the building include security cameras to assist surveillance?

- **Server security**   Are servers within locked rooms in all locations? Is the access to server rooms monitored and protected? Are the servers themselves physically secured within locked cabinets? Is physical server access controlled? This should apply specifically to domain controllers. Windows Server 2003 supports the use of smart cards for administrator accounts. You should assign smart cards to all administrators. With the new low-cost smart card options, there are few reasons not to implement this policy. Aladdin Knowledge Systems (http://www.ealaddin.com/), for example, offers the eToken, a USB smart card that does not require the extraneous reader to function.

- **BIOS security** All computing devices should have some level of BIOS security. For servers, this should also include power-on passwords. For all systems, BIOS settings should be password protected, and, like all passwords, these passwords should be highly protected and modified on a regular basis. New DMI management tools allow the centralization of BIOS password management.

> **QUICK TIP**
>
> *Though all computer brands (HP, Dell, IBM, and so on) include DMI software, few organizations take the time to put it in place and use it to its full extent. This is unfortunate because it is an important part of a security strategy.*

- **Staging security** Are all physical security policies extended to staging rooms where systems are installed? It doesn't do to have highly secure computer rooms when the staging facilities are wide open.

- **PC security** Are workstations and mobile devices secure? Are hardware identification systems such as biometrics and smart cards used for mobile devices? Is data on the mobile devices secure when the device is in transit? Are external connections from the mobile devices to the internal network secure? Is your hardware tagged with non-removable identifiers?

- **Network security** Is the network and its services secure? Is it possible for someone to introduce rogue DHCP servers, for example? With Windows Server 2003, as with Windows 2000, DHCP servers must be authorized to allocate addresses, but only if they are Windows-based DHCP servers. Is there a wireless network in place? Is it secure? Can rogue wireless users penetrate the network? Are all wireless communications encrypted?

- **Physical redundancy** Are your critical systems redundant? This should include all systems—data systems, fire protection, Internet and WAN connections, air conditioning, electrical, and so on. More on this in Chapter 9.

All of the physical aspects of your installations must be maintained and documented. In addition, appropriate aspects of the physical protection plan must be communicated to employees at all levels. Finally, physical protection must be supplemented by a surveillance program. Once again, this is a part that can be played by personnel at all levels. Each employee must be aware that they can and should participate in the surveillance of any suspicious activity or the notification of any untoward event that may compromise your information systems.

Level 3: Operating System Hardening

The object of operating system hardening is to reduce the attack surface of your systems. To do so, you need to remove anything that is not required on a system. Windows Server 2003 does a good job of this right from the start because it installs about 20 services less than Windows 2000. Remember, the list of installed services can be found in the Server Data Sheet (on the companion Web site). In addition, IIS is not installed by default which ensures that systems that do not require it do not have it.

But limiting the number of services is not the only activity you need to perform during system hardening. You will also need to cover the following:

- System security configuration
- Antivirus strategy
- Active Directory security
- File system security
- Print system security
- .NET Framework security
- IIS security
- System redundancy

Each of these is described in the following sections.

System Security Configuration

System Security Configuration involves the application of security parameters during the machine staging process. As mentioned in Chapter 2, when you install a machine, especially a server, you need to perform some modifications to the default installation to ensure that your machine is protected. These activities are performed on two levels:

- The first level focuses on performing some post-installation configuration modifications for security purposes.
- The second level involves the application of security templates to the server by server role. This second portion of the system configuration process uses the Security Configuration Manager (SCM) to automatically apply security settings to your system.

Many of the items that are in your Post-Installation Checklist can be automated through the application of security templates.

Post-Installation Security Checklist

Chapter 2 outlines the post-installation activities you should perform on a newly staged server. Chapter 4 outlines the minimum security configuration for a domain controller. This should also include the following:

- Rename the administrator account. Although this has been mentioned in Chapter 2, it is essential to repeat it here. This is also an activity that can be performed through a security template because it is a Group Policy object setting. Remember to use a complex account name and assign a complex password.

> ▶ **QUICK TIP**
>
> *A complex password is your best defense system. In fact, a 15-character password (WS03 supports up to 127 characters) that includes letters in both upper- and lowercase, numbers, and special characters is well nigh impossible to crack. Well-known password cracking tools such as L0phtcrack and John the Ripper only work up to 14 characters. If there is one feature that you implement to secure your servers, it should be complex passwords because they provide a better defense than renamed accounts.*

- Copy the administrator account to create a backup account. Use a complex account name and a complex password.

- Create a dummy administrator account and assign only guest access rights to it. Use a complex password for this account. Creating a dummy administrator account serves as a trap for users who want to try to access the real administration account.

- Verify that the guest account is disabled and that a complex password has been assigned to this account.

- Verify the list of running services and make sure they are well documented. Shut down any service you deem unnecessary for this server role. Test the role before deploying it.

- Verify the list of open ports and shut down the ports you deem unnecessary for this server role. You can identify the list of open ports by using the netstat command. Use the following command:

```
netstat -a -n -o
```

The -a switch asks for all ports; the -n switch asks for numeric output for the ports; and the -o switch asks for the process associated with the port.

That's about it for basic security. Everything else can be performed through the Security Configuration Manager.

▶ **CAUTION**

Though a complex password is your best defense system, it can also be your worst nightmare because complex passwords are hard to remember. One of the things you can do is use real words or phrases, but replace letters with numbers and special characters and mix up the cases, for example, Ad/\/\ln1$traT!on (Administration). You should also use different passwords for different locations.

Using Security Templates

The security settings of Group Policy objects are stored in two locations in Windows Server 2003. The first is in the Group Policy object itself under Windows Settings | Security Settings in both User and Computer Configurations. The second is in a Security Template file. In many cases, it is best to store a setting in a security template file because it automatically forms a backup file for the setting. Security settings from a template can be applied in two ways.

The first is directly through a GPO by importing the template into the GPO. This is done by selecting Import Policy from the context menu displayed when you right-click on Computer Configuration | Security Settings in the Group Policy Object Editor. This displays a dialog box that lists available templates.

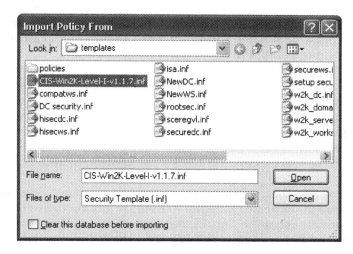

Imported templates can either be merged with or replace all security settings in the GPO. The difference is applied through the "Clear this database before importing" option in the Import Policy From dialog box. Selecting this option will automatically clear all security settings in the GPO and apply only those found in the template.

The second manner is through the secedit command. This command applies the settings in a template to the Local Policy found on all Windows computers. Using this command does not affect Group Policy; it only affects Local Policy objects.

Through security templates, you can configure the following security areas:

- **Account Policies**   Password, lockout, and Kerberos policies.

- **Local Policies**   Audit, user rights assignments, and security options.

- **Event Log**   Settings for system, application, security, directory, file replication, and DNS service logs.

- **Restricted Groups**   Control group membership.

- **System Services**   Startup modes and access control for the services on each system.

- **Registry**   Access control for registry keys.

- **File System**   Access control for folders and files (only NTFS, of course).

The WS03 Help System offers comprehensive information about each of these security settings.

The latter three (system services, registry, and file system settings) are ideally suited to locally applied security templates because they control the access to specific object types. The application of access control rights to files, folders, the registry, and the configuration of system services can be quite time consuming. Therefore, it is best to keep these settings in local security templates rather than setting them directly at the GPO level because local security templates are applied manually (or automatically through schedules you control) while GPOs are constantly being reapplied on the systems in an Active Directory domain. (Remember: GPOs are refreshed every five minutes on DCs and every 90 minutes on servers and workstations). Make sure that your GPO strategy does not affect these three areas if you choose to set them through local security templates because of the application order for GPOs. Local security templates are set as local policies and local policies are always overridden by Group Policy objects.

Windows Server 2003 also includes some default templates that are provided with the system. There are four types of templates. *Basic* templates are designed for non-secure workstations, servers, and domain controllers. Few people, if any, use these templates. *Compatibility* templates are used to reset security settings to a Windows NT level to allow legacy applications to run. Again, these are not recommended. *Secure* templates are designed for computers, servers, and domain controllers in a secure environment such as an internal network. *Highly secure* templates are designed for computers, servers, and domain controllers in a non-secure environment such as an external or perimeter network.

If you use the default templates, you should only use the secure or highly secure templates. In addition, Microsoft provides role-based templates with the Security Operations Guide for Member Servers in general, domain controllers, Application Servers, File and Print Servers, Network Infrastructure Servers, and Web Servers running IIS. These are all based on a baseline template. Two baselines exist: one for Member Servers and one for domain controllers. In addition to the Member Server baseline, there are three incremental templates for each Member Server role identified above, though the template for the Application Server role is empty because it needs to be customized for each type of Application Server.

The SOG is not the only source of baseline security templates. The U.S. National Security Agency (NSA) offers templates for download as well as offering complete security documentation on a number of Windows 2000 services and features (Windows Server 2003 will surely follow). These templates are available at http://nsa2.www.conxion.com. The NSA documentation and templates are an excellent source for security recommendations.

The Center for Internet Security (CIS) is also an excellent source for security templates. Its templates are role-based and include the coverage of the basic operating system for both workstations and servers as well as coverage of Internet Information Server. Its templates can be found at http://www.cisecurity.org/.

Finally, templates can be acquired from commercial vendors such as NetIQ, Bindview, Quest, and many others.

▶ *CAUTION*

Careless application of security templates, especially templates you are not familiar with, may break running systems. Because security templates will modify default security settings on computer systems, it is essential that you apply them in a test environment before putting them on production systems. In fact, you should test every server and computer function before releasing a security template to production.

Creating Baseline Templates for Local Application

When you create templates for local application—during computer installation, for example—you will ideally start from a baseline template that you acquired from the NSA, CIS, or the Security Operations Guide. As in the SOG, you will need to create a minimum of two baseline templates: one for domain controllers and one for Member Servers. These baseline templates should include only three types of settings: file system, registry, and system service settings. (Other security settings will be covered with templates for import into Group Policy objects.)

You may require the use of two domain controller templates, especially if you use multipurpose servers in your network. Regional servers tend to have multiple functions such as File and Print, domain controller, Network Infrastructure, and Application Server all rolled into one. These servers may require a special baseline template.

You will need to identify which settings best fit your organization, but here are some recommendations for each of the three categories:

- The registry should be as secure as possible. First, make sure that access to the registry editor is controlled in your network. This is done by restricting access to both REGEDT32.EXE and REGEDIT.EXE through a Group Policy object. (Go to User Configuration | Administrative Templates | System: Prevent access to registry editing tools.)

- Secure specific keys in the registry itself. The easiest way to secure registry keys and hives is to propagate inheritable permissions from the parent key to subkeys. In some cases, this may not be possible.

- Secure files and folders. Ideally, you will secure folders rather than files. Propagation is preferable, but not always applicable here.

- Be careful when securing files and folders not to modify security settings on objects that are automatically secured by WS03. For example, it is not a good idea to replace security settings on the Documents and Settings folder since WS03 must manage these settings every time a new User Profile is created.

- Secure the local security account database (SAM) with the syskey command. Search for article number Q143475 at http://support.microsoft.com/ for more information.

- You may decide that you do not have to replace the Everyone group with Authenticated Users in WS03 since restrictions are now applied to Everyone (no Anonymous users) because it is applied everywhere by default.

- Set system services to the appropriate start mode: automatic for services that must start when the computer boots; manual when a user or process is allowed to start a service, but it does not have to start automatically; and disabled when the service is not required. You might consider removing services that are in a disabled state. Ensure that this is fully documented.

- Finally, you can apply security to each service limiting the access rights for starting, stopping, and otherwise controlling services. If you set security on services, be sure that you always include both the Administrators group and the System account or you may encounter problems starting services. By default, three objects have this access: Administrators, the System account, and the Interactive group.

> ▶ **QUICK TIP**
>
> *WS03 now includes a new "system" account: the NetworkService account. This account has fewer privileges than the LocalSystem account and should be used to start services on high-risk servers. Thus if someone manages to take control of a service and wants to use it to take control of a machine, they will not have the privileges to do so.*

Configuring Security Templates

Once you have identified the registry keys, files, folders, and services you want to modify, you can move on to the creation or modification of your security templates. The first thing you need to do is create a Security Template console.

1. Move to the Start Menu, select Run and type **MMC**, and then press ENTER.

2. In the MMC console, select File | Add/Remove Snap-in.

3. In the Add/Remove Snap-in dialog box, click Add. In the Snap-in dialog box, select Security Templates, click Add and then click Close. Click OK to return to the console. Move to the File menu to select Save, name the console Security Console, and click Save.

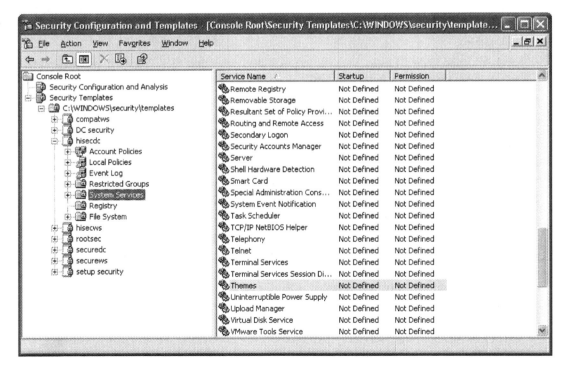

4. The Security Template console automatically lists all of the templates available on your system. The WS03 Help and Support Center lists more information on each of these. If the system is a domain controller, this list should at least include:

   - **Setup security.inf**   The template that was created at system installation.

   - **DC security.inf**   The template that was created during the promotion of the domain controller.

   - **Compatws.inf**   The legacy application compatibility template.

   - **Securews.inf and Securedc.inf**   Templates for workstations and servers as well as domain controllers in a secure environment (for example, they use only newer authentication protocols to increase security).

   - **Hisecws.inf and Hisecdc.inf**   Templates for workstations and servers as well as domain controllers in a highly secure environment (for example, it requires server-side Server Message Block [SMB] signing, refuses both LAN Manager and NTLM authentication protocols and enables restricted group memberships).

   - **Rootsec.inf**   The default permissions applied to the root of the system drive.

   - **Notssid.inf**   A template that can be used to remove Terminal Server security identifiers from file and registry permissions. The Terminal Server practices outlined in Chapter 7 eliminate the need for this template because Terminal Services are run in Full Security mode.

5. You can add your own templates to the list. Templates are located in the %systemroot%/ security/templates directory. To create a new template from an existing template, right-click on it to select Save As and rename it. Once it has been renamed, you can add your own settings. You can also create a new template by right-clicking on the directory name in the left pane and selecting New Template, but doing so means you're starting the template from scratch and need to redefine all settings.

▶ *CAUTION*

The content of this directory is critical. Ensure that it is protected at all times and that templates are not modified without your knowledge.

6. Move to your new template and modify its settings. Begin by right-clicking on the template name and selecting Set Description to modify the description. Type in the appropriate information and click OK. Expand the template to view its components.

7. To set registry security, right-click on Registry and select Add Key. In the Add Key dialog box, locate the key you want to secure and click OK. Decide if you want to propagate permissions to subkeys, reset permissions on subkeys, or block permission replacement on this key. Use the Edit Security button to set the appropriate security rights and click OK. Repeat for each key or subkey you want to secure.

8. To set file or folder security, right-click on File System and select Add File. In the Add File dialog box, locate the file or folder you want to secure and click OK. Set the appropriate security rights and click OK. Decide if you want to propagate permissions to the file or folder, reset permissions on the file or folder, or block permission replacement on the file or folder. Repeat for each file or folder you want to secure.

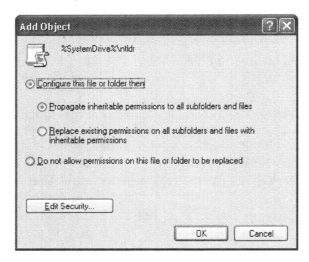

9. To set security on system services, select System Services. Double-click on the appropriate service in the right pane, select Define this policy setting in the template, select the start mode, and, if required, click Edit Security to modify the security settings. Click OK when done. Repeat for each service you want to modify.

10. Make sure you right-click on the template name and select Save before you exit the console.

Using Local Security Templates

Local security templates can be applied in two manners: through a graphical tool called the Security Configuration and Analysis or through a command-line tool called secedit. Both have their uses. Both can be used to analyze and configure a system based on a security template.

The Security Configuration and Analysis is an MMC snap-in that provides a graphical view to system configuration and analysis. This can be quite useful since it provides the same interface that you use to either create templates or modify Group Policy objects. The console you use for the use of this tool must be created. In fact, it is a good idea to include both the Security Templates and the Security Configuration and Analysis snap-ins into the same console. You can also add the Group Policy Editor snap-in. This way, you have a single tool to create, modify, apply, analyze, and import Security Policy Settings.

To analyze a computer and compare it to a given security policy, use the following procedure:

1. Right-click on Security Configuration and Analysis inside your Security Console and select Open Database.

2. In the Open Database dialog box, either locate the appropriate database or type in a new database name, and then click OK. The default path setting is My Documents\Security\Databases.

3. You will need to select the security template you want to use for analysis. This must be a template that has been prepared in advance. Select the appropriate template and click OK.

4. To analyze your system, right-click on Security Configuration and Analysis and select Analyze Computer Now.

5. Since every analysis or configuration operation requires a log file, a dialog box appears to ask you the location of the log file. The default path setting is My Documents\Security\Logs and the default name is the same as the database. Either type in the name of a new log file, use the browse button to locate an existing file, or click OK to accept the default name.

6. The analysis will begin.

7. Once the analysis is complete, you can see the difference in settings between the template and the computer. Simply move to a setting you wish to view and select it. Differences (if any) will be displayed in the right pane.

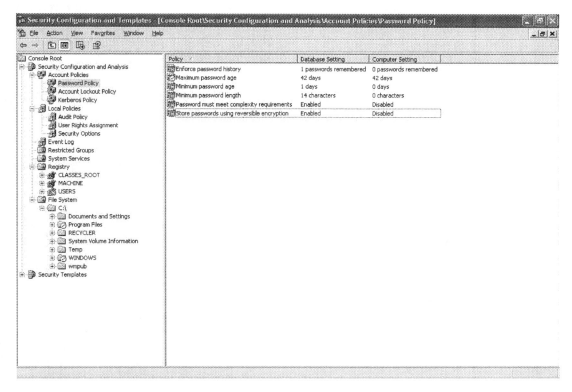

8. You can also view the log file. To do so, right-click on Security Configuration and Analysis and select View Log. The log file will be displayed in the right pane. To return to the database, simply deselect View Log in the context menu.

9. You can modify database settings to conform to the values you want to apply by moving to the appropriate value and double-clicking on it. Select Define this policy in the database, modify the setting, and click OK.

10. Right-click on Security Configuration and Analysis and select Save to save the modifications you make to the database.

11. To configure a computer with the settings in the database, select Configure Computer Now from the same context menu. Once again, you will need to specify the location and name of the log file.

12. Close the Security Console when done.

▶ **QUICK TIP**

You should never create a template from scratch since there are numerous templates on the market and you can use Security Configuration and Analysis to capture the settings from an existing machine. To do so, you need to modify all the settings you need on the model machine, create a new database, import a template, analyze the computer, verify that all settings are appropriate, and export the resulting database to a new template file. Export Template is once again found on the context menu of the Security Configuration and Analysis snap-in.

You can also automate the application of templates to different machines through the use of the secedit command. Use the following command to do so:

```
secedit /configure /db filename.sdb /log filename.log
```

In addition, the /verbose switch can be used to create a log file that is highly detailed. If no log file is specified, secedit will automatically log all information to the scesrv.log file in the %windir%\security\ logs directory.

Since the local security template affects only the file system, the registry, and system services, you should ensure that the command you use applies to only those portions of the template. To do so, use the following command:

```
secedit /configure /db filename.sdb /log filename.log /areas REGKEYS FILESTORE
SERVICES /quiet
```

▶ **QUICK TIP**

This secedit command can be inserted in an automated system installation to ensure that computers are secured as soon as they are installed (through the Unattend.txt response file—see Chapter 2).

This command will ensure that only the appropriate areas are applied, guaranteeing the application of your written security policy. In addition, the /quiet switch will ensure that no comments are output during the application of the template.

Secedit is also useful for regular security setting verification since it includes the /analyze switch. Both analysis and configuration can be automated through the Task Scheduler in the Control Panel. The secedit command must be captured in a script for automation to work.

These are not the only operations that can be performed through secedit. You can find out more on this command through the WS03 Help and Support Center or simply by typing secedit at the command prompt.

> ### QUICK TIP
>
> *You can also use the secedit command to reset security settings on a machine. To do so, you need to apply the original Setup Security.inf template for a workstation or server, or DC Security.inf for a domain controller. You can also use RootSec.inf to reset only the root of the system disk.*

Security Template Best Practices

There are a few things to remember when using security templates:

- Settings entered in a security template are not stored into the GPO until the security template has been imported into the GPO.

- The security template can be reapplied on a regular basis to ensure that settings that may have been modified are reset to appropriate values.

► CAUTION

This should be a recurring security task. Once every quarter, security personnel should go through critical servers and verify them against approved templates. Once every year, you should question the strength of your templates and make them evolve as necessary.

- Applying a template through secedit applies it only to the local policy. Any conflicting setting applied through Group Policy will override the local policy setting. For this reason, you should limit local settings to files, folders, the registry, and services.

- If you decide to use the Clear database option when importing templates into GPOs, this means that you will never modify security settings in your GPOs directly because these modifications will be overridden when you import a template.

- Always document your GPO changes even if they are stored in a security template.

► CAUTION

The application of GPO settings should be centralized. All GPOs should be fully documented and changes should be versioned to ensure that everyone is always aware of the changes applied to each GPO.

- At minimum, use the Hisecws.inf or the Hisecdc.inf templates in the parallel network since this network only contains the Windows XP or Windows Server 2003 operating systems.

Antivirus Strategies

A second layer of security on all systems is the antivirus (AV) engine. Implementing a complete security environment requires the use of a comprehensive antivirus solution. This is not a function of Windows Server 2003, but WS03 does offer special application programming interfaces (API) to support file and object scanning on a system. In addition, Microsoft has worked extensively with antivirus manufacturers to ensure that their solutions work well under stress and reliably in any situation.

A complete antivirus solution should include the following elements:

- Central management of both clients and servers
- Automatic installation and deployment to client and server machines
- A Microsoft Management Console for AV management tasks
- Automatic download of new virus signatures
- Variable download schedule to distribute the download workload
- Automatic deployment of signatures to AV clients
- Automatic system scanning
- Central collection of all scanning results
- Alert generation on virus find
- Central quarantine of found viruses and automatic machine cleanup
- Detection of unusual behavior to locate unknown viruses
- Provide policy-based management
- Support for email and database system inspection
- Support from the manufacturer for virus cleanup

One of the best solutions on the market today is Symantec AntiVirus Corporate Edition from Symantec Corporation (http://enterprisesecurity.symantec.com/). It is so simple to deploy that an administrator with no experience in the product can have it deployed and fully functional including automatic update management within a single hour. Once it is deployed, there should be little else to do because it automatically updates all systems. The only thing to do is to make sure it is installed on any new system that joins the domain.

Whatever the solution you select, ensure that it is in place and fully functional *before* you provide any means to connect to the outside world in your parallel network.

Using Software Restriction Policies

Your antivirus strategy cannot be complete without support from Windows Server 2003 and Group Policy. WS03 includes a special set of GPO settings that identify the code that is allowed to run and operate within a network. These are the Software Restriction Policies (SRP).

This set of GPO settings allows you to control unknown code in your network. Though the SRPs allow you to control over 38 file types—basically anything that is seen as code—there are two file types that you should absolutely control: scripts and macros. Most unknown viruses come in the form of either one of these two file types. Thus, since you control what occurs in your network, you should explicitly identify the scripts and macros that are authorized within it.

The easiest way to do this is to digitally sign your scripts and macros. Signing places a PKI certificate within the code. You can then define SRPs that block all scripts and macros except those that are signed with your certificate. SRPs are defined in Computer Configuration | Windows Settings | Security Settings | Software Restriction Policies. This section is empty by default. You must begin by selecting New Software Restriction Policies from the context menu. Then you must identify the extensions that you want to disallow, change the basic policy, and identify the certificate to trust. Make sure that you do not include the SRP within the Default Domain Policy. That way, if you have to deactivate it for some reason, you will not deactivate your Global Domain Security Policy. A good place to enable Software Restriction Policies is in the Global PC GPO that is applied at the PCs OU level.

▶ *CAUTION*

If there is a single best practice that you follow in this chapter, it should be using SRPs to block unauthorized scripts.

General Active Directory Security

The Active Directory is also an area that requires considerable security. In fact, the entire design of the Active Directory that you have created to date has been done with security in mind. The concept of the Protected Forest Root Domain (PFRD) and of child production domains is one of the first steps towards the creation of an Active Directory. The concept of creating Organizational Units and delegating certain management activities to other people in your organization is also an important part of the security foundation for Active Directory. But no matter which security measures you put in place in your directory, you will always have one caveat: you must trust your administrators implicitly. Of course, the AD allows you to limit the rights you grant to different levels of administrators, something you couldn't do in Windows NT. Nevertheless, the administrators you designate must be trustworthy, otherwise everything you do to secure the directory will be useless.

A good place to start is by changing administrative habits. AD administrators should use limited access accounts for their everyday work and use the Run As command to perform administrative tasks. Since WS03 supports the use of smart cards for administrators, it is also a good idea to implement it. This means two-factor authentication for all administrators in the enterprise network. WS03 fully supports this and eases the smart card administration burden because of the new features such as auto-enrollment and auto-renewal for public key certificates. You might even consider giving the token to one person and the password to another in highly secure environments. This way, access is always documented.

To make sure that your AD is secure, you need to perform the actions outlined in the active Directory security checklist illustrated in Figure 8-5. Many of these activities have been covered in

The Active Directory Security Checklist

❑ Design the Active Directory with security in mind (Chapter 3)
❑ Ensure that each domain contains at least two domain controllers to protect the data in the domain (Chapter 3)
❑ Run forests in native mode to profit from the latest security features (Chapters 3, 4)
❑ Position Operation Masters for maximum service efficiency (Chapters 3, 4)
❑ Ensure that all services related to the directory use directory integrated d ata storage (for example, DNS) (Chapter 4)
❑ Ensure that you use a structured Group Policy Strategy (Chapter 5)
❑ Create read only custom consoles as much as possible (Chapter 5)
❑ Distribute consoles through Terminal Services and assign only read and execute permissions to them (Chapters 5, 7)
❑ Ensure that all directory data is protected and can be modified only by the right people in your organization (Chapter 6)
❑ Manage groups effectively to assign permissions in the directory (Chapter 6)
❑ Make sure that sensitive information stored within the domain is hidden from prying eyes (Chapter 7)
❑ Ensure that your domain controllers are physically protected
❑ Ensure that your domain controllers have specific local security policies applied to them
❑ Configure the two Default Domain Group Policies before creating child domains to profit from policy propagation at domain creation
❑ Manage your trusts properly to ensure rapid service response where required
❑ Delegate only the administrative rights that are required and nothing else to both service and data administrators
❑ Tightly control the Modify Permissions and Modify Ownership permissions
❑ Implement a strong Global Account Policy within the directory
❑ Audit sensitive object access within the directory
❑ Use spot checks at irregular intervals to ensure that your administrative audits cannot be set to a pattern
❑ Protect the directory restore password
❑ Ensure that you have a comprehensive directory backup policy (Chapter 9)

Figure 8-5   The Active Directory Security Checklist

previous chapters. A few will also be covered in coming chapters. The others are covered both in this section and in Layer 4.

Security Within the Directory

Chapter 7 outlined how you could hide objects within the directory through the use of discretionary access control lists (DACLs). Chapters 5 and 6 used the same approach for OU delegation. These examples demonstrate how the Active Directory uses DACLs to apply security on its principals. Like the Windows NTFS file system, the directory also provides security inheritance. This means that all child objects inherit the parent's security settings. What is particular to the directory is the way permissions are inherited.

Explicit permissions always override inherited permissions, even deny permissions. This means that it is possible to define a deny permission on a parent object and define an allow permission on its child object. For example, you can deny the List Contents permission on an OU and define an allow List Contents on a child OU within the previous OU. The people who are denied access to the parent OU will never be able to see or modify its contents, nor will they be able to navigate the directory to the child OU, but they will be able to search the directory to locate contents within the child OU.

Like the NTFS file system, the directory offers two levels of permission assignment. The first regroups detailed permissions into categories such as full control, read, write, execute, and so on. To view security settings for an object, you must right-click on it and select Properties (within one of the AD consoles).

> ► **QUICK TIP**
>
> *You need to enable Advanced Features in the View menu of the console in order to be able to view the Security tab in the object's Properties dialog box.*

The second level lets you assign specific and detailed permissions. Clicking on the Advanced button of this dialog box leads to the detailed security permissions. Several types of information are available in this dialog box. To begin, it gives you access to special security features such as Permissions, Audit, Owner, and Effective Permissions.

Each tab outlines different information. The Permissions tab, for example, identifies if permissions are inherited and if so, from which container, or whether they are explicit. The Auditing tab identifies the audit policies that are applied to the object. The Owner tab lists the various owners of this object. Finally, Effective Permissions lets you identify the resultant permissions for a given security principal. Click on Select to locate the user of the group for which you want to view effective permissions.

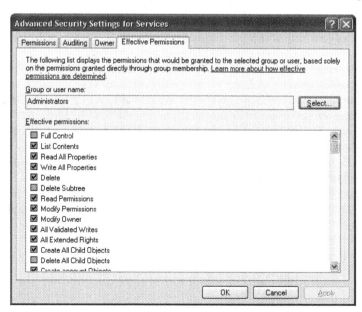

If you want to view or assign specific permissions, return to the Permissions tab and click Add or Edit. This displays the Permissions Entry dialog box. Here you can assign specific permissions to users or groups. (Remember, it is always preferable to assign them to groups rather than users.) This level of detail can make managing directory permissions quite complex. Always keep your directory permissions as simple as possible and try to use inherited permissions as much as possible. Detail specific permissions when you delegate control of an OU.

File System Security

The file system is also a portion of Operating System Hardening that supports a secure environment. There is no doubt that NTFS is an absolute must and a pillar of the WS03 Castle Defense System. Chapter 7 covered NTFS and share permissions extensively. All of Windows Server 2003's advanced disk and file operations are based on the use of its latest storage and NTFS features. The same applies to file encryption. Without NTFS, there is no encryption.

One of the important aspects of secure file management is the ability to log all file changes and alert organizations when unauthorized changes occur. This can be done in some form with file access audition, but for critical data files, professional help is required. This help comes in the form of a utility such as Tripwire for Servers (http://www.tripwire.com/products/servers/). Tripwire monitors all file changes even down to the file's checksum properties. Therefore, it can alert administrators when critical files have been modified by unauthorized personnel. Tripwire does require resources so you should plan for its use.

The Encrypting File System

The Encrypting File System (EFS) is a part of NTFS that also plays a significant role in the Castle Defense System. It is very powerful because its operation is transparent to users once it is enabled. It also provides more file protection than permissions do because if a malicious attacker gains physical access to encrypted files, he or she will not be able to view their content. This is not necessarily the case with files that only include NTFS permissions (if they use NTFS for DOS, for example). The ideal security level is one which uses both NTFS permissions and encryption.

Encryption is activated through the file or folder properties, just like permissions. It can also be performed with the cipher command. Encryption is a file property, thus it cannot be applied if the file has also been compressed. These two properties are mutually exclusive. Files that are part of the operating system cannot be encrypted nor can files found in the %SYSTEMROOT% folder. WS03 supports the encryption of data contained in folder shares. But data that is contained in encrypted files located on network shares is not necessarily encrypted when transported from the file share to the local computer. If full encryption, even to the communications level, is required, additional technologies such as IPSec must be used.

WS03 supports the encryption of offline files. This property can be set at the GPO level and applied along with Folder Redirection policies. Encrypted files will become decrypted if copied to non-NTFS volumes so users should be warned of best practices for secure files. In addition, encryption does not prevent deletion of files; it only prevents unauthorized users from viewing their content. If users have permissions to a directory containing encrypted files, they will not be able to view them, but they may be able to delete them. Encrypted files are displayed in green within Windows Explorer. This helps users quickly identify secure files. Once again, this information should be part of your user security communications program.

Encrypting a file is very simple:

1. Open Windows Explorer.

2. Right-click on the folder you want to encrypt and select Properties.

3. Click the Advanced button on the General tab.

4. Click Encrypt contents to secure data and click OK.

5. Click OK to close the Properties dialog box.

6. EFS will ask you to confirm the setting you wish to apply. Select Apply changes to this folder, subfolders and files and click OK.

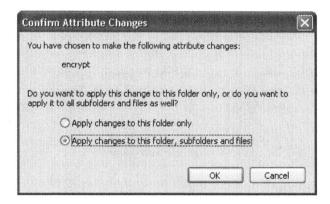

7. If folder tasks have not been turned on, EFS will ask you to turn them on. Click Yes. Folder tasks are part of the new Windows themes interface. Encrypted files will now appear in green in Windows Explorer.

EFS is as simple as that, but there are guidelines:

• You should encrypt folders rather than individual files.

• You should ensure that offline files are encrypted.

• The entire My Documents folder should be encrypted.

• Both %Temp% and %Tmp% should be encrypted to make sure all temporary files are encrypted as well. Use a script based on the cipher command during system setup to set these folders as encrypted.

• You should encrypt the spool folder on Print Servers.

- You should combine EFS with IPSec to ensure end-to-end data encryption.
- You should use Group Policy to control the behavior of EFS in your network.
- You should protect the recovery agent and limit the number of recovery agents in your network.
- You should use a WS03 Public Key Infrastructure to manage EFS certificates and recovery agents.

EFS uses public and private keys (certificates) to manage the encryption and recovery process. The best way to manage these certificates is to use Windows' PKI features. In addition, to ensure the safety of encrypted files, you should move recovery agent certificates to removable media such as floppy disk or CD to ensure a two-factor process when recovering files.

▶ **NOTE**

More information on EFS is available at the Microsoft security Web site. Search for EFS at http://www.microsoft.com/security/.

Print System Security

Print System Security is also important. As seen in the previous section, if files are encrypted on user systems, they should also be encrypted in printer spooling shares. Security for the print system has already been covered in Chapter 7, but it is important to recall here that giving users management permissions to printer spoolers means that you trust them with potentially confidential data. Use the data categorization that you performed while working with Level 1 of the Castle Defense System to determine which printer spoolers must be protected and encrypted.

.NET Framework Security

The .NET Framework is another aspect of Operating System Hardening. First, it is included as a core element of the WS03 operating system. Second, it provides core functionalities for Web services. As such, it provides the engine for both operation and execution of Web services. It is this engine's responsibility to determine if the code it is about to run can be trusted. The Common Language Runtime (CLR) applies security in two different manners; the first is for managed code and the second is for unmanaged code.

Managed code security is at the heart of the CLR. Two aspects of the code are evaluated by the CLR before allowing it to run: the safety of the code and the behavior of the code. For example, if the code uses a method that expects a 4-byte value, the CLR will reject an attempt to return an 8-byte value. In other words, the CLR ensures that managed code is well-behaved as well as safe.

The advantage of using this approach to security is that users need not worry if code is safe before they run it. If it is, the CLR will execute it. If it isn't, it simply won't run. This applies only to managed code. Unmanaged code is allowed to run as well, but it does not benefit from these security measures. To run unmanaged code, the CLR must use a specific set of permissions—permissions that can be controlled but that must be declared globally. One day, all the code you run will be managed code and its security application will be entirely controlled by the CLR.

The Evaluation Process for Managed Code

The CLR uses a ten-step evaluation process for managed code. This process is illustrated in Figure 8-6.

1. When an assembly (a piece of managed code) calls upon another assembly, the CLR evaluates the permission level to apply to the new assembly.

2. The first thing the new assembly must do is provide evidence. This evidence is a set of answers to questions posed by the CLR's Security Policy.

3. Three questions are asked about the source of the assembly:

   - *From which site was the assembly obtained?* Assemblies are automatically downloaded to the client from a Web site.

   - *From which URL did the assembly originate?* A specific URL address must be provided by the assembly.

   - *From which zone was the assembly obtained?* This applies to Internet Explorer zones such as Internet, intranet, local machine, and so on. Some zones are more trusted than others.

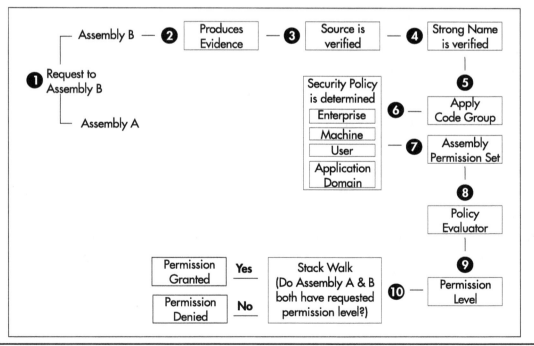

Figure 8-6   The .NET Framework Security Allocation Process

4. The assembly must also provide a cryptographically strong identifier called its *strong name*. This identifier is unique and must be provided by the author of the assembly. The identifier does not necessarily identify the author, but it does identify the assembly as unique.

5. Evidence is gathered from a series of different sources including the CLR itself, the browser, ASP.NET, the shell, and so on. Once the evidence is provided, the CLR begins to determine the security policy to apply. First, it applies the evidence against standard *code groups*. These groups contain standard policies depending on the zone from which the assembly originates. The .NET Framework includes basic code groups, but administrators can add their own or modify the default groups.

6. Once the code group is determined, the policy is defined. This policy can be defined at three levels: enterprise, machine, and user, in this order. A fourth level involves the application domain. This domain provides an isolated environment for the application to run in. An application contained within a domain cannot interfere with any other domain on the same machine.

7. Once the policy has been set, an initial set of permissions is created. The assembly can fine-tune this set of permissions in three ways:

   • First, it can identify the minimum set of permissions it requires to run.

   • Second, it can specify optional permissions. These are not absolutely required.

   • Third, a very well-behaved assembly can refuse permissions it doesn't require and deem too risky, actually reducing the permission set it is assigned by the CLR.

8. All of these factors are reviewed by the policy evaluator.

9. A final set of permissions is created for the assembly.

10. The final stage is the *stack walk*. The CLR compares the permission set to those of other assemblies that are involved in the original call for this assembly. If any of these assemblies do not have permission to run with this permission set, the permission to execute is denied. If everything is okay, the permission to execute is granted.

Administering Code Access Security

The entire CLR security allocation process is referred to as *Code Access Security* (CAS). Two tools are available for .NET Framework administration in Administrative Tools: the .NET Framework Configuration Console and the .NET Framework wizards. The latter contains three wizards that walk you through a configuration process: Adjust .NET Security, Trust an Assembly, and Fix an Application. Security can be performed either through the wizards or the configuration console. If you choose to use the console, you need to move to the Runtime security policy section of the console tree. As you will see, the task pane of the console provides a lot of online help and assistance.

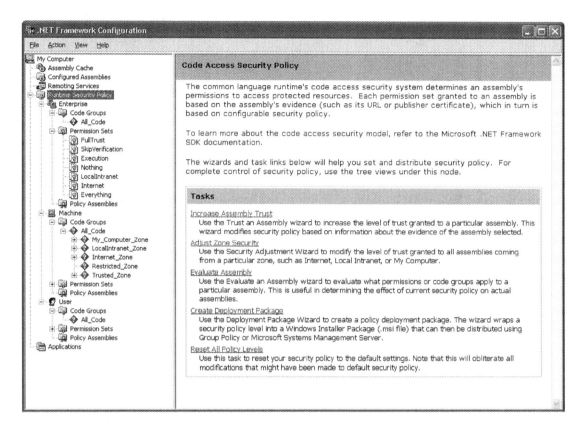

Keep in mind that the wizards only work for two policies: the machine and user policies. Remember also that policies are always applied in the same order: enterprise, machine, and user. In addition, you can set a default level of policy for the CLR to apply by telling the .NET Framework to stop policy application at a specific level. For example, if you consider that your enterprise policy is secure enough, you can tell the CLR to stop policy processing at the enterprise level. This will cause the CLR to ignore both the machine and the user policies.

If you browse through the default policies in the .NET Framework Configuration console, you will see that the default set of policies is quite extensive. Right-clicking on the objects listed in the console tree will give you access to all of the features of the console. CLR security is rather granular and can be applied at a number of levels. Code Access Security works in conjunction with role-based access (more at Level 4) to provide a complete .NET security model.

A Code Access Permission Set can include permissions for all levels of the .NET Framework. This includes everything from local access to the file system to access to the registry. You can also create your own permission sets. For example, you might determine that you prefer a higher level of trust for applications originating from within your intranet. The best way to determine what works best for your environment is to try them out. Begin with the default security policies and refine them as you become more familiar with the .NET Framework. The most important recommendation for use of the .NET Framework is to migrate all code to managed code.

The security policies of each level are stored in local XML files. Three files are created, one for each level of policy:

- **Enterprise**   %windir%\Microsoft.NET\Framework\v1.0.3705\config\enterprisesec.config

- **Machine**   %windir%\Microsoft.NET\Framework\v1.0.3705\config\security.config

- **User**   %userprofile%\Application Data\Microsoft\CLR Security
  Config\v1.0.3705\security.config

The version number of each folder may vary according to the version of the .NET Framework you are working with. The advantage of these XML files is that you can define a single .NET Framework set of policies and deploy them to each and every machine in your network.

▶ | **QUICK TIP**

You should include custom versions of these files at machine staging, ensuring once again that you have a secure machine as soon as it is installed.

Internet Information Server 6.0

Internet Information Server (IIS) has been seen as Windows' weakest point for some time. This is not the case with WS03. IIS is locked down by default in WS03. In fact, the following characteristics of IIS have been modified in Windows Server 2003:

- IIS is no longer installed by default on most versions of WS03; it must be explicitly selected for installation. Of course, this does not apply to Windows Server 2003, Web Edition. The very purpose of this bare-bones version of WS03 is to run as a Dedicated Web Server. But even if IIS is installed by default on this version, it still profits from the other security features that have been applied to IIS 6.0.

- Once installed, IIS only serves static Web pages. All other features must be turned on explicitly to work.

- When you open the IIS Management console, the first thing you need to do is finalize the configuration of the service and enable the features you require. This ensures that you know exactly what is enabled on your IIS servers. You should make sure that you document this configuration as soon as you complete running the wizard.

- The account running IIS services has fewer privileges than in Windows 2000. WS03 uses the NetworkService account to run IIS. NetworkService is a lower privilege account than LocalSystem.

- No samples are installed by default. Samples contain code that may be used to attack a Web server. If you feel you need the sample sites, you can install them on a more secure, internal machine.

- All of the IIS components are secured by default, even at the NTFS level.

- URLScan can also be added to your IIS configuration. It is used to authorize requests from given URLs. Beware, though: URLScan is simply an initialization file. If it is not properly secured through NTFS, it can be used to perform a denial-of-service attack. To do so, simply modify it to deny all URLs. No errors will be reported in the IIS error logs since IIS will think it is behaving properly. Because of this, this is a good file to monitor with the Tripwire tool mentioned earlier in the NTFS section.

▶ | *QUICK TIP*

To obtain the latest version of URLScan, go to http://www.microsoft.com/downloads/ and search for URLScan.

- In addition, the execution mode for IIS is completely different in WS03. Each application running in IIS 6.0 runs in its own execution environment and is completely isolated from other applications. If an application wants to perform illegal operations, it cannot affect other applications running on the same server. IIS can also automatically restart applications after crashing, limiting the damage a denial-of-service attack can have on each application.

- Finally, the core IIS system, HTTP.SYS, runs in the WS03 kernel and is isolated from applications. It only accepts requests that originate from the operating system itself. This secures the basic operation of IIS and links it directly to the operating system.

These are the major new features for IIS security. Altogether, IIS is a much more secure and stable Web platform than it ever has been before.

Keep in mind, though, that IIS is no longer required on most of your servers. In addition, you should not place IIS on any of your domain controllers if at all possible. There may be some circumstances where you have no choice in this matter (for example, in the case of multipurpose servers).

Additional IIS Security Activities

To install IIS on the Windows Server 2003 Standard, Enterprise, or Datacenter editions, you need to use the Manage Your Server console. The role you choose is the Web Application Server (IIS). This installs IIS in Web Application mode, which means that the installation wizard will propose to activate ASP.NET. You can determine if this is the configuration you require. If not, deselect ASP.NET from the wizard.

You can also install IIS from the Windows Components portion of the Add/Remove Programs in the Control Panel. If you choose to install it from the Manage Your Server console, you will be given two consoles to manage IIS: the normal IIS console found in Administration Tools, and a new

Application Server console that regroups the management of the .NET Framework, IIS, and
COM+ Components.

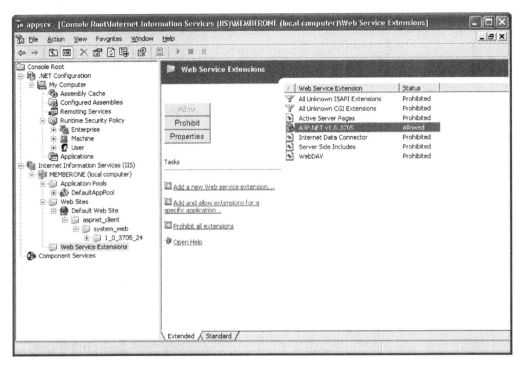

IIS security is an issue in and of itself. It should be locked down and synchronized with the
security you implement in the file system. One of the best places to start for additional IIS security
is the Security Operations Guide. It includes a list of strong recommendations for tightening IIS
server security.

Final Operating System Hardening Activities

Two additional activities are required for you to finalize the hardening of your operating systems:
creating system redundancy and putting in place recurring security maintenance operations. System
redundancy means building resilience into your servers and into the services they deliver. A lot of
resiliency was covered in Chapter 7, especially through the use of the Distributed File System. More
will be covered in Chapter 9. Here you will build additional resilience through cluster servers and
backup operations.

You also need to cover security maintenance. In addition, you will need to implement server and
workstation patch management at the enterprise level. If you are using SMS, see http://www.microsoft
.com/smserver/evaluation/overview/featurepacks/default.asp for more information.

Level 4: Information Access

Level 4 deals with user identification and the attribution of permissions, allowing them to operate within your network. Much of this has been covered in Chapter 6 in the discussion on User and Group Management. Like Windows 2000, Windows Server 2003 includes a number of different security protocols for authentication and authorization. The most important of these for an internal network is Kerberos, even though NTLM is still supported. But in the parallel network, there is little need for NTLM since all machines are using the latest operating systems and the forests are in native mode.

A lot has been said on the Kerberos protocol. It has many advantages over NTLM. It is faster, more secure, more widely accepted, and simpler to use. One of its best features is the fact that once it has authenticated users, they do not need to return to the server for authorization. Whereas in NTLM, the user is constantly returning to the server for rights and permission validation, in Kerberos, the user caries rights and permissions within the access token that is granted by the Kerberos server. This access token is in the form of the Kerberos *ticket* that is granted to the user at logon. In addition, with Kerberos, the server authenticates to the client, making sure that it is authorized to grant user access within the domain. Finally, Kerberos supports two-factor authentication. This two-factor authentication can be in the form of a smart card or a biometric device such as a fingerprinting device.

One of the key elements of a Kerberos realm (realm is the term used to designate the notion of a domain in Kerberos) is the timestamp. Time synchronization is essential in Kerberos because the authentication server matches the time of the client's request with its own internal clock. If the time differs by more than the allotted time, the Kerberos server will not authenticate the user. This is one reason why Microsoft has integrated the time service into the PDC Emulator master of operations role in Active Directory and it is the reason why the processes outlined in Chapter 2 for forest-wide time synchronization are so important.

Smart Card Authentication

One of the most important places for smart card authentication is with administrative accounts. If you want to design a highly secure infrastructure, you should take advantage of this feature for all accounts that are granted administrative authority. In addition, your administrators should have two accounts: a user-level account for everyday operations and an administrative account for administrative operations. They should be logged on as users and should perform their administrative activities through the Run As command using their smart card to log on. You will need a Public Key Infrastructure to assign certificates to the smart cards.

There may be some occasions where Run As is insufficient to perform administrative tasks. The best way to circumvent this is to place administrative tools on a server and to allow administrators to access these tools through Terminal Services. This way, you only have to manage administrative tools on a few servers and you don't need to worry about creating special workstations for administrative purposes.

Securing User Identification

User identification happens on many levels within a WS03 enterprise network. The most obvious authentication is through the Active Directory domain. For this, you need to set Global Account Policies for the entire forest and refine them within each domain. In addition, authentication occurs in cross-forest scenarios. Remember, WS03 extends the notion of transitive trust from inside the forest as was found in Windows 2000 to multiple forests. For this, you need to establish trusts. Two other areas of authentication are found in WS03: Web server and Web service or .NET Framework authentication. Web server authentication is performed through IIS and uses a series of authentication techniques. New to WS03 is the ability to perform Microsoft Passport authentication in IIS. .NET Framework authentication is role-based and can be specific to each application. Each of these authentication areas are covered in the following sections.

User Authentication in Active Directory

In Windows networks, each security principal is identified by a unique number, the Security ID or SID. Security principals include everything from computers to users to groups and so on. The user SID is included in the access token for each user. When the information in the access token is used to determine if a user has access to an object, the user's SIDs are compared with the list of SIDs that make up the object's DACL to identify the level of permission the user has to the object. In other words, every security principal in WS03 is identified as a number, not a name.

The impact of this is that ownership of objects is identified by SIDs. When you recreate an object such as a user account, you assign it a different SID. Thus when you create the parallel network, you *must* transfer accounts from the originating domain to the new production domain otherwise all of your users will have new SIDs. If this occurs, your users will not have access to their files and folders when they are transferred from originating file servers to the file servers in the parallel network. Chapter 10 will outline some of the procedures you can use for this process. They are one of the keys to a successful implementation of a parallel network.

Securing Level 4 Through Group Policy Objects

The best way to manage authentication, authorization, and auditing is through Group Policy. Authorization has been covered to some extent in the discussion on Operating System Hardening, and especially in access control of directory, file system, and registry objects. As you have seen, the latter two can be configured through the Security Configuration Manager. Directory objects are secured as you create them. For example, the delegation procedures you use when creating your OU structure are part and parcel of directory object access management.

The best way to control authentication processes is to define their boundaries through Group Policy. So far, you have created several different GPOs for object management purposes. Now, you can review these policies and see if they can be reused for security purposes. This will also allow you to identify if additional security policies are required. Table 8-1 outlines the GPOs created to date. Each GPO lists the OU it can be found in, its name, and its purpose. Three new GPOs are included here: the two default GPOs and a new one, the Baseline GPO. The latter is designed to provide baseline security for all Member Servers. New GPOs are listed in bold.

OU	GPO	Policy Type	Notes
Domain	**Default Domain Policy**	Computer	Contains Global Account Policies
Domain	**Intranet Domain GPO**	Computer	Contains global settings for all systems, for example, Printer Location Tracking and Software Restriction Policies
Domain Controllers	**Default Domain Controllers Policy**	Computer	Contains settings specific to DCs throughout each domain of the enterprise network
PCs	Global PC GPO	Computer	Applies to all PCs
Desktops	Global Desktop GPO	Computer	Includes specifications for desktop workstations
Kiosks	Special Kiosk GPO	Computer	Special features for kiosk computers
Mobile Systems	Global Mobile GPO	Computer	Includes specifications for mobile devices
External	Global External GPO	Computer	Includes basic settings for PCs not controlled by the organization
People	Global People GPO	User	Applies to all users
Special Workgroups	SWG GPO	User	Mostly designed to let SIG users have access to their own remote desktop
Services	**Baseline GPO**	Computer	Baseline security settings for all Member Servers
File and Print	Global File and Print GPO	Computer	Controls all aspects of file sharing, Distributed File System, and printing
Application Servers and Dedicated Web Servers	Global Application Server GPO	Computer	Controls database servers, general purpose Web Servers, .NET Framework, and corporate applications
Terminal Servers	Global Terminal Server GPO	Computer	Contains Server-side Terminal Services settings
Collaboration Servers	Global Collaboration GPO	Computer	Contains settings for Real-time Communications Services, Exchange Server, SharePoint Portal Server, Content Management Server, and Streaming Media Services; these may be segregated into more GPOs to refine service management
Network Infrastructure	Global Infrastructure GPO	Computer	Contains settings for DHCP, WINS, RIS as well as operational servers such as Microsoft Operations Management, Systems Management Server, Internet Security & Acceleration Server, and so on; these may be segregated into more GPOs to refine service management

Table 8-1   Global Production Domain GPO List

In all, 16 GPOs are required to manage and secure the production domain, as is illustrated in Figure 8-7. Each contains both security and management information. You might consider creating a GPO for each purpose, but this will practically double the number of GPOs you need to manage for little reason. What is important is to fully document each GPO and use a structured change management approach for modifications. Perform modifications in the appropriate GPO. For example, to encrypt offline files, assign the modification to the Global File and Print GPO because it is the GPO that controls file management and this security modification is related to file management.

> ► **QUICK TIP**
>
> *In WS03, you must use the gpupdate command to manually refresh GPO settings. The secedit command is no longer used for this purpose.*

In addition, every other domain in your enterprise network will also contain at least two policies: Default Domain and Default Domain Controller Policies.

Configuring the Default Domain Policy

Chapters 3 and 4 outlined the importance of configuring the two default domain policies (Default Domain and Default Domain Controllers) at the Protected Forest Root Domain. The reason for this is so that the content of these policies will propagate to child domains as soon as they are created. This means the default policies should be customized as soon as the forest root domain has been created.

The Default Domain Policy is the *account policy* for the domain. Since only one policy can contain account information, this information should be defined in a single area. You might consider creating a separate domain policy because the Default Domain Policy cannot be deactivated. Therefore, if you make a mistake while editing this policy, you will be affecting the entire domain. This is one reason for a structured Group Policy Change Management Strategy. In fact, what you should do is define the policy in the root domain so that it is as complete as possible. This policy should correspond to the settings required by your Single Global Child Production Domain. It will propagate to child domains upon their creation. You can then make modifications as Required in each child domain. (Remember, generic accounts are created only in development, training, and testing domains.) This is no reason for lax security in domains other than the production domain.

The elements that need to be covered in this account policy are outlined in Table 8-2. All of the elements outlined in this table are from the Computer Settings | Windows Components | Security Settings branch of Group Policy. Once again, remember to document all of your GPO settings.

> ► **QUICK TIP**
>
> *All of the settings for Kerberos Policy are set at the default WS03 default, but setting them explicitly assists your Group Policy operators in knowing what the default setting actually is.*

All of these settings are applied at the domain level to ensure that they affect every object within the domain. In fact, the account policy is a computer policy. This means that the user configuration portion of the GPO can be disabled. Remember to fully document all changes you make to these GPOs.

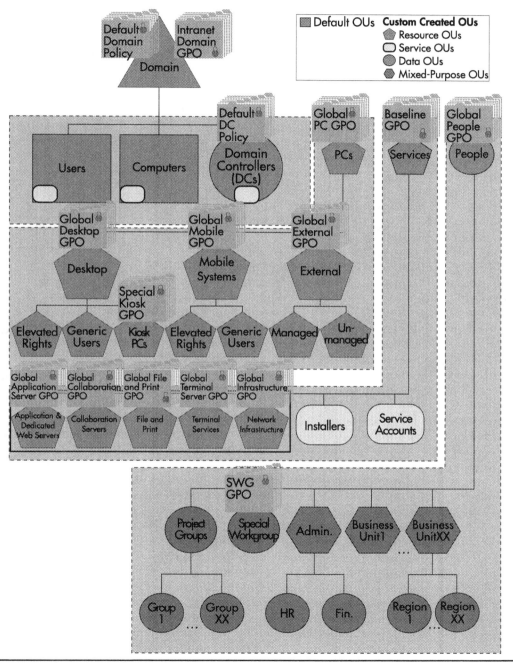

Figure 8-7   The intranet domain GPOs

Section	Setting	Recommendation	Comments
Account Policy/ Password Policy	Enforce password history	24 passwords	At the rate of one password change per month, this setting remembers two years worth of passwords.
	Maximum password age	42 days	This is approximately a month and a half.
	Minimum password age	2 days	This stops users from changing their passwords too often.
	Minimum password length	8 characters	This is the threshold where password crackers start taking longer to break passwords.
	Password must meet complexity requirements	Enabled	This ensures that passwords must contain both alphabetic and numeric characters, both upper- and lowercase, as well as special symbols.
	Store passwords using reversible encryption	Disabled	Enabling this setting is the same as storing plain text passwords. This setting should *never* be enabled.
Account Policy/ Account Lockout Policy	Account lockout duration	120 minutes	This setting determines how long an account is locked after several bad logon attempts. The shorter the time, the more attempts that can be made against the account.
	Account lockout threshold	3 invalid logon attempts	After three bad logon tries, the account is locked out. Set this value higher if you use two-factor authentication.
	Reset account lockout counter after	120 minutes	This must be equal to or greater than the account lockout duration.
Account Policies/ Kerberos Policy	Enforce user logon restrictions	Enabled (default)	This ensures that users have the right to access either local or network resources before granting them a Kerberos ticket.
	Maximum lifetime for service ticket	600 minutes (default)	This sets the duration of the session ticket that is used to initiate a connection with a server. It must be renewed when it expires.
	Maximum lifetime for user ticket	10 hours (default)	This must be greater than or equal to the previous setting. It must be renewed when it expires.
	Maximum lifetime for user ticket renewal	7 days (default)	This sets the duration of a user's ticket granting ticket. The user must log on again once this ticket expires.
	Maximum tolerance for computer clock synchronization	5 minutes (default)	Kerberos uses timestamps to grant tickets. All computers within a domain are synchronized through the domain controllers. This value can be shorter in a network with high-speed WAN links.

Table 8-2   Account Policy Elements

Section	Setting	Recommendation	Comments
Restricted Groups	*Domain*/Enterprise Admins	Individuals only	Select trusted individuals should be members of this group.
	Domain/Domain Admins	Individuals only	Select trusted individuals should be members of this group.
	Domain/ Administrators	Enterprise Admins Domain Admins	This group should contain only trusted groups.

Table 8-2   Account Policy Elements *(continued)*

▶ *CAUTION*

It is very important to ensure that you have a strong communications program to keep users aware of the importance of having a comprehensive account policy within your enterprise network. It is also important that you indicate to them the settings in your account policy. Finally, educating them on the protection of passwords and the immediate renewal of passwords they think may be compromised will ensure that your account policy is supported by the very people who use it.

The Default Domain Controller Policy

The Default Domain Controllers Policy should also be modified, but the required modifications are too numerous to be listed here. The DC Promotion process will automatically secure different aspects of the local system and create the DC Security.inf template, but in most cases, additional DC security is required. In addition, it will be essential to ensure that all your domain controllers remain in the Domain Controllers organization unit, otherwise they will not be affected by your default DC policy. This is one reason why directory auditing is also very important to implement. You can look to several sources of information for applicable security templates:

- The two built-in default templates: Securedc.inf and Hisecdc.inf
- The Security Operations Guide for a Baseline DC template
- The NSA DC security templates
- Commercial templates

Whatever template you use, make sure that you secure the following areas:

- Focus on Kerberos authentication rather than NTLM, even NTLM version 2
- DC to DC communications
- Use data signing for LDAP queries

- Remove down-level client support
- Secure the NTDS.DIT storage file

There are other security features that are applied by these templates. Review them carefully and select those that are appropriate for your environment. You must determine whether you will place all settings in the default DC policy (DDCP) or use local policy. If you choose to use a local policy in addition to the default DC policy, remember to apply the local policy to domain controllers only once they are promoted.

> ### QUICK TIP
>
> *You should always verify the templates located on the various Web sites since they are updated regularly. For Microsoft templates, search for the Security Operations Guide at http://www.microsoft.com/security/.*

The best practice is to modify the DDCP to set security parameters that will not affect the three local policy areas (file system, registry and services). One element that is useful in the DDCP is data transport encryption or rather, using IPSec to communicate between servers.

The Member Server Baseline Policy

Another security policy that is global to a group of objects is the Member Server baseline policy. This policy includes a variety of settings that are applied to all servers. It is located in the Services OU and because it is the parent OU for all Member Servers, it is applied to all of them. Because of this, each specific server role GPO includes only incremental security settings as well as the settings it requires for its role to function properly. For example, in order to provide additional security, you can include the Prevent IIS Installation setting (from Computer Configuration | Administrative Templates | Windows Components | Internet Information Services) in this baseline template. This way no one will be able to install IIS on any of your Member Servers. Then you can disable this setting in the incremental GPO that you apply to the Application Servers and Dedicated Web Servers OU.

Managing Trusts

Windows 2000 introduced the concept of automatic two-way transitive trusts within an Active Directory forest. Windows Server 2003 brings this concept even further with the addition of transitive trusts between forests. But despite the fact that trusts are now mostly automatic, some degree of management is still required because whenever a trust is created, you give access to your forests or domains to people and objects in other AD containers.

There are several types of trusts in Windows Server 2003. They are outlined in Table 8-3.

Trust Type	Directions and Nature	Comments
Parent and Child	Two-way transitive	These are the automatic trusts that are established when a child domain is created.
Tree-root	Two-way transitive	These are the automatic trusts that are established when a new tree is created.
Forest	One- or two-way transitive	Extends the transitivity of trusts from one forest to another.
Shortcut	One- or two-way transitive	Creates a shortcut path for authentication between two domains. The domains can use this path for authentication instead of having to traverse the forest hierarchy.
Realm	One- or two-way transitive or non-transitive	Creates an authentication link between a domain and a non-Windows Kerberos realm (such as UNIX).
External	One- or two-way non-transitive	Creates an authentication link between a WS03 domain and an NT4 domain.

Table 8-3   WS03 Trust Types

> **QUICK TIP**
>
> *To enable forest trusts, your forest must be in native WS03 forest mode. All domains must also be in WS03 native mode.*

The trusts you will mostly use in your parallel network will be forest, shortcut, and external. The latter is used to link your parallel network to the legacy network if it is based on NT4. Shortcut trusts will be used to improve validation performance between child domains that require high levels of interaction. Forest trusts can be used primarily between your infrastructure forest and partner forests.

Giving access to resources from other domains or forests through trusts is a two-step procedure. First, you must establish the trust. Second, you must insert User Groups from one forest or domain into User Groups in the other in order to give users access to resources (see the UGLP Rule from Chapter 6 for more information). Use the following procedure to create shortcut trusts:

1. Open the Active Directory Domains and Trusts console.

2. Right-click on the domain you want to assign the trust to and select Properties.

3. Move to the Trust tab in the Properties dialog box and click New Trust.

4. This will launch the New Trust Wizard. Click Next.

5. Type in the name of the domain or forest you wish to establish the trust with. Domain names can be in NetBIOS format, but forest names must be in DNS format. Click Next.

6. Select the type of trust you wish to create (two-way, one-way: incoming or one-way: outgoing).

7. If you have administrative rights in both domains, you can select Both this domain and the specified domain to create both sides of the trust at the same time. Click Next.

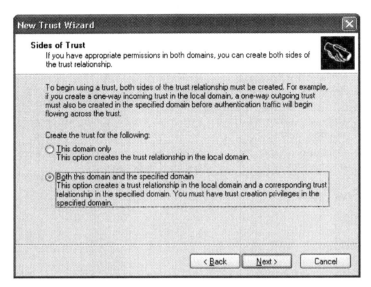

8. Type in your administrative credentials for the target domain or forest. Click Next.

9. The wizard is ready to create the outgoing trust in the target domain or forest. Click Next. Once finished, it will ask you to configure the new trust. Click Next.

10. It will ask you to confirm the outgoing trust. Select Yes, confirm the outgoing trust and then click Next. Confirming trusts is a good idea because it ensures that the trust is working properly.

11. It will ask you to confirm the incoming trust. Select Yes, confirm the incoming trust and then click Next.

12. Review your changes and click Finish when done.

Use the same procedure to create other types of trusts. The wizard will automatically change its behavior based on the values you input in its second page.

Working with Active Directory security can be complex, but you will reduce the level of complexity if you keep a structured, well-documented approach to change management. Ensure you use standard operating procedures at all times and ensure that these documented procedures are provided to all personnel who require them.

Web Server Access Control

Another area where authentication is required is at the Web server. IIS provides several different authentication types from anonymous logon to full certificate-based authentication. Table 8-4 lists the authentication modes available in IIS 6.0.

Mode	Security	Limitations (If Any)	Client Support	Comments
Anonymous	None	No security	All	Works in any scenario
Basic	Low	Clear text password, use only with SSL	All	Works in any scenario
Digest	Medium		IE5 and higher	Works in any scenario
NTLM	Medium	Doesn't work over proxies	Internet Explorer only	Works only in the intranet
Kerberos	High		IE 5 on W2000 or XP in domain infrastructure	Works only in the intranet, DC needs to be accessible by the client
IIS Client Certificate Mapping	High	WS03 provides auto-renewal for certificates	All newer browsers	All
AD Client Certificate Mapping	Very High	WS03 provides auto-enrollment and auto-renewal for certificates	All newer browsers	Works in any scenario
Microsoft Passport	Very High	Passport is stored on the Web	All newer browsers	Works in any scenario, but may be risky for intranet implementation

Table 8-4   Authentication in IIS

Basically, you need to determine which authentication mode works best for you and for the Web server requirement. Internal and external solutions will be different and there will also be differences between the solutions you implement on the Internet and in the extranet because you will most likely want more secure authentication in the latter.

Table 8-5 outlines some recommendations.

Scenarios	Requirements	Recommendations
Intranet (parallel network)	All clients have Windows accounts stored in your directory All clients use Internet Explorer 6 or more There is a strong level of password encryption	Use Kerberos through Integrated Windows Authentication
Internet	You need to support multiple browser types and multiple versions Most of the information on your servers is public Some data or business logic may require a secure login You do not have control over user computers and you do not want to be intrusive Some situations may require delegation	Anonymous Basic over SSL Passport

Table 8-5   Web Server Authentication Recommendations

Scenarios	Requirements	Recommendations
Extranet	This requires very secure solution You might require mutual authentication You may need a third party to manage the relationship between your server and the certificate holder The operation should be seamless to the client	Certificate Passport

Table 8-5 Web Server Authentication Recommendations *(continued)*

IIS authentication is defined in the IIS console under the Web site's properties. In the Directory Security tab, there is an Authentication and Access Control section. Click Edit to modify this Web site's settings. Select and apply the appropriate authentication mode for each site.

.NET Framework Authentication

Since the .NET Framework uses Web services, authentication models rely heavily on IIS, but there are some core functionalities within the framework itself since it provides role-based security (RBS). The RBS in the framework can rely on three different types of authentication: forms-based authentication (generates a cookie), IIS authentication, and Windows authentication. The first must be programmed within the Web service. The second and third methods are administered by network operations.

The easiest way to authenticate users and authorize access to Web resources within the intranet is to assign roles to them. Roles are groups that have different access levels within each application. These groups are application-specific, but they can be mapped to the Active Directory. Authorization stores must be created prior to group assignation. This can be done through the Authorization Manager console which is launched by running the azman.msc command. Developers must create the initial store and link it to an application, then administrators can assign users and groups to it. The store can be located in Active Directory, but the developer must have store creation rights within the AD to do so. This is a new security model that is very powerful and requires less management than former application authorization schemes. Ensure that your developers endeavor to use this approach when creating Web services for internal use.

Access Audition and Monitoring

The final aspect of Level 4 is audition. It is important to track resource use and monitor log files to ensure that users have appropriate access rights and that no user tries to abuse their rights. Audition is a two-step process in WS03. First, you must enable the auditing policy for an event. Then, for given types of objects, you must turn on the auditing for the object you want to track and identify who you want to track. WS03 lets you audit several different types of events: account logon events, account management, directory service access, logon events, object access, policy change, privilege use, process tracking, and system events.

Audition is controlled through the Audit Policy, which is located in the security settings of Group Policy. Enabling the Audit Policy can have significant impact in your network. Audited objects and events slow down the system, so it is important to audit only those events or objects you deem critical in your network.

To define the Audit Policy, move to the appropriate GPO and select Computer Configuration | Windows Settings | Security Settings | Audit Policy. Double-click on the event you want to audit and modify the policy. You can audit either the success or the failure of an event or both.

If you want to audit object access, such as accessing a container in AD or a file on a server, you must turn on auditing for that object and identify who you want to audit. To do so, you must view the object's security properties and use the Advanced button. In AD, you must enable Advanced Features from the View menu of the AD consoles to do this.

Once again, turn to the security guides mentioned earlier to identify the audit policies you want to implement in your network.

Level 5: External Access

Level 5 focuses on the perimeter network and the protection of your internal network from outside influences. In today's connected world, it is impossible to create internal networks that are completely isolated from the external world. Thus you need to secure the internal network as much as possible, in fact, creating a barrier that must be crossed before anyone can enter. This barrier can take several different forms, but in the case of the parallel network, it is based on the continued use of your perimeter environment. This environment is often called the demilitarized zone (DMZ).

Perimeter networks can contain any number of components. These can be limited to a series of firewalls that protect your internal network or they can include and contain your Internet servers as well as your extranet services. If this is the case, this network will be fairly complex and will include defenses at every level of the Castle Defense System.

The perimeter also includes all of the links between your internal network and the outside world. Too many administrators forget that their network includes internal modems that users can use from

▶ **QUICK TIP**

Microsoft provides a very extensive outline of a complex perimeter network through its Prescriptive Architecture Guide for Internet Data Centers. In fact, this guide is extremely complete and provides specific instructions for the implementation of the network for both Nortel and Cisco network devices. It is located at http://www.microsoft.com/solutions/idc/techinfo/ solutiondocs/default.asp.

within the enterprise to connect to the outside world and do not include these in the analysis of perimeter requirements. Do not make this mistake.

It is not the purpose of this chapter to review all of the features of a perimeter network. What is important at this level for the internal network is the implementation of a Public Key Infrastructure.

Designing an Internal Public Key Infrastructure

PKI implementations can be quite complex, especially if you need to use them to interact with clients and suppliers outside your internal network. The main issue at this level is one of authority: are you who you say you are and can your certificates be trusted? When this is the case, you must rely on a third-party authority specializing in this area to vouch for you and indicate that your certificates can and should be trusted. WS03 can play a significant role in reducing PKI costs in these situations. Since it includes all the features required to implement a PKI service, all you need to do is acquire the root server certificate from an external source. This certificate will then be embedded into every certificate issued by your infrastructure. It will prove to your clients, partners, and suppliers that you are who you are and you won't have to implement an expensive third-party PKI solution.

But you don't need this type of certificate for the purposes of the internal network since you control all of the systems within the network and you don't need to prove yourself or your organization to them. The Windows PKI services support several types of security situations. You can use them to:

- Secure Web services, servers, and applications
- Secure and digitally sign email

- Support EFS
- Sign code
- Support smart card logon
- Support virtual private networking (VPN)
- Support remote access authentication
- Support the authentication of Active Directory replication links over SMTP
- Support wireless network authentication

WS03 provides two types of certificate authorities (CA): standalone and enterprise. The latter provides complete integration to the Active Directory. The advantage of enterprise CAs is that since their certificates are integrated to the directory, they can provide auto-enrollment and auto-renewal services. This is why the PKI service you implement in the internal network should be based on enterprise CAs.

PKI best practices require very high levels of physical protection for root certificate authorities. This is because the root CA is the core CA for the entire PKI hierarchy. If it becomes corrupted for some reason, your entire Public Key Infrastructure will be corrupted. Therefore, it is important to remove the root CA from operation once its certificates have been issued. Since you will remove this server from operation, it makes sense to create it as a standalone CA (removing an enterprise CA from the network will cause errors in AD).

▶ **QUICK TIP**

Root CAs should be removed from operation for their protection. Many organizations find it difficult to justify a physical machine as root CA because the machine is basically always off the network. This may be a good opportunity to use virtual machines using technologies such as VMware GSX Server (http://www.vmware.com/) if budgets do not permit a physical machine. Taking a virtual machine offline is much easier than for a physical machine. In addition, the virtual machine can be placed in a suspended state indefinitely, making it easier and quicker to bring back online. It can also be copied to DVD and physically removed from the site.

PKI best practices also require several levels of hierarchy. In fact, in PKI environments that must interact with the public, it makes sense to protect the first two levels of the infrastructure and remove both from the network. But in an internal PKI environment, especially one that will mostly be used for code signing, encryption, smart card logon, and VPN connections, two levels are sufficient. Subordinate CAs should be enterprise CAs so that they can be integrated to AD. In order to add further protection to the subordinate CA, do not install it on a domain controller. This will reduce the number of services on the server. An example of both an internal and an external PKI architecture is illustrated in Figure 8-8.

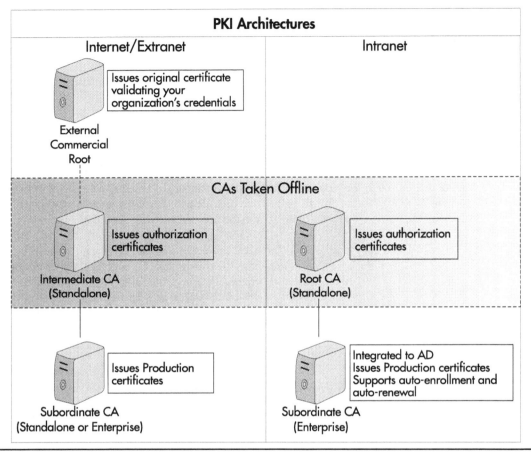

Figure 8-8   A PKI architecture

Even if your PKI environment will be internal, you should still focus on a proper PKI design. This means implementing a seven-step process as is outlined in the internal PKI Implementation Checklist illustrated in Figure 8-9. Consider each step before deploying the PKI. This is not a place where you can make many mistakes. Thoroughly test every element of your PKI architecture before proceeding to its implementation within your internal network. Finally, just as when you created your security policy to define how you secure your environment, you will need to create a certification policy and communicate it to your personnel.

The Internal PKI Implementation Checklist

❏ Review WS03 PKI information and familiarize yourself with key concepts
   An excellent place to start is with the "Designing a Public Key Infrastructure" chapter of
   the Windows Server 2003 Deployment Guide in the WS03 Resource Kit
❏ Define your certificate requirements
   ❏ Identify all the uses for internal certificates
   ❏ List them
   ❏ Define how they should be attributed
❏ Create your PKI architecture
   ❏ How many levels of certificate authorities will you require?
   ❏ How will you manage offline CAs?
   ❏ How many CAs are required?
❏ Create or modify the certificate types you require
   ❏ Determine if you need to use templates
     Templates are the preferred certificate attribution method
❏ Configure certificate duration
   Duration affects the entire infrastructure
   Root CAs should have certificates that last longer than subordinate CAs
❏ Identify how you will manage and distribute certificate revocation lists
❏ Identify your operations plan for the certificate infrastructure in your organization
   ❏ Who will manage certificates?
   ❏ Who can provide them to users?
   ❏ If smart cards are in use, how are they attributed?
   ❏ Who can revoke certificates?

Figure 8-9   The Internal PKI Implementation Checklist

Managing the Security Policy

The Castle Defense System provides a structured approach to the design of a security policy. But it cannot stand alone to defend your critical resources. It must be supplemented by a defense plan, a plan that includes both reactive and proactive defense measures. This means additional defenses at several levels, especially in terms of system resilience. This will be covered in Chapter 9.

There are also ongoing operations that must take place at regular intervals to ensure that your defense system is constantly monitored and that your reaction plans work properly. Simulations and fire drills are good practice. You will see how you respond and also if your response plan is adequate. You do not want to find yourself in a situation where the only response is unplugging a system. One of the keys to a solid response plan is ensuring that everyone in the organization knows and understands their role in the plan. Windows Server 2003 and Active Directory bring considerable change to the enterprise network. It is important that these changes are fully understood by your staff. It is also important that you identify each new role within your operations as well as the modifications you must bring to existing roles. Finally, to support your security policy to its fullest, you need to limit the delegated rights you assign to both administrators and operators within your network. These items will be covered in Chapter 10.

Best Practice Summary

This chapter recommends the following best practices:

- Implement a Security Policy.
- If you do not have a security model in place, use the Castle Defense System.
- Add support to the Castle Defense System by preparing a defense plan as outlined in the Enterprise Security Policy Design Blueprint.
- Round out security management activities by implementing security testing and monitoring.
- Ensure that you have comprehensive user awareness programs in place.

Layer 1: Critical Data

- Inventory and categorize all information in your network.
- Ensure that your applications make use of the security features within the engine they use to run. If you create applications using SQL Server, make sure you use the security features of SQL Server in addition to other security measures in your network.

Layer 2: Physical Protection

- Ensure that the physical protection aspects of your network are well documented and include redundant systems.
- Use two-factor authentication devices for administrators.

Layer 3: Operating System Hardening

- Secure your servers and computers at installation with the secedit command.
- Use security templates and the Security Configuration Manager to apply security settings to files and folders, the registry, and system services. Use GPOs for all other security settings.
- Remember to fully test all of your security configurations before deploying them, especially with corporate applications, because securing certain elements may stop applications from working.
- Protect your systems with an antivirus program and apply Software Restriction Policies.
- Always keep your directory permissions as simple as possible and try to use inherited permissions as much as possible.
- Ensure that all personnel with administrative rights to the directory can be fully trusted.
- Encrypt all offline data.
- Protect encrypted data through Windows PKI.

- Begin with the default security policies for managed code in the .NET Framework and refine them as you become more familiar with the use of this powerful application tool.

- If you intend to make extensive use of the .NET Framework, migrate all code to managed code as soon as you can. It will give you more granular security processes.

- Keep Internet Information Server off your servers unless it is an Application Server.

- Do not install IIS on domain controllers.

- When IIS is installed, configure its security level to the minimum required for the server role. Make this the first step in your configuration activities.

- At a minimum, use the IIS security template from the Microsoft Security Operations Guide to secure your IIS servers.

- Globally secure your IIS servers through Group Policy.

Layer 4: Information Access

- Modify the default policies within the Protected Forest Root Domain *before* creating child domains.

- Manage trusts carefully and use the UGLP Rule to assign permissions to users.

- Use a comprehensive authentication and authorization plan that covers Windows, Web servers, and the .NET Framework.

- Modify the Default Domain Policy to include a high-security Global Account Policy.

- Ensure that your developers use role-based authorization plans for the Web services they design.

- Enable auditing on key events within your network and monitor those audits.

Layer 5: External Access

- Create the root certificate authority of your Public Key Infrastructure as a standalone CA and remove it from the network once its certificates have been issued.

- Use a two-level CA hierarchy for internal purposes and make all second-level CAs enterprise CAs.

- Plan your PKI environment carefully before you implement it. Test it in a lab environment before deploying to your internal network.

- Ensure that communications between your domain controllers are encrypted through IPSec tunneling.

General Security

- Ensure that your security policy is always up to date and that all of your users are aware of it. Continue to provide regular communications to your user base on security issues.

Chapter Roadmap

Use the illustration in Figure 8-10 to review the contents of this chapter.

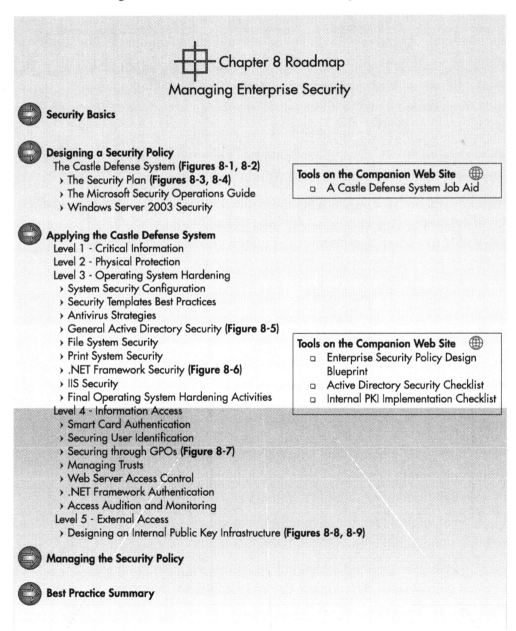

Figure 8-10 Chapter Roadmap

CHAPTER 9

Creating a Resilient Infrastructure

IN THIS CHAPTER

A significant element of security is system resiliency: ensuring that your services will not fail, even in the event of a disaster or a security breach. Several elements of system resiliency have already been covered to date:

- **Active Directory**   Resiliency here is created through the distribution of domain controllers throughout your network. It is also based on the multimaster replication system and the creation of an appropriate replication topology.

- **DNS**   By integrating the DNS service within the directory, you ensure that your network naming service will always function because it has the same resiliency as the directory service.

- **DHCP**   Your address allocation infrastructure has resilience built in because of the way you structured it with redundant scopes. In addition, if you place your DHCP servers in different sites, you also have a solution that would continue to work in the event of a disaster.

- **WINS**   Your legacy name resolution servers are redundant since the service is offered by the same servers as the DHCP service.

- **Object management infrastructure**   Your object management structure is resilient since it is based on the OU structure in the directory and the directory service offers system resilience.

- **Domain DFS roots**   Your file shares are resilient because they are distributed through the directory, making them available in multiple sites. They include automatic failover—that is, if the service fails in one site (or server), it automatically fails over to the other site (or server).

- **Volume Shadow Copies**   Your shared files, shared databases, Exchange stores, and other shared information deposits are protected through the Volume Shadow Copy feature, taking system snapshots on a regular basis and even allowing users to recover files themselves. This feature is described in Chapter 7.

- **Terminal Services**   The Terminal Services servers you deployed offer resilience through the Session Directory Server, but this server can be a single point of failure since it is the only server hosting this service.

Despite the fact that several of your systems are resilient, there remain areas that could cause significant impact on your operations if they failed. Remember, one of the most popular hacker attacks is *Distributed Denial of Service* (DDoS). This type of attack can succeed for two reasons: first, the server hosting the service is not protected; second, the service is hosted by a single server, so there is no failover service. This is not the only type of attack you may face, but it demonstrates the need for protection at several levels. Chapter 8 showed you how to protect your systems through the Castle Defense System. Now you need to add additional resiliency to the network through two strategies: system redundancy and system recovery.

Planning for System Redundancy

System redundancy relies on the implementation of methods and measures that ensure that if a component fails its function will immediately be taken over by another, or at the very least, the procedure to put the component back online is well documented and well known by system operators. A Windows 2000 News survey (http://www.w2knews.com/index.cfm?id=142&search=current%20admin%20headaches) identified that the most common administrator headaches at the beginning of 2002 were network security and disaster recovery. It's not surprising since, at that time, 9/11 was still fresh in everyone's mind. It is sad that such an event is required to remind people that these issues are at the very core of the enterprise network. Nevertheless, the issue stands: no matter what you do, you must ensure that your systems are protected at all times.

Once again, the Castle Defense System can help. Layer 1 helps you identify risk levels because it helps you determine the value of an information asset. Risk is determined by identifying value (the importance of an asset) and multiplying it by the risk factor that is associated with it. The formula looks like this:

```
risk = asset value * risk factor
```

For example, an asset that is valued at $1 million with a risk factor of .2 has a risk value of $200,000. This means that you can invest up to $200,000 to protect that asset and reduce its risk factor.

While these calculations can be esoteric in nature, what remains important is to invest the most in the protection of your most valued assets. This is one reason why it is so important to know what you have. Figure 9-1 is a good reminder of this principle.

By focusing on Physical Protection, Layer 2 also helps you plan for system redundancy. This is where some of the elements covered in Chapter 2's Server Sizing Exercise become important. Random arrays of inexpensive disks (RAID) and random arrays of inexpensive network (RAIN)

interface cards, for example, provide direct, hardware-level protection for your systems. It is also important to include uninterrupted power supply (UPS) systems at this level. This can either be individual USB-connected UPS devices (for regional servers) or centralized power management infrastructures that protect entire computer rooms (usually at central sites).

> **QUICK TIP**
>
> *The American Power Conversion Corporation (APC) provides information on three power protection architectures (central, zonal, and distributed) at http://www.apc.com/solutions/pps.cfm.*

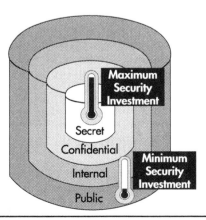

Figure 9-1 Information asset categories

The redundancy you build into your Physical Protection layer is only part of the solution. You'll need to ensure that you also have service redundancy. That can be accomplished through service clustering, either at the network level or the server level. Finally, you'll need to provide data redundancy. This is done through the elaboration and implementation of backup and recovery systems. Here it will be important to choose the right type of backup solution since you need to protect data that is stored not only in the file system, but also within databases such as the Active Directory.

Building redundancy in your systems is valuable only if you know it works. It's not enough to be prepared; you need to know that your preparation has value. To do so, you'll need to test and retest every redundancy level you implement in your network. Too many organizations have made the fatal error of backing up data for years without testing the recovery process, only to find out that the recovery doesn't work. This is not a myth. It actually happens. Don't let it happen to you. Test all your systems and document your procedures. In fact, this is an excellent opportunity for you to write standard operating procedures as outlined in Chapter 1.

Preparing for Potential Disasters

There are two types of disasters: natural and man-made. Natural disasters include earthquakes, tornadoes, fires, floods, hurricanes, and landslides. They are very hard to predict and even harder, but not impossible, to prevent. The best way to mitigate the impact of these types of disasters is to have redundant sites: your core servers and services are available at more than one site. If one is impaired for any reason, your other site takes over. This is also where the concept of the *Failsafe Server* introduced in Chapter 1 comes into play. This server is a standby server that is dormant, but can be activated quickly if required.

There are also man-made disasters: terrorist attacks, power failures, application failures, hardware failures, security attacks, or internal sabotage. These attacks are also hard to predict. Some require the same type of protection as for natural disasters. Others, such as application and hardware failures and security attacks, can be avoided through the Castle Defense System.

To determine the level of service protection you need to apply, you can use a service categorization that is similar to the Layer 1 categorization for data:

- *Mission-critical systems* are systems that require the most protection. Interruption of service is unacceptable because it affects the entire organization and its ability to function.

- *Mission-support systems* require less protection than mission-critical systems, but interruptions should be minimized as much as possible. These interruptions do not impact the entire organization.

- *Business-critical systems* are systems where short service interruptions can be acceptable because they impact only a portion of the business.

- *Extraneous systems* are deemed non-critical and can have longer lasting interruptions.

What most people seldom realize is that the basic network infrastructure for your enterprise network is, in many cases, part of the mission-critical level because if it does not work, nothing works.

Using WS03 Clustering Services

One of the areas that can add service resiliency is service clustering. Clustering services are, in fact, one of the major improvement areas for Windows Server 2003. Microsoft clustering services support three types of clusters:

- **Network Load Balancing (NLB)**   This service provides high availability and scalability for IP services (both TCP and UDP) and applications by combining up to 32 servers into a single cluster. Clients access the NLB cluster by using a single IP address for the entire group. NLB services automatically redirect the client to a working server.

- **Component Load Balancing (CLB)**   This service allows COM+ components to be distributed over as many as 12 servers. This service is not native to WS03; it is provided by Microsoft Application Center Server.

- **Server Clusters**   This service provides resilience through resource failover: if a resource fails, the client is automatically transferred to another resource in the cluster. Server Clusters can be composed of two to eight nodes.

These three clustering services work together to provide a complete service structure as is illustrated in Figure 9-2. It is important to note that clustering services are installed by default in the appropriate

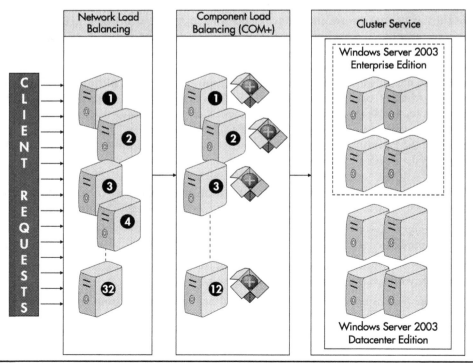

Figure 9-2   A complete clustering service structure

editions of WS03. Table 9-1 outlines the features and supported services for each clustering mode. Since CLB clustering is not native to WS03, it is not covered in this table.

▶ **NOTE**

You can view a complete cluster at work for yourself. Microsoft has a satellite and topographical map of the United States available at http://terraserver.homeadvisor.msn.com/.

As you can see, NLB and Server Clusters are rather complementary. In fact, it is not recommended to activate both services on the same server; that is, a Server Cluster should not also be a member of a NLB cluster. In addition, NLB clusters are designed to support more static connections. This means that it is not designed to provide the same type of failover as a Server Cluster. In the latter, if a user is editing a file and the server stops responding, the failover component will automatically be activated and the user will continue to perform his or her work without being aware of the failure (there may be a slight delay in response time). This is because the Server Cluster is designed to provide a mirrored system to the user. But an NLB cluster will not provide the same type of user experience. Its main purpose is to redirect demand to available resources. As such, these resources must be static in nature since they do not include any capability for mirroring information deposits.

Clustering Service	Network Load Balancing	Server Clusters
WS03 Edition	Web Standard Enterprise Datacenter	Enterprise Datacenter
Number of nodes	Up to 32	Up to 4 for WES Up to 8 for WDS
Hardware	All network adapters must be on the WS03 Hardware Compatibility List, especially RAIN NICs	Cluster hardware must be designed for WS03
Server role (as identified in Chapter 1)	Application Servers Dedicated Web Servers Collaboration Servers Terminal Servers	Identity Management (domain controllers) Application Servers File and Print Servers Dedicated Web Servers Collaboration Servers Network Infrastructure Servers
Applications	Web farms Internet Security and Acceleration Server (ISA) VPN servers Streaming Media Servers Terminal Services	SQL Servers Exchange servers Message Queuing servers

Table 9-1   WS03 Clustering Services

Both clustering services offer the ability to support four service requirements:

- **Availability**   By providing services through a cluster, it is possible to ensure that it is available during the time periods the organization has decreed it should be.
- **Reliability**   With a cluster, it is possible to ensure that users can depend on the service because if a component fails, it is automatically replaced by another working component.
- **Scalability**   With a cluster, it is possible to increase the number of servers providing the service without affecting the service being delivered to users.
- **Maintenance**   A cluster allows IT personnel to upgrade, modify, apply service packs, and otherwise maintain cluster components individually without affecting the service level of the cluster.

An advantage that Server Clusters have over NLB clusters is the ability to share data. Server Cluster resources can be tied to the same data storage resource, ensuring the transparency of the failover process. In fact, it is often a very good idea to tie Server Clusters to large-capacity data storage devices such as a storage area network (SAN) or network attached storage (NAS). In addition, WS03 includes several powerful storage management features and improvements over Windows 2000. It fully supports remote storage and offline storage management because, for the first time, it provides a single set of unified APIs for storage management.

NOTE

See "Redefining Windows Storage," by Ruest and Ruest, .NET Magazine *(May 2003) at http:// www.fawcette.com/dotnetmag/.*

Clusters do have disadvantages. They are more complex to stage and manage than standalone servers and services that are assigned to clusters must be cluster aware in order to take advantage of the clustering feature.

QUICK TIP

More information on WS03 clustering can be found at http://www.microsoft.com/technet/ treeview/default.asp?url=/technet/prodtechnol/ windowsserver2003/proddocs/SCCon_BP.asp.

Network Load Balancing

The basis of the NLB cluster is a virtual IP address: client systems connect to the virtual IP address and the NLB service redirects the client to a cluster member. If a cluster member fails or is taken offline, the NLB service automatically redirects requests to the other cluster members. When the member comes back online, it automatically rejoins the cluster and requests can be redirected to it. In most cases, the *failover* process—the process of redirecting clients to other cluster resources when a member fails—takes less than ten seconds. This delay is directly proportional to hardware power—the more powerful the hardware, the shorter the delay.

NLB cluster members do not share components. They are independent servers that host the same applications and local copies of the data client systems access. This is why NLB is best suited to *stateless* applications—applications that provide access to data mostly in read-only mode. NLB servers normally use two network interface cards. The first is dedicated to cluster network traffic and the second is for communications with clients and other normal network communications. Cluster network traffic from the member is mostly in the form of a heartbeat signal that is emitted every second and sent to the other members of the cluster. If a member does not send a heartbeat within five seconds, the other members automatically perform a convergence operation to remove the failed member from the cluster and eliminate it from client request redirections.

Since each cluster member uses identical data, it is often useful to optimize the server hardware to support fast read operations. For this reason, many organizations planning to use NLB clusters do not implement RAID disk subsystems because redundancy is provided by cluster members. Disk access is optimized because there is no RAID overhead during read and write operations. It is essential, however, to ensure that all systems are fully synchronized at all times. Whether or not you decide to construct NLB servers without RAID protection is a decision you will make when designing your NLB architecture. It will depend mostly on your data synchronization strategy, the type of service you intend to host on the server and the number of servers you intend to place in your NLB cluster.

The core of the NLB service is the wlbs.sys driver. It is a driver that sits between the network interface card and network traffic. It filters all NLB communications and sets the Member Server to respond to requests if they have been directed to it.

NLB is very similar to round robin DNS, but it provides better fault tolerance. Since the NLB service is hosted by every cluster member, there is no single point of failure. There is also immediate and automatic failover of cluster members.

▶ | **QUICK TIP**

You can combine round robin DNS with NLB to create multiple clusters supporting 32 members each.

Multicast versus Unicast Modes

NLB clusters operate in either Multicast or Unicast mode. The default mode is Unicast. In this mode, the NLB cluster automatically reassigns the MAC address for each cluster member on the NIC that is enabled in cluster mode. If each member has only one NIC, member to member communications are not possible in this mode. This is one reason why it is best to install two NICs in each server.

When using the Multicast mode, NLB assigns two multicast addresses to the cluster adapter. This mode ensures that all cluster members can automatically communicate with each other because there are no changes to the original MAC addresses. There are disadvantages to this mode though, especially if you use Cisco routers. The address resolution protocol (ARP) response sent out by a cluster host is rejected by these routers. If you use Multicast mode in an NLB cluster with Cisco routers, you must manually reconfigure the routers with ARP entries mapping the cluster IP address to its MAC address.

Whether you use one mode or the other, you should use two NICs on each member. One advantage of doing so is that it allows you to configure one card to receive incoming traffic and the other to send outgoing traffic, making your cluster members even more responsive. You can also ensure that if your NLB cluster is only the front end of a complex clustering architecture such as the one illustrated in Figure 9-2, all back end communications are handled by the non-clustered NIC.

If your NLB members are expected to handle extremely high traffic loads, you can use Gigabyte Ethernet cards to improve communication speed and host only the essential networking services on each card (for example, Client for Microsoft Networks should definitely be turned off on clustered NICs). If even higher loads are expected, you can also add more NICs in each member and bind the NLB service to each one, improving the overall response time for each member.

Single Affinity versus No Affinity

NLB clusters work in affinity modes. Each refers to the way NLB load balances traffic. *Single affinity* refers to load balancing based on the source IP address of the incoming connection. It automatically redirects all requests from the same address to the same cluster member. *No affinity* refers to load balancing based on both the incoming IP address and its port number. Class C affinity is even more granular than single affinity. It ensures that clients using multiple proxy servers to communicate with the cluster are redirected to the same cluster member. No affinity is very useful when supporting calls from networks using network address translation (NAT) because these networks only present a single IP address to the cluster. If you use single affinity mode and you receive a lot of requests from NAT networks, these clients will not profit from the cluster experience since all of their requests will be redirected to the same server.

However, if you use an NLB cluster to provide VPN connections using either L2TP/IPSec or PPTP sessions, you must configure your cluster in single affinity mode to ensure that client requests are always redirected to the same host. Single affinity should also be used for any application that uses sessions lasting over multiple TCP connections to ensure that the entire session is mapped to the same server. Finally, single affinity must be used if your client sessions use the secure sockets layer (SSL) to connect to NLB servers.

Single affinity does not give the same load balancing results as no affinity. Consider the type of requests your cluster will handle before deciding on your cluster architecture.

QUICK TIP

Microsoft provides detailed information on the deployment of NLB clusters in the Windows Server 2003 Deployment Guide*: "Deploying Network Load Balancing."*

Installing and Configuring NLB Clusters

NLB cluster installation is fairly straightforward. One great advantage is that the servers hosting your NLB applications do not have to have identical hardware, but each member should have enough disk space to host the application and each should have at least two network interface cards. You will also need to have some information on hand before you begin the installation though. The information you require is detailed in Figure 9-3.

The NLB Cluster Preparation Checklist

What you need on hand before creating the NLB cluster:

❑ The cluster's Internet name: the DNS name you intend to use for the cluster.

❑ The cluster's virtual IP address and the appropriate subnet mask: the address that will be linked to the DNS name.

❑ The current IP addresses and subnet masks for each cluster member.

❑ The cluster casting mode you want to use: Unicast or Multicast.

Note: If you use Multicast, you will also want to use IGMP Multicast to reduce the number of ports used to address cluster administration traffic and restrict it to the standard class D range; that is, 224.0.0.0 to 239.255.255.255.

❑ The cluster affinity mode you want to use: Single affinity, Class C or No affinity.

❑ Whether or not you want to enable remote control of the cluster using the NLB.EXE application.

Note: It is highly recommended not to enable this feature because it can cause a security risk. Any user with access to the NLB.EXE application can control a cluster. It is best to use the Network Load Balancing Manager console to administer your NLB clusters. Access to this console can be controlled better than access to NLB.EXE.

❑ The unique IDs you want to assign to each cluster member.

❑ The TCP and UDP ports for which you want NLB to handle traffic.

❑ The Load Weight or Handling Priority you will apply to the cluster.

Note: Load weight is used when you filter traffic to multiple cluster members. Handling priority is used when traffic is filtered only to a single cluster member.

Figure 9-3   The NLB Cluster Preparation Checklist

Now you're ready to set up your NLB cluster.

1. Begin by launching the Network Load Balancing Manager. Move to the Start Menu, select Administrative Tools, and click Network Load Balancing Manager.

2. This opens the NLB Manager MMC. To create a new cluster, right-click on Network Load Balancing Clusters in the left pane and select New Cluster.

3. This opens the Cluster Parameters dialog box. Type in the cluster's IP address and subnet mask, the cluster's DNS name, and indicate whether you want to use Unicast or Multicast mode. If you

choose Multicast mode, you should also enable IGMP Multicast. When you do so, WS03 gives you a warning message. Click OK to close it and then click Next.

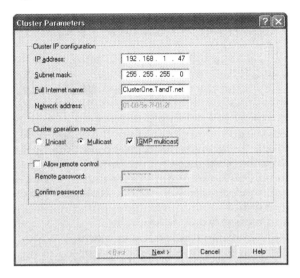

4. Here you can determine if you want to use more than one IP address for the cluster. Add IP addresses if required. Click Next when done.

5. The third dialog box allows you to define port rules for the cluster and the affinity mode for each rule. By default, all cluster members handle all TCP and UDP ports in Single Affinity mode. To modify this rule, click Edit. To add new rules, click Add. Click Next when done.

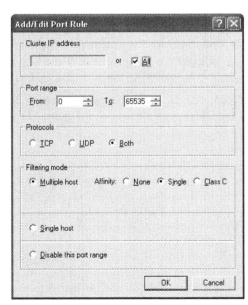

6. Now you can add cluster members. Type in the member's DNS name and click Connect. WS03 will locate the server and add it to the server list. Repeat for each member of the cluster. Click Next when done.

7. The final step is the configuration of each cluster member. Here you need to assign the Priority Number (1 to 32), the IP address and subnet mask, and the Default State for the NLB service. By default, the Default State is Started. Click Finish when done.

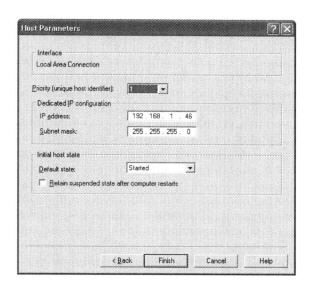

8. When you complete the process, the NLB service will perform a convergence to bring all the cluster members online.

You're done. From now on, you can manage the cluster—adding, deleting, and configuring members—through this console. You can even automate the setup of NLB clusters during the staging of the server using either Unattended or Disk Imaging installations with SysPrep.

▶ | **QUICK TIP**

Microsoft provides information on the automation of NLB cluster member setup at http:// www.microsoft.com/technet/treeview/default.asp?url=/technet/prodtechnol/windowsserver2003/ deploy/confeat/NLBclust.asp.

NLB Clusters will be very useful for load balancing Terminal Services, Streaming Media, Web application, and virtual private network servers within the enterprise network.

Multiple-Node Server Clusters

Server Clusters offer the same type of availability services as NLB clusters, but use a different model. Whereas in NLB clusters servers do not have to be identical, it is the purpose of the Server Cluster to make identical servers redundant by allowing immediate failover of hosted applications or services. As illustrated in Figure 9-2, Windows Server 2003 supports either four-node (with the Enterprise edition) or eight-node clusters (with the Datacenter edition).

Server Clusters can include several configurations. You can design the cluster so that each node will perform different tasks, but will be ready to fail over any of the other nodes' services and applications. Or you can design the cluster so that applications operate at the same time on each of the nodes. For example, you could design a four-node financial database cluster so that the first node managed order entry, the second order processing, the third payment services, and the fourth the other accounting activities. To do so, your application must be fully cluster aware—completely compliant with all of the Microsoft Cluster Services (MSCS) features. Not all applications or even WS03 services are fully cluster aware.

Cluster Compatibility List

Not all products are cluster compatible. In fact, even in Microsoft's own product offering, there are some particularities. Cluster compatibility can fall into one of three categories:

- **Cluster aware** A product or internal WS03 service that can take full advantage of the cluster service. It can communicate with the cluster API to receive status and notification from the Server Cluster. It can react to cluster events.

- **Cluster independent (or unaware)** A product or internal WS03 service that is not aware of the presence of the cluster, but that can be installed on a cluster and will behave the same way as if it was on a single server. It responds only to the most basic cluster events.

- **Cluster incompatible** A product or internal WS03 service that does not behave well in the context of a cluster and should not be installed on a Server Cluster.

Table 9-2 categorizes Microsoft's .NET Enterprise Servers and WS03 functions in terms of cluster compatibility.

Product or Service	Cluster Aware	Cluster Independent	Cluster Incompatible	Comment
Print services	X			Fully compliant
File sharing	X			Fully compliant
DFS	X			Standalone DFS roots only
Distributed Transaction Coordinator	X			Fully compliant

Table 9-2 Cluster Compatibility List

Product or Service	Cluster Aware	Cluster Independent	Cluster Incompatible	Comment
Microsoft Message Queuing	X			Fully compliant
SQL Server 2000 and above	X			Fully compliant
Exchange 2000 and above	X			Fully compliant
Project Central	X			Only the SQL Server portion
Active Directory	X			Compliant, but not recommended
DNS		X		Compliant, but not recommended
DHCP-WINS		X		Compliant, but should run as single instance
BizTalk Server		X		BizTalk 2000 has its own clustering mechanism, but can take advantage of a clustered SQL Server backend
Terminal Services		X		NLB clusters are preferred
IIS		X		NLB clusters are preferred
Content Management Server		X		Only the SQL Server portion
COM +		X		Component Load Balancing clusters preferred
SMS 2003		X		Under special conditions
Remote Installation Services			X	Not supported
Microsoft Operations Manager			X	Not supported
ISA Server 2000			X	NLB clusters are preferred, but supports its own clustering through server arrays
SharePoint Portal Server 2001			X	Not supported; coexistence with SQL or Exchange not recommended
Commerce Server			X	Component Load Balancing clusters preferred
NLB			X	Network Load Balancing should not be installed on a MSCS cluster
SharePoint Team Services			X	Only the SQL Server portion; IIS portion should use NLB

Table 9-2   Cluster Compatibility List *(continued)*

The information in Table 9-2 is subject to change, but it serves as a good starting point for determining what you can install on your clusters.

> **CAUTION**
>
> *You can also test your own applications for cluster compliance. See "How to pretest applications for Cluster Service Requirements" in the WS03 Help and Support Center.*

Server Cluster Concepts

The nodes in a Server Cluster can be configured in either active or passive mode. An *active* node is a node that is actively rendering services. A *passive* node is a node that is in standby mode, waiting to respond upon service failure. It goes without saying that, like the Failsafe Server role presented in Chapter 1, the passive node is an expensive solution because the server hardware is just waiting for failures. But if your risk calculations indicate that your critical business services require passive nodes, then you should implement them, because they provide extremely high availability in certain scenarios.

Most organizations use the active-active cluster mode. In fact, the most popular implementation of MSCS is the two-node active-active cluster. This is called a *cluster pack* because the cluster nodes share data. This cluster pack can be configured to either run exactly the same services at the same time (for example, Microsoft Exchange Server running on both nodes) or run different services on each node. In this configuration, each node is configured to run the same applications and services, but half are activated on the first node and half are activated on the other node. This way, if a service fails, the other node can provide immediate failover because it can run the service temporarily until the failed node can be repaired.

In active-active scenarios that run the same applications on all nodes, the applications must be fully cluster aware. This means that they can run multiple instances of the application and share the same data. Many applications include their own internal capabilities for supporting this operating mode. Applications that are not fully compliant—that are only cluster independent—should run in single instances. In either case, the servers you choose to create your Server Cluster should be sized so that they can take on the additional load node failures will cause. You can use the Server Sizing Exercise outlined in Chapter 2 to help identify the components you require for your cluster nodes. Properly sizing servers is essential to support application failover. This failover process is illustrated in Figure 9-4. It details how each node of a four-node cluster must be able to absorb the failure of each other node, until a single node is left. This is, of course, a worst case scenario.

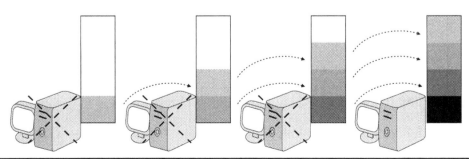

Figure 9-4   Node failover in a four-node cluster

You can configure your Server Clusters in many ways. In addition, on multiple node clusters, you can use a mix and match of multiple instance services or applications with single instance functions. If the application is mission-critical and cannot fail under any circumstances, you can configure it as a multiple instance on some nodes, and host it in passive mode on other nodes to have the best possible availability for the application.

Finally, be careful with your failover policies. A two- to four-node cluster can easily use random failover policies—the failed service is randomly distributed to the other available nodes—because the possible combination of resources is relatively small. But if you have more than four nodes in the cluster, it is a good idea to specify failover policies because the possible combination of resources will be too great and nodes may become overloaded during failover. The illustration in Figure 9-4 is an example of a random failover policy.

▶ *CAUTION*

Single instance applications are best suited for two-node clusters where one node runs the service and the other hosts the service in standby mode. That way, if the service fails on the running node, the second node can fail it over.

Cluster Configurations

Your cluster configuration will require the ability to share information about itself between the nodes. This is called a *quorum resource*. By default there is a single quorum resource per cluster. Each node of the cluster can access the quorum resource and know the state of the cluster. This resource is usually in the form of a shared storage system. Shared storage systems can be in the form of shared SCSI or fiber channels. SCSI systems are only supported in two-node clustering. Arbitrated loop fiber channel is also only supported for two-node clustering, but provides better scalability than SCSI systems because it can host up to 126 devices.

Switched fabric fiber channel is the only supported technology for clusters that includes more than two nodes. Here devices are connected in a many-to-many topology that supports the high availability and complex configuration requirements of multiple-node Server Clusters.

As in the NLB cluster, Server Cluster nodes should have two NICs: one for communication within the cluster, and one for communication with client systems and other network resources.

Geographically Dispersed Clusters

Windows Server 2003 supports the dispersion of clusters over multiple physical sites. This means that in addition to application or service resiliency, you can also add disaster recovery. If an entire site fails for some unforeseen reason, the cluster will continue to provide services to its client base because failover will occur in the other site or sites that contain cluster nodes. Geographically dispersed clusters are more particular than same-site clusters to configure because of the added difficulty of maintaining cluster consistency. In fact, if you want to create a multi-site cluster, you need to ensure that your WAN connection latency is not over 500 milliseconds. In addition, you need to configure a virtual LAN that regroups the multi-site nodes. If you can't meet these two conditions, you should not design multi-site clusters.

When configuring multi-site clusters, you need to use a new WS03 feature: *majority node sets*. Majority node sets are required because the multi-site cluster cannot share data sets since the nodes are not located in the same physical site. Therefore, the cluster service must be able to maintain and update cluster configuration data on each storage unit of the cluster. This is the function of the majority node set.

Figure 9-5 illustrates the difference between a single site and a multi-site cluster (or geo-cluster) in terms of storage and configuration data management.

> ### QUICK TIP
>
> *Testing server clusters is not simple because it requires a lot of hardware. Once again, you can use VMware's virtual machine technology to test both NLB and server clusters right on your own desktop or laptop. For information on how to use VMware Workstation to create server clusters, go to http://www.winnetmag.com/Articles/Index.cfm?ArticleID=37599. You will need a subscription to* Windows & .NET Magazine *to obtain the article.*

Final Server Cluster Considerations

Cluster server installation and deployment is not a simple task. It requires special hardware—hardware that is qualified to support Windows Server 2003 Server Clusters. For this reason, it will be essential for you to verify with the Windows Hardware Compatibility List (http://www.microsoft .com/hwdq/hcl/) that your cluster hardware is fully compatible with WS03. Then proceed with caution to ensure that your clusters are properly constructed. Ask for support from your hardware manufacturer. This will make sure your Server Clusters take full advantage of both the hardware's and WS03's high availability and reliability features.

In addition, you should take the following considerations into account:

- **Majority Node Clustering**   WS03 supports only two-site Majority Node Clustering. The WS03 majority node feature does not manage data replication for applications; this function must be available within the application itself. It is also important to note that majority node sets cannot survive with a single node. They need to have a majority of the nodes available to

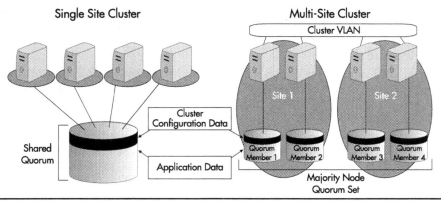

Figure 9-5   Single versus multi-site cluster configurations

continue operating. Single quorum clusters can, on the other hand, survive with just one node because the quorum data is stored in a single location.

• **Clustering Identity Servers**   It is *not recommended* to cluster domain controllers because of the nature of this service. For example, the Flexible Single Master of Operations roles cannot be failed over and may cause service outages if the hosting node fails. In addition, it is possible for the DC to become so busy that it will not respond to cluster requests. In this situation, the cluster will fail the DC because it will think it is no longer working. Carefully consider your options when deciding to cluster DCs.

• **Cluster Server Security**   The clustering API only uses NLTM authentication. Therefore, it does not provide mutual authentication between the client and the server during remote administration. For this reason, cluster operations have been highly secured in WS03. In fact, only the cluster administrator has the rights to manage and view cluster data. This is different from Windows NT and Windows 2000. It is important to note that WS03 clusters should be clean installations because upgrades from NT and 2000 will carry over their existing security modes. This could allow unauthorized personnel to view cluster data.

These are not the only considerations to take into account when creating and installing Server Clusters, but they provide a good reference and foundation before you begin. The best thing to do is to determine where Server Clusters will help you most. Use the details in both Tables 9-1 and 9-2 to help you make the appropriate clustering decisions.

QUICK TIP

Microsoft provides detailed information on the deployment of Server Clusters in the Windows Server 2003 Deployment Guide*: "Designing Server Clusters." Another chapter, "Installing on Cluster Nodes," outlines all of the activities required for cluster server installations. Finally, Microsoft provides information on the automation of Server Cluster member setup at http:// www.microsoft.com/technet/treeview/default.asp?url=/technet/prodtechnol/windowsserver2003/ deploy/confeat/MSCclust.asp.*

Server Consolidation

As mentioned in Chapter 1, Windows Server 2003 offers some exceptional opportunities for server consolidation. This leads to fewer servers to manage. These servers, though, have a more complex structure because they include more services than the single purpose server model used in the NT world.

But server consolidation does not necessarily mean more complex server structure; it can just mean more with less. For example, Microsoft has tested two-node Server Clusters that manage upwards of 3,000 printers. This means that you could greatly reduce the number of Print Servers in your organization, especially in large office situations where network connections are high speed and printer management can be centralized.

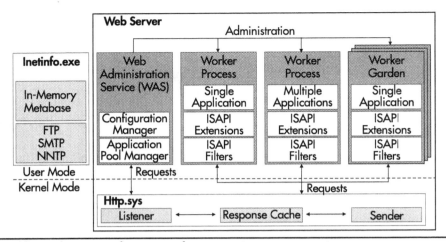

Figure 9-6   The architecture of Internet Information Server version 6

The same goes for file servers. The same WS03 server can manage up to 5,000 domain DFS roots. A Server Cluster can manage up to 50,000 standalone DFS roots—another opportunity for massive server consolidation and considerable cost savings.

Internet Information Server (IIS) also offers great consolidation opportunities because of its WS03 architecture. By placing the HTTP.SYS driver within the WS03 kernel, Microsoft has isolated it from the general operation of IIS services, making it more stable. This segregation now supports worker process isolation, meaning that any hosted Web site can operate completely independently from all of the others. In fact, Microsoft states that worker process isolation is so powerful, an Internet service provider (ISP) could actually host Web sites from highly competitive firms on the same server without their knowledge and without any impact on each other. The new IIS architecture, as shown in Figure 9-6, outlines how each worker process is completely isolated. In addition, this isolation allows the creation and operation of *Web gardens*, special affinity groups that can be assigned to specific server resources such as CPUs and memory. The Web garden concept allows you to ensure that critical Web sites get the resources they need even if they share server hardware. This again provides an excellent opportunity for consolidation.

Consolidation Through Server Baselining

The best way to identify consolidation opportunities is to create server baselines and base your service level agreements on them. Server baselines tell you what level of operation is acceptable for a given service under normal workloads and conditions. As you migrate services from your existing network to the new parallel network, you have the opportunity to re-architect and redesign them. Operations that used multiple small servers in your existing network can easily be consolidated into Server Clusters in the new network so long as they meet the performance baselines of the older network.

To do so, you need to have established baselines and standard measurement systems. This is where performance monitoring comes into play. Windows Server 2003 uses System Monitor to evaluate server performance. System Monitor is accessed through the Performance shortcut in Administrative Tools.

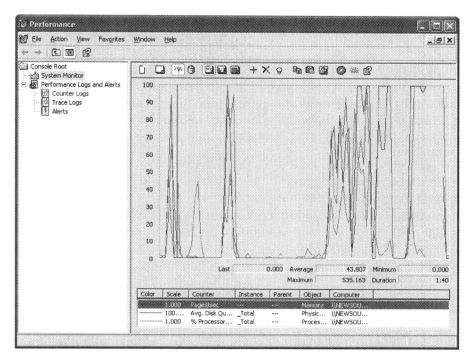

System Monitor manages three performance object counters by default: pages per second, average disk queue length, and percent processor time. These are the three core monitors for establishing a server baseline, but there are more. Some of the important object counters to monitor while creating baselines are:

- Free disk space (percent free physical disk space and percent free logical disk space)
- Disk usage time (percent physical disk time and percent logical disk time)
- Disk reads and writes (physical disk reads per second and physical disk writes per second)
- Disk queuing (average disk queue length)—*active by default*
- Memory usage (available memory bytes)
- Memory paging (memory pages per second)—*active by default*
- Paging file activity (percent paging file usage)
- Processor usage (percent processor time)—*active by default*
- Interrupts (processor interrupts per second)
- Multiple processor usage (system processor queue length)
- Server service (total server bytes per second)
- Server work items (server work item shortages)
- Server work queues (server work queue length)
- Server paged pool (server pool paged peak)

Use the Explain button in System Monitor to learn what each setting refers to. Monitor these settings over time in the older network to identify what has been deemed acceptable to date. Set up your consolidated servers in your lab environment and stress test them to see if their performance fits within the parameters you have identified. When you deploy your servers, ensure that you continue to monitor their performance. You can use System Monitor or Microsoft Operations Manager (MOM) to do so. MOM actually includes several "management packs" that allow you to monitor special server roles. This facilitates the monitoring and baseline exercise. Keep in mind that performance evaluation itself affects server performance in your calculations. More information on MOM can be found at http://www.microsoft.com/mom/.

Once you are confident that you know how your servers should perform, set or adjust your service level agreements based on this performance. Then, if you see long-term performance deviations, you can increase server capacity through its growth mechanisms.

QUICK TIP

Microsoft provides stress testing tools for its Windows platforms. It can help out in the server baselining process, especially in the evaluation of server interrupts per second. Just search for "stress tool" at http://www.microsoft.com/technet/default.asp.

Planning for System Recovery

Even though you have done your best to ensure high availability for your servers and services, disasters can always happen and servers can always go down. This is why it is important to prepare for system recovery. No system is perfect, but the more protection levels you apply to your systems, the less chance you have of losing data and experiencing downtime. Therefore you need to implement data protection strategies.

Backing up and restoring WS03 data is a complex process, but it has been greatly simplified by new WS03 features such as the Volume Shadow Copy Service. In fact, the built-in backup tool automatically initiates a shadow copy before taking a backup. Backups are an important part of the recovery operation, but they are not its only component. WS03 offers several different recovery strategies. Some of these will be familiar to you if you've worked with Windows NT before (or Windows 2000), but WS03 also includes new features that are specific to this operating system.

Recovery Planning for the Enterprise Network

Recovering enterprise systems is never an easy task. The best way to avoid having to recover systems is by using a multilayered protection strategy. But if you do get to the stage where a recovery operation is required, you must have a detailed strategy to follow. Like every other operation in the enterprise network, recoveries must be planned. Your recovery strategy must begin with an understanding of the operating system's own recovery capabilities. Next, once you're familiar with the tools the operating system offers to help you recover systems, you can outline or adjust your recovery strategy. Finally, you can integrate your troubleshooting strategy to the new or updated recovery strategy.

Recovery Strategies for Windows Server 2003

Recovery strategies for WS03 depend on the type of problem you encounter, of course, but they include:

- **Driver rollback**   If you install an unstable driver on your system, you can use the driver rollback feature to restore the previous version of a driver so long as you can still log into your system. This is done by viewing the device properties in the Device Manager (System Properties | Hardware tab), moving to the Driver tab, and selecting Roll Back Driver.

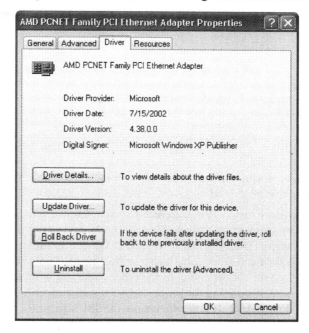

- **Disabling devices**   You can also disable devices that are not operating properly. This is done by moving to the Device Manager, locating the device, right-clicking on it, and selecting Disable from the context menu.

- **Last Known Good Configuration**   Just like Windows NT and 2000, WS03 includes a Last Known Good Configuration startup choice. This reverts to the last configuration saved in the registry before you applied changes. This is done by pressing the F8 key during system startup. This will also give you access to a number of different startup modes, Safe Mode, Safe Mode with Networking, and so on. These are also operation modes you can use to repair WS03 installations.

- **Recovery Console**   In Chapter 2, you installed the Recovery Console as part of your standard WS03 server staging process. This console allows you to perform recovery operations such as disabling services, copying device drivers or other files to the system, and otherwise repairing an installation. Installing the console saves you from requiring the Windows Server 2003 original installation CD to perform a repair because the Recovery Console is listed as an operating system in your startup choices.

- **Windows PE** Chapter 2 also outlined how to use Windows PE to create a bootable CD that will boot into a character-based Windows environment. This is also an excellent recovery tool because Windows PE will give you access to both network drives and local NTFS drives during your repair process.

- **Emergency Management Services** As described in Chapter 2, if you have appropriate hardware, you can use Windows Server 2003's Emergency Management Services (EMS) to remotely manage and administer servers when problems arise. EMS is mostly oriented to "headless" servers— servers without monitors or human interface devices such as keyboards and mice.

> ## CAUTION
>
> *Anyone who has physical access to a server and the administrator password for that server can use these tools and technologies to severely damage the server. Make sure that physical access to servers is tightly controlled as outlined in Layer 2 of the Castle Defense System.*

- **Volume Shadow Copy** Users and administrators can restore any data file that is still available within the shadow copy store.

- **Backup and restore** Using the default backup tool included within Windows Server 2003, you can backup and restore data to removable medium or to spare disk drives.

- **Automated System Recovery** The Automated System Recovery (ASR) option is a tool that allows you to reconstruct a non-working system. It is composed of two portions: ASR Preparation Wizard and ASR Restore. The Preparation Wizard captures everything on a system, from disk signatures to system state and other data. It also creates an ASR boot floppy disk. Then if you need to restore the system because none of the other strategies outlined in this section work, you simply start system setup using the proper WS03 installation CD, press F2 when prompted, and insert the ASR floppy. ASR Restore will restore the disk signatures, install a minimal version of Windows, and restore all system and data files. It is not 100 percent perfect, but it is the best recovery tool to date to come with Windows. More on ASR will be covered later in this chapter.

- **Third-party backup and restore tools** There are a number of third-party tools that are designed for backup and restore for Windows Server 2003 systems. When selecting a third-party product, there are three key elements you must consider: integration to the Volume Shadow Copy APIs to take advantage of this feature, complete system recovery from floppy disk (comparable to the ASR), and integration to Active Directory. The latter is the most important aspect because tools that integrate directly to AD are rare. This issue will be discussed more in detail later in this chapter.

System Recovery Strategies

A system recovery strategy should include the following activities:

- Service interruption is detected.

- The interruption type is identified and has been categorized through your troubleshooting strategy.

- Risk has been evaluated and identifies the level of response.

- The recovery plan for this problem and level of risk is put into action.
- A "Plan B" is ready in case the main recovery plan does not work for some reason.
- The results of recovery actions are fully tested to ensure everything is back to normal.
- Secondary recovery actions are performed; for example, broken servers that were taken offline are repaired, or users are notified that their files are back online.
- The incident is documented and the procedure is updated, if required.

A recovery strategy is based on the activities outlined in Figure 9-7. Here, it is important to detail the actual recovery plan for each type of situation. This is one reason why risk evaluation is so important. You may not have time to document recovery processes for every single disaster situation, but if you have taken the time to evaluate risks, you can ensure that the most critical situations are documented. In the end you will have multiple recovery plans that will "plug into" your recovery strategy. All of these should be SOPs.

If possible, you should also have the Failsafe Server, geo-clusters, or a hot site—a separate site that mirrors your production site and that can take over in the case of a disaster.

Troubleshooting Techniques

The final element of the system recovery process is a sound troubleshooting strategy. This is the strategy your operations staff will use to identify the type of disaster they are facing. It is essential that this strategy be clear and standard, because it is critical to the recovery process. If the issue you are facing is wrongly identified, it may cause a worse disaster.

In general, help requests and problem reports should be dealt with through an organized, scientific approach that treats system errors as always being causal—that is, problems don't just happen. Problems are deviations from a norm that have distinct, identifiable causes. The troubleshooting technician's job is to logically deduce causes of problems based on his or her knowledge of how the system works. The best way to do this is to use a standard procedure. The steps outlining the troubleshooting procedure are illustrated in Figure 9-8. Note that complex problems (more than one cause-effect relationship) may require several iterations of this process.

One of the important aspects of troubleshooting is problem classification. In clearly defining errors, it is often helpful to categorize errors according to the circumstances surrounding the occurrence. Table 9-3 provides a non-exhaustive list of problem classifications.

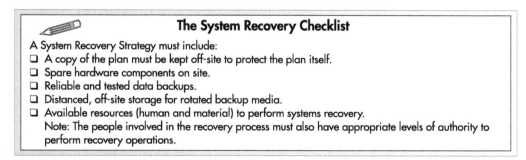

The System Recovery Checklist

A System Recovery Strategy must include:
- ☐ A copy of the plan must be kept off-site to protect the plan itself.
- ☐ Spare hardware components on site.
- ☐ Reliable and tested data backups.
- ☐ Distanced, off-site storage for rotated backup media.
- ☐ Available resources (human and material) to perform systems recovery.
  Note: The people involved in the recovery process must also have appropriate levels of authority to perform recovery operations.

Figure 9-7   The System Recovery Checklist

✏️   **The Troubleshooting Checklist**

❑ Document appropriate information: for example, the time, date, machine, and user information.
❑ Document all relevant information concerning the problem. Refer to baseline system operation information if necessary.
❑ Create itemized problem description. Answer these questions:
   ❑ Is the problem reliably reproducible or random?
   ❑ Is it related to the time of day?
   ❑ Is the problem user-specific?
   ❑ Is it platform specific?
   ❑ Is it version specific?
   ❑ Is it related to hard disk free space?
   ❑ Is it network traffic related?
   ❑ What is it *not?*
❑ Research similar occurrences in your internal troubleshooting databases and other sources.
❑ Create a reasonable hypothesis based on all of the available information.
❑ Test the hypothesis and document the results.
   Note: If the test successfully cures the problem, document and close the case. If unsuccessful modify the hypothesis or, if necessary, create a new hypothesis. Repeat the hypothesize-then-test cycle until resolved.

Figure 9-8   The Troubleshooting Checklist

▶ | **QUICK TIP**

When identifying problems, review the Windows Server 2003 Help and Support Center. Also, review external troubleshooting databases such as Microsoft TechNet (http://www.microsoft.com/technet/) and the Microsoft Knowledge Base (http://support.microsoft.com/default.aspx?scid=fh;[ln];kbhowto). It is also a good idea to draw on the expertise of your coworkers and of course, Microsoft Premier Support at https://premier.microsoft.com/ (you need an account with the latter).

Problem Classifications	Key Characteristics
Installation	Procedure, media, hardware/software requirements, network errors
Peripherals	Keyboard, video display, hardware components, drivers
Network	Adapter configuration, traffic, cabling, transmission devices
Bootstrap	Missing files, hardware failures, boot menu
Logon	User accounts, validating server, registry configuration, network access
User Configuration	Redirected folders, User Profiles, group memberships
Security	File encryption, access rights, permissions
Service Startup	Dependent services, configuration
Application	Application-specific errors
Procedural	User education, control processes

Table 9-3   Sample Problem Classifications

As you can see, the troubleshooting procedure outlined here is not only used in disasters. It can be used in all troubleshooting situations. But, for disasters, the key to the troubleshooting and recovery strategy is the quality of your backups. This is why the backup strategy is one of the most important elements of your system resiliency design.

Data Protection Strategies

Backing up your systems will mean backing up several types of information: user data, corporate data, databases, documents, system state information for your servers, and Active Directory data. As mentioned earlier, you can use either the WS03 Backup Utility (in either graphical or command-line mode) or a third-party backup tool to perform these backups. Whichever one you use, make sure that you use a standard backup strategy, creating backup sets of specific data types—for example, creating only user data backups in one backup set and only system data in another. This will simplify the restoration process.

Data backups are rather straightforward: select the data drive and back it up. Remember that WS03 will automatically create a shadow copy before backing up the data. In fact, the backup set is created from shadow copy data. This avoids issues with open files. Shadow copy also has special APIs that enable it to work with databases such as SQL Server and Exchange Server, making the snapshots valid even for databases.

Figure 9-9 outlines a sample data, System State, and Automated System Recovery backup strategy. Basically both data and System States should be backed up on a daily basis. ASRs should be taken on a weekly basis. System States and data backups can be incremental or differential during weekdays. Differentials are preferred; they take more space, but are faster to restore since they include all the new data on the same backup set. On weekends, you can take full backups of both. ASR backups are full backups by default.

▶ **CAUTION**

The System State backups shown in Figure 9-9 include both the System State and system and boot volumes. In the case of an enterprise network server, this means backing up the System State and drive C.

You need to support your backup strategy with both a remote storage solution and offsite media storage. WS03 includes several features to support remote storage, but the solution you use will depend on the overall storage technology you will have in place. If you use a SAN or NAS, it will include remote storage capabilities. You will need to ensure that you have a safe offline storage space for media. You should rotate offsite media on a regular basis. For example, every second complete backup should be stored offsite in a controlled environment.

The schedule proposed in Figure 9-9 outlines a four-week retention strategy. This means that you retain backup media for a period of four weeks. If you keep every second copy offsite, then you are always only a week away from complete disaster. In addition, your archiving schedule will outline which copies you should keep offsite on a permanent basis.

System State Backups

System State backups are more complex for administrators because these are the tools that protect the operating system itself (remember, system and data drives were separated at system staging in Chapter 2).

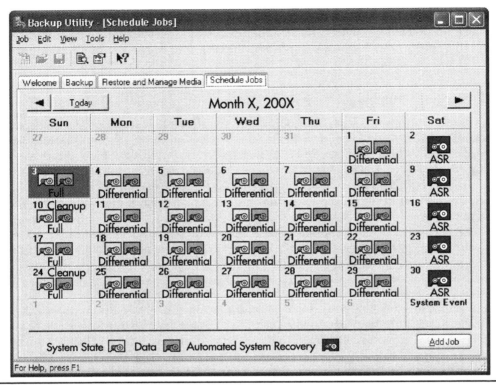

Figure 9-9 Sample data, System State backup, and ASR strategy

It is thus important to fully understand what is found in a System State backup. There are nine potential elements to a System State backup. Some are always backed up and others depend on the type of server you are backing up. They are identified as follows:

- The system registry
- The COM+ class registry database
- Boot and system files
- Windows File Protection System files
- Active Directory Database (on domain controllers)
- SYSVOL folder (on DCs as well)
- Certificate services database (on certificate servers)
- Cluster service configuration information (on Server Clusters)
- IIS metadirectory (on Web Application Servers)

System State data is always backed up as a whole; it cannot be segregated. The System State backup is performed by selecting System State in the Backup Utility screen, under the Backup tab.

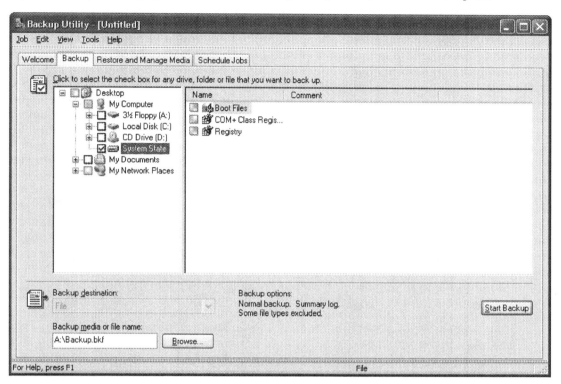

> ## QUICK TIP
>
> *Launch NTBackup through the shortcut in All Programs | Accessories | System Tools from the Start Menu. By default, the backup tool starts in wizard mode. To ensure that you always start in Advanced mode, uncheck the Always start in wizard mode box.*

Selecting Third-Party Backup Tools

One of the most important aspects of the selection of a third-party backup tool is its awareness of the System State data. Many backup tools, especially backup tools that are designed to back up Windows data and store it on central mainframe servers, are "dump" backup tools. All they do is copy a file from the Windows server to the mainframe. You need to use the NTBackup utility in WS03 to first create a backup to file on a data disk, and then the mainframe backup tool takes a copy of this backup file. While the merit for this backup strategy is debatable because it is true that mainframe storage is all right to use in certain scenarios, especially in organizations that have not moved to central Windows storage systems such as storage area networks (SAN) or network attached storage (NAS), this strategy becomes inviable when it is time to restore a Windows server.

As you know, restoring Windows servers can be complex. As stated earlier, it is much easier now with the coming of the ASR, but it is still a complex process. Restoring a server from a backup that is stored on a mainframe is well-nigh impossible. First, you must recover the backup file from the mainframe, then you must begin the restore process, often installing a limited version of Windows, then restore the data, and finally, restart the server hoping everything is all right. In fact, in these situations, it is often useful to have a second operating system already installed on the server to make the restoration process simpler, but as mentioned in Chapter 8, this second copy of an OS can be a security risk.

It is often much simpler and faster to use Remote Installation Services (RIS) to reinstall the server from scratch and simply restore the data portion of the server. If this is the case, your expensive mainframe-based backup solution does not fit the bill.

▶ **QUICK TIP**

If you need to choose a third-party backup tool, make sure the restore process is part of your evaluation criteria.

There are a number of third-party backup solutions on the market that are specifically designed for Windows Server 2003. They all meet specific criteria, which must include:

• Being aware of System State data
• Being integrated to the Volume Shadow Copy (VSC) feature, triggering a VSC before launching a backup operation
• Enabling complete system recovery from a simple process comparable to the ASR
• Being Active Directory aware

Meeting these four basic criteria is essential. There are others, of course, such as integrating with massive storage products that are supported by Windows, including special drivers for SQL Server and Exchange, and so on. But the four listed here are the core requirements for an intelligent third-party backup solution.

Using NT Backup

The Backup utility found in Windows Server 2003 (NTBackup) has greatly improved with this edition of Windows. It now includes a comprehensive graphical interface that includes three operating modes:

• The Backup Wizard, which takes users through a backup or restore operation
• The Advanced Backup interface, which is more appropriate for enterprise system administrators
• The command line backup tool

It is the Advanced Backup interface that has changed the most. The startup screen now includes an ASR button instead of the Emergency Repair Disk button found in Windows 2000.

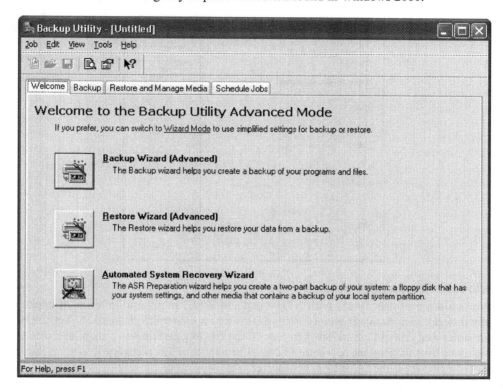

In addition, it includes the Schedule Jobs tab. This tab allows you to schedule backups directly within the graphical interface, making it much easier than in Windows NT where you had to create a command line script and integrate the script with scheduled tasks.

NTBackup also includes the Automated System Recovery feature which creates a comprehensive system backup and supports system restoration from a single restore floppy disk. Creating an ASR backup is simple. Just click on the ASR button on the Advanced Backup startup screen.

Once the backup is complete, you can view a report of the backup operation. In fact, this displays the backup log. You should store these logs in a safe place because they are very useful for quickly locating files that need to be restored. They are simple text files that can be searched much faster than a restore through the Backup utility. With the addition of the ASR, NTBackup becomes a much more viable backup solution than ever before, but it is not, by far, an enterprise backup solution.

Authoritative Active Directory Restores

One of the most significant issues with NTBackup and WS03 in general in terms of backup and especially restoration is Active Directory. Active Directory is a complex database. Often, the best way to restore a downed domain controller is to rebuild the DC to a certain level, then let multimaster replication take over to bring the server up to date. The impact of this recovery strategy is that it taxes the network, especially if the DC is a regional server. It all depends on the level to which you rebuild the server and the obsolescence of the data it contains.

Fortunately, WS03 lets you stage DCs with offline media. This means that you can create an Active Directory Database backup on compact disk and use it to stage or restore DCs. The more recent the CD, the less replication is required. Recoveries of this type are not too complex. These recoveries assume that the data within the other replicas of the Directory Database is *authoritative*—it is valid data. It also means that there was no critical and unreplicated data within the downed DC.

The issue arises when there is critical data within a downed DC, data that is not within the other replicas, or when an error occurs and data within the directory is damaged and must be restored. In this case, you must perform an authoritative restore. This is where you begin to find the limitations of NTBackup.

Active Directory manages directory replication through update sequence numbers (USNs). They can be thought of as change counters and represent the number of modifications on a domain controller since the last replication. Values for objects and properties that have the highest USN are replicated to other domain controllers and replace the values that are in the copies of the Directory Database located on the target DCs. USNs are also used to manage replication conflicts. If two domain controllers have the same USN, then a timestamp is used to determine the latest change. Thus, when you perform a normal AD restore, data that is restored from backup is updated according to the information in other domain controllers. In fact, it is overwritten if the USN for the data in other DCs is higher than the USN for the data in the restored DC.

When you need to restore data from a crashed DC that included critical data—data that is not found in the current version of the directory (for example, someone deleted an entire OU and it has been replicated to all DCs)—you need to perform an *authoritative* restore. In this restore, the information you will recover from backup will take precedence over the information in the directory even if the USNs are of a lower value.

To perform an authoritative restore, you must begin with a normal restore. Then once the data is restored and the domain controller is still offline, you use the NTDSUTIL tool to make the restore authoritative. The authoritative restore can include all or just a portion of the restored AD data. Here's how:

1. Repair the server if required and start it up. During startup, press F8 to view the startup modes.
2. Select the Directory Services Restore Mode and press ENTER.
3. This will boot into Windows. Log into the local administrator's account.
4. Launch the backup utility and perform the restore.
5. Once the restoration is finished, reboot the server.
6. Press F8 once again to select Directory Services Restore Mode and press ENTER.
7. Log into the local administrator's account.
8. Launch the command prompt and type **ntdsutil**.
9. In the NTDSUTIL tool, type the following commands:

```
authoritative restore
restore database
```

10. Type **quit** and restart the server in normal mode.

Once the server is restarted, the replication process will start and the restored information will be replicated to other domain controllers.

If you want to restore only a portion of the directory, use the following restore command:

```
restore subtree ou=ouname,dc=dcname,dc=dcname
```

For the Services OU in the Intranet.TandT.net domain, you would use the following command:

```
restore subtree ou=services,dc=intranet,dc=tandt,dc=net
```

As you can see, restoring information that can be deleted from a simple operator error can be quite complex when using the default WS03 backup utility. This is one of the key reasons why you would consider using a comprehensive backup technology, a technology that is specifically designed to integrate and support all of Windows Server 2003's features.

CommVault Galaxy

CommVault Systems, a Microsoft Gold Certified Partner, produces a backup technology called Galaxy (http://www.commvault.com/products.asp). Galaxy is an enterprise data protection technology that is fully integrated with Windows Server 2003. It fully supports backing up and restoring System State data; it is integrated with the Volume Shadow Copy Service; it provides a feature similar to the ASR, allowing administrators to restore downed servers from scratch using a recent backup; and it fully knows and understands Active Directory. It also includes intelligent agents for SQL Server and the Web Store, the database used to store both Exchange and SharePoint Portal Server data.

What this means is that you can perform object and attribute restorations directly within the Active Directory without having to go through the complex operations required to perform traditional authoritative restores. In addition, Galaxy can restore single objects directly within the Exchange Web Store. This means you can restore single email messages without the hassles normally required to perform such an operation.

Galaxy is one of the only data protection tools on the market that can perform restores to the Active Directory without having to take the domain controller offline. If an operator makes a mistake and modifies the wrong data or even performs a modification that must be reversed, you simply use the Galaxy Recovery Console to select the item to be restored, restore it, and it appears in the directory within moments. It is automatically assigned a new USN, which means that it will automatically replicate to other domain controllers and restore the AD to the desired state.

As can be seen in Figure 9-10, Galaxy offers agent modules for a comprehensive list of products, including Active Directory, SQL Server, Exchange, SharePoint Portal Server, and SAN/NAS hardware.

Figure 9-10   During installation, Galaxy displays the different agents it supports

> **QUICK TIP**
>
> *Enterprise data protection technologies are also very useful for data migration. One of the best ways to migrate data from the legacy network to the parallel network is through backups and restores. Back up the data with security properties from the old network (NT or Windows 2000) and restore it to the new network (WS03). It will retain its security properties and users will have appropriate access rights through SID history.*

Finalizing Your Resiliency Strategy

Choosing the right data protection technology is a core element of your resiliency strategy, but as you have seen here, it is not the only element. You need to design and implement the proper processes and ensure they are followed. This is an excellent opportunity for the design of standard operating procedures.

In addition, you must ensure that your data protection strategies complement your system redundancy strategies. One of the key elements of the former is integrated and regular testing: your backup tapes or other media must be tested on a regular basis. Fire drills are also an excellent testing procedure.

Resiliency is at the core of the enterprise network. It is also at the final preparation stage of the parallel network. Now your network is ready to provide complete services to your enterprise. Two key elements have yet to be covered before the parallel network is fully operational:

- The migration of both users and data into the parallel network as well as the decommission of the legacy network.

- The modification of operational roles within your IT organization to cover new and sometimes integrated administrative activities for the new network.

Both of these elements will be covered in the final chapter of this book, Chapter 10.

Best Practice Summary

This chapter recommends the following best practices:

- Use the risk calculation formula to determine the appropriate system resilience design for each type of resource and service.

Network Load Balancing Clusters

- Do not install both Network Load Balancing services and Server Clusters on the same machine.
- Ensure that you use NLB clustering with resources that are static in nature.

- Use at least two NICs in each NLB cluster member.
- If you use Multicast mode in an NLB cluster with Cisco routers, ensure that you manually reconfigure the routers with ARP entries mapping the cluster IP address to its MAC address.
- If you use an NLB cluster to provide VPN connections using either L2TP/IPSec or PPTP sessions, you must configure your cluster in single affinity mode to ensure that client requests are always redirected to the same host.
- Do not enable remote control for NLB clusters; use the NLB Manager console for all administrative operations.

Server Clusters

- Use active-active clusters to reduce costs while increasing availability.
- If you use multiple instance applications, you must ensure that they are cluster aware.
- For essential services that need added resilience, use two-node clusters in active-active mode and configure the services to run in single instances on each node.
- If you configure multi-site clusters, make sure that you configure a VLAN to regroup the cluster nodes and that the WAN connection latency is below 500 milliseconds.
- Monitor majority node clusters carefully because they always require a majority of the nodes to continue operation during system failures.
- If at all possible, avoid clustering domain controllers. DCs provide their own redundancy system through multimaster replication.
- Secure your Server Clusters carefully and ensure that cluster administrative accounts are well protected.
- Use Microsoft Clustering Services to consolidate services and reduce the number of servers in your enterprise. Ensure that you create server performance baselines to evaluate your consolidation opportunities.

System Recovery

- Begin by learning and understanding the operating system's potential recovery features.
- Design or update your recovery strategy based on what you learned about the operating system's recovery features.
- Integrate your troubleshooting strategy to the recovery process.
- Create standard problem classifications and use them to categorize problems. Use these categories in your risk analysis process.

Backup and Restore

- Separate System State and data backups in your backup strategy; it will be easier to restore data in this manner.

- Make sure you educate users about the Shadow Copy feature and self-service restoration of files; this will greatly reduce your restoration workload.

- Use an enterprise data protection technology. If your information is critical to your business, you cannot afford to rely on the default backup utility even if it is more intelligent in Windows Server 2003.

- When you choose a third-party data protection technology, make sure the restore process is part of your evaluation criteria. Ensure that it is integrated to Active Directory and supports inline restores to the attribute level.

- Test all of your backups to make sure they work to recover data. Perform these tests on a regular basis.

- Ensure that you document all of your resiliency procedures. This is an excellent opportunity for the creation of SOPs.

 # Chapter Roadmap

Use the illustration in Figure 9-11 to review the contents of this chapter.

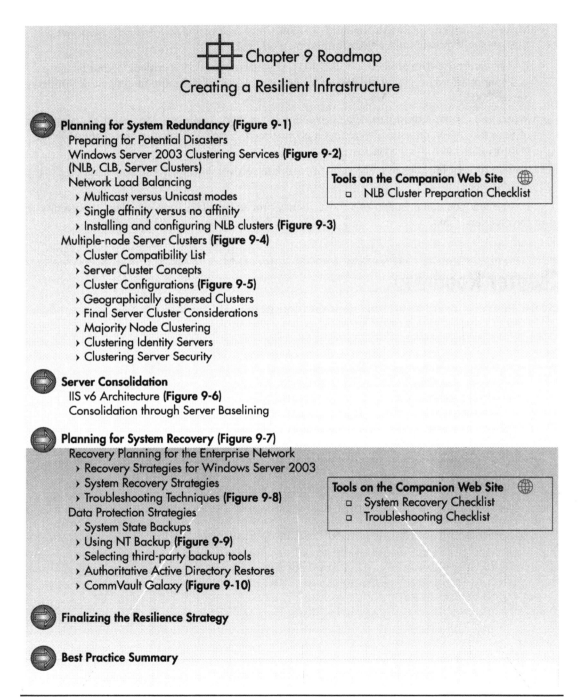

Chapter 9 Roadmap
Creating a Resilient Infrastructure

Planning for System Redundancy (Figure 9-1)
Preparing for Potential Disasters
Windows Server 2003 Clustering Services **(Figure 9-2)**
(NLB, CLB, Server Clusters)
Network Load Balancing
› Multicast versus Unicast modes
› Single affinity versus no affinity
› Installing and configuring NLB clusters **(Figure 9-3)**
Multiple-node Server Clusters **(Figure 9-4)**
› Cluster Compatibility List
› Server Cluster Concepts
› Cluster Configurations **(Figure 9-5)**
› Geographically dispersed Clusters
› Final Server Cluster Considerations
› Majority Node Clustering
› Clustering Identity Servers
› Clustering Server Security

Tools on the Companion Web Site
□ NLB Cluster Preparation Checklist

Server Consolidation
IIS v6 Architecture **(Figure 9-6)**
Consolidation through Server Baselining

Planning for System Recovery (Figure 9-7)
Recovery Planning for the Enterprise Network
› Recovery Strategies for Windows Server 2003
› System Recovery Strategies
› Troubleshooting Techniques **(Figure 9-8)**
Data Protection Strategies
› System State Backups
› Using NT Backup **(Figure 9-9)**
› Selecting third-party backup tools
› Authoritative Active Directory Restores
› CommVault Galaxy **(Figure 9-10)**

Tools on the Companion Web Site
□ System Recovery Checklist
□ Troubleshooting Checklist

Finalizing the Resilience Strategy

Best Practice Summary

Figure 9-11 Chapter Roadmap

CHAPTER 10

Putting the Enterprise Network into Production

IN THIS CHAPTER

The final technical preparations for the parallel network are now done. It is almost ready to go online. Now you need to migrate all users, PCs, data, and services to the parallel network and decommission the legacy environment. It is at the end of this operation that you will have completed your migration to Windows Server 2003. You will then move on to the operation of the new network. At this stage you will discover there are changes in the way you need to administer and operate a native WS03 network.

As you performed all of the operations outlined in the previous chapters, you noticed that several traditional IT tasks have been modified and that new tasks have been added to the operational roster. Thus, as you prepare to place the parallel network online and complete the user migration from the legacy network, there is one final activity you must perform. It is the review of administrative and operational roles within your enterprise network. Once this review is done, your network will be ready for prime time.

Migrating Data, Users, and PCs to the Parallel Network

Your network is ready to be launched into the production environment. So far, every operation you followed has been (or should have been) within a laboratory environment. Even this final procedure must be thoroughly tested before you move to the production network. To migrate users, PCs, and data to the new network, you'll need to perform the following activities:

1. **Create trusts** The first step is to create a two-way trust relationship between the production domain and your legacy domain. This two-way trust serves to support the operation of both networks at the same time. Refer to Chapter 4 (Figure 4-3) for a visual representation of these trusts.

2. **Nest groups** The second step is to nest the appropriate Global groups into the Domain and Domain Local groups that are required to grant joint access to resources from both domains. For example, if you are migrating a select group of users and the migration cannot be completed all at once, you need to ensure that both sets of users—the ones located in the legacy network and the ones already migrated to the new network—have access to joint resources so they can continue to work together for the duration of the migration. This approach will need to extend to all users of public folders because they must share resources for the duration of your migration.

3. **User account migration** Next, you'll need to migrate user accounts from the legacy network to the new environment. As you know, migrating accounts from NT to WS03 will only give you the username and password. Users should be given authority to modify their own personal information through the use of a user data modification Web page as discussed in Chapter 6. The Active Directory Migration Tool (ADMT) included with Windows Server 2003 will provide great help here since it migrates user accounts, passwords, groups and group memberships, service accounts, computer accounts, and more.

▶ **NOTE**

This is an excellent opportunity to clean up your SAM database as it is imported into the new production domain. It will be especially important here to ensure that only appropriate data is included in comments because users can now view comments stored in the Active Directory (which they couldn't in NT).

4. **Service account migration** You shouldn't need to migrate service accounts since they have been recreated into the new network as new services have been activated.

5. **User Data Migration** You can then proceed to migrate user data that is located on network shares such as home directories. This is where it is important to use the proper tool for user account migration because each account that is migrated is assigned a new security identifier (SID). This SID is different from the SID used to create the information in the legacy network. This means that it is possible for users not to have access to their data once it has been moved to a new network. But ADMT can either maintain a SID history when it migrates a user account, giving the account the ability to present a legacy SID when accessing data in the new network, or it can perform SID translation, replacing the legacy SID with the new SID on the object to avoid this problem.

6. **PC migration** Next, you'll need to migrate PCs. If PCs do not need to be restaged (they are already running Windows XP or at least Windows 2000), then you can use the ADMT to migrate computer accounts and reset security descriptors on each system. If, on the other hand, they are not up to date and need to be staged, you will need to first recover all user data from the system, reinstall the system, join it to the domain during reinstallation, and then restore user data to the system. This will be a good time to use the User State Migration Tool (USMT).

▶ **NOTE**

Microsoft has designed the Automated Purposing Framework to assist in the staging and migration of massive numbers of PCs (and servers as well). More information is available at http://www.microsoft .com/serviceproviders/deployment/automated_purposingP67545.asp.

7. **Decommission legacy network** The last step will consist in the legacy network decommissioning. This will be the step that identifies that the migration is complete. It requires the removal of group nesting, the removal of the two-way explicit trusts, and the decommission of the machines in the legacy domain.

These seven steps are illustrated in Figure 10-1. Once they are complete, your migration will be finalized and you'll be ready to move on to the administration and optimization of your new network.

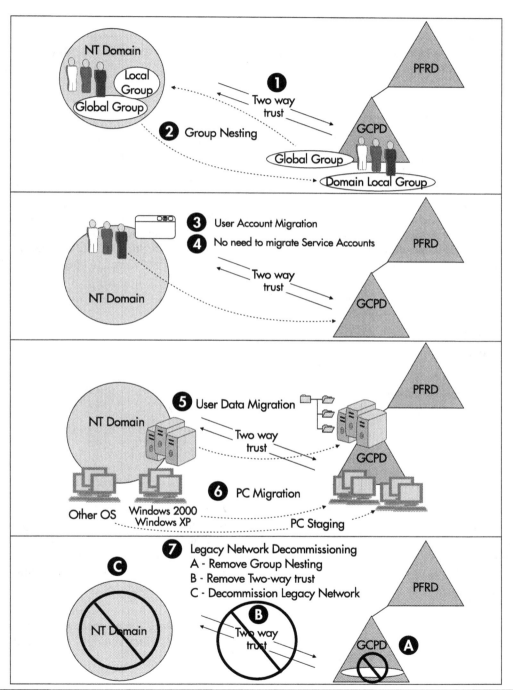

Figure 10-1   The User, Data, and PC Migration Process

▶ *NOTE*

Using a commercial migration tool avoids many of the migration hassles because it takes all of these situations into account.

Using the Active Directory Migration Tool

The ADMT offers several features for the support of the Parallel Network Migration Approach. It is fairly simple to use. Its installation is based on a Windows Installer file (as are the Support Tools, the Resource Kit, the Group Policy Management Console, and other WS03 add-ons and installable components) that is located on the WS03 CD in the |i386|ADMT folder. Simply double-click on the ADMIGRATION.MSI file for installation.

Once it is installed, you can launch the ADMT console by moving to Administrative Tools and selecting Active Directory Migration Tool. You need Enterprise Administrator rights to be able to use this tool. The operation of the ADMT basically consists of right-clicking on Active Directory Migration Tool to access the context menu and selecting the appropriate wizard to operate. ADMT offers several wizards:

- User Account Migration
- Group Account Migration
- Computer Migration
- Service Account Migration
- Security Translation
- Trust Migration
- Group Mapping and Merging
- Exchange Directory Migration
- Reporting

The operation of the wizards is straightforward. You need to identify the source domain, the target domain, the objects you want to migrate, the container you want to migrate them to, and how you want to perform the migration. In addition to performing account or group migration, ADMT supports migration of Exchange objects such as user mailboxes, distribution lists, and so on. ADMT also migrates trust relationships between domains and it can perform group mapping or merging.

▶ *CAUTION*

The ADMT should be run in test mode first. Choosing this mode allows you to test migration results before actually performing the operation. Simply select "Test the migration settings and migrate later?" when you use one of the wizards.

The best way to use ADMT in the Parallel Network Migration Process is to migrate groups of users. When ADMT migrates a group, it can also migrate the users that are contained within that group, making it easier for you to determine what to migrate. But before you can move users and computers from one network to another, you need to ensure that the data you will migrate will be filtered and that all obsolete records will be removed. You don't want to input obsolete data into your brand new WS03 network!

Creating Domain Data Reports

To filter data from your source domain, you need to use ADMT's Reporting Wizard. This reporting tool can support the creation of several different report types to summarize the results of your migration operations:

- Migrated Users and Groups
- Migrated Computers
- Expired Computers
- Impact Analysis
- Name Conflicts

The Expired Computers report lists the computers with expired passwords. Name Conflicts does the same with potential objects that will have the same name in the target domain. The report that allows you to identify obsolete objects is the Impact Analysis report. It provides a detailed list of the user, group, and computer objects that are found in your source domain. You can use this report to identify what must be removed from this database.

You can perform this removal in several ways:

- You can remove the objects from the source domain, and then migrate the accounts.
- You can create new groups that contain only valid objects in the source domain and migrate objects by using these groups.
- You can move the accounts to a specific OU, clean them up, and then move them to their destination OUs.

▶ **NOTE**

Reports must be generated before you can view them. Many reports are generated from information that is collected from computers throughout your network. This will impact their performance, therefore you may decide to use dedicated servers for this function. Also, reports are not dynamic; they are point in time reports and must be regenerated to get an updated picture.

The last approach may be your best bet since the ADMT will allow you to control the way accounts are treated after the migration. In fact, you can ensure that no account is activated until you perform a cleanup operation on the newly migrated accounts.

▶ **NOTE**

The ADMT is also available from http://www.microsoft.com/windows2000/downloads/tools/admt/ default.asp. In addition, you can refer to Chapter 9 of the Microsoft Domain Migration Cookbook for more information on account and other object migration at http://www.microsoft.com/technet/ prodtechnol/windows2000serv/deploy/cookbook/cookchp9.asp. Finally, a summary of the operations required to run ADMT can be found in the Microsoft Knowledge Base article number Q260871 at http://support.microsoft.com/default.aspx?scid=KB;en-us;260871&.

Special ADMT Considerations

There are a few items you must keep in mind when using the ADMT. The first is related to the security identifier (SID). As mentioned earlier, all of a user's data is associated with the SID that represents the user at the time the object is created. Thus all of a user's data will be associated with the user's *legacy* SID. When you transfer this data to the new network, you must use a special technique that will either carry over the user's legacy SID or translate the SID on the object to the user's new SID (the one generated by the new network).

The best way to do this is to ensure that the user's legacy SID is migrated to the new domain (using the appropriate check box in the Account Migration wizards) and then to use SID translation. The latter is performed through the use of the ADMT's Security Translation Wizard. But in order for security translation to work properly, *you must make sure that all of a user's data has been migrated to the new network first*, otherwise you will need to perform the SID translation again once this is done.

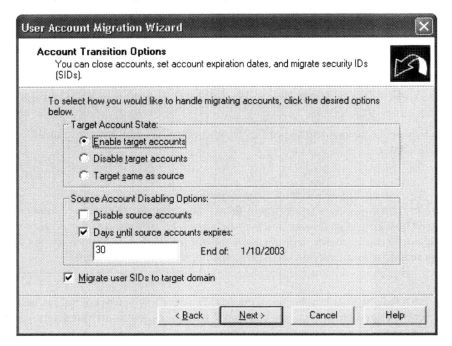

It is also important to note that for SID history migration to work, a Password Export Server (PES) is required. The PES is installed on a domain controller in the legacy network. It is best to use a dedicated server for this operation because it is resource intensive. Therefore, you must stage a new domain controller (BDC in Windows NT or simply a DC in Windows 2000) and dedicate it to this task. Installing the PES is simply a matter of launching the PES installation file found in the PWDMIG folder under ADMT on the WS03 installation CD. This installation will also support password migration if this is what you choose to do (you can also regenerate passwords during the migration). There is no doubt that password migration is easiest on your users even if you force them to reset passwords at their first login to the network. It is also more secure than password regeneration because in regeneration mode, you must find a private way to communicate the new password to users. This can be an opportunity for account theft.

Your network also needs to meet the following conditions before you can perform password migration or SID translation:

- Auditing must be enabled on the source domain. If it isn't, ADMT will offer to turn it on during the migration.

- Your target domain must be in native mode, but this shouldn't be an issue since it was set to native mode during its creation in Chapter 4.

- You must also activate legacy access in the target domain by inserting the Everyone group into the Pre-Windows 2000 Compatible Access group.

▶ *CAUTION*

It is recommended to activate legacy access only for the duration of a migration operation and to deactivate it as soon as the operation is complete because it is a potential security risk. This means that you activate it, perform a user or group migration, and then deactivate it. Do not activate it for the duration of the domain migration because this can last quite a while depending on your migration strategy and the size of the legacy domain.

There are other prerequisites you must take care of before performing a migration (such as service pack level for the source domain machines). ADMT will also require some additional settings, but it can automatically perform the modifications during a migration operation.

Thus, you can use the ADMT to perform most of the operations identified above to support your network migration, including:

- Create a source domain object report for filtering purposes.

- Migrate user accounts, groups and computer accounts (if the systems are already running Windows XP or at the very least Windows 2000).

- Perform security translations to give users access to their data.

The only operation it does not handle is the migration of user data that is stored on network shares. As mentioned earlier, it is important to migrate user data before you perform security translations.

Transferring Networked User Data

Migrating networked user data will involve the copying of data found on server shares within the legacy network. It should include public, group, project, and user data. User data should include home directory data if they were in use within the legacy network.

This operation consists mostly of relocating shared data from one network onto the other. In most cases, it will mean moving the data from a specific share on one server to the same share on another server. This may even give you the opportunity to consolidate server processes and regroup file shares on fewer servers. In addition, if you used the practices provided in Chapter 7, you will be now using DFS shares instead of mapped drives. Thus you will have to ensure that your migration program includes a user information program showing them how to access the new shares. This user information program should also include the procedure to use to access personal user data because this process has changed.

> **QUICK TIP**
>
> *Now that your new network is using DFS, it will support simplified migrations since you can ensure that all networks use the same DFS naming strategy.*

The parallel network no longer uses the home directory concept. It uses redirected folders. There is a catch, though: redirected user folders are not created until the user has logged on at least once (in fact, three times before the redirection process is complete). You cannot simply move the user's home folder files from one server to another because the user's destination folder won't be created until later. Thus, you must devise a special personal user Data Migration Strategy. There are three possibilities:

- You can ask all users to move all of their home directory files into their My Documents folders on their desktop. Then, when they migrate to the new network and log on for the first time, the contents of their My Documents folders will automatically be moved to the new shared folder thanks to the Folder Redirection Group Policy. This process will require two additional logons before completion if you are using Fast Logon Optimization.

> **QUICK TIP**
>
> *You may consider turning off Fast Logon Optimization for the duration of the migration in order to simplify the creation of redirected folders.*

- If you need to stage PCs because they are not running either Windows XP or Windows 2000, you can add an operation to the User State Migration process since it will be required on all systems. The operation you need to add is similar to the first approach: script a process that takes all of a user's home directory data and copies it to the My Documents folder before performing the backup portion of the USMT. The data will automatically be redirected when the recovery portion of the USMT runs at a user's first logon to the new network and the Folder Redirection GPO is applied.

- You can migrate data to a holding folder and, using a special one-time logon script, move the files to the user's newly created redirected folder once the user is logged on and the Group Policy has been applied.

Of these three strategies, the third is the best, though it requires operations that occur during a user's first logon. The first would also work, but it has a major flaw: you must rely on operations that are out of your control for the process to complete. It will not work unless you have a well-trained user base and you provide them with excellent instructions. The second only works if the user's PCs must be staged. Thus, if your network does not meet these two conditions, you must use the third option.

Finally, you may need to migrate Roaming User Profiles if they were in use in the legacy network. Remember that the new network does not use Roaming Profiles, but relies on Folder Redirection instead. To migrate Roaming Profiles, simply turn the feature off in the legacy network (only for users targeted for migration). The profile will return to the local machine. If the machine is already running Windows XP or 2000, the profile will automatically be transformed to Folder Redirection when the machine is joined to the new domain and the user logs on because the GPOs will activate Folder Redirection. If the machine needs to be staged, the profile will be captured through the use of the User State Migration Tool.

Using a Commercial Migration Tool

The ADMT is a very powerful tool, especially in its second edition, but it does not do everything in a migration. If you find that you have several thousands of users and several gigabytes of data to migrate in multiple locations, you may decide that using the ADMT is not enough. In this case, you may decide to use a commercial migration tool. There are several on the market and all of them include the capability to migrate both accounts or other directory objects and networked user data. Thus, using a commercial migration tool facilitates the migration process because it offers professional tools and support for every aspect of this process.

The NetIQ Migration Suite is the product suite upon which is based on the Active Directory Migration Tool. When you begin to use the Domain Migration Administrator (DMA), you will see the similarities between both products. But there are subtle differences. While DMA also supports the migration of user accounts, groups, and computer accounts from one domain to another, it does so in a much more intelligent way. For example, during the migration of accounts, you can tell DMA to ignore accounts in the source domain that have been marked as disabled, performing a database cleanup as you perform the migration instead of having to do it beforehand or afterwards as with the ADMT. It also provides more comprehensive reports when analyzing source domain data. It provides better support for Microsoft Exchange migrations. Finally, it provides extensive cleanup capabilities. For example, it will allow you to remove SID histories from your target network once all the security translations are performed.

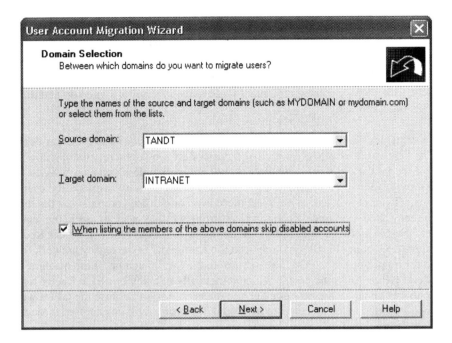

In addition, the NetIQ suite includes Server Consolidator, a tool that is designed to migrate files, folders, shares, printers and printer settings, and the appropriate access permissions from one server to another. It is not only designed to migrate data, but also to help in the consolidation process, allowing you to regroup resources on larger servers and even Server Clusters.

▶ **NOTE**

More information on the NetIQ Migration Suite can be found at http://www.netiq.com/products/ migrate/default.asp.

Commercial tools such as NetIQ's DMA and Server Consolidator can be expensive, but there are ways to reduce costs for their use. For example, Microsoft Consulting Services (MCS) has a special usage license for these products. If you hire an MCS consultant to assist in your migration, they may be able to provide you with the Migration Suite under certain circumstances. Another way to acquire the Migration Suite is to acquire other products from NetIQ. For example, if you acquire the NetIQ Administration Suite—a set of tools that is designed to assist ongoing administration of WS03 networks, you may be able to obtain the Migration Suite for free.

NetIQ isn't the only provider of such tools. Several other manufacturers offer migration support tools. Both Aelita Software (http://www.aelita.com/products/ControlledMigration.htm) and Quest Software (http://www.quest.com/solutions/microsoft_infrastructure.asp#deploy) offer very powerful migration and administration tools. Both also offer programs that give you access to their migration suites at special rates.

▶ *NOTE*

Microsoft offers information on products that integrate with WS03 and support migrations at http://www.microsoft.com/windows2000/partners/amatlsrv.asp.

Decommissioning the Legacy Network

Once everything has been migrated from the legacy network to the new network, you can proceed with the decommissioning of the legacy network. This process involves the following tasks:

1. Begin by removing embedded groups. You only need to do this in the new domain. Thus, you can remove Legacy Global groups from your production Domain Local groups.

2. Remove the trust relationships. Once again, you only need to remove trusts from the new production domain. Use the AD Domains and Trusts console to perform this activity.

3. Now you can move on to the decommissioning of the legacy domain itself. But before you do so, it is a good idea to perform full backups of the PDC (if it is a Windows NT network) or the DC (if it is Windows 2000).

4. When the backups are complete, store them in a safe place, then shut down the legacy domain's final domain controller (PDC or DC).

5. If you need to recover this server within the new network, you can reinstall it in a new role in your new production domain. But it is a good idea to hold on to this server as a backup for a while as you iron out the operation of the new network.

You might consider having a celebration at this stage because you certainly deserve it. You and your migration team have done a lot of hard work preparing the new network and migrating every legacy resource to the new environment. Congratulations!

Celebrations aside, it will also be a good idea for you to perform a post-migration review to ensure that you can reuse this process and improve upon it if you ever need it again.

Revising the IT Role Structure

As you prepared to place the new network online, you probably realized that a review of administrative and operational roles is also required. In fact, this review of operational roles focuses on the third quadrant of the Service Lifecycle illustrated in Figure 1-1 (in Chapter 1), Production, since the activities of the first two quadrants are now complete (Planning and Preparation). The operations outlined in the Production quadrant require a new organizational structure because many of them will be delegated to users who do not have administrative privileges.

New and Revised AD IT Roles

One of the areas where IT roles are modified the most is in terms of Active Directory management. If you're migrating from Windows NT to Windows Server 2003, most of these roles are new. If you're already using Windows 2000, you know that all of these roles are necessary. The relationship of AD IT roles is illustrated in Figure 10-2. This figure was originally drawn from the Microsoft Best Practice Active Directory Design for Managing Windows Networks guide (www.microsoft.com/windows2000/techinfo/planning/activedirectory/bpaddsgn.asp), but has been enhanced with additional IT roles. The responsibilities of each role are outlined in Table 10-1. Depending on the size of your organization, you may combine roles. What is important here is that each *function* be identified within your IT group. It will also be important to ensure that no unnecessary privileges are given to administrators and operators within the Active Directory.

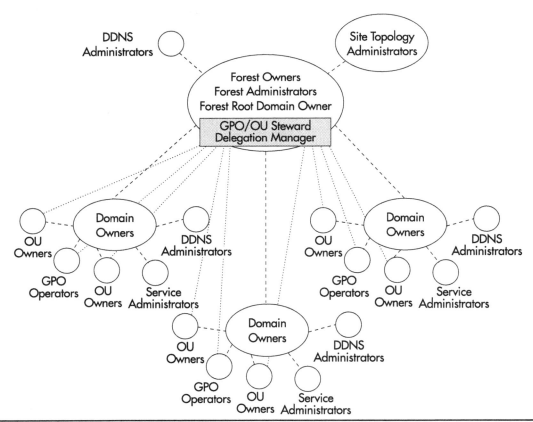

Figure 10-2   AD IT role relationships

Role	Department	Role Type	Responsibilities
Forest Owner	IT Planning and Enterprise Architecture	Service Management	Ensure that all forest standards are maintained within the forest Responsible for the forest schema Identify and document new standards
Forest Administrator	IT group	Service Management	Ensure that the forest is operating properly Responsible for the forest configuration Enforce all forest standards Responsible for Forest Root Domain administration Responsible for Forest-wide Operation Master roles Responsible for Root Domain-centric Operation Master roles Responsible for the analysis/recommendation of the implementation of operational software that modifies the schema Responsible for Global Catalog content
Domain Owner	IT group/ training/IS	Service Management	Ensure that all domain standards are maintained within the domain Identify and document new standards
Domain Administrator	IT group	Service Management	Service administrator who ensures that the domain is operating properly Enforce all domain standards Ensure that all DCs within the domain are sized appropriately Responsible for Domain-centric Operation Master roles
DDNS Administrator	IT group	Service Management	Ensure the proper operation of the forest namespace Administer and manage internal/external DNS exchanges
Site Topology Administrator	IT group	Service Management	Monitor and analyze forest replication Modify site topology to improve forest replication
Service Administrators	IT group	Service Management	Responsible for a given service in the domain Has limited rights in the domain (only to the service they manage)
GPO Operators	IT group	Service Management	Design and test GPOs for use in production environments Use the Group Policy Management Console to manage, debug and modify GPOs Report to the GPO/OU steward
Root Domain Owner	IT Planning and Enterprise Architecture	Data ownership	Responsible for Universal Administrative Groups Responsible for root domain standards Can be the same as the forest owner

Table 10-1   AD IT Roles

Role	Department	Role Type	Responsibilities
GPO/OU Steward	IT Planning and Enterprise Architecture	Data ownership	Responsible for the proper operation of all OUs within the production forest Must ensure that all OUs are justified and that each has a designated owner Must maintain the GPO registry (all GPO documentation) Must ensure that all GPOs conform to standards Must manage the GPO production release process
Delegation Manager	IT Planning and Enterprise Architecture	Data ownership	Responsible for the proper documentation of all delegation rights Must ensure that all delegations are justified and that each has a designated officer Must ensure that all delegations conform to standards Must include all custom management consoles in the delegation documentation Must manage the production delegation process Can be the same as the GPO/OU steward
OU Owners	Entire organization	Data ownership	Responsible for all information delegated within the OU Must report regularly to the GPO/OU steward

Table 10-1   AD IT Roles *(continued)*

All of these roles will need to interact with each other during ongoing operations. A regular roundtable discussion is an excellent way for each of the people filling these roles to get to know each other and begin the communication process. The frequency of these meetings does not need to be especially high. Gauge the number of meetings you need per year according to the objectives you set for your directory. There could be as few as two meetings per year. A possible organizational structure of these new and reformed IT roles is displayed in Figure 10-3.

> ▶ **QUICK TIP**
>
> *Microsoft offers a very complete Active Directory Operations Guide. It is in two parts and is available at http://www.microsoft.com/technet/treeview/default.asp?url=/technet/prodtechnol/ ad/windows2000/downloads/adopsgd.asp. It also outlines which role should perform which operation.*

Designing the Services Administration Plan

The management and administration of an Active Directory, especially a NOS-centric AD, is concentrated mostly on the delegation of specific administrative rights to both service operators and security officers. Chapter 5 identified the requirement for local or regional security officers. If you

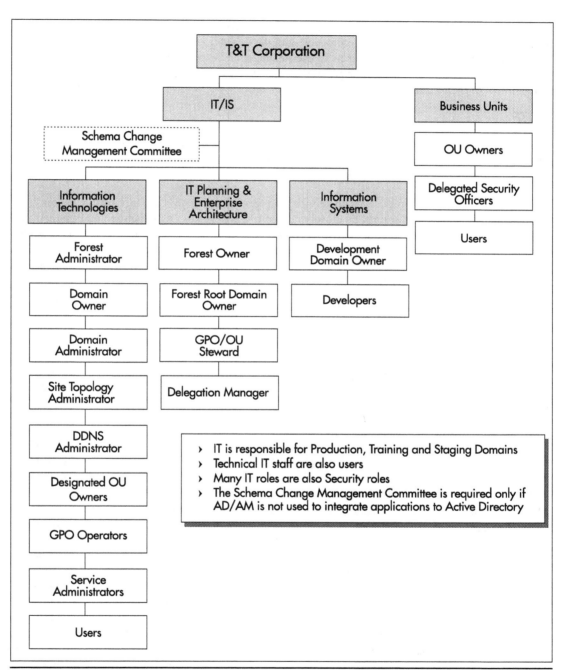

Figure 10-3   The organizational structure of AD IT roles at T&T Corporation

have decided to delegate specific IT operations related to both the management of PCs and the management of users, you will need to proceed with the delegation of appropriate rights to these officers as outlined in Chapter 5. In terms of user management especially, you will also need to proceed with the identification of your group managers and give them appropriate rights for the management of their User Groups as outlined in Chapter 6.

▶ **NOTE**

The procedure for creating custom MMC consoles and delegating rights is outlined in Chapter 5. The procedure for creating appropriate administrative groups is outlined in Chapter 6.

Finally, you will need to proceed with service management delegation as outlined in Chapter 7. Service management activities must be closely related to the Services OU structure you designed during the preparation of the parallel network's enterprise services. It is also closely tied to the seven core server roles identified in Chapter 2, but additional operations are also required, as you well know—system backup, performance monitoring, security management, problem management and user support, and so on. The core roles to cover here include:

- File and Print operators
- Application Server operators
- Terminal Server operators
- Collaboration Server operators
- Infrastructure Server operators
- Dedicated Web Server operators

These six operator groups require appropriate rights and delegation of the appropriate OU. As with the Services OU structure, these operational groups may be subdivided into smaller, more focused groups that are responsible for specific technologies (Identity Management Server operators are your Domain Administrators and have been identified earlier).

▶ **QUICK TIP**

Several administrative tasks are either new or have been changed especially between Windows NT and WS03 networks. A sample list of changed or new tasks per administrative or operational role is available at http://www.Reso-Net.com/ WindowsServer/. It can help you identify which operations require modification before you activate the WS03 enterprise network.

In fact, many of the enterprise management and operations tasks you will have to review will be closely related to the new Server Construction Model you have implemented in the parallel network: the PASS model as illustrated in Chapter 1 (Figure 1-2). Because of its modular and layered design, this model helps you identify the relationship between each layer and management or operational technologies and activities. Some of these relationships are illustrated in Figure 10-4.

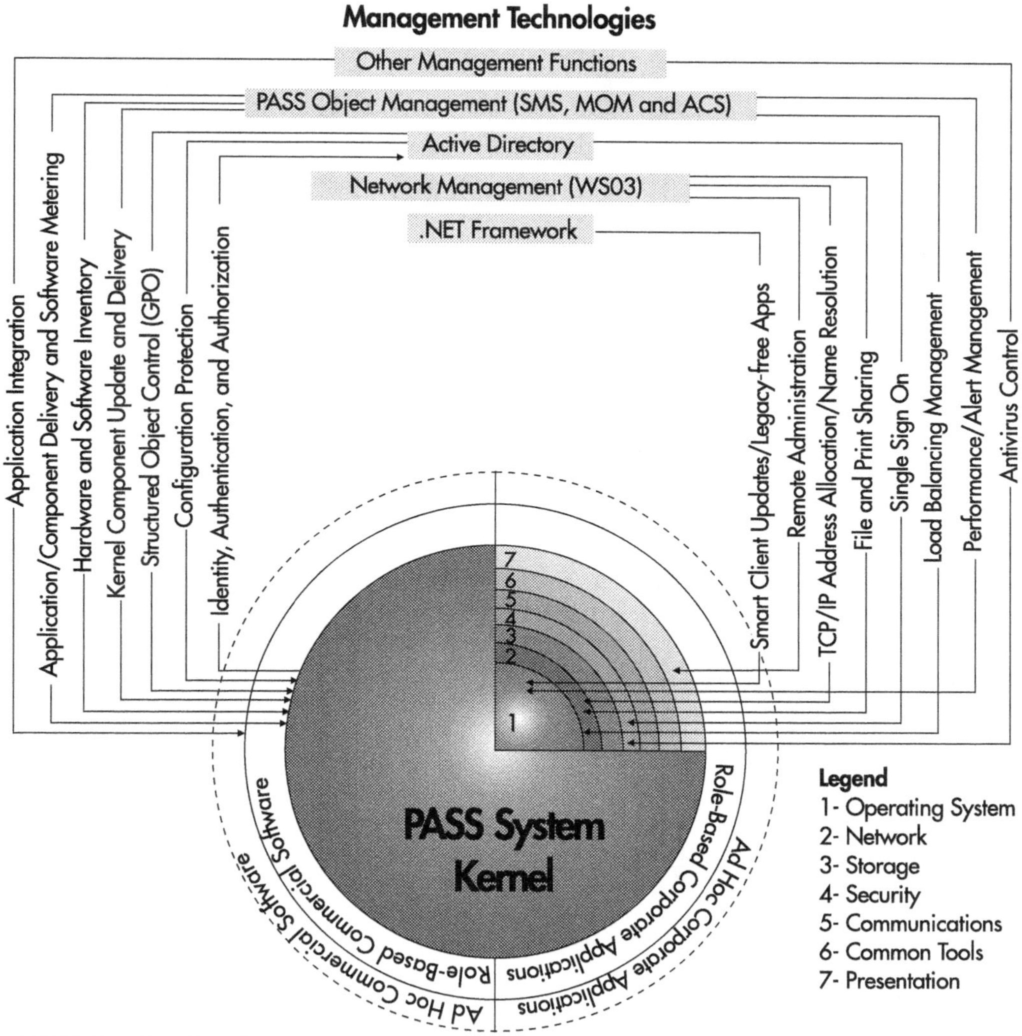

Management Technologies

Other Management Functions

PASS Object Management (SMS, MOM and ACS)

Active Directory

Network Management (WS03)

.NET Framework

Application Integration

Application/Component Delivery and Software Metering

Hardware and Software Inventory

Kernel Component Update and Delivery

Structured Object Control (GPO)

Configuration Protection

Identity, Authentication, and Authorization

Smart Client Updates/Legacy-free Apps

Remote Administration

TCP/IP Address Allocation/Name Resolution

File and Print Sharing

Single Sign On

Load Balancing Management

Performance/Alert Management

Antivirus Control

7
6
5
4
3
2
1

PASS System
Kernel

Role-Based Corporate Applications

Ad Hoc Corporate Applications

Role-Based Commercial Software

Ad Hoc Commercial Software

Legend
1- Operating System
2- Network
3- Storage
4- Security
5- Communications
6- Common Tools
7- Presentation

Figure 10-4   The relationship between management technologies and PASS model layers

It does not show an exhaustive list of the relationships between network support technologies and each individual server or workstation, but it outlines the basic concept of relationships.

Several of the management and administrative activities you need to cover will require special technologies. Systems Management Server will support application deployment, inventories and software usage habit analysis. Microsoft Operations Manager (MOM) will support performance and alert management within the network, especially with critical services. Application Center Server (ACS) will support component-based application deployment and advanced load balancing. But whether your legacy network is running Windows NT or Windows 2000, you are most likely already using these or similar technologies. If you moved from Windows NT, your biggest change will still focus on Active Directory and, especially, Group Policy Management. If you've already been using Windows 2000, it doesn't hurt to review your AD operations. Here, you will use the Group Policy Management Console (GPMC) or a similar tool to facilitate the administration and standardization of your GPOs.

WS03 Administrative Tools

Windows Server 2003 includes a whole series of new and improved management and administration tools. Several are located directly within the operating system and consist of command-line tools. WS03 includes over 60 new command-line tools and over 200 command-line tools in general. All are well documented in the WS03 Help and Support Center. In addition, just like previous versions of Windows, WS03 includes an Administrative Tool Pack, a Support Tool Pack, and a Resource Kit. The most useful of these are the Support Tool Pack and the Resource Kit.

▶ **QUICK TIP**

An excellent source of information on these tools is the Windows XP Power Toolkit *(Microsoft Press, 2002).*

Support tools are divided into several management tool categories:

- Active Directory
- Disk and data
- File and folder
- Hardware
- Internet services
- Network services
- Performance monitoring
- Printer and fax
- Process and service
- Remote administration
- Security
- Software and system deployment
- System management

The same type of categories applies to the Resource Kit tools. The advent of these new tools greatly enhances the operational management of the enterprise network. In fact, the inclusion of new command-line tools allows you to script several operations.

> ▶ **QUICK TIP**
>
> *A listing of all administrative and support tools is available at http://www.Reso-Net.com/ WindowsServer/. This listing includes a rating for each tool indicating when to use it and how useful it can be.*

Chapter 1 outlined the importance of standard operating procedures (SOP). In many cases, the best SOP is a script because it ensures that the operation is *always* performed in the same manner. Since technical personnel often prefer not to write documentation, but rather to create automations and programs, the use of well-documented scripts (documented within the script itself) and a complete script inventory makes it easier to implement an SOP approach.

Remember, though, that all scripts must be digitally signed before they are introduced into the production network (you should be using Software Restriction Policies to ensure that only signed scripts are allowed).

> ▶ **QUICK TIP**
>
> *Microsoft provides excellent scripting support in the TechNet Script Center at http://www .microsoft.com/technet/treeview/default.asp?url=/technet/scriptcenter/default.asp. Also, if you find that you need to create a lot of your own scripts, you might elect to acquire a scripting tool. There are several on the market. Many require their own scripting engines, but if you decide to use the Windows Scripting Host, you should consider using Primal Script as your scripting tool. It is an inexpensive tool that provides very powerful scripting support in several scripting languages and includes many of the features found in the most powerful programming languages, such as IntelliSense-like automatic entries, code samples, source control (to avoid duplicate scripts) and project management. Primal Script is available from Sapien Technologies Inc. at http://www.sapien.com/.*

Also, you should be careful who you give access to both Support and Resource Kit Tools. They are powerful tools that can cause a security risk if misused. One of the best ways to control their access is to store them on servers only and to use Terminal Services to give access to both sets of tools. An additional advantage of this approach is that you do not need to create and maintain administrative or operational workstations for your IT staff. Their workstations can be similar to other power users within your enterprise and focus on productivity tools. Then, when they need to perform an administrative task, they can log onto an administrative server using Terminal Services to access the appropriate tool.

This can also help increase security. Since the administrative tools are not on the operators' PCs, they can use their *user* account to perform their daily tasks. Then when an administrative task is required, they can log in with their *administrative* account in the Terminal Services session. An additional layer of security can be added through the use of smart cards for administrative logons. Since WS03 supports the use of smart cards for administrators, you can ensure that two-factor authentication is required for the performance of all administrative tasks.

Final Recommendations

This book has provided you with a structured approach for the migration toward a new Windows Server 2003 enterprise network. As such, it tried to focus on the best features WS03 has to offer for the enterprise. Since you are only beginning to use this technology, you will surely discover additional ways to use it.

Learn from WS03. It is by far the most powerful operating system Microsoft has ever delivered. Microsoft began the move toward the enterprise with Windows 2000, but this move is only really becoming a reality with WS03 because both users and providers have learned about the needs and requirements an enterprise network demands from a Windows operating system. Thus, with a version two product, Windows Server 2003, Microsoft begins to offer real potential in this arena.

WS03 is also the first Windows OS that supports the Itanium and AMD-64 chips operating at 64 bits. As you have noticed, not all features run on the 64-bit version of WS03. If you decide that you want to move to this type of server, you'll find that you will need to refine your understanding of the 64-bit capabilities of Windows Server 2003. You'll also need to refine the way you structure your servers to ensure that only compatible services are hosted on these servers. It is a good idea to begin this move, since the 32-bit microchip is bound to be phased out eventually.

You might also find that you want to begin using IP version 6, but as was mentioned in Chapter 4, WS03 does not offer the possibility of a pure IPv6 network since WS03 still requires the installation of IPv4 on each server. Once again, it will be a good idea to begin experimenting with this technology because IPv4 is bound to be phased out as well.

> ### QUICK TIP
>
> *A good reference is* Understanding IPv6 *(Microsoft Press, 2002).*

One of the things you will realize as you work with your new network is that the more things change, the more they stay the same. Even though you've had to review your entire network in order to recreate it in a parallel environment and you've had to adjust old concepts to new technologies, you'll find that service management remained the same all along. Your job is to deliver services to your user base. That's what the legacy network did before and that's what the new WS03 network is designed to do again. From now on, what you'll need to concentrate on is how to improve service delivery and how to simplify network management. Even though your network is now ready for prime time, *your* journey is just beginning.

Best Practice Summary

This chapter recommends the following best practices:

User, Data, and PC Migration

- Create a trust relationship between the legacy and the new network. Also, nest groups between the two domains to give users access to resources in both networks.

- Keep the trusts and group nesting on for the duration of your migration.

- At the very least, use the Active Directory Migration Tool to migrate accounts from the legacy domain to the new network.

- Perform a cleanup operation during the account migration process.

- Migrate users, then user data, then user PCs, in that order.

- Create a special process to migrate personal user data.

- Create user documentation to inform them of new practices and steps they may have to perform during the migration.

- Use a commercial migration tool if you can because it simplifies the migration process.

- Remember to remove nested groups, turn off trusts, and create an extensive backup before you decommission the legacy network.

- Celebrate when you're done. You and your team deserve it.

IT Role Structure

- Review and revise your IT role structure to prepare for the new roles AD brings to your network.

- Prepare your Services Administration Plan. Refine it as you learn more about WS03.

- Use all of the available tools to minimize administration tasks.

- Use scripts wherever possible to automate operations and ensure that they are standardized.

- Begin to experiment and use the latest WS03 features once the network is stabilized. You will need to familiarize yourself with technologies such as IPv6 and 64-bit computing in the very near future.

 # Chapter Roadmap

Use the illustration in Figure 10-5 to review the contents of this chapter.

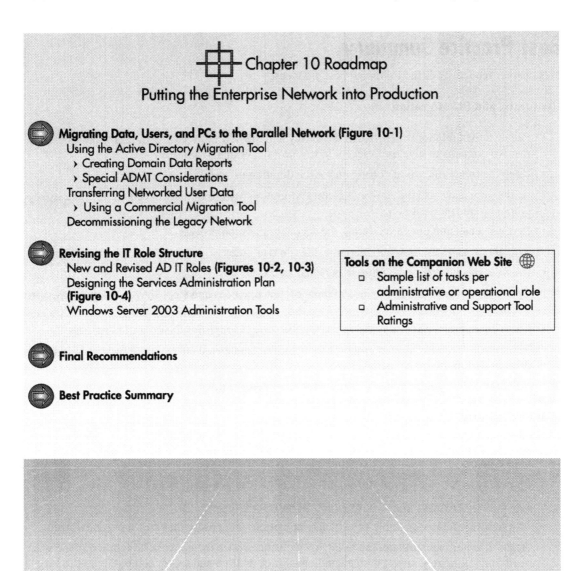

Chapter 10 Roadmap
Putting the Enterprise Network into Production

Migrating Data, Users, and PCs to the Parallel Network (Figure 10-1)
Using the Active Directory Migration Tool
> Creating Domain Data Reports
> Special ADMT Considerations
Transferring Networked User Data
> Using a Commercial Migration Tool
Decommissioning the Legacy Network

Revising the IT Role Structure
New and Revised AD IT Roles **(Figures 10-2, 10-3)**
Designing the Services Administration Plan
(Figure 10-4)
Windows Server 2003 Administration Tools

Tools on the Companion Web Site
❑ Sample list of tasks per administrative or operational role
❑ Administrative and Support Tool Ratings

Final Recommendations

Best Practice Summary

Figure 10-5   Chapter Roadmap

Index

IIS, 384–386
information access, 352, 387–399, 405
migrations and, 45–46
.NET Framework, 357, 380–384
operating system hardening, 352, 362–386,
 404–405
passwords. *See* passwords
physical protection, 352, 361–362, 404,
 410–411
policies, 351
Post-Installation Checklist, 363–364
Print System, 380
risk levels, 410
SANS Institute, 357
social engineering, 356
users and, 263–264
viral attacks, 356
WS03 features, 357–359
Security Configuration and Analysis tool, 370–372
security groups, 93, 258
security identifier (SID), 263–264, 388, 448,
 452–453
Security Operations Guide (SOG), 356–357,
 361, 366
security plan, 355–356
security policies, 81, 403
Security Policy filtering, 207
security templates, 325, 364–374
Security Translation Wizard, 452
server administration password, 154
server baselines, 426–428
server bases, 48
Server Clusters, 412–414, 420–425, 442
Server Consolidator tool, 456
Server Data Sheet, 45–46, 54
Server Kernel, 25–26
server lifecycle, 3–5, 51
server positioning, 118–126
Server Preparation Worksheets, 154
server roles
 configuring, 26–27
 described, 287–288

hardware requirements, 339–340
servers. *See also* WS03 Server
 Application. *See* Application Servers
 Bridgehead Servers, 128–132
 capacity of, 49
 Collaboration Servers, 26, 287, 337, 341
 configuring, 4, 154–158, 167
 consolidation, 23–24, 425–428, 456
 customizing, 60–65
 DC, 154, 156
 DHCP. *See* DHCP servers
 DNS, 159–162
 dynamic addressing for, 156
 Enterprise Network Server, 149–150
 Exchange Server, 115, 341
 Failsafe Server, 27, 411
 File Servers, 26, 287–288, 296–304, 345
 Identity Servers, 39–41, 425
 IIS, 384–386, 396–398
 Infrastructure Servers, 346
 installing. *See* installing servers
 life expectancy of, 51
 location of, 48–49
 maximum load of, 48
 Member Servers, 37, 41–44
 moving, 185–189
 multiprocessing, 49
 multipurpose, 288
 naming, 72–73
 Network Infrastructure. *See* Network
  Infrastructure Servers
 number of users per, 48
 physical location of, 50
 placement of, 27
 Print Servers, 26, 287–288, 312,
  319–323, 345
 production forest, 121
 putting in place, 75
 Reference Servers, 65–70, 73–74
 repairs to, 4
 RIS Servers, 70–75, 337–339
 role of, 22–23

INTERNATIONAL CONTACT INFORMATION

AUSTRALIA
McGraw-Hill Book Company Australia Pty. Ltd.
TEL +61-2-9900-1800
FAX +61-2-9878-8881
http://www.mcgraw-hill.com.au
books-it_sydney@mcgraw-hill.com

CANADA
McGraw-Hill Ryerson Ltd.
TEL +905-430-5000
FAX +905-430-5020
http://www.mcgraw-hill.ca

GREECE, MIDDLE EAST, & AFRICA
(Excluding South Africa)
McGraw-Hill Hellas
TEL +30-210-6560-990
TEL +30-210-6560-993
TEL +30-210-6560-994
FAX +30-210-6545-525

MEXICO (Also serving Latin America)
McGraw-Hill Interamericana Editores S.A. de C.V.
TEL +525-117-1583
FAX +525-117-1589
http://www.mcgraw-hill.com.mx
fernando_castellanos@mcgraw-hill.com

SINGAPORE (Serving Asia)
McGraw-Hill Book Company
TEL +65-6863-1580
FAX +65-6862-3354
http://www.mcgraw-hill.com.sg
mghasia@mcgraw-hill.com

SOUTH AFRICA
McGraw-Hill South Africa
TEL +27-11-622-7512
FAX +27-11-622-9045
robyn_swanepoel@mcgraw-hill.com

SPAIN
McGraw-Hill/Interamericana de España, S.A.U.
TEL +34-91-180-3000
FAX +34-91-372-8513
http://www.mcgraw-hill.es
professional@mcgraw-hill.es

UNITED KINGDOM, NORTHERN,
EASTERN, & CENTRAL EUROPE
McGraw-Hill Education Europe
TEL +44-1-628-502500
FAX +44-1-628-770224
http://www.mcgraw-hill.co.uk
computing_europe@mcgraw-hill.com

ALL OTHER INQUIRIES Contact:
McGraw-Hill/Osborne
TEL +1-510-596-6600
FAX +1-510-596-7600
http://www.osborne.com
omg_international@mcgraw-hill.com

www.ingramcontent.com/pod-product-compliance
Lightning Source LLC
Chambersburg PA
CBHW080133060326
40689CB00018B/3769